T0302002

# Retail Supply Chain Management

## Second Edition

# Retail Supply Chain Management

## Second Edition

James B. Ayers
Mary Ann Odegaard

CRC Press
Taylor & Francis Group
Boca Raton  London  New York

CRC Press is an imprint of the
Taylor & Francis Group, an **informa** business

A PRODUCTIVITY PRESS BOOK

CRC Press
Taylor & Francis Group
6000 Broken Sound Parkway NW, Suite 300
Boca Raton, FL 33487-2742

First issued in paperback 2021

© 2018 by Taylor & Francis Group, LLC
CRC Press is an imprint of Taylor & Francis Group, an Informa business

No claim to original U.S. Government works

ISBN-13: 978-1-4987-3914-6 (hbk)
ISBN-13: 978-1-03-217896-7 (pbk)
DOI: 10.1201/9781315151410

This book contains information obtained from authentic and highly regarded sources. Reasonable efforts have been made to publish reliable data and information, but the author and publisher cannot assume responsibility for the validity of all materials or the consequences of their use. The authors and publishers have attempted to trace the copyright holders of all material reproduced in this publication and apologize to copyright holders if permission to publish in this form has not been obtained. If any copyright material has not been acknowledged please write and let us know so we may rectify in any future reprint.

Except as permitted under U.S. Copyright Law, no part of this book may be reprinted, reproduced, transmitted, or utilized in any form by any electronic, mechanical, or other means, now known or hereafter invented, including photocopying, microfilming, and recording, or in any information storage or retrieval system, without written permission from the publishers.

For permission to photocopy or use material electronically from this work, please access www.copyright.com (http://www.copyright.com/) or contact the Copyright Clearance Center, Inc. (CCC), 222 Rosewood Drive, Danvers, MA 01923, 978-750-8400. CCC is a not-for-profit organization that provides licenses and registration for a variety of users. For organizations that have been granted a photocopy license by the CCC, a separate system of payment has been arranged.

**Trademark Notice:** Product or corporate names may be trademarks or registered trademarks, and are used only for identification and explanation without intent to infringe.

Publisher's Note

The publisher has gone to great lengths to ensure the quality of this reprint but points out that some imperfections in the original copies may be apparent.

**Library of Congress Cataloging-in-Publication Data**

Names: Ayers, James B., author. | Odegaard, Mary Ann, author.
Title: Retail supply chain management / James B. Ayers and Mary Ann Odegaard.
Description: Second Edition. | Boca Raton, FL : CRC Press, [2017] | Revised edition of the authors' Retail supply chain management, c2008. | Includes index.
Identifiers: LCCN 2017015349| ISBN 9781498739146 (hardback : alk. paper) | ISBN 9781315151410 (ebook)
Subjects: LCSH: Business logistics. | Retail trade--Management. | Industrial procurement--Management.
Classification: LCC HD38.5 .A947 2017 | DDC 658.8/700687--dc23
LC record available at https://lccn.loc.gov/2017015349

**Visit the Taylor & Francis Web site at**
**http://www.taylorandfrancis.com**

**and the CRC Press Web site at**
**http://www.crcpress.com**

To the men and women in the retail supply chain—designing, manufacturing, and delivering products that enrich our lives.

# Contents

## SECTION V   ACHIEVING FINANCIAL SUCCESS IN THE RETAIL SUPPLY CHAIN

# Preface

In 2008, when the first edition of this book was published, most retail supply chain businesses operated as if specialization was a good thing. However, the retail world and the accompanying supply chains have experienced a revolution in the last 5 years. The basic supply chain mission of matching supply and demand requires new skills and organization alignment.

The previous model saw retailers and their supply chain partners organized into separate stand-alone functional departments like sales, merchandising, distribution, human resources, store management, accounting, and finance. Retailers' suppliers—including distributors and manufacturers—also had similar specialization but with different functions needed to fulfill their supply chain roles. The effectiveness of such approaches has deteriorated as prodding for higher service levels from the retailers they serve has grown rapidly. Customarily, retailers, distributors, logistics companies, and manufacturers still perform the traditional functions, but they now face requirements for greater delivery speed, shorter lead times, and smaller quantities as well as new sets of requirements necessitated by the increased demands of omnichannel retailing.

In 2008, a consequence of specialization had been weak processes that crossed department and company boundaries. This has been the central problem addressed by the supply chain management (SCM) discipline at that time and was discussed extensively in the first edition. Managers and employees practiced their specialty with too little appreciation for the supply chains within which they needed to operate.

Vast technological change has enabled personalization of the customer experience across multiple channels. This is referred to as omnichannel retailing. It enables the customer to decide exactly where and when he or she will shop and how the merchandise, goods, and services will be delivered. The SCM discipline still requires a process view across the boundaries. New process designs go beyond tinkering and are shifting the paradigm again, upsetting whole industries.

In 2008, the industry leaders in distribution were companies like Wal-Mart and Dell who had reputations for expeditious delivery of product to brick-and-mortar stores or directly to the customer. Now, Amazon has set a new standard for delivery speed for online shoppers that competes with brick-and-mortar stores.

In the early era of Internet sales, an accepted assumption was that online sales would prosper for products that are identical and do not have to fit the customer. Examples are music CDs and books. But that is no longer the case. Customers get shoes from Zappos—a company that differentiates itself by its 10 core customer service values—in a day or two. To address the "fit problem," Zappos' shoes arrive with documentation for easy customer return of the product with a minimum of inconvenience. Nordstrom, the large Northwest retailer recognized for its outstanding customer service, has created an environment where customers select where they buy, order, and receive a wide range of products. Such requirements are becoming the norm.

This book is aimed to help managers, strategists, and any others who are responsible for managing a link in the supply chain. For retail trading partners to operate as a supply chain, rather than individual companies, they will continue to have to invent new approaches for performing the tasks necessary for supply chain success in the rapid and demanding omnichannel world. The five major tasks currently facing supply chain members include the following:

1. *Revising supply chains for strategic advantage in an omnichannel world.* This task creates *business models* that erect barriers to competition.
2. *Implementing collaborative relationships inside the organization.* For many, this task is the hardest of the five. One reason is that specialization produces local department optimums but substandard service and profits at the company and supply chain levels.
3. *Forging supply chain partnerships with trading partners up and down the supply chain.* This is an "unnatural act" but increasingly a competitive must as companies rely on outside partners.
4. *Managing supply chain information.* The claims for new software confound potential users. There are many providers, and performance claims are hard to evaluate. The need for investments raises the risk involved.
5. *Making money from the supply chain.* Process improvement aimed at cost reduction retains its importance, but processes are multicompany along the supply chain and require collaboration to increase value and reduce costs.

Successful retailers spread prosperity back through their supply base. To that end, the authors are continuing their own partnership. Our collaboration brings together two skill sets: one in operations and another in managing retail businesses. Our mission is to match the challenges and opportunities in the retail industry with the solutions available from the SCM discipline. Their challenges include deciding what solutions to pursue and communicating to others up and down the chain what they require and why. Meanwhile, the customer craves greater and greater personalization and value for their money. This book should ease the work.

# Authors

**Mary Ann Odegaard, PhD,** is an experienced consultant and has completed assignments for major companies that include Apple, IBM, Toshiba, Cardinal Health, and Sunset Magazine and Books, and numerous retailers and shopping malls. She is an emeritus senior lecturer in marketing and international business at Michael G. Foster School of Business and a former lecturer in pharmacy at the University of Washington. She also served as the director of External Management Programs and, in this capacity, founded and directed the Retail Management Program, the Business Fundamentals Program, and the Pharmacy Management Program. Her specialties include marketing strategies in consumer products environments and supply chain implications for distribution companies. She has held board positions at several retailers and has served as president, vice president, and secretary of the University Book Store Board of Trustees. Her current research spans the gamut of retail strategy and includes market identification and strategic response, supply chain planning for private label products, information processing, financial implications of retail data, and the impact of sustainability considerations on retail management. Dr. Odegaard holds a BA in history, an MBA, and a PhD in business from Stanford University.

**James B. Ayers** is a principal with CGR Management Consultants, Los Angeles. He has instructed and consulted in strategy and operations improvement for clients in a variety of manufacturing, distribution, and service companies. The latter include clients delivering services in transportation, healthcare, engineering, utility, and financial industries. He has authored articles and has presented courses on product and process development as well as supply chain management. A prior book, *Improving Competitive Position: A Project Management Approach*, was published by the Society of Manufacturing Engineers (SME). Books in the supply chain management series include the first and second editions of the *Handbook of Supply Chain Management* (2001, 2006), *Making Supply Chain Management Work: Design, Implementation, Partnerships, Technology, and Profits* (2003), and *Supply Chain Project Management: A Structured Collaborative and Measurable*

*Approach* (2004, 2010). Jim is also the editor of the *Encyclopedia of Supply Chain Management* (2011).

Jim earned a BS degree with distinction from the U.S. Naval Academy and MBA and MS industrial engineering degrees from Stanford University. As a naval officer, he served on submarines. He is a Certified Management Consultant (CMC) through the Institute of Management Consultants (IMC).

# THE RETAIL SUPPLY CHAIN

The five chapters in Section I frame what we include in the retail "industry" defined in the broadest sense. Section I describes the retail supply chain components and describes the industry's impact on people around the globe—in both developed and developing countries.

| # | Chapter Name |
|---|---|
| 1 | Defining the Retail Supply Chain |
| 2 | Success in a Retail Business |
| 3 | Types of Retail Supply Chain Businesses |
| 4 | A Changing World: Moving toward Comparative Advantage |
| 5 | Corporate Social Responsibility, Sustainability, and the Retail Industry |

Chapter 1 points out that the retail supply chain has many players and most certainly is "more than stores." In fact, stores are the proverbial tip of the iceberg. A network of distributors, service providers, and manufacturers supports each point of sale, and the types of these points of sale have multiplied since the first edition of this book. In many cases, the ties between these contributors are quite loose— with trading partners living in different worlds, although those worlds have been converging to meet today's needs. One mission of this book is to provide advice and assistance to those charged with bringing those worlds closer together. Another objective is to assist supply chain participants in understanding each other's roles and business needs.

A profit model for retailers is the subject of Chapter 2. Many readers, in particular those playing roles in the supply chain upstream from retailers, may have little knowledge of the methods retailers use to achieve profitability and the importance of margin maintenance and strict inventory planning in attaining that state. Chapter 3 uses the profitability framework described in Chapter 2 to illustrate the wide range of business models pursued by various retailers and provides U.S. Census data on the participants in the U.S. retail supply chain. Although only United States data are profiled, other regions and markets are likely to grow networks of a similar scale as world markets further develop and as the rapidly growing omnichannel market strategies impact global markets with full force.

Globalization, the subject of Chapter 4, addresses the economic impact of the changes occurring because of this trend, the concept of both geographic and cultural distance associated with doing business across country boundaries, and a methodology for doing the math when it comes to making global sourcing decisions.

Chapter 5 addresses the growing importance of corporate social responsibility (CSR) for retailers and their supply chain's role in activities to improve society. This chapter covers a variety of causes behind these developments ranging from environmental impacts to social conditions in factories that produce merchandise. The chapter goes on to suggest some directions for confronting these issues and describes how to pick and choose in setting a direction for CSR that is consistent with a retailer's own strategy.

# Chapter 1

# Defining the Retail Supply Chain

This chapter describes a reference model shown in Figure 1.1 for the retail supply chain and the supply chain terminology that goes with it. Common definitions play an important role in dealing with a subject like this. The simplified retail supply chain model shown in Figure 1.1 includes, starting from right to left, the following:

1. Customers or end users—on the right
2. Retailers—white diamond shapes
3. Distributors—gray diamond shapes
4. Original equipment manufacturers (OEMs)—large rectangle
5. First-tier suppliers—gray circles
6. Second-tier suppliers—white circles
7. Service providers—not shown

Not shown for the sake of simplicity is a wide range of supply chain service providers (#7 above). Examples include warehouse operators, process and information technology providers, various consultants, transportation companies, trading companies, and customs brokers. Some service providers, such as contract manufacturers, may play roles as second-tier suppliers.

Growth rates are high in developing *omnichannel* supply chains. As the name implies, these have multiple paths to customers and end users. The OEM (square at the center of the figure) is an example. The OEM products can reach consumers through dealers/resellers, distributors, and stores, and by direct delivery. Omnichannel retailing provides the customer choices in channels at different points in the buying process. For example, initial research might be online, and actual purchase might be in the store—or vice versa; and returns could be accomplished in store, by mail,

3

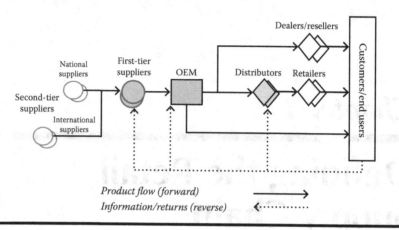

**Figure 1.1 Retail supply chain.**

or by pickup from a transportation agent. This obliges OEMs to have the flexibility to deliver product-related information, goods, and services through the channels favored by a particular customer. The party responsible for paying for transportation, in many cases the retail company, usually determines the type and vendor to be used.

The term *retail* refers to final sales to *consumers* who are customers or end users. However, businesses also purchase through retail supply chains. Retail transactions can be identified as business to consumer (B2C) or business to business (B2B). Because supply chains for consumers can be long, they consist of both B2B links, like those between first- and second-tier suppliers, and B2C links, like those between retailers and customers.

Successful retailers do three things well. First, the retailer must identify its target market segment offerings, preferably in those segments with growing demand. Second, retailers must design and develop an effective retail format. For example, retailer Tommy Bahama sells Hawaiian/Caribbean attire to men, women, and children at premium prices in stores decorated in a tropical theme. Third, the retailer must establish a sustainable competitive advantage. Rarely is price sufficient to compete—more must be offered. Costco and Wal-Mart emphasize low prices, but they have to augment this with the other aspects of the retail mix. Wal-Mart uses its size to bargain hard for low prices, while offering a very wide variety of products, and Costco buys in bulk when good deal opportunities come along, carrying a much narrower product assortment.

Research indicates that competitive positions built on virtues like brand, style, reliability, or availability result in better financial performance than positions built on lower price.[1] The authors surveyed the return on assets (ROA) of 25,000 companies that were publicly traded in U.S. stock exchanges from 1966 to 2010. Top-tier "miracle workers" were in the top 10% in terms of ROA. In retail categories, these were Abercrombie & Fitch, Wrigley, Weis Markets, and Maytag. All had nonprice strategies; none had a simple price-based strategy.

Colleges and universities have raised the profile of supply chain management (SCM) in their offerings. The website for Material Handling & Logistics publishes its list "10 Best Schools for a Supply Chain Education."[2] These are U.S. universities; similar lists are available for institutions outside the United States. Table 1.1 lists the institutions with a summary of reasons for their inclusion.

In introducing the results, author Dave Blanchard cites Kevin O'Marah of SCM World, a supply chain research organization. Mr. O'Marah notes that, unlike other disciplines, SCM knowledge and practice originates with practitioners, not academia. So academia must be educated by industry practitioners.

**Table 1.1   Best U.S. Schools for Supply Chain Education**

| Rank | School | Contributions Summary |
|------|--------|----------------------|
| 1 | Michigan State University | Research institute focused on value chain management |
| 2 | Pennsylvania State University | Department of Supply Chain Management offers undergraduate, master's, PhD, and executive programs |
| 3 | Massachusetts Institute of Technology | Established MIT Global SCALE (Supply Chain and Logistics Excellence) Network |
| 4 | Arizona State University | In 2014, offered Master of Science in Supply Chain Management and Engineering |
| 5 | Georgia Institute of Technology | Established the Supply Chain and Logistics Institute (SCL) to develop the next-generation supply chain workforce |
| 6 | University of Michigan | Ross School of Business offers a Master of Supply Chain Management degree |
| 7 | Stanford University | School of Business Value Chain Innovation Initiative that brings together student and faculty from multiple schools |
| 8 | University of Tennessee | Global Supply Chain Institute that conducts research projects; twice-yearly Supply Chain Forums |
| 9 | Ohio State University | Fisher College of Business supported by faculty in Marketing and Logistics Management Science Departments |
| 10 | Harvard University | Influential articles in *Harvard Business Review*; ongoing research in supply chain management |

## 1.1 More Than Stores

Retail supply chains are more than stores and technically begin with the original sourcing of raw materials for product manufacture. The supply chain will vary among product types and the preferences of customers and end users. According to Figure 1.1, customers or end users can acquire products and services from retail and online stores, directly from OEMs, and from dealers or resellers who also deal with the OEM. Retailers and distributors may refer to OEMs as the *manufacturer*, the *vendor*, or the *resource*.

Some retail supply chains include more than one intermediary distributor. This is especially true of the food industry, where freshness is mandatory, and for frequently purchased consumer goods like over-the-counter (OTC) medications For example, milk may be produced on a farm, then sold to a cooperative, which sells it to a processor, who in turn sells it to a distribution brand; it is then sold to a retailer, who sells it to the consumer. A supply chain analogy is the fire brigade, where it is faster to pass the bucket along a chain of people than to have one person carry it the entire distance.

Another appropriate analogy is the iceberg. As customers or end users, we participate in the last transaction in the chain. We see the part of the iceberg that sticks out of the water while most of the iceberg is hidden. Also, there is often a difference between *customers* and *end users* at the end of the supply chain. In this book, the customer makes buying decisions and purchases goods and services, while the end user actually consumes or uses the product or service. For example, a wife and mother who shops is the customer for her household; family members are end users and may wield strong influence over what is actually purchased. A purchase of a product like a computer will likely be accompanied by what are called "extended product" services. Examples include financing, warrantees, delivery options, software, and training,

Both customers and end users combine with other influencers to make purchase decisions. For example, a father may have health concerns for his children and insist that the mother purchase low-fat milk even though he is neither a consumer nor a shopper.[3]

Most of us buy much of what we use or consume at stores, but alternatives are many due to the growth of omnichannel distribution. Consumers also order out of catalogs, go online, or purchase from dealers or salespersons who guide them in their selections. The store, direct, and dealer/reseller paths in Figure 1.1 are *channels of distribution*.

Each level in a supply chain (e.g., distributor, OEM, or supplier) is called an *echelon*. Bypassing an echelon is a process called *disintermediation*. Disintermediation, in some cases, can lower cost, inventory, and lead times. Many supply chain participants, particularly distributors, are wary of disintermediation paths that bypass them. Firms employing a disintermediation strategy must be judicious in setting up a direct path to customers that alienates existing trading partners.

Recently, well-known apparel brands have opened up their own brand-centered specialty stores near retailers who carry their lines. Notable examples include the previously cited Tommy Bahama and Eileen Fisher, a seller of women's apparel. Eileen Fisher seeks to "make women feel good with premium products." In Seattle, the Eileen Fisher store is located directly across the street from the Nordstrom flagship store, which also carries the Eileen Fisher brand. By varying the merchandise in the company-owned stores so they are not in direct competition, the two coexist successfully.

Apparel companies who operate their own stores and/or websites are said to be *vertically integrated*, controlling the supply chain from beginning to end. A manufacturer that engages in retail activities would be *forwardly integrated*, whereas a retailer engaged in production would be considered *backwardly integrated*. Backward integration has become a necessity for retailers to attain desired margins, regardless of retail format. Costco, Wal-Mart, Macy's, Kroger, and most others have turned to producing their own products to stay competitive. Costco's establishment of the Kirkland brand has been very successful. These private label goods are known to be very good-value items, dependable because Costco has selected them as their own.

The OEM also often provides the *brand* identity for the products sold by the retailer. However, as with Costco, brand identity might be associated with the retail enterprise through *private label* brands designed and sold exclusively by that retailer. Gap is another example of a company that carries private label merchandise and uses it to develop its retail image and a long-term competitive advantage. Gap maintains stores under the identities of Gap, Old Navy, Banana Republic, and Athleta retail outlets. Customers can purchase merchandise outright, buy a gift card, reserve merchandise to pick up in the store, and create a wish list for future purchases. Gap-branded merchandise is sold only by Gap and is not carried in other apparel stores.

In some cases, components of a product are branded for inclusion in other products sold at retail. Intel chips and Microsoft operating systems in computers are sold by computer OEMs across a range of *form factors* (e.g., desktop, laptop, notebook).

Brand identity is enhanced by extended product features—up to a point. Supply chain design must support these strategies. Lack of extended product features narrows the basis of competition to price. Earlier, this chapter reported that nonprice strategies resulted in superior performance measured by ROA. Gap, Tommy Bahama, and Eileen Fisher also distinguish themselves with nonprice supply chain features.

Starbucks, with Internet access and comfortable places to linger, delivers an extended product that supports sales of base products such as coffee, other beverages, merchandise, and light food. Starbucks' growth is based on consumers' perceptions of the coffee shops as a relaxing third place to go, the others being the place of work and home.

A retailer with a good reputation for after-sales services provides an extended product in the form of customer risk reduction. The customer is certain that he or she can use the product with confidence, return unsatisfactory merchandise, or have problems fixed promptly. Section 1.4 further explores how supply chain networks create value. Chapter 6, Section 6.3, further describes the importance of extended product features.

Some companies have expanded their breadth of brand offerings too far. In 2014, Proctor and Gamble announced it was drastically reducing its number of brand offerings to focus on its 70 to 80 best-selling brands. Growth, reliable cash flow, and profit generation motivated this reduction. There can be too many brand differentations.[4]

*Globalization* is an important supply chain topic. Figure 1.1 shows second-tier sources of product components as either national or international. Globalization also opens international markets for base and extended products that fuel sales growth. Wal-Mart not only imports many of its products, but it also has opened stores in foreign countries, including many in China. This book deals with globalization again in Chapter 4 and Chapter 6, Section 6.4. The rapid and complex globalization of online retailer Amazon is without precedent in retail history and is impressively described in detail in MWPVL International's paper on the subject.[5]

In June 2016, a referendum, labeled "Brexit" in Great Britain called for the United Kingdom to exit the European Union. Major issues for the British were open-border immigration into the United Kingdom that threatened resident jobs and its accompanying economic malaise. After the referendum passed, the *Los Angeles Times*[6] posed the question of the moment, "Will 'Brexit' mark the end of the age of globalization?" The article maintained that the vote "signals a new era for the post–World War II globalization drive." It identified the public backlash to lower trade barriers and open borders. This same theme formed a major plank of the U.S. Republican Party's platform in the 2016 presidential election.

A potential source of confusion is the use of the terms *upstream* and *downstream* in the supply chain context. In this book, upstream relates to operations that precede a point of reference. For example, in Figure 1.1, distributors are upstream of retailers. For customers and end users, all operations are upstream. Downstream operations, on the other hand, follow points of reference. So distributors are downstream of OEMs in Figure 1.1.

Some companies refer to upstream trading partners as their *supply chain* and downstream trading partners as their *demand chain*. A common practice—that has great potential for harm—is to label sourcing and purchasing functions as the "supply chain" domain. Those that do so view the supply chain as the upstream links and fail to consider the whole supply chain as depicted in Figure 1.1. This book is dedicated to promoting the view that supply chain should be defined as end-to-end process steps from raw materials to the arrival in the customer's hands—and the return cycle.

## 1.2 Defining *Supply Chain* and *Supply Chain Management*

As mentioned in the last section, there are many working definitions of supply chain, varying with the viewpoint of the definer. A common interpretation mentioned in the previous section is where organizations define supply chain as procurement only, distribution, or a collection of information system applications. These viewpoints usually reflect the need for operating efficiency in running the supply chain. This often ignores strategic advantage from supply chain design.

To understand the variation and commonality in definitions, the staff of DC Velocity (*DC* stands for *Distribution Center*) questioned a panel of 11 supply chain practitioners, whom they referred to as logistics profession "rainmakers." Table 1.2 summarizes the responses to the question, "How do you define supply chain management as it relates to logistics operations?"[7]

Table 1.2 responses prove that perspectives on SCM vary. They range from broad, planning-oriented definitions (such as #1, #3, #4, #5, and #7) to operational ones (e.g., #2, #8, and #9). The rainmakers' responses reflect their roles, with those of academics and executives being broader in nature and operating executives' responses more focused on physical flows of concern to logistics management.

This book recommends a broad view that includes the potential for strategic contribution from SCM; first, a broader definition, of the term supply chain is presented here.[8]

Supply chain:
> Product life-cycle processes comprising physical, information, financial, and knowledge flows whose purpose is to satisfy end-user requirements with physical products and services from multiple and linked suppliers.

This definition says that the supply chain is made up of *processes*, as emphasized in Table 1.2, definition 5. Figure 1.1 is a high-level snapshot of these processes. They include sourcing material, designing products, manufacturing, transporting, fixing, and selling physical products or services at supply chain enterprises.

In addition to the widely accepted marketing definition of the term *product life cycle*, the term has at least two meanings when examined in the supply chain context: the selling life cycle and the usage life cycle. For long-life, or *durable*, products as well as many services, these aren't the same. The selling time window may be far shorter than the product's useful life. Examples of products with extended lives are automobiles, computers, life insurance policies, and 30-year mortgages.

All must be supported long after newer products take the place of older ones. For this reason, product support after the sale can be an important—if not *the* most important and profitable—supply chain component. In these cases, the prospects for seller longevity, another extended product feature, is important to customers. Service after purchase may be a very important component of the product choice.

**Table 1.2    Practitioner Definitions of the Term *Supply Chain Management***

|   | *Thought Leader* | *Definition Summary* |
|---|---|---|
| 1 | Theodore Stank, University of Tennessee (Knoxville) | Orientation to conduct business across multiple firms to improve end-customer value |
| 2 | Tim Krishner, president, SeayCo Integrators, Inc. | How best to use tools and reports to enhance productivity |
| 3 | James Stock, University of South Florida | Management of a relationship network between independent organizations and business units |
| 4 | John Sidell, founder of ESYNC, supply chain execution systems and consulting | The end-to-end management of inventory and information from sourcing through manufacturing/assembly to distribution to customer delivery and, depending on the business model, through to the end consumer |
| 5 | Jeffrey Karrenbauer, founding director of Insight, Inc., optimization and simulation applications | Integration of key business processes from end user through original suppliers, which provides products, services, and information that add value for customers and other stakeholders |
| 6 | Philippe Lambotte, Kraft Foods | Management of goods and information flows from the retail shelf to suppliers |
| 7 | Chad Autry, Texas Christian University | Business process integration across and through the boundaries of multiple firms acting together to create value |
| 8 | Michael Fostyk, American Eagle Outfitters | Getting the right goods to the customer, at the right time, consistently, accurately, at the right value to the organization |
| 9 | John Gentle, formerly Owens Corning leader for transportation affairs | Begins with material planning and is translated back into transportation requirements of inbound materials, warehousing of both raw and finished materials, and the transportation of the finished goods to the customer |

*(Continued)*

**Table 1.2 (Continued)    Practitioner Definitions of the Term *Supply Chain Management***

|   | *Thought Leader* | *Definition Summary* |
|---|---|---|
| 10 | Jeffrey Camm, University of Cincinnati | The old standard definition ... getting the right quantities to the right locations at the right time in a cost-effective manner |
| 11 | Dick Ward, Material Handling Industry of America | Flow of all goods and materials from the beginning of the chain to the end, being the final consumer, and even beyond, when you consider returns |

*Physical, information,* and *financial* flows are frequently cited supply chain dimensions. However, the common viewpoint of the supply chain as a purchasing or physical distribution network is limiting. *Information* and *financial* components are often as important as *physical* flow in supply chains as are *reverse* flows that go in the opposite direction, shown in Figure 1.1.

Often omitted from supply chain definitions is the role of *knowledge* inputs into supply chain processes. Knowledge is the driver behind new products and new processes, the source of growth through innovation. Designing supply chain processes for new products requires coordination of intellectual input (the design) with physical inputs (components, prototypes, factories, distribution channels, and the like). In the retail industry, such knowledge can produce better-designed, more user friendly, and more stylish products. Increasingly, products sold to consumers rely on software to distinguish them; such features are currently highly influential in automobile choices made by customers. The knowledge component of our definition includes that software.

Organizations experiencing turnover have particular challenges in managing the knowledge component. An article centered on passing knowledge in distribution describes OPPTY, an acronym for observation, practice, partnering, and taking responsibility.[9] The technique calls for internal experts, usually senior acknowledged experts, to mentor aspiring newer employees interested in their area of expertise. The recommended interaction includes observation, practice, joint problem solving, and delegating responsibility.

Another framework for passing on knowledge applies to areas where the firm "doesn't know what it knows." The method is called MASK (Method for Analyzing and Structuring Knowledge). Like OPPTY, acknowledged internal experts, perhaps more than 100 in an organization—who may not be aware of the knowledge they hold—are queried. The knowledge is assembled into a *Knowledge Book* with sections on topics like craft specifications, concepts, process, history, know-how, and evolution.[10]

The supply chain should support the satisfaction of *end-user requirements*. These requirements give rise to the fundamental mission of supply chains—matching supply and demand. As noted later in this chapter and in Chapter 7, there may be a range of customer or end-user groups who constitute market *segments*. An integral part of SCM is tailoring supply chain networks to satisfy the varying needs of these segments.

A supply chain also has *multiple, linked suppliers*. From the customer or end-user viewpoint, a supply chain exists when there are multiple enterprises backing the last link that delivers the product or service. Under this definition, the neighborhood barber would not constitute a supply chain, while a chain of barbershops would.

As mentioned previously, the supply chain has a two-way flow. Many consider supply chains only in terms of *forward* flow from suppliers to end users, so SCM definitions take on a limited sourcing-logistics flavor. For the physical processes, this is largely true. Only one definition in Table 1.2 (#11) mentions *reverse* flows in the form of returns.

But supply chain design must include backward flows for product returns, payments and rebates, replenishment orders, repair, and other reasons. The European Union has passed regulations that hold companies responsible for the disposal of the products they sell. For example, computer manufacturers have to take back and recycle parts and materials from the products that they have sold. Chapter 22 deals with reverse flows in more detail.

Services also have supply chains. Production planning for the research and development department, which produces designs, not products, can benefit from the same techniques used by product manufacturers.

Federal Express and United Parcel Service (UPS) operate service businesses, but they employ complex supply chains to move customer shipments. A software company like Microsoft is challenged to continuously improve its product through upgrades, so it too has a supply chain for its knowledge-based product.

With the term supply chain defined, SCM is simply the following.

Supply chain management:
> Design, maintenance, and operation of supply chain processes, including those for base and extended products, for satisfaction of end-user needs.

Although easy to define, SCM is a challenge to practice. Applying the above definition, effective SCM requires the management skills to perform the following five tasks:

*Task 1. Designing supply chains for strategic advantage.* This task creates new business models that shift the basis of competition. Definition 1 in Table 1.2 comes closest to recognizing this need. The presence of needed skills to perform this task is rare in many organizations.

*Task 2. Implementing collaborative relationships inside the organization.* Specialization in focused departments of a retailer or its trading partners produces local optimums with substandard service and productivity in the retail supply chain overall.

*Task 3. Forging supply chain partnerships with trading partners up and down the supply chain.* This is an "unnatural act" but often a necessary one to gain competitive advantage. Many of the definitions in Table 1.2 recognize this need. Section 1.4 describes the value within a network.

*Task 4. Managing supply chain information.* The claims for new software applications may confound potential users. The confusion is the consequence of having many providers and the difficulties of evaluating their claims or adapting their "solutions" to one's business. Chapter 10 describes a resource for dealing with this complexity.

*Task 5. Making money from the supply chain.* Well-managed process improvement retains its importance, but processes that cross department and company boundaries have to be defined and addressed, not just those in a department.

Note that the tasks range from strategy making to collaborating effectively and to running efficient operations. The tools and techniques in this book will help readers improve their skills in performing these tasks.

## 1.3 The Importance of Customer Segments

Figure 1.1 shows customers and end users as a single block. However, customers or end users are seldom as homogeneous as the figure implies. The block often is made up of individual customer/end-user groups, called *segments*. Each segment sells to those who share buying habits and product preferences and have common needs for supply chain performance. This performance includes features like cost, quality, and responsiveness that are built into the supply chain's design.

Marketers define four variables that control how products are presented to different market segments. These *four Ps* are product, price, place, and promotion. Management's decisions on these four variables will drive retail supply chain design. Needless to say, the number of variations for any product line is huge. The SCM "art" is in designing supply chains to support targeted-segment retail strategies without overdoing it, as mentioned earlier with regard to Proctor and Gamble's discovery that they had unprofitably oversegmented the market. Subsequent chapters, particularly those in Section III, describe variations in strategy and the types of supply chain designs needed to support them.

## 1.4 Adding Value along the Chain

A term that is often interchanged with supply chain is *value chain*, a term from strategist Michael Porter that reflects profitability at different echelons along the chain.[11] Porter uses the expression in the same context in which the term supply chain is used. *Value* in a supply chain like the one in Figure 1.1 is reflected by the profit earned at each echelon. Greater value brings higher profits and return on investment.

Many criticize retailer Wal-Mart for its market power over suppliers through aggressive cost negotiations. Wal-Mart customers appreciate the resulting lower prices. Distributors may fear disintermediation because their operations may not be seen as *adding value* to the supply chain. The same is said of retail stores whose businesses suffer in the face of direct sales by OEMs or distributors.

For technology products, second-tier suppliers may enjoy outsized profits, adding the greatest value to supply chain products. Technology companies in particular possess proprietary *core competencies* that drive innovation in the end products. Microsoft and Intel are examples for personal computers. For other supply chains, the OEM may be the most profitable trading partner. This advantage could derive from the OEM's distribution system, its investment in manufacturing plants, or its product development capabilities.

Resellers in other supply chains could also enjoy high profits. This would be the case where complex systems have to be assembled from relatively inexpensive components. Another source of a profitable business comes from after-sales replacement parts and support. Examples are consumables like printer cartridges and razor blades.

In mid-2016, a book and accompanying webinar pointed out the premium value that lies in networks. This is relevant since supply chains are a form of network. The book's authors' firm, OpenMatters, LLC, had conducted a survey of companies in the S&P 1500. These authors maintain that "networks are eating the world."[12] They point to the market values of traditional companies compared to those with business models that utilize networks.

For example, transportation provider Uber, a network example light on fixed assets, has a market capitalization of $63 billion. General Motors, a capital-intensive company, has a stock value of $30 billion. Netflix, another network company, has a value of $40 billion, while the cinema chain Regal Cinemas' is about $3 billion. The common thread is that the higher-value companies have digital, not brick-and-mortar, business models. Table 1.3 summarizes OpenMatters' research including their identification of four business models.

**Table 1.3  Business Models and the Value of Networks**

| Business Model | Description | % of Companies |
| --- | --- | --- |
| Asset builders | Make one, sell to one | 64% |
| Service providers | Hire one, sell to one | 24% |
| Technology creators | Make one, sell to many | 11% |
| Network orchestrators | Make many, sell to many | 1% |

**Table 1.4  Business Model and Value**

| Business Model | Scaling (cost of added capacity) | Price/Revenue Multiplier |
|---|---|---|
| Asset builders | High marginal cost | 1.8 |
| Service providers | Moderate marginal cost | 2.7 |
| Technology creators | Low marginal cost | 5.3 |
| Network orchestrators | Near zero marginal cost | 8.0 |

Asset builders are the most common model. Examples include large retail chains and automotive manufacturers. Growth must be supported by a proportional investment in the number of outlets for stores or manufacturing plants for the asset builders. Service providers are similar, but the added capacity requires a lower marginal cost. The technology creators, like the publisher of this book, transfer knowledge from its book writers to audiences interested in the writers' knowledge and insights. Facebook and Twitter are network orchestrators because they have built a bridge between multiple sources and multiple users with very low investment.

Table 1.4 shows the value of each model as expressed in its stock value-to-revenue multiplier. Mr. Libert noted in his webinar that the network orchestrators are rewarded by high valuations because they provide tools that maximize asset utilization. For example, ride sharing with Uber enables a car owner to earn money lost when his or her vehicle is not needed for his or her own needs.

The authors maintain that all four models exist in any industry and that a path exists to multiply the value of an industry's players by changing their business model. The SCM methodologies and tools in this book can support these efforts.

# References

1. Raynor, Micheael E. and Ahmed, Mumtaz, "Three Rules for Making a Company Truly Great," *Harvard Business Review*, April 2013, pp. 108–117.
2. Blanchard, Dave, "10 Best Schools for a Supply Chain Education," *Material Handling & Logistics (MHL)*, August 21, 2015.
3. Zikmund, William G., and d'Amico, Michael, *Creating and Keeping Customers: Effective Marketing*, Cincinnati: South-Western College Publishing Company, 1998.
4. Coolidge, Alexander, "P&G to Shed More Than Half Its Brands," *Cincinnati Enquirer*, August 1, 2014.
5. "Amazon Global Fulfillment Center Network," MWPVL International, August 2016.
6. Lee, Don, "Will Brexit Mark the End of the Age of Globalization?," *Los Angeles Times*, June 25, 2016, p. A1.

7. DC Velocity Staff, "The Rainmakers," *DC Velocity*, July 2006, pp. 33–49.
8. Ayers, James B., *Handbook of Supply Chain Management*, 2nd ed., Boca Raton: Auerbach Publications, 2006.
9. Leanard, Dorothy, Barton, Gavin, and Barton, Michelle, "Make Yourself an Expert," *Harvard Business Review*, April 2013, pp. 127–131.
10. Van Berton, Philippe and Ermine, Jean-Louis, "Applied Knowledge: A Set of Well-Tried Tools," *Journal of Information and Knowledge Management Systems*, vol. 36, #4, pp. 425–431, 2006.
11. Porter, Michael E., *Competitive Advantage: Creating and Sustaining Superior Performance*, New York: The Free Press, 1985.
12. Libert, Barry, Beck, Megan, and Wind, Jerry, *The Network Imperative: How to Survive and Grow in the Age of Digital Business Models*, Boston: Harvard Business Review Press, 2016.

# Chapter 2

# Success in a Retail Business

Achieving success in the retail industry (usually judged by profitability) requires having the right product in the right place at the right time, happy customers, and collaboration with key supply chain partners. Chapter 2 identifies financial success factors for a retail enterprise. The factors apply to retail chains and physical and online stores of any size. Achieving success as a retailer—or as a supplier to retailers—requires a range of skills, with the five supply chain management (SCM) tasks listed in Chapter 1, Section 1.2, among them. Recent goals and objectives that have universal appeal include the following:

- Timely deliveries to excel at customer service
- High margins and frequent inventory turns along the supply chain
- For sustained success, great products updated promptly as fashion and technology change

Trading partner collaboration with retailers will be aided by an understanding of how the retailer makes decisions. Larger retailers, who manufacture as well as sell, should employ these measures across their operations. IKEA, in fashionable but proprietary home furnishings, and Zara, known for its rapid turnover of fashion clothing, are examples.

## 2.1 Financial Statements and Analysis

Financial statements are the basic foundation for retail decision making. Two universally employed reports are as follows:

1. The income statement (Table 2.1) that reports financial results over a specified time period, often quarterly or yearly
2. A balance sheet (Table 2.2) that reports assets and liabilities at a point in time—also quarterly or yearly

These two reports include the numbers needed to assess profitability and return on investment and also may identify opportunities to improve performance. The use of income statements and balance sheets is not limited to retailers. Trading partner companies use similar reporting.

**Table 2.1  Retailer Income Statements (Millions of U.S. Dollars)**

|   |   | Discounter | High-End |
|---|---|---|---|
| 1 | Gross sales | 1000 | 35 |
| 2 | Less: returns | 50 | 5 |
| 3 | Net sales | 950 | 30 |
| 4 | Less: cost of goods sold (COGS) | 750 | 10 |
| 5 | Gross margin | 200 | 20 |
| 6 | Less: operating expense | 90 | 15 |
| 7 | Less: interest expense | 50 | 12 |
| 8 | Total expense | 140 | 27 |
| 9 | Net pretax profit | 60 | 3 |
| **Popular Ratios (Percent)** | | | |
| 10 | Gross margin (#5/#3) | 21 | 67 |
| 11 | Expense ratio (#8/#3) | 15 | 90 |
| 12 | Pretax profit margin (#9/#1) | 6 | 9 |
| 13 | Returns ratio (#2/#1) | 5 | 14 |

**Table 2.2   Retailer Balance Sheets (Millions of U.S. Dollars)**

|  |  | *Discounter* | *High-End* |
|---|---|---|---|
| **Assets** | | | |
| ***Current Assets:*** | | | |
| 1 | Accounts receivable | 15 | 10 |
| 2 | Merchandise inventory | 150 | 5 |
| 3 | Cash | 10 | 1 |
| 4 | Total current assets | 175 | 16 |
| ***Fixed Assets:*** | | | |
| 5 | Buildings, equipment (at cost) | 1000 | 5 |
| 6 | Less: accumulated depreciation | 400 | 1 |
| 7 | Net fixed assets | 600 | 4 |
| 8 | Total assets | 775 | 20 |
| **Liabilities** | | | |
| 9 | Accounts payable | 80 | 7 |
| 10 | Long-term liabilities | 300 | 1 |
| 11 | Other liabilities | 5 | 0 |
| 12 | Total liabilities | 385 | 8 |
| 13 | Owners' equity | 390 | 12 |
| 14 | Total liabilities and owners' equity | 775 | 20 |
| **Popular Ratio** | | | |
| 15 | "Quick" ratio[a] (#1 + #3)/#9 | 0.3 | 1.6 |

[a] Also called acid test, or current ratio.

## 2.1.1  Retailer Income Statements

Table 2.1 shows fictitious income statements for two retailers, the first for a company called *Discounter*, a chain, with annual revenues of $1 billion, and the other for a smaller chain called *High-End*, with annual revenues of $35 million. Tax rates vary widely from company to company and are not relevant to the themes in this chapter, so after-tax figures are not included.

The two companies are on opposite ends of the retail value–service spectrum. Discounter caters to value-seeking consumers in search of low prices. High-End customers are service seeking and attracted to style and luxury. Discounter has a significantly higher cost of goods sold (COGS) relative to sales (row 4 of Table 2.1) and far lower gross margins, 21% versus 67% for High-End (row 10). High-End delivers more service for the sales dollar—83% versus 15% for Discounter, reflected in the expense ratio (row 11). These services include help with selection, customer education about product choices, consumer credit to finance sales, a luxurious shopping environment, and ample inventory from which to choose.

Pretax profit margin (row 12) is 50% higher for High-End. To determine if this is good or bad, one must consider the required investment from the balance sheet shown in Table 2.2. The returns ratio (row 13 of Table 2.1) highlights potential customer service or product quality problems, or could reflect a more generous return policy appropriate for this kind of retailer.

To improve income statement performance, retailers have four fundamental options:

1. Decreasing expenses
2. Increasing margins by
   a. Obtaining merchandise at a lower cost
   b. Raising prices
3. Selling more merchandise

While stating the available solutions is simple, execution may be difficult. For example, consultants from McKinsey & Company report "holes in the pocket" for retailers, which show up as leaks in income.[1] The authors note that small leaks in income statement categories can produce large drags on earnings. This is reflected in row 11, which shows that a 1% decrease in *Discounter's* merchandise, operating, and interest costs increases pretax profit from 6% to 7%, a 17% improvement in profitability. Thus, attention to detail on the cost side will produce significant improvements in profitability. Leaks identified by McKinsey include the following:

■ Online order discounts
■ Delivery to the customer without appropriate charges
■ Discounts that discourage rapid payment or are granted without fast payment
■ Cooperative advertising with the manufacturer that is ineffective
■ Ineffective market development incentives to promote brands or sales to customer groups

Several lines on the income statement are supply chain related. These include the Cost of Goods Sold (COGS), the largest expense, for products purchased from original equipment manufacturers (OEMs) or distributors. Inbound freight is added to the COGS as part of merchandise cost. Many operating expenses are also supply chain costs. Examples are the cost of distribution facilities, inventory handling, and inventory carrying costs. Improving supplier quality might also reduce returns. Customer support processes to match products with customer needs may also be a good investment. This could reduce a revenue leak from returns, particularly for a company like High-End with a 14% return rate.

## 2.1.2 Retailer Balance Sheets

As described above, the income statement reports performance *over a period of time* like a month, quarter, or year. The balance sheet reports the financial condition *at a point in time* (end of the year, quarter, or month). Assets in Table 2.2 include the credits extended to customers in the form of accounts receivable (row 1), inventory to support sales (row 2), and cash (row 3). These are referred to as *current* or short-term assets because they have expected lives of less than 1 year.

Fixed assets like buildings and equipment (rows 5–7) have longer lives. They are often valued at cost with accumulated depreciation deducted as it is on row 6. This figure may not reflect current market values but, rather, the costs incurred at time of purchase. Sometimes investors buy a company because physical asset values have increased and aren't reflected in the company's value.

In the example, Discounter owns many of its stores and related equipment. High-End relies on short-term leases for its stores and equipment and, therefore, has few assets on its balance sheet. Some companies also report long-term leases as liabilities.

The liabilities side of the balance sheet includes both short-term, current (accounts payable, row 9), and long-term (rows 10 and 11) liabilities. For Discounter, these liabilities include the loans taken to purchase the stores it owns. High-End has few long-term liabilities because management has chosen to lease store space. This practice raises the risk of losing a lease, resulting in relocation costs and additional marketing expenses to inform the public of the move or in large rent increases.

Owner's equity (OE) is the difference between assets and liabilities. Because long-term assets are recorded on the balance sheet at historical costs, owner's equity doesn't necessarily reflect market values.

To make funding decisions when evaluating strategic options, companies calculate the "cost of capital." This company-specific interest rate is determined by weighting rates paid for various sources of debt and equity capital. To be approved, company investments must generate enough cash flow to meet this hurdle rate. Chapter 19, Section 19.2, describes the application of the cost of capital to investment decisions.

Some lenders require borrower *liquidity* as determined by the balance sheet. A popular ratio derived from the balance sheet is the acid test or quick ratio (row 15). Usually, the ratio assumes that inventory values are 0—the acid test.

Ratios greater than 1 might be a lender test of the borrower's capacity to repay a loan. In Table 2.2, Discounter has a low ratio (0.3) whereas High-End has a higher one (1.6).

Anand Khokha, president of a turnaround company, has led several retailers in financial trouble with their lenders to more profitable paths. He points to several opportunities to improve retailer cash flow and profitability:

1. Making sound merchandising decisions about what to buy remains the best way to increase sales and reduce inventory. It is no surprise that poor financial performance is the product of poor merchandising decisions.
2. Getting the product on time is vital, particularly for retailers who rely on seasonal sales, such as at Christmas, or who sell seasonal products like skis, fashion apparel, and bathing suits. Company processes may not assure timely deliveries.
3. Owned real estate is often neglected when turning around a company. A lot of this value can be turned into cash. This could be the case for Discounter. When real estate values are escalating, selling the real estate may have a higher yield than operating the retail business.
4. Retailers often select too many stock-keeping units (SKUs), raising inventory and tying up capital. Merchandisers may seek to offer a full product range, but many products are unprofitable. A strategic analysis is required to determine the appropriate assortment width (number of product lines carried) and depth (number of SKUs within the product category).
5. Measuring category profitability is not done well. The retailer does not know what is profitable and what is not.[1]

This chapter and Chapter 19 address items #1, #4, and #5. Applications include all products, product lines, stores, and individual products.

## 2.1.3 Financial Analysis

A financial analysis is a starting point for turnaround experts like Mr. Khokha. The analysis seeks to uncover opportunities for improvement and requires calculation of performance measures that combine income statement and balance sheet items. Table 2.3 provides common measures for analyzing supply chain performance. The numbers aid discovery of ways to improve cash flow and profitability. The following paragraphs interpret these measures and identify opportunities to apply the SCM methodologies and tools in this book.

*Inventory turns and days of supply (rows 1 and 2).* Retailers are particularly interested in inventory turnover. The ratio tells them how many times a year the company has used and reused its inventory investment dollars, garnering the products' contribution margins with each turn of the inventory. Unless objectives for

**Table 2.3  Financial Analysis**

| | Name | Factors | Equation | Discounter | High-End |
|---|---|---|---|---|---|
| 1 | Inventory turns | COGS/inventory[a] | #4/#2 | 5.0 | 2.0 |
| 2 | Inventory days of supply | *Inventory/daily COGS* | #2/(#4/365) | 73 | 183 |
| 3 | A. Receivable days<br>B. Payable days | *Receivables/daily net sales*<br>*Payables/daily COGS* | #1/(#3/365)<br>#9/(#4/365) | 6<br>39 | 121<br>255 |
| 4 | Cash-to-cash cycle (days) | Receivable + inventory days – payable days | #2 + #3A – 3B | 40 | 49 |
| 5 | Return on equity (percent) | *Pretax profit/owners' equity* | #9/#13 | 15 | 25 |
| 6 | Return on total capital (percent) | *Pretax profit/total assets* | #9/#8 | 8 | 15 |
| 7 | Return on working capital (percent) | *Pretax profit/(receivables + inventory + cash – accounts payable)* | #9/(#1 + #2 + #3 – #9) | 63 | 33 |

*Note:* Balance sheet items are in italics, and income statement items are in regular type.

a Some companies calculate inventory turns as net sales/inventory.

inventory turns are met, the company can find itself short of cash to pay its expenses and, in extreme cases, bleeding to death by depleting inventory to pay other bills.

Inventory is a common target for cost reduction efforts. Many retailers employ rules for the optimum inventory (days of supply) that maximizes turns, minimizes order costs, and eliminates stockouts. Solutions include purging slow-moving items through inventory analysis, sharing forecasts with suppliers, negotiating delivery schedules, requiring suppliers to hold inventory, direct shipments to stores, more frequent replenishment, and more accurate forecasting. Since accuracy in forecasts may be as good as it gets, shifting from forecast-driven to demand-driven replenishment can be a solution. Chapter 17 describes approaches to achieving demand-driven supply chains.

*Receivable and payable days (rows 3A and 3B).* Excess receivables may be symptomatic of loose credit practices or providing too much credit to customers. This is one of the leaks identified by the McKinsey consultants. "Firing" or denying future credit to slow-paying customers may improve cash flow. Payables, on the other hand, provide a source of working capital. High-End makes ample use of supplier credit to finance its business. Should suppliers' willingness to perform this service change, High-End's business model would be threatened.

*Cash-to-cash cycle (row 4).* This cycle captures the effect of coordinating the three working capital accounts for receivables, inventory, and payables. Dell (computers) and Toyota (automobiles) have sought to minimize this measure. Early in their company's life, cash was in short supply. Dell's direct model took an order payment from the customer and only then acquired the parts necessary to build the computer. Toyota has a "sell one, make one" mentality exemplified by its *pull* replenishment systems. Dell's and Toyota's demand-driven approach, sometimes referred to as *Lean* manufacturing, has been rewarded with high profits and market share. Many supply chain reengineering efforts use the cash-to-cash cycle to set their goals. One such company, described in Chapter 10, Section 10.1, is furniture maker Herman Miller.

*Return on capital (rows 5, 6, and 7).* Most companies use metrics that relate profits to investment. The three shown here are common. The first includes only owners' equity in the base, the second total assets, and the third working capital only. The total assets approach is the broadest. Many investors might consider the 8% return on total capital for Discounter marginal. On the other hand, High-End's 25% return on equity (ROE) would be attractive to many.

As noted above, where private capital investors are acquiring retailers and other distribution firms, possible acquisition candidates are identified by examining income statements and balance sheets. The goal is to convert assets into cash to pay for the acquisition. Discounter might be such a candidate. Their substantial real estate holdings may be such a source of funds. Shortening the 40-day cash-to-cash cycle through inventory reductions, dropping slow-moving merchandise, faster collections, and having suppliers finance Discounter's inventories are other opportunities.

## 2.2 Merchandise Replenishment and Budgeting

The merchandising function at the retailer level establishes a plan for buying merchandise, allocating it to stores, and planning replenishment. Retailers often utilize a form of the *Strategic Profit Model* in this task. Financial executives at E.I. DuPont de Nemours and Company (DuPont) developed such a model during World War I to evaluate internal performance. At the time, the company, founded in July 1802, was already over 100 years old. The model is particularly useful for retailers because it takes into account common goals for inventory turnover and margins in merchandising decision making.

The DuPont Company broke down ROE into three ratios: return on sales, sales turnover, and the ratio of assets to equity.[2] They then demonstrated the relationship between them as follows:

Return on equity = (return on sales) × (sales turnover) × (financial leverage)

or, algebraically, with income statement parameters in regular type and balance sheet items in italics:

$$(\text{Profit}/equity) = (\text{profit}/\text{sales}) \times (\text{sales}/assets) \times (assets/equity)$$

A subset financial parameter under the control of the retail merchandising decision maker is the *gross margin return on investment* (GMROI). GMROI is the *gross margin percentage* of the merchandise multiplied by *sales-to-stock* ratio. The equation is as follows:

$$\text{GMROI (\%)} = (\text{gross margin/net sales}) \times (\text{net sales}/average\ inventory\ valued\ at\ cost)$$
$$= \text{gross margin (\%)}/average\ inventory\ valued\ at\ cost$$

This measure, expressed as a percentage, is employed for a merchandise category in order to plan stock ordering to support expected sales. The purpose is to assure that gross margins are earned by a not-too-heavy investment in inventory. This tells the buyer how much margin is achieved for every dollar invested in inventory.

GMROI is also useful in evaluating the performance of merchandise buyers and in making decisions about whether to continue a product or group of products. There are variations in the way GMROI is calculated. Consistently applied by a company, this should not be a problem for evaluating profitability. The table is a reference showing a range of gross margin percentages and a range of net sales-to-average inventory ratios. The shaded rows have GMROI values greater than 200%. Readers can use the table to look up GMROIs when they have the component values. It is also useful for mapping multiple measures when comparing products or locations.

| | Gross Margin Return on Investment (GMROI) (%) | | | | | | | | | |
|---|---|---|---|---|---|---|---|---|---|---|
| **Gross Margin Percentage** | Net Sales/Average Inventory | | | | | | | | | |
| | **1** | **2** | **3** | **4** | **5** | **6** | **7** | **8** | **9** | **10** |
| **90%** | 90% | 180% | 270% | 360% | 450% | 540% | 630% | 720% | 810% | 900% |
| **80%** | 80% | 160% | 240% | 320% | 400% | 480% | 560% | 640% | 720% | 800% |
| **70%** | 70% | 140% | 210% | 280% | 350% | 420% | 490% | 560% | 630% | 700% |
| **60%** | 60% | 120% | 180% | 240% | 300% | 360% | 420% | 480% | 540% | 600% |
| **50%** | 50% | 100% | 150% | 200% | 250% | 300% | 350% | 400% | 450% | 500% |
| **40%** | 40% | 80% | 120% | 160% | 200% | 240% | 280% | 320% | 360% | 400% |
| **30%** | 30% | 60% | 90% | 120% | 150% | 180% | 210% | 240% | 270% | 300% |
| **20%** | 20% | 40% | 60% | 80% | 100% | 120% | 140% | 160% | 180% | 200% |
| **10%** | 10% | 20% | 30% | 40% | 50% | 60% | 70% | 80% | 90% | 100% |

There is a view that there are better ways than GMROI to perform the measurement task.* The authors from the Profit Planning Group in Colorado point out the advantages of GMROI. These include being easy to use and simple to understand. Objections include the following:

■ GMROI is biased. It overstates the performance of items with a low gross margin percentage while understating the performance of items with a high gross margin percentage.
■ GMROI treats the two levers—margin and turnover—equally. Gross margin is stronger.
■ An item might have a high GMROI and be unprofitable.

To address these concerns, the Profit Planning Group recommends direct product profit (DPP) as a better measure than GMROI for measuring the financial results of individual items, merchandise categories, or departments. This approach, described in Chapter 19, entails assigning direct costs to the product. This can be challenging in a brick-and-mortar store, where it is difficult to measure direct selling effort, and online, where IT costs play a critical role. A recommendation is to use both. Use GMROI to screen products, categories, and stores for opportunities and then apply the more detailed DPP or similar approach for a detailed analysis.

## 2.2.1 The Importance of Replenishment Models in Retail Supply Chains

Using merchandise budgeting, the merchandise managers and buyers plan the amount of money to spend on a product line or category in a defined budget

---

* "Saying Goodbye to GMROI," Boulder, CO: Profit Planning Group, 2014.

period. Once the amount is set, the planner must select the merchandise items to order.

Juggling financial variables to optimize merchandise plans is formidable. The following discussion is in two steps. Step 1 describes the concept behind merchandise replenishment and budgeting and includes an example. Step 2 describes how numbers required to complete the budget are collected and calculated.

## 2.2.2 Merchandise Types—Staple versus Fashion

Merchandise budgeting methods consider whether the merchandise is a "staple" product with predictable sales patterns or a "fashion" product with less sales history and greater demand uncertainty. In our examples, Discounter specializes in staple products, High-End in fashion products. Other labels for these categories include *functional* and *innovative*. For simplification, we assume that our retailers do not mix these categories; in practice, many retailers have both types of merchandise.

Staples, or functional products, are those consumers buy every day or with some regularity. Examples include common grocery products, basic clothing, and hardware items. Examples of fashion or innovative products include stylish apparel, just-released movies, new electronic gadgets, upgraded cellphone models, and expensive, limited-production automobiles. For the fashion category, the merchandise planner needs to track sales more closely and adjust replenishment plans more frequently. For staples, computer inventory maintenance and ordering software may monitor volumes and automatically replenish supplies by generating replacement orders when volumes indicate such a need.

### 2.2.2.1 Staple or Functional Products

Retailer Discounter specializes in this product category. A merchandise budget will provide planning rules, often in software, to ensure that the category meets profitability goals from GMROI targets or Direct Product Profie (DPP). Staples have lower margins—probably less than 50% in the GMROI table—than fashion/innovative products. To satisfy a GMROI objective, inventory should be closely managed. Systems for staples compute recommended *order points* and *order quantities* based on sales history and forecasts. The order point is the minimum inventory level required to avoid an out-of-stock situation. Upstream suppliers who reduce order lead time can lower safety stock requirements for this category.

Systems for staples also often factor in *forecast error*, or the difference between actual demand and the forecast. They then employ formulas to take uncertainty into account. Overstocking staples may not lead to markdowns. Most will be sellable at some point when the excess stock is worked down, but capital is tied up in these products until they are sold.

Most retailers use electronic data interchange (EDI) computer language to interact with supply chain partners. Computer systems continuously track sales by store and region and maintain accurate inventory counts. This visibility enables automatic generation of orders without human intervention.

Michael Hugos, in his work *Essentials of Supply Chain Management*, classified staple inventories into three categories[3]:

1. Cycle inventory: inventory needed between orders to meet demand, like regular quantities of men's underwear. These items are often reordered in fixed quantities when the reorder point is reached.
2. Seasonal inventory: inventory purchased and stored for anticipated future demand in a particular period like summer or Christmas.
3. Safety inventory: extra inventory to adjust for uncertain demand during the reorder period and variations in lead times.

Hugos suggests four ways to reduce safety stock:

1. Improve forecasting, lowering forecast error.
2. Deliver more frequently to reduce lead times and inventory.
3. Add predictability to decision making using fixed intervals for making decisions about demand and inventory levels.
4. Work with suppliers to ensure product availability including shared forecasts and access to stock level data.

## 2.2.2.2 Fashion or Innovative Products

Retailer High-End specializes in selling these products. They are higher margin, so meeting GMROI objectives requires attention to insure sufficient inventory to avoid lost sales without overbuying, which results in markdowns, thereby reducing overall margins. Fashion/innovative products have one or more of the following characteristics:

- Are sold in limited time windows—seasonal, new product introductions with limited life cycles—or are tied to promotional events
- Are harder to forecast accurately due to limited selling histories, placing a premium on supply chain flexibility capable of responding to fluctuating demand
- Have higher profit margins and may be in the market introduction or growth phases of the product life cycle
- May be recurring new models or upgrade products with a common distribution channel, such as music, movies, software, electronic gadgets, or new food items on the menu
- May have multiple paths to end users and customers

## 2.2.2.3 Merchandise Budget: An Example

The merchandise budget, such as that shown in Table 2.4, plans the movement of merchandise. The table presents an example of a seasonal fashion category product to be sold in a 4-month period, or *window*. In Table 2.4, inputs from the planner are in bold with shaded cells on the spreadsheet format. Initial data include the following:

1. Beginning end-of-month (EOM) inventory shown on line 8 in the initial stock column ($70,000). This is a planned initial purchase from the OEM manufacturer or distributor.
2. Planning assumptions. These assumptions in the right-hand column include forecast sales (line 2) of $250,000; monthly reductions for samples, promotions, shrinkage, and employee discounts (line 4) of $25,000, or 10% of sales; and desired average beginning-of-the-month (BOM) *stock-to-sales* ratio (line 6). Setting the stock-to-sales target ratio considers objectives for GMROI.
3. Monthly distributions for sales and reductions in percentages (lines 1 and 3). The planner will estimate forecast sales distribution in line 1 based on the timing of promotions for the product, seasonality factors if any, and the rate of market acceptance. The approach to reduction estimates on line 3 is similar.
4. Desired End of Month (EOM) inventory at the end of the promotion in month 4. This is $0 in the example, a seasonal category with few sales expected after the end of the 4-month selling period.

From these inputs, the spreadsheet calculates expected inventory, needed replenishments, and the actual average BOM stock-to-sales ratio. Although the average stock-to-sales ratio needs to be 2.0 to meet the GMROI objective, this plan shows extra stock for the first 2 months of the sales period. The planner makes this decision to have a stock-to-sales ratio of 2.5. The example shows that the actual ratio for the 4 months matches that allowed by the budget (2.0).

The calculation for additions to stock (line 9) establishes an EOM inventory (line 8) sufficient as a beginning of month (BOM) inventory (line 7) for the next month. An understanding of this procedure enables suppliers to collaborate with the retailer on initial inventory and the replenishment schedule.

## 2.2.2.4 Merchandise Budget Follow-Up

Several ongoing activities unfold as the merchandise budget plan goes into effect and the marketplace responds to the products.[4] These include the open-to-buy system, allocation of stock to stores, analyzing merchandise performance, sell-through

**Table 2.4  Merchandise Budget Plan for Fashion Category**

| | | Initial Stock | Months 1 | 2 | 3 | 4 | Planning Assumptions |
|---|---|---|---|---|---|---|---|
| 1 | Sales distribution (percent) | | 15 | 25 | 40 | 20 | 100 |
| 2 | Forecast sales (dollars) | | 37,500 | 62,500 | 100,000 | 50,000 | 250,000 |
| 3 | Reductions (percent) | | 30 | 30 | 25 | 15 | 100 |
| 4 | Monthly reductions (dollars) | | 7,500 | 7,500 | 6,250 | 3,750 | 25,000 |
| 5 | Total consumption (dollars) | | 45,000 | 70,000 | 106,250 | 53,750 | 275,000 |
| 6 | BOM stock-to-sales ratio | | 2.5 | 2.5 | 2.0 | 1.0 | 2.0 |
| 7 | BOM inventory (dollars) | | 70,000 | 175,000 | 212,500 | 53,750 | |
| 8 | EOM inventory (dollars) | 70,000 | 175,000 | 212,500 | 53,750 | – | |
| 9 | Additions to stock (dollars) | | 150,000 | 107,500 | (52,500) | – | |
| | | | | | Actual average BOM stock-to-sales ratio: | 2.0 | |

*Note:* Figures are in U.S. dollars except where indicated otherwise.

analysis, and supplier evaluation. Open-to-buy systems continuously assess needs to reach the EOM stock levels planned in the budget and serve as a monthly "checkbook" for the buyer. This activity tracks goods on order and decides what should be purchased to achieve the stock levels required to meet objectives.

Store analysis tracks how specific items are doing at various locations. It also reallocates stock to stores in the case of supply chain problems. The sell-through analysis looks at specific merchandise SKUs to tune the plan to add or reduce specific SKU items and to make price changes as needed. The analysis can lead to markdowns of slow-moving SKUs before the end of the selling period.

## 2.3 Online Retailers' Inventories

The most important change in the retail industry in the last 10 years is the growth in importance of the online store. This has had significant impacts on inventory procurement methods. Brick-and-mortar stores quickly became aware that online shopping was becoming a necessity to compete successfully in today's marketplace. Consumers expect to be able to shop when and where they please, so a store's merchandise must be available at all times, if not in the store, then on mobile platforms and computers.

Nordstrom was an early entrant into online retailing, driven primarily by the advantages it provides in shoe retailing, the historic founding block of the company's business. For each store, Nordstrom had to carry any particular style in a range of sizes, with varying widths in a selection of different colors. Thus, to have one pair of shoes available in three colors might require 12 sizes in 4 widths, or 144 different pairs of shoe (SKUs). In popular sizes, the stores would carry at least three or four pairs, requiring a huge inventory. Such inventories had to be maintained in each Nordstrom store for each style sold, resulting in cash-consuming inventories or the failure to service the needs of some of their customers.

Imagine being able to consolidate some of that inventory in a central location! Nordstrom took the most unusual sizes out of the stores entirely and maintains them in a central location from which online customers can order their size, or the Nordstrom brick-and-mortar stores could have them sent upon customer request. This also allowed for smaller in-store inventories.

Another early online shoe store success is onlineshoes.com, founded in 1996. Today, the company offers over 300 different brands of high-quality footwear in multiple sizes and colors and provides free shipping and exchanges, a 365-day return policy, extensive customer service, and a 110% price guarantee in over 100 countries. Without the online platform, such extensive selection and market coverage would not be possible.

Zappos took the strategy one step farther and provided very rapid delivery of ordered shoes with quick and easy returns. Consumers responded with enthusiasm but often order one style in several sizes to assure that they receive the proper size. They then return those that don't fit, complicating Zappos financial picture. But Amazon has since acquired Zappos and is applying some of the new company's operating principles to other products.

Today's online marketplace is complex and multilayered. Amazon, the reigning king of e-retail, was founded in 1994 and went live as a functioning web-based retailer in 1995. Founder Jeff Bezos selected an introductory merchandise category with little variation and social risk but with wide appeal to sell first—books. From that simple base, Amazon today, after more than 20 years in business, sells many categories of goods.

The expansion into so many areas has been made possible by drop-shipping merchandise. Although Amazon does maintain very large and complex inventories, a larger percentage of sales comes from drop shipments. Amazon takes an order and has the merchandise shipped directly from the manufacturer of the product who, in addition to merchandise cost, charges a fee such as $5 for performing this service. Thus, Amazon has no inventory to maintain of these products. When Amazon does maintain an inventory, their ordering procedures would be modified versions of those discussed earlier in the chapter. In addition, the company's practice of using associated companies has resulted in a vastly expanded product offering.

Drop shipping has become the norm for most online retailers. Costco, Wayfair, and many others have integrated the practice into their strategies. In the extreme, some companies simply take suppliers' entire catalogs and integrate the products into their online offerings, thereby providing a very wide variety of products without the normal vast investment inventory. For example, Wayfair incorporates several rug manufacturers' catalogs into their web offerings and simply forwards orders as received to the manufacturer for drop shipping. Thus, they are able to offer a far greater selection of products than most brick-and-mortar retailers can physically hold.

There are some important requirements for a company to successfully use drop shipping. The online retailer must provide some sort of value added, either by providing expertise in a niche or by providing customer service of unusual quality for that niche or providing helpful content, tutorials, etc. Costco, for example, maintains its ability to offer very attractive pricing, even when using drop shipping, through advantageous procurement contracts with the drop-shipping manufacturer.

## 2.4 Summary

Understanding what makes a retailer financially successful is important to all retail supply chain participants. Retailers will be motivated by cooperative efforts to improve GMROI; suppliers who can help that effort will be appreciated. Suppliers can do much to improve supply chain links to ensure reliable, rapid replenishment of the retailer.

# References

1. Marn, Michael V., Roegner, Eric V., and Zawada, Craig C., "The Power of Pricing," *The McKinsey Quarterly*, No. 1, 2003, pp. 27–36.
2. Bruner, Robert F., Eaker, Mark R., Freeman, R. Edward, Sjpekman, Robert E., Teisberg, Olmsted, Elizabeth, and Venkataraman, S., *The Portable MBA*, 4th ed., Hoboken, NJ: John Wiley & Sons, 2003, p. 477.
3. Hugos, Michael, *Essentials of Supply Chain Management*, 2nd ed., Hoboken, NJ: John Wiley & Sons, 2006, pp. 60–63.
4. Levy, Michael and Weitz, Barton A., *Retailing Management*, 5th ed., New Delhi: Tata McGraw-Hill Publishing Company Limited, pp. 415–425, chap. 13.

# Chapter 3

# Types of Retail Supply Chain Businesses

This chapter, which provides data related to the U.S. retail supply chains, describes higher-level government sector classifications and includes data from five company financial reports. The companies are

- Wal-Mart Stores, Inc.
- Costco Wholesale Corporation
- Gap Incorporated
- West Marine, Inc.
- McKesson Corporation

Current data reported in recent annual reports are compared with similar data from the first edition published in 2008.

Every 5 years, the U.S. Census Bureau documents all industries, including the *retail trades*[1] sector, in detail. The report is called the North American Industry Classification System (NAICS, pronounced "nakes"). Data in the bureau's *Economy Wide Statistics Brief* document the U.S. retail industry's size and structure. Retailing supply chain sectors link with sister sectors as shown in Figure 3.1.

Information in this chapter is useful to those in other countries for two major reasons. First, many countries export to the United States, and knowledge of the landscape is important. Second, other markets, even though smaller, could mirror U.S. supply chains as they develop. Copying good features and avoiding bad ones may have value to many.

An article in the *Wall Street Journal* profiled the potential for growth of what it referred to as "organized retailing."[2] This is measured by chain store penetration. The article quotes a study by the firm Technopak Advisors, an Indian consumer

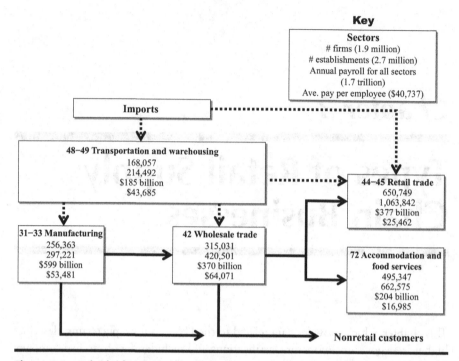

**Figure 3.1 Principal U.S. supply chain sectors. (From Caruso, Anthony, Statistics of *U.S. Businesses; Employment and Payroll Summary: 2012*, U.S. Department of Commerce, released February 2015.)**

product consultancy. The study describes the different levels of organized retailing penetration in different countries—for example, there is 3% in India and 20% in China compared to 85% in the United States.

Lower levels of chain penetration, as in India and China, hold promise for growth unavailable in mature economies. In the United States, the business press frequently reports examples of this movement. For example, at the time of this writing, Apple's CEO Tim Cook is in India seeking opportunities for expansion.

The last chapter section summarizes a *Wall Street Journal* article that addresses the need for revitalizing U.S. manufacturing and manufacturing's related supply chain sectors like transportation, warehousing, and retail trade.[3]

## 3.1 Supply Chain Component Data

The statistics derived from the 2012 NAICS survey reveal the relative size of the sectors that comprise the retail supply chain. Figure 3.1 is a top-down flowchart showing participating sectors in the retail supply chain.

In NAICS data, the first two digits define broad sectors similar to those shown in Figure 3.1. Subsequent three-, four-, five-, and six-digit classifications provide data at lower subsector levels. The top view includes the following supply chain sectors with their two-digit NAICS codes:

- Manufacturing (31–33)
- Wholesale trade (42)
- Retail trade (44–45)
- Transportation and warehousing (48–49)
- Accommodation and food services (72)

These sectors represent 33% of U.S. businesses, 36% of the establishments (stores and other outlets), 40% of employment, and 32% of annual payroll. But the retail supply chain is "more than stores." Manufacturing, transportation and warehousing, and wholesale trade bring total U.S. supply chain employment to about 15 million.

Figure 3.1 shows that the retail industry involves large numbers of participants. There are about 1.9 million *enterprises*, defined as "a business organization consisting of one or more domestic establishments under common ownership or control." These enterprises maintain about 2.7 million *establishments*, These are defined as "a single physical location where business is conducted or where services or industrial operations are performed."

The profile illustrates the "many-to-many" situation in retail supply chains. The approximately 700,000 manufacturers and distributors in the wholesale trade sector provide goods for sale to the estimated 2.7 million retail establishments. Average payroll at an establishment in these sectors is about $600,000. Independent or captive intermediary distribution warehouses and other service providers, about 200,000 in the transportation and warehousing sector, provide logistics services. This is the glue that connects the pieces. In fact, financial analysts track transportation and warehousing sector companies to gauge the future of the U.S. economy to make investing decisions.

Much of what is ultimately sold at retail consists of imports of final products and raw materials. This is shown as inputs into the supply chain. Within the box for each sector are statistics that include the following:

- The number of firms and establishments or locations
- The annual payroll for each sector in billions of dollars
- Sector annual payroll
- Average annual pay per employee in the sector

## 3.2 Retail Supply Chains in the United States

The retail trade categories shown in Figure 3.1 include 12 retailer three-digit subsectors from 441 through 454. Table 3.1 lists these subsectors along with brief descriptions. These classifications are broken down further with four- and five-digit categories. For example, the first category (441) breaks down as follows:

> 441. Motor vehicles and parts
>   4411. Automobile dealers
>     44111. New car dealers
>     44112. Used car dealers
>   4412. Other motor vehicle dealers
>     44121. Recreational vehicle dealers
>     44122. Motorcycle, boat, and other vehicle dealers
>   4413. Automotive parts, accessories, and tire stores
>     44131. Automotive parts and accessories stores
>     44132. Tire dealers

Table 3.2 profiles the 12 retail trade subsectors with data like those in Figure 3.1. All subsectors but the last are *fixed point-of-sales* locations. The last (454) is the nonstore category. Note that most of the descriptions in Table 3.1 list needs for equipment, advice, displays, repair facilities, and other expertise to facilitate customer purchases. These are examples of extended products as defined in Chapter 1. Retailers' markets are not only limited to consumer sales but also serve business and institutional customers.

Table 3.2 shows retail trade sector employment by three-digit sector. The industry had $377 billion in sales. There are about 15 million paid employees, and average annual earnings are about $25,000. The table compares current (2012) with first-edition figures. Some sectors have grown; others have retreated.

## 3.3 Selected Supply Chain Company Returns

Table 3.3 displays data from five companies that were profiled in the first edition. Table 3.3 data come from recent annual reports available at the time of writing; figures from the first edition are included for comparison so that the reader can assess each company's business success or the lack thereof in recent years. The companies' figures illustrate the diversity that exists in various retail sectors in terms of financial success factors. Understanding the differences is important for upstream and downstream collaboration to improve supply chain processes.

Table 3.3 also calculates gross margin return on investment (GMROI) in column G. and the cash-to-cash cycle (column H). Chapter 2 describes how to calculate these parameters. The calculations use end-of-period inventory (column E) rather than average inventory prescribed in some definitions of GMROI.

**Table 3.1   Definition of NAICS Categories**

| Code | Descriptions of Product Category | Description |
|------|----------------------------------|-------------|
| 441 | Motor vehicles and parts | Retail motor vehicles and parts from fixed point-of-sale locations. Typically operate from showrooms or open lots. |
| 442 | Furniture and home furnishing stores | Sellers of new furniture and home furnishings from stores. Usually operate showrooms and have substantial areas for presentation of products. Many offer interior decorating. |
| 443 | Electronics and appliance stores | Electronics and appliances from point-of-sale locations. Use floor displays to demonstrate products. Staff is knowledgeable in features and warranties and may include trained repair persons. |
| 444 | Building material and garden equipment and supplies | New building material and garden equipment and supplies from fixed locations. Display equipment designed to handle lumber and related products and garden equipment and supplies. Staff knowledgeable in use of products for construction, repair, and maintenance of the home and associated grounds. |
| 445 | Food and beverage stores | Sell retail food and beverages from stores. Have equipment (e.g., freezers, refrigerated display cases, refrigerators) for displaying food and beverages. Staff trained in the processing of food products to guarantee the proper storage and sanitary conditions. |
| 446 | Health and personal care stores | Retail health and personal care merchandise from stores. Staff may include pharmacists, opticians, and other professionals advising customers, or fitting the product sold to the customer's needs. |
| 447 | Gasoline stations | Retail automotive fuels (e.g., gasoline, diesel fuel, and gasohol) and automotive oils with or without convenience stores. Have specialized equipment for the storage and dispensing of automotive fuels. |

*(Continued)*

**Table 3.1 (Continued)    Definition of NAICS Categories**

| Code | Descriptions of Product Category | Description |
|------|----------------------------------|-------------|
| 448 | Clothing and clothing accessories stores | New clothing and accessories. Establishments have display equipment and staff knowledgeable in fashion trends and the proper match of styles, colors, and combinations of clothing and accessories. |
| 451 | Sporting goods, hobby, book, and music stores | Provide expertise on use of sporting equipment or other leisure activities, such as needlework and musical instruments. Bookstores also included. |
| 452 | General merchandise stores | Unique establishments in that they have the equipment and staff capable of retailing a variety of goods. Include varied display equipment and staff trained to provide information. |
| 453 | Miscellaneous store retailers | Retail merchandise from stores that are different from those of other sectors. Many are unique. Examples include florists, used merchandise stores, pet and pet supply stores, and others. |
| 454 | Nonstore retailers | Nonstore examples that include broadcasting of infomercials, the broadcasting and publishing of direct-response advertising, the publishing of paper and electronic catalogs, door-to-door solicitation, in-home demonstration, selling from portable stalls, and distribution through vending machines. Establishments include mail-order houses, vending machine operators, home delivery sales, door-to-door sales, party plan sales, electronic shopping, and sales through portable stalls (e.g., street vendors, except food). Also includes direct sale of products, such as home heating oil dealers and newspaper delivery. |

*Source:* North American Industry Classification System (NAICS).

**Table 3.2    Retail Supply Chain Management Category Volumes**

| The Top Numbers are for 2007 and Appeared in the First Edition Published in 2008. The Lower Numbers are 2012 Data. | | | | |
| --- | --- | --- | --- | --- |
| *A* | *B* | *C* | *D* | *E* |
| *NAICS Code* | *Products* | *Annual Payroll (millions of dollars)* | *Paid Employees* | *Annual Payroll per Employee ($)* |
| 441 | Motor vehicles/ parts | 64,549 71,632 | 1,845,496 1,718,800 | 34,977 41,675 |
| 442 | Furniture and home furnishings | 12,843 11,695 | 535,029 422,595 | 24,004 27,674 |
| 443 | Electronics and appliances | 9,330 10,495 | 391,015 428,298 | 23,861 24,503 |
| 444 | Building material/ garden equipment | 30,067 35,202 | 1,160,016 1,170,402 | 25,919 30,077 |
| 445 | Food and beverage | 48,686 60,873 | 2,838,653 2,872,426 | 17,151 21,192 |
| 446 | Health and personal care | 20,226 32,570 | 1,024,429 1,010,173 | 19,744 32,242 |
| 447 | Gasoline stations | 13,701 15,903 | 926,792 862,630 | 14,783 18,435 |
| 448 | Clothing and accessories | 21,391 28,267 | 1,426,573 1,630,575 | 14,995 17,336 |
| 451 | Sporting goods, hobby, books, and music | 8,703 9,132 | 611,144 511,983 | 14,241 17,837 |
| 452 | General merchandise | 42,647 60,091 | 2,524,729 2,871,931 | 16,892 20,924 |
| 453 | Miscellaneous retailers | 12,835 14,502 | 792,361 712,624 | 16,198 20,350 |
| 454 | Nonstore retailers | 17,094 26,676 | 571,438 595,521 | 29,914 44,795 |
| **Total/average:** | | $302,072 $377,038 | 14,647,675 14,807,958 | $20,623 $25,486 |

**Table 3.3  Selected Public Company Supply Chain Performance Data**

| | A | B | C | D | E | F | G | H |
|---|---|---|---|---|---|---|---|---|
| | Reporting Year | Annual Revenue (millions of dollars) | Cost of Sales (millions of dollars) | Gross Margin (percent) | End-of-Period Inventory (millions of dollars) | Sales-to-Stock Ratio | GMROI | Cash-to-Cash Cycle (days) |
| 1 Wal-Mart Stores, Inc. | 2006 | 312,300 | 240,000 | 23 | 32,200 | 9.7 | 225 | 13 |
| | 2016 | 482,130 | 362,000 | 25 | 44,469 | 10.6 | 61 | 10 |
| 2 Costco Wholesale Corporation | 2005 | 51,900 | 46,300 | 11 | 1,470 | 35.3 | 381 | 19 |
| | 2014 | 110,212 | 98,458 | 11 | 8,456 | 13.1 | 128 | 4 |
| 3 Gap, Inc. | 2005 | 16,023 | 10,154 | 37 | 1,696 | 9.4 | 346 | 20 |
| | 2014 | 16,435 | 4,206 | 13 | 1,889 | 8.7 | 113 | 2 |
| 4 West Marine, Inc. | 2005 | 700 | 495 | 29 | 312 | 2.2 | 66 | 206 |
| | 2014 | 676 | 483 | 28 | 214 | 3.2 | 88 | 105 |
| 5 McKesson Corporation | 2006 | 88,050 | 84,188 | 4 | 6,920 | 12.7 | 56 | 12 |
| | 2015 | 179,045 | 167,634 | 6 | 14,296 | 11.9 | 77 | 10 |

Manufacturers, distributors, and retailers should assess products, categories, markets, and other companies using measures like these. Achieving excellence in the metrics requires savvy merchandise selection, targeting attractive customers, logistics skills, and collaboration with upstream and downstream trading partners.

Wal-Mart Stores, Inc., is the world's largest retail company measured by sales and operates over 6000 locations.* Its strategy has centered on offering value-for-price to its customers. The 2017 report to shareholders recognized the major challenge to retailing as transformative change made possible by rapidly emerging technology. For its success, the company points to rapidly evolving omnichannel customer service, supplier financing, buying direct from manufacturers, and limiting the number of product stock-keeping units (SKUs) carried. The negative cash-to-cash cycles for Costco signal that customer payments are in advance of supplier payments.

Gap is a clothing retailer with over 3000 stores. Its branded chains include Gap; Banana Republic; Old Navy; Athleta; Intermix; and Gap, Inc., Direct. The last (Direct) operates the websites for the brands, an example of an omnichannel retailing. Gap enjoys the highest gross margins in this selection as it did in the first edition. The Gap CEO has congratulated the 140,000 employees for this and points out challenges in the areas of global growth, product, customer experience, and employee talent.

West Marine, with 260 stores at the time of writing, focuses on the recreational boating industry. It has the lowest sales-to-stock ratio in the group, reflecting the high price tags for its products. The firm, in its recent financial disclosure, notes the background and success of its CEO. The executive, Matthew Hyde, was recruited from recreational retailer REI, where he implemented the company's award-winning omnichannel strategy.

McKesson, a pharmaceutical distributor and healthcare information technology company, here illustrates the role of the distributor. This company uses GMROI to measure product performance; it has the lowest gross margin (column D). It also carries 30 days of inventory, resulting in the lowest GMROI in the group. However, distributors succeed on volume, and McKesson is one of the largest. Its use of supplier credit produces a short cash-to-cash cycle of 10 days.

Dick's Sporting Goods is a Pittsburgh-based retailer in the United States; its store count has increased from 300 to over 600 since the first edition. The company, on its website, claims to be "largest full-line U.S. retailer in the sporting goods industry." The company claims a market share of 10% of a $67 billion market.

Dick's Sporting Goods' mission is as follows:

> *To be recognized by our customers as the #1 sports and fitness specialty omnichannel retailer that serves and inspires athletes and outdoor enthusiasts to achieve their personal best through the relentless improvement of everything we do.*

---

* In 2015, Amazon surpassed Wal-Mart as number one in market capitalization, but Wal-Mart remains sales leader.

The CEO since 1984, Edward Stack, has predicted more consolidation in sporting goods retailing, where the top five companies control only 16% of the market. Very recently, Dick's Sporting Goods acquired the brand name and intellectual property of bankrupt Sports Authority. All communications to Sports Authority are now directed to the Dick's website, increasing its significance and potential market share in that industry. The results of this merger are not yet visible.

## 3.4 Revitalizing U.S. Manufacturing

As cited at the beginning of this chapter, a *Wall Street Journal* article has provided a strategy for revitalizing U.S. manufacturing. The article acknowledges that revitalizing manufacturing will lift other industries and include the sectors shown in Figure 3.1. The author notes the 5.7 million decline in U.S. manufacturing jobs between 2000 and 2010. Acknowledging the challenge, he lists ideas "for getting U.S. manufacturing back on track." He cites experts* who have shown that lifting manufacturing boosts other sectors. So the strategies for manufacturing companies profiled in Table 3.4 would lift many boats along the supply chain.

Whether these strategies have political and financial support is uncertain. Some may find early acceptance; others may never be enacted. Also, many require time to put into place. However, readers will benefit from knowledge of these options that might be proposed and debated. Recently, U.S. President Donald Trump has pledged political support to U.S. companies that keep their production facilities in the United States.

## 3.5 Summary

An important lesson is that there are virtually infinite options for participating in retail supply chains. This chapter captures the breadth and depth of that participation.

---

\* Sources include Daniel J. Meckstroth, MAPI Foundation, and the U.S. Bureau of Economic Analysis.

**Table 3.4  Strategies for Revitalizing U.S. Manufacturing**

| | |
|---|---|
| 1. | Make exports more valuable by providing certificates to exporters that importers must buy |
| 2. | Impose value-added taxes on imports that are waived for exports |
| 3. | Deal with overvalued currency by imposing market access charges on investments in the United States |
| 4. | Examine the real cost of offshoring and make companies aware of hidden cost factors |
| 5. | Purge duplicate regulations to reduce the cost of not complying with no-longer-needed regulations |
| 6. | Encourage trade jobs by promoting modern complementary labor-saving technologies |
| 7. | Enlist community colleges in providing workers in the skilled trades |
| 8. | Boost government-funded research and development (R & D) financing to improve process technology |
| 9. | Create centers of excellence for developing and performing basic manufacturing processes |

# References

1. Caruso, Anthony, Statistics of U.S. *Businesses; Employment and Payroll Summary: 2012*, released February 2015 by the US Department of Commerce.
2. Tita, Bob, "How to Revitalize U.S. Manufacturing," *Wall Street Journal*, June 8, 2016, p. R1.
3. Bellman, Eric and Hudson, Kris, "Wal-Mart to Enter India in Venture," *The Wall Street Journal*, November 28, 2006, p. A3.

# Chapter 4

# A Changing World: Moving toward Comparative Advantage

Few supply chain topics resonate more than the effects of globalization. Chapter 3 reported the lack of organized retailing penetration in large countries such as India and China. These countries are fertile grounds for retail chains seeking growth, and many Western companies like Microsoft are moving to expand to these areas. At the other end of the supply chain, original equipment manufacturers (OEMs) and their suppliers in emerging economies manufacture many products. Chapter 3 listed nine proposals for retaining U.S. production. Several call for strengthening U.S. capabilities; others are openly protectionist.

Supply chains that stretch across national borders bring political debates over whether such changes are good or bad. In rich countries, globalization means lower-cost imported goods. Consumers in these countries appreciate a good deal, and the developing country has ample capacity to produce to demand. On the darker side, changes in sources displace domestic producers and cost many employees their jobs.

For the low-cost countries, exports bring the promise of jobs and middle-class prosperity for its citizens. C. K. Prahalad, a business professor at the University of Michigan, suggests a "different set of lenses," referring to globalization as "importing competitiveness."[1] In this view, working across national boundaries spurs changes all along the supply chain to remain competitive.

A *global* supply chain as defined in this book simply means a supply chain that crosses international boundaries. Figure 1.1 in Chapter 1 shows physical and information flows in a typical supply chain. The OEM in Figure 1.1 imports components from international second-tier suppliers and sells its product into national and international markets.

Although the picture of low-cost countries as suppliers is a common one, retailers are also eyeing these emerging markets, with their growing working classes, as opportunities for new sales growth. Products in the supply chain might even take a U-turn from factory to retailer to consumer, all in the same country. Press anecdotes have identified China as a target domestic market and as an outlet for Chinese manufacturers.

Current retail figures in China support the growing importance of that country as a market for consumer goods. Since the beginning of 2016, retail sales in China have grown 10.2% over last year, and online sales have risen 27.7% in that same time period. China is converting to a consumer society from an export-driven nation.[2]

However, this process is not automatic and depends upon political and economic conditions in these countries. In instances in which the retailer is based in the developed world, developing countries provide the "brawn" to make the product, and the retailer, the "brains" to design, brand, source, and merchandise it. As each side of this balance between brain and brawn adding value seeks to broaden its contribution, the equilibrium point is sure to shift industry by industry, challenging supply chains to adjust.

Thomas Friedman, in his widely read best seller, *The World Is Flat*, asserts that the availability of jobs in emerging countries is not enough to bring third-world countries strongly into the world economy. He goes on to say:

> Countries grow out of poverty … when they also create an environment that makes it easy for their people to start businesses, raise capital, and become entrepreneurs and when they subject their people to at least some competition from beyond—because companies and countries with competitors innovate more and faster.[3]

Another Friedman, Milton, identified his favorite work on the topic,[4] "Protection or Free Trade" by American economist Henry George (1839–1897). George pointed out that trade is not compulsory but requires the mutual consent of the trading partners. Nation A sells to nation B only if nation B has the money to buy nation A's outputs. How does nation B get those funds? By selling its outputs to nation A and others. Nation A tariffs blocking nation B imports result from political favors dispensed by nation A favor seekers. Such political favors "will inevitably go not to the deserving but to the strong and unscrupulous."

The remainder of this chapter summarizes the concept of comparative advantage—a driver behind globalization—and describes the CAGE framework for decision making, sourcing, and marketing in other countries. This framework calls for assessing *distance* between trading partners along four dimensions: cultural, administrative, geographic, and economic.

# 4.1 Primer on Comparative Advantage

Adam Smith's *Wealth of Nations*, published in 1776, described the economics for trading across national boundaries. Smith urged any country to trade for, rather than make, goods that other countries can make more cheaply than that country could. These lower-cost countries would have an *absolute* advantage because they are more efficient at making those goods. Trading between countries with absolute advantages in certain products rewards both trading partners because each country sells to its trading partner the products it makes more efficiently.

Smith likened this concept to a "private family" situation. For example, in a doctor's household, the practice of medicine would be the "product" it produces most efficiently. Under absolute advantage, the doctor's family should trade for other things it needs—such as groceries, house repairs, and furniture.

It would not make sense for the doctor to spend time growing crops for food, doing house repairs, or building furniture. Because the doctor earns more practicing medicine, time spent on creating these other necessities doesn't make sense; also, the doctor needs to maintain his medical skills. Without the doctor buying other goods and services, his patients couldn't pay him.

Economist David Ricardo coined the term *comparative advantage* in 1817. It is counterintuitive because comparative advantage says that, even if a country has an absolute advantage in producing a good or service, it is to its benefit to buy that good or service. So the doctor should stick with healthcare even if that doctor was the very best as a farmer, repairman, or furniture maker. This is because the doctor's highest contribution comes from the practice of medicine, not from the other pursuits.

Ricardo's example, also a classic in economics, describes the relationship between two trading partners, Portugal and England, who exchange just two products: wine and wool. Portugal had an absolute advantage in both products in Ricardo's day. Despite this absolute advantage, the theory of comparative advantage calls for Portugal to specialize in wine while purchasing its wool from England. This is because dedicating itself to wine produces more overall value than diverting a portion of its winemaking capacity to wool production.

With this arrangement, English wool makers would keep themselves busy and have money to purchase Portuguese wine. The Portuguese, in turn, were clothed while earning more than they would if they diverted winemaking resources to wool production.

The absolute form of advantage is easier to understand than the comparative form. If a country does everything well, why not do everything? This may seem especially true if you are a wool maker in Portugal or a winemaker in England. According to comparative advantage, both of these "misfits" must pursue another trade.

The *Wall Street Journal*, in an editorial, points out the reality that labor and capital are far more mobile than they were back in Ricardo's day.[5] Citing economist Matthew J. Slaughter at Dartmouth University in the United States, this increased speed means that trade is no longer a *zero-sum game*. That is, the loss of a job in the United States through outsourcing and offshoring to places like India or China is not an overall loss to the United States. This is despite the consequence of losing some industries, like winemaking in England.

A concept called *complementarity* holds that outsourcing and offshoring brawny jobs to developing countries create complementary requirements for brainy jobs in developed countries. These expand the scale and the scope of the multinational enterprise. World developments since the 2008 recession suggest that the loss of too many jobs can have a deleterious effect on the countries losing the jobs until substitute forms of employment are developed. In addition, the rapid expansion of technologically based business solutions has resulted in a mismatch between workers' previous training and the current requirements of the job market.

*Scale* refers to growth in the functions performed in global companies due to their larger size. *Scope* refers to the mix of activities done in the home country, with a focus on higher-skilled activities—such as product design, branding, merchandising, and supply chain management. These displace the low-skill work transferred elsewhere. Conflict comes because those doing the low-skill work are not prepared to do the high-skill work. During the 2016 presidential election, candidate Donald Trump called for building a wall along the U.S.–Mexico border and after his election continued to argue for its construction. The purpose was to restrict migration and protect local markets from competition.

Through research, Slaughter has verified the benefits of globalization. The findings show that, from 1991 to 2001, U.S. companies that added 2.8 million workers in overseas affiliates also added 5.5 million jobs in the United States. This growth was faster than that of less global competitors. The editorial's conclusion is that, at the company level, jobs created overseas generate jobs at home. Simultaneously, the trade brings consumers "greater quantity and variety of goods and services for lower prices."

Although the Slaughter study examined U.S. companies, the lessons aren't lost on companies in the developing world. *Forbes Magazine* reports the case of Indian company Gujarat Heavy Chemicals Limited (GHCL Ltd.) and its acquisition of Dan River, Inc., in Danville, Virginia.[6] Dan River, founded in 1882, designs, manufactures, and distributes textile products for home fashion and apparel fabric markets.

At the time of purchase, the company had $250 million in sales, three plants, and 3000 workers in Danville. It was also in bankruptcy, a situation attributed to globalization forces. Indian companies, recently freed to pursue overseas investments, have cast about for companies like Dan River. However, GHCL was not after more factories (Dan River's brawn); it sought in Dan River its customers, distribution network, brands, and designers (its brains).

With customers such as Bed Bath & Beyond and the now defunct Linens 'n Things, GHCL expected a rapid payback. It intended to extend its reach by acquiring retailers around the world—having purchased $200 million chain Roseby's, a 300-store home furnishing retailer in the United Kingdom, in mid-2006. (Roseby's went out of business in 2008.) The vision is a vertically integrated chain for towels, sheets, and related products from "concept to consumer" in one supply chain.

Comparative advantage makes globalization inevitable for retailers and manufacturers in retail supply chains. This will be one of the drivers of supply chain change, as described in Chapter 6, Section 6.4.

Four of the public companies profiled in Chapter 2 have pursued international business. Those that have not emphasized stores in international markets provide online stores available worldwide. A brief summary of their progress or lack thereof follows.

Wal-Mart Stores, Inc.
 Wal-Mart in the United States had $298 billion in 2016 sales; Wal-Mart International, with 800,000 associates, primarily operates in Mexico and Canada and had $123 billion in sales. China is another market where the company has operations. Other services include online grocery businesses in Mexico, Canada, and the United Kingdom.

Costco Wholesale
 Costco had about $32 billion outside the United States in fiscal 2015, slightly less than 30% of revenue as reported on The Motley Fool website. The United States is considered its best-performing market. International sales dropped 8% in Canada and 6% elsewhere. One reason has been the strong dollar.

Gap, Inc.
 In 2015, Gap, Inc., had about 3700 stores and $16 billion in sales through four store chains: Gap, Old Navy, Athleta, and Banana Republic. Revenues have been basically flat since 2005, and profits have declined. Seventy-seven percent of revenues are in the United States, with Gap and Old Navy providing the largest share. Asia, Canada, and Europe provide most of the other revenue.

West Marine
 West Marine is a U.S.-based boating supplies retailer, operating through some 300 company-owned stores. It has a port supply wholesale business and direct-to-customer website, catalogs, and call center. Most are in the United States. Others are in Canada and Puerto Rico. Five stores are franchised in Turkey. Its direct-to-consumer channel markets 75,000 boating products worldwide. A separate port supply business provides wholesaling and distribution to commercial, government, and industrial customers.

Dick's Sporting Goods

In 2015, Dick's, a U.S.-focused chain, announced a plan to increase market share in the United States through growing its store base in new and under-penetrated U.S. markets. The plan would increase the base to 735–750 stores by the end of fiscal 2017, an increase from the 603 stores at the end of fiscal 2014. The company plans to grow e-commerce sales to approximately $1.0 to $1.2 billion in fiscal 2017, from $628 million in fiscal 2014.

The following sections describe a methodology for assessing the viability of building a retail supply chain capability in a candidate country. Companies seeking to shrink their global footprints by dropping countries from their market portfolios can also use the same method to evaluate their alternatives.

## 4.2 Concept of Distance

Globalization usually means doing business at some distance across international boundaries. Distance, in this context, means physical distance—between a retailer in the United Kingdom like Roseby's, for example, and a factory in China. Because the physical distance crosses international boundaries, there are other important dimensions to consider, e.g., culture, language, political systems, logistics, tariffs, currency exchanges, legal systems, and even the climate. This section describes research into the effect of these other attributes of distance.

In assessing the attractiveness of foreign markets, some companies use a conventional tool called *country portfolio analysis* (CPA). This analysis weighs alternative market opportunities using market size measures such as per-capita consumption, income, population, and market size for a particular product or product category. Analysis of these data produces a ranking of each country's attractiveness in terms of the market size.

Because application of CPA may ignore the costs and risks in a new market that are harder to identify, Pankaj Ghemawat recommends taking the concept of distance into other dimensions in addition to those just listed.[7] His framework utilizes research from economists Jeffrey Frankel at Harvard and Andrew Rose at the University of California, Berkeley. Their research identifies other patterns in global trade. These include not only geographic but also cultural, administrative, and economic distance—producing the acronym CAGE.

Table 4.1 lists the four CAGE distance types and aspects of each. In their research, Frankel and Rose found that factors other than geographic distance and income were determinants of the level of trade between pairs of countries. For example, a country with links unrelated to geography, a *colony–colonizer* relationship, resulted in a 900% increase in trade over that observed without such a relationship.

Table 4.2 lists attributes and their impacts on trade documented by the research. For example, for item #1 in Table 4.2, a 1% increase in the gross domestic product (GDP) of a country such as Mexico will produce a 0.7% increase in trade with that

**Table 4.1  CAGE Distance Dimensions**

| Type of Distance | Description of Factors Involved |
|---|---|
| Cultural | Languages, ethnicities, religions, social norms |
| Administrative | Colonial ties, common currencies, political harmony, trading agreements, government policies, institutional strength (legal, financial systems) |
| Geographic | Proximity, common border, size of country, transportation/communication links, climate |
| Economic | Income similarities, cost and quality of natural resources, worker availability, infrastructure, raw materials and components, knowledge/information resources |

**Table 4.2  Attributes and International Trade-Level Impacts**

|  | Attributes Related to Distance | Effect on International Trade | CAGE Factor |
|---|---|---|---|
| 1. | 1% increase in gross domestic product (GDP) per capita | +0.7% per 1% gain | Economic |
| 2. | 1% increase in GDP | +0.8% per 1% increase | Economic |
| 3. | 1% increase in physical distance | −1.1% per 1% increase | Geographic |
| 4. | 1% increase in physical size | −0.2% per 1% increase | Geographic |
| 5. | Access to ocean | +50% | Geographic |
| 6. | Common border | +80% | Geographic |
| 7. | Common regional trading block | +330% | Administrative |
| 8. | Colony–colonizer relationship | +900% | Cultural |
| 9. | Common colonizer | +190% | Cultural |
| 10. | Common polity (form or system of government) | +300% | Administrative |
| 11. | Common currency | +340% | Administrative |

country. A common border has a much larger impact, increasing trade by 80%, as shown by item #6.

What this means is that the market potential for a U.S. retailer in Mexico based solely on GDP per capita—the CPA approach—will underestimate the potential of the market that a common border has. Ghemawat cites the case of Tricon Restaurants International (TRI), formerly based in Dallas, Texas, and now doing business out of Louisville, Kentucky, as YUM! Brands, Inc. The company's popular food chains include Kentucky Fried Chicken (KFC), Pizza Hut, and Taco Bell.

Measuring only per-capita fast food consumption, TRI found Mexico to rank 16th out of 20 countries it served in market potential. Because of outsized debt, TRI was faced with the need to prune the number of countries in which it operated. Applying the factors in Table 4.2, TRI found that Mexico advanced in market potential from 16th to a tie for 2nd by adjusting for the following:

- Geographic closeness to its base in Dallas
- A common border between the countries
- Membership in a trade agreement (North American Free Trade Agreement, or NAFTA)

The analysis also deducted for lack of a common language. After the analysis, Mexico tied for second with the United Kingdom. (Canada ranked first.) These insights enabled TRI to focus its scarce resources on the most profitable countries—in this case, those closest to home.

Because trade is a two-way flow, this concept can be extended to decisions regarding sourcing. Ghemawat explains that different distance factors will have different impacts on individual industries. Electricity, for example, is highly sensitive to administrative and geographic factors, but not at all to cultural factors. Preferential trading agreements in the administrative distance category affect textile fibers, where such agreements are common, more than they affect footwear, where such agreements are less common.

## 4.3 Applying the Framework

Experts caution against blindly chasing "low cost" as the primary goal of going global. James Womack, who coined the term *Lean* (now employed not only to manufacturing operations but also to supply chains), recommends application of "Lean math" in making such decisions.[8] In his article, Womack listed several costs that the purchasing department often omits, including the following:

- Correction for allocated overhead costs that will not be reduced by international sourcing
- Added inventory costs to cover the distances involved

- Cost of added safety stocks to protect against disruptions
- Cost of expedited shipments that may be necessary
- Added warranty costs due to supplier learning curve delays
- Cost of engineering and social audit visits to ensure product quality and workplace standards
- The time of managers to establish and maintain the supply chain link
- Costs of lost sales and out-of-stocks due to longer lead times for material
- Costs of written-off product due to the need for longer-term forecasts that are more likely to result in excess stock
- Risk due to suppliers becoming competitors

Levy and Weitz, in *Retailing Management*, cite other hidden costs more directly of concern to retailers.[9] These include the following:

- The panache or style associated with higher-priced goods from a country with a better reputation for quality.
- The technical reputation of the source country.
- Foreign currency fluctuations.
- Tariffs and other taxes. The authors note that free trade zones in some countries also offer tax relief.
- Logistics costs, including the holding cost of inventories and transportation.
- Extra costs for quality assurance, including qualification of suppliers and inspections.
- The flexibility gained through quick response to changes in demand and frequent deliveries.
- Preference of customers for products made in their own country.
- Cost of policing human rights and child labor laws.

To take these factors into account, CAGE can be blended with other techniques to assess risks and opportunities in doing business in other countries. Gross margin return on investment (GMROI), an approach described in Chapter 3, provides a first-cut ranking of profitability; factors listed below should help to confirm the first-cut ranking.

Table 4.3 uses a financial statement approach to list operating *factors of production* for application with the CAGE approach. In any analysis of sourcing, the hidden cost factors listed previously should be captured in the applicable categories in the table.

Each category applies in varying degrees to different kinds of supply chain companies—to retailers, distributors, and manufacturers. The same cost categories recommended are employed in Chapter 19, Section 19.2, for the purpose of analyzing activity-based process costs for reduction efforts.

An example using a transportation service illustrates the issues faced. An OEM that manufactures a bulky, low-value item could face higher costs for transportation

**Table 4.3 Impact of Globalization on Factors of Production in the Retail Supply Chain**

| Improvement Categories | Description | Globalization Opportunity |
|---|---|---|
| Revenues | Sales of products through retail outlets or distribution channels, or direct from manufacturing sites. | Expanded sales or production in new countries, including supplier countries that manufacture for the retailer. |
| **Workforce Costs** | | |
| Direct labor | Labor that "touches" the product. Examples: retail employees, purchasing, factory workers, and logistics providers. | Lower direct-cost labor is often the motivator for outsourcing or offshoring. |
| Indirect labor | Labor that supports the direct labor component. Includes store support functions. | These functions coordinate supply chain functions and will likely increase because globalization adds complexity. |
| Administrative/ clerical | Detached from direct activity. Managers, assistants, accounting staff, receptionists, and sales administration. | These tasks, especially if they are routine or don't require face-to-face interaction, are often moved to lower-cost locales. |
| Technical- professional | Engineers, merchandising staff, information technology support, logistics planners, and other white-collar functions. | Essential group, custodians of *core competencies*. May also experience outsourcing and offshoring to lower-cost locales. Also, additions needed to support operations in new countries. |

*(Continued)*

**Table 4.3 (Continued)    Impact of Globalization on Factors of Production in the Retail Supply Chain**

| Improvement Categories | Description | Globalization Opportunity |
|---|---|---|
| Recurring costs | Annualized costs of capacity—stores, manufacturing plants, and equipment and inventory. Rent, interest on debt. Other fixed expenses. | Avoiding capital expenditures may or may not be a good reason for sourcing globally. With automation, some processes may best be performed in the home country. |
| **Purchased Goods and Services Costs** | | |
| Professional services | Manufacturing, accounting, consulting, transportation, and engineering support. | Routine tasks may be off-loaded. Their absence in an offshore location can be a deterrent to globalization. |
| Standard services | Transportation and other logistics, janitorial, local services, and security. | These are locally purchased. The amount and quality should be weighed in a globalization decision. |
| Specialized material/ merchandise | Material or merchandise made to company specification. Other unique components in the product. | This category is often the subject of partnerships among trading partners. The availability of sources is a major consideration. |
| Commodity material/ merchandise | Products or material bought by many companies. Low-technology, off-the-shelf design. | Industries depending on commodities may locate close to the source to reduce the cost of logistics. Sufficient local capability should be confirmed. |

under the standard services category in Table 4.3 if they enter another country to sell or make their product. Applying CAGE, longer shipping distances (a geographic distance) would penalize a distant country as a candidate for making or marketing this product in that country.

A high-value, complex product might be penalized by language differences (cultural distance) if end users require detailed instructions and technical support. Such a manufacturer might favor trading partners in countries who communicate in the local language.

Another option for the manufacturer would be to mitigate the effects of the added distance. For example, for the manufacturer of bulky merchandise, the strategy could be to manufacture locally to supply the market in that country.

A retailer seeking to expand in a new country requires ample qualified store staff and related facilities. Logistics services and infrastructure are also vital. So is a legal system that assures predictability in contracts.

Table 4.4 correlates factors of production with distance attributes. The purpose is to assist readers in tailoring the CAGE application to their situation. A particular retail chain may be more concerned with income and GDP levels and the availability of a skilled workforce for its stores. These are economic and administrative factors. A manufacturer, on the other hand, may be more concerned with the cost of logistics, which is a geographic factor.

The correlations are "+" or "−" depending on the direction of the impact. For example, a common language is a positive influence on the ability to integrate the workforce. So a retail user of this matrix might credit a particular country with a 200% increase in potential if it values easy communications with the home office.

If it is not important to the business, then a credit may not be justified. Another example for both retailers and manufacturers is the negative correlation of geographic factors (physical size, access to ocean, common border) with the cost of transportation, which is a standard service. So a business that is affected by transportation costs would penalize locations accordingly.

The following sections describe some of the many considerations for applying the methodology. The user can start with the correlations in Table 4.4 and modify them according to products, competitive position, and objectives.

### 4.3.1 Revenue

The matrix shows positive correlations, as one might expect, with income level and GDP. Participation in a regional trading block offers added revenue potential because tariffs and better logistics likely make a product more competitive. These effects should be available to both the retailer intending to open stores in the country and the OEM seeking distribution and retailers as customers there. They are less of a factor if the OEM is evaluating whether to manufacture in the county—unless sales there are dependent on having a manufacturing presence.

**Table 4.4  Applying CAGE to Factors of Production**

| Factors of Production | Income Level | GDP | Attributes Related to Distance | | | | | | | | | |
|---|---|---|---|---|---|---|---|---|---|---|---|---|
| | | | Physical Distance | Physical Size | Access to Ocean | Common Border | Common Language | Regional Trading Block | Colony–Colonizer | Common Colonizer | Common Polity | Common Currency |
| **Revenues** | + | + | | | | | | + | | | | |
| **Workforce Costs** | | | | | | | | | | | | |
| Direct labor | | | − | | | | + | | + | + | + | |
| Indirect labor | | | − | | | | + | | + | + | + | |
| Administrative/clerical | + | | − | | | | + | | + | + | + | |
| Technical–professional | + | | − | | | | + | | + | + | + | |
| **Recurring costs** | + | + | | | | | | | | | + | |
| **Purchased Item Costs** | | | | | | | | | | | | |
| Professional services | + | + | | | | | + | + | | | + | + |
| Standard services | + | + | | − | + | + | + | + | | | + | + |
| Specialized material/merchandise | + | + | | | + | + | | + | | | + | + |
| Commodity material/merchandise | + | + | | | + | + | | | | | + | + |

### 4.3.2 Workforce Costs

The retailer or OEM that requires higher skills could find that higher income levels signal the availability of such people. Ease of doing business is certainly improved by a common language for all types of employee. Physical distance is likely to have a negative impact if personal contact is needed across country boundaries. Colonization categories and common polity (defined as the form of civil government) are marked because these signal shared value systems and heritage.

### 4.3.3 Fixed Costs

Fixed costs include facilities (stores, warehouses, and factories), interest paid, process equipment, and transportation investments. Income level and GDP are indicative of local wealth that could be a source of financing. A common polity would provide familiar approaches to contracts and legal recourse to better assure secure investments.

### 4.3.4 Purchased Item Costs

Income level is an indicator of the presence of skilled professionals. Higher levels of GDP reflect the availability of all categories of purchased items—in addition to purchasing power for the retailer's or manufacturer's products. Physical distance and physical size point to increased transportation cost under standard services. Access to the ocean and common border should make transportation and logistics less expensive for any given amount of product movement whether it is subcontracted or commodity-type material. A common language should aid communications with service professionals and technical staff. Common polity and common currency should benefit contracting relationships for materials and services.

## 4.4 Summary

This chapter explains comparative advantage theory and a method for assessing where to go, or where not to, if alternatives for doing business in new countries exist. The method recognizes that physical distance and local income may not be sufficient to understand risks in extending a supply chain to a new region. The methodology should help decide *where* and *where not* to pursue cross-border expansion.

## References

1. Prahalad, C.K., "The Art of Outsourcing," *The Wall Street Journal*, June 8, 2005, p. A14.
2. "China Retail Sales Up 10% in May," *Xinhua Online Edition*, June 13, 2016.

3. Friedman, Thomas L., *The World Is Flat: A Brief History of the Twenty-First Century*, New York: Farrar, Straus and Giroux, 2005, p. 318.
4. Powell, Jim, "Milton Friedman's Favorite Book on Trade," *Wall Street Journal*, June 11–12, 2016, p. A11.
5. Outsourcing 101 (Editorial Board), The *Wall Street Journal*, May 27, 2004, p. A20.
6. Bahree, Megha, "The Multinational, Updated," *Forbes*, October 2, 2006, pp. 103–104.
7. Ghemawat, Pankaj, "Distance Still Matters: The Hard Reality of Global Expansion," *Harvard Business Review*, September 2001, pp. 137–147.
8. "Move Your Operations to China? Do Some Lean Math First," Interview in *Lean Directions*, the e-Newsletter of Lean Manufacturing, Society of Manufacturing Engineers, April 9, 2003.
9. Levy, Michael and Weitz, Barton A., *Retailing Management*, 5th ed., New Delhi: Tata McGraw-Hill Publishing Company Limited, 2004, pp. 441–447.

# Chapter 5

# Corporate Social Responsibility, Sustainability, and the Retail Industry

In 2004, the authors participated in a Sloan Foundation workshop at the University of Washington.[1] The workshop topic was the role of intermediaries in global supply chains. The 16 academic attendees, mostly professors or lecturers at U.S. universities, represented economics (3 attendees), sociology (7 attendees), and business (6 attendees) disciplines. One active discussion centered on the distribution of power among *intermediaries* that served as links in the supply chain. Several attendees argued that retailers hold the strongest hand in the supply chain, creating a *monopsony* where they control product access to the markets.

Not unexpectedly, Wal-Mart Stores, the largest retailer at the time, was a center of discussion. The question pondered by the group amounted to, "Is Wal-Mart good or bad?" The sociologists appeared to argue for "bad" because of Wal-Mart's reputed low wages and benefits and lack of employee union representation. Others, like the business representatives, argued in favor of "good" for bringing low prices to consumers and, measured by sales, doing the best job of delivering what customers wanted.

For years, unions have attempted to organize Wal-Mart workers, but in elections, the employees have opted to keep the unions out. The company, in spite of its problems, has a stock option plan for its employees and encourages attendance at annual and management meetings. Recently, in 2015, Wal-Mart has made changes to its compensation and insurance plans to improve working conditions, partially as a result of pressures nationally for all retailers to pay workers a $15-an-hour minimum wage.

Later in the year of the Sloan Conference, some attendees provided their viewpoints in a Public Broadcasting System (PBS) *Frontline* documentary, "Is Wal-Mart Good for America?"[2] The documentary echoed the workshop themes and described Wal-Mart's success and methods of doing business. Topics included its rapid growth, its leverage in gaining low prices from suppliers, its sophisticated logistics, an implied bait and switch using low-price loss leaders in its stores, and the zeal of associates in promoting high-margin merchandise. To some in society, these features of the Wal-Mart model may seem like sharp-elbow, nefarious business practices; to others, they are commonsense marketing strategies, well executed.

Although targeting a broader but still price-conscious market, Costco has risen in popularity during this same period and has earned a reputation for paying its employees well over $20 an hour on average. The societal push toward establishing a $15 minimum wage that began gaining momentum in 2014 has brought additional criticism of Wal-Mart, a situation that, as previously stated, they are now addressing.

This trend, the workshop, and the documentary all remind us that the role of business is defined by its society and it is likely to change fairly often. Brian Nattrass and Mary Altomare describe the present situation in their book, *Dancing with the Tiger*. They present sustainability as one of today's foremost challenges requiring changes in the current business operating paradigm described by the following:

> *Obsessed by the tyranny of the financial markets, driven to relentlessly increase sales and profits quarter by quarter, forced to match every competitor's advance …, determined to seize market share from adversaries …, today's corporations leave the actions needed to ensure long-term survival to someone else.*[3]

Few companies draw the same amount of attention as Wal-Mart, However, companies in retail supply chains increasingly need to define and refine their own company's role. This chapter describes the scope of what is now labeled *corporate social responsibility* (CSR) and the responses of companies in retail supply chains.

According to Wikipedia, CSR "is a form of corporate self-regulation integrated into a business model." CSR policy functions as a self-regulatory mechanism where each business monitors and ensures its compliance with the spirit of the law, ethical standards, and national or international norms. These strategies are intended to benefit stakeholders, including customers, employees, investors, and the community.

This chapter describes methods of aligning CSR initiatives with strategy to the benefit of society and the stakeholders. Like globalization, described in Chapter 4, the push for CSR will bring change to retail companies and their supply chains. Far-flung supply chains put retailers on the spot, not only for their own behavior but also for that of their trading partners. For example, apparel manufacturers are now held responsible for the behavior of companies upstream in the supply chain. Societal expectations have a direct effect on brand value. Fabrics, even though not manufactured as a result of direct contract with the apparel manufacturer, must be produced in factories with humane conditions paying a fair day's wage. This is part of society's CSR expectations for many U.S. companies, not a result of any legal action. Failure to comply can have immediate consequences on brand value and thereby upon profitability.

CSR efforts need not collide with economic realities. An article described economic issues behind a movement to use factories closer to customers.[4] The article cites examples of Adidas in Germany, Nike, Apple, and Jabil Circuits (electronic component subcontractor). All are using "on-shoring" accompanied by automation to cut lead times and increase flexibility. A further benefit to this practice is avoiding overproduction that leads to inventory write-offs.

The CSR push has also taken the form of international standards for transparent reporting of CSR goals and accomplishments. The vision for achieving this transparency has been to place CSR on the same level as financial reporting. Many companies like environmentally conscious REI now have executives designated as CSR watchdogs.

The Global Reporting Initiative (GRI) (http://www.globalreporting.org), an international interindustry group, has promulgated a reporting standard for assuring sustainability. The standard, described in its *Sustainability Reporting Guidelines*, encompasses what GRI calls the "triple bottom line" for economic, environmental, and social reporting. Guideline updates appear periodically; the version at the time of writing was *G4*.

This chapter describes current CSR reporting and provides an overview of the initiative and its reporting requirements. It then describes a framework for focusing CSR on issues of strategic importance to the retailer and its supply chain trading partners. Finally, a case, that of Boots Ltd. in the United Kingdom, will describe their approach to setting priorities and reporting and regularly updating progress in employing the GRI G4 guidelines.

## 5.1 CSR at Retailers

Table 5.1 summarizes Wal-Mart's framework in the form of stakeholder perspectives for its 152-page *Global Responsibility Report* for 2016. The table contains categories for Wal-Mart's efforts and the areas stakeholders have identified for policies

**Table 5.1  Wal-Mart *Global Responsibility Report 2016***

| Stakeholder Perspectives | Identified Areas | Business Relevance | How Wal-Mart Can Help |
|---|---|---|---|
| Environmental | Climate | Cost; energy; carbon Reputation | Work to reduce energy intensity, adopt renewable energy, and reduce emissions in Wal-Mart operations and supply chains, including with customers |
| | Natural resources | Supply security Cost structure Growth | Collaborate with suppliers and others to create more restorative supply chains in food and other commodities with less environmental impact |
| | Waste | Cost Revenue streams | Eliminate waste in own operations and help "close the loop" on waste throughout production and consumption |
| | Animal welfare | Customer trust Cost | Encourage suppliers to support Five Freedoms in food production |

*(Continued)*

**Table 5.1 (Continued)  Wal-Mart Global Responsibility Report 2016**

| Stakeholder Perspectives | Identified Areas | Business Relevance | How Wal-Mart Can Help |
|---|---|---|---|
| Social | Inclusive economic mobility | Associate engagement<br>Productivity<br>Growth<br>Retention<br>Reputation | Expand customer access to affordable food and other products through retail and e-commerce<br>Continue to provide opportunity for associates, with wages, upskilling, and other practices that support mobility<br>Support local manufacturing; help women-owned, diverse suppliers grow; support smallholder access to markets |
| | Worker dignity in supply chains | Customer trust<br>Supply security<br>Reputation | Continue responsible sourcing practices and collaborate with others on initiatives that support healthier, safer work conditions free from forced labor |
| | Community resilience | Customer trust<br>Associate engagement<br>Reputation<br>Cost | Support local community causes through volunteerism and giving<br>Help communities prepare for and respond to disasters |

**Table 5.2  GRI G4 Reporting Elements**

| # | Indicator Category | |
|---|---|---|
| 1 | In-accordance option (core or comprehensive) | |
| 2 | How material aspects were defined | |
| 3 | Identify boundaries where impacts occur | |
| 4 | Organization's approach to managing material aspects | |
| 5 | Indicators for each material aspect corresponding to the in-accordance option (#1) | |
| 6 | GRI content index to locate relevant content for aspects and boundaries | |

and actions. As described in the report, gathering stakeholder perspectives was an impressive effort (Table 5.2).

> *Over the past year, to sharpen our social and environmental priorities, programs and reporting, we heavily engaged our stakeholders—customers, associates, suppliers, advisory councils, community leaders, grantees, other NGOs, government leaders and investors—in dialogues, working sessions and surveys about their perspectives on Walmart's role in society.*
>
> *These included interviews and a 1,750-respondent survey conducted by Sustainalytics. The Sustainable Development Goals recently released by the United Nations also informed our discussions.[5]*

Participants were solicited to identify "societal changes" and their relevance to Wal-Mart's business. As shown in Table 5.1, summaries of what is needed in the way of action are also provided. They are based on the following approaches, or themes, intended to "use our strengths to support and improve the social and environmental systems upon which we all rely."

■ *Whole-system change* for broad, not incremental, improvement.
■ Shared value for the business and society
■ *Leading through the business* by integrating social and environmental priorities into processes
■ *Focus on actions that leverage Wal-Mart's strengths* by virtue of its size and reach
■ *Using philanthropy to complement business initiatives* including $1 billion in in-kind and financial gifts
■ *Collaborating with others* by supporting other organizations and tools like the Consumer Good Forum and the Sustainability Index

GRI's guidance recommends that reports be tailored to the needs of the specific business reporting.[6] The guidance calls for defining "Aspects" and "Boundaries." (These terms are capitalized in the standard.) Aspects are issues that are material to the business. Businesses will differ regarding which ones are material. Boundaries define whether an Aspect has an impact inside (in company operations) or outside (in suppliers or distributors). Two GRI documents explain the expectations for reporting:

■ Part 1. Reporting Principles and Standard Disclosures (97 pages)
■ Part 2. Implementation Manual (260 pages)

Part 1 contains reporting principles, standard disclosures, and the criteria to be applied by an organization to prepare its sustainability report. Part 2 explains how to apply the reporting principles, how to prepare information to be disclosed, and how to interpret the guideline concepts.

## 5.2 CSR Link to Strategy

Academics and consultants recommend making societal concerns integral to company plans for its processes and its products. Many of these are actually the unintended negative financial consequences of profit-driven activities like carbon emissions, excessive consumption of resources, and overproduction of waste. The CSR movement requires substantive, formal processes for managing what will likely be multiple, simultaneous efforts at different levels of the organization. This section describes two frameworks for linking CSR with strategy provided by prominent management thought leaders.

### 5.2.1 Link between CSR and Competitive Advantage

Michael Porter, the widely read strategy thinker at Harvard University, and Mark Kramer, a cofounder with Porter of the FSG Social Impact Advisors and the Center for Effective Philanthropy, recommend making CSR strategic.*[7] "FSG" is derived from the organization's former name, Foundation Strategy Group. Michael Porter was also the originator of the term *value chain* and developer of the activity system tool described in Chapter 13.

In their award-winning article, Porter and Kramer note that most CSR efforts are disconnected from business needs. Essentially, they are reactive to external stakeholders or critics, reactivity necessitated by the need to protect the brand and

---

\* The article in Ref. 5 was the 2006 first place winner of the annual McKinsey Award for the best article in the *Harvard Business Review*.

not necessarily to generate more profit. There is little in the way of a *shared value*, a form of win–win, for society and the enterprise.

A core reason is that activists target visible, usually successful, corporations to attract attention, even if those corporations can make little impact on the causes they support. Company responses, according to the authors, have been cosmetic public relations and media campaigns. Even worse, such criticism may develop a reaction in the company that puts it at odds with CSR goals, initiating a zero-sum game with no net gain for society. In this environment, the company does what it has to do to look good, and the private businesses fall short in fulfilling their potential to benefit society while adding value for shareholders and employees.

The authors, Porter and Kramer, examine the current ways companies justify CSR initiatives and find them wanting. They identify four common methods: *moral obligation, sustainability, license to operate, and reputation.* The moral obligation assumes that doing good is good for business. Sustainability is associated with minimizing environmental damage. The license to operate applies to industries such as mining where approvals are needed to set up operations. In the absence of this necessary approval, the "license" justification devolves into responding to pressure groups, forfeiting control over the CSR agenda.

Unfortunately, these four justifications are outside in and provide no framework for setting CSR priorities that support company strategy. Porter and Kramer point to a common weakness of all the four approaches: each justification approach focuses on the "tension between business and society rather than their interdependence." Successful businesses need a healthy society that provides the climate for successful operations. Likewise, a healthy society needs successful businesses to satisfy peoples' needs and efficiently use resources. A shared-value CSR effort that also includes inside-out priorities should benefit both society and the enterprise. This leads to a healthier company that provides jobs, pays taxes, produces products society needs, and avoids activities that damage the world around it.

Porter and Kramer recommend thinking of social issues as being of three types:

1. *Generic* issue. Response to social issues in this category is "good citizenship." They do not affect company operations or its competitiveness, at least in the short term. Global warming and AIDS prevention are examples.
2. Value chain impact (including activities this book defines as the supply chain). Affects company day-to-day activities. There are two types—*mitigation of harm* and *strategic transformation of the value chain*. The boundary is either inside the company or along its chain in the upstream or downstream direction. An example is recycling material to reduce costs at a manufacturing plant. Another is developing a product that uses recyclable components that can be efficiently manufactured with minimal raw material and energy consumption.

3. *Strategic philanthropy.* Issues that affect an underlying driver of company competitiveness in locations where the company works. This category changes the *competitive context.* The authors cite Microsoft's partnership with the American Association of Community Colleges to relieve the shortage of information technology workers. Another example is Starbucks' support for redevelopment of city parks in the company's home town, Seattle. The latter produces positive local feelings for a company that has a significant city impact, thereby increasing appreciation for the brand itself.

Porter and Kramer note that a car manufacturer might consider CSR investments to reduce the spread of AIDS as a type 1 generic impact, whereas a pharmaceutical company might consider it a type 3 competitive context impact. One test of the type 3 situation is that the company investment will be seen as a means to differentiate it from competitors, certainly effective for differentiating Starbucks, who originally faced stiff competition from local competitors Seattle's Best Coffee and Tully's. Seattle's Best Coffee is now a wholly owned subsidiary of Starbucks, and Tully's sold its bean distribution business to Green Mountain Coffee Roasters in 2008, and after filing Chapter 11 in 2012, the rest of the company was sold to Global Baristas.

Authors Porter and Kramer then divide CSR initiatives into *responsive* and *strategic* categories. Table 5.3 summarizes the split between the two types. Addressing generic issues is responsive. It is likely the case with many efforts pursued in the absence of links between CSR and strategy. A type 2 mitigation effort may make the company less of a polluter or violator of human rights, but it is mostly intended to help the company stay out of trouble and is not strategic. Some type 2 efforts can reinforce a strategy, like a strategy developed with the activity system tool described in Chapter 13. A type 3 effort will use company capabilities to improve in some way the environment in which the company competes. It is also likely to "move the envelope" by providing distinctive ways of serving society that distinguish the company.

**Table 5.3   Responsive and Strategic CSR**

| Type | Social Issue | Responsive CSR | Strategic CSR |
|------|--------------|----------------|---------------|
| 1 | Generic | • | |
| 2 | Value chain mitigations | • | |
| 3 | Value chain strategy reinforcement | | • |
| 4 | Competitive context | | • |

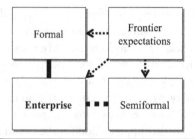

**Figure 5.1   Social issues environment.**

### 5.2.2 *Private Companies and Social Issues*

In another article, consultants from McKinsey & Company urge companies to anticipate the changing CSR landscape.[8] The authors call attention to the constantly moving nature of the *social contract* between society and the business enterprise. Figure 5.1 shows three categories of CSR responsibilities in this environment: *formal, semiformal,* and *frontier* expectations. The formal contract includes regulation, taxes, contract structures, and product liability. Laws, treaties, and the like put these in place. The heavy line symbolizes the mandatory nature of the group. The informal contract lies in expectations, not laws or regulations, and these are shown by a heavy dotted line. An example is the responsibility to maintain labor standards in the supplier base.

Frontier expectations have less direct threads to the enterprise. They may evolve into formal or semiformal requirements or could be directly imposed. An example is the responsibility of food manufacturers for obesity. If people eat too much or the food is "overcaloric," where does the responsibility lie—with the food producer, the restaurant, or the consumer? Or at the movies, is it healthy to serve a 32 oz. small soda? This practice was originally brought about by the theater's need to generate more income. The cost to the theater of renting the movies to show is so high that ticket sales are not enough to cover expenses; setting higher ticket prices would result in a lower number of attendees, as this market is thought to be highly elastic. Therefore, theater food must be marked up by high percentages to achieve profitability. The solution has been to sell huge sizes of sodas, popcorn, candy, and other food items so the theater can generate more income, resulting in the sale of unhealthy portions and contributing to the societal obesity problem. Today's frontier expectations can turn into tomorrow's formal and informal social contract, as shown by arrows in Figure 5.1. The authors argue for more business intervention in the shaping of these expectations.

## 5.3   Framework for Classifying CSR Activities

The previous sections suggest a way toward better management of CSR activities. Table 5.4 consolidates the ideas presented in this chapter for the purpose of

**Table 5.4  Boots CSR Activity Classification**

| A # | B Name of Boots CSR Activity | C GRI Category | D. Type of CSR 1. Good Citizen 2. Mitigation 3. Strategic Process 4. Strategic Philanthropy | E. Origination Outside-In (O) Inside-Out (I) | F. Driver Formal (F) Semiformal (S) Frontier Expectation (E) | G. Reporting 1. Influences 2. Influences Greatly 3. Controls |
|---|---|---|---|---|---|---|
| 1 | Pension plan obligations | EC | 2 | O | F | 3 |
| 2 | Total materials used | EN | 2 and 3 | I | S | 3 |
| 3 | Energy-efficient products and services | EN | 3 | I | S | 3 |
| 4 | Skills management/lifelong learning | LA | 3 | I | S | 2 |
| 5 | Supplier human rights screening | HR | 1 and 2 | O | S | 2 |
| 6 | SunSmart campaign | PR | 4 | I | E | 1 |
| 7 | Change One Thing antismoking campaign | – | 1 and 4 | I | E | 1 |

*Note:* The GRI categories are EC (economic), EN (environmental), HR (human rights), LA (labor practices), PR (product responsibility), and SO (society).

gaining control over the company's CSR agenda. For a company in the retail supply chain that has undertaken or plans to undertake CSR initiatives, the classification approach will assist in the following ways:

- Provides an inventory of existing efforts to facilitate coordinated responses
- Produces a list of candidate issues to address in the future through research or brainstorming
- Leads to setting new priorities, such as dropping some efforts and initiating or renewing others
- Assists in communicating with internal and external stakeholders

The columns provide for listing existing and proposed CSR efforts. Then the type, driver, and reporting requirement under GRI guidelines can be discussed and determined. Some examples from Boots Ltd., the United Kingdom's leading pharmacy-led health and beauty retailer, which dates back to the nineteenth century, are shown in the columns and discussed in the next section.

## 5.4 Boots Ltd.—CSR/Financial Report Convergence

In early 2006, Boots reported in some detail about its CSR efforts. This was not Boots' first report, but it was one that clearly explained its efforts in terms of the GRI guidelines. Subsequently, Boots delivered an update.* The report described progress in the four areas listed below with examples:

- *Community*, to be the recognized champion of healthy communities wherever we operate
- *Environment*, including new refrigeration and landfill reduction
- *Marketplace*, with the use of environmentally ingredients in its products
- *Workplace*, with teams to deliver the best available service

By way of background, a merger in 2006 resulted in a company with 3000 retail outlets in 17 countries. Boots supported 125,000 retail customers with its wholesale and distribution business. Many of these were independent pharmacists. Products included bath and body, skin care, cosmetics, and hair care categories. Its gross margin ROI (GMROI), an important retail supply chain metric described in Chapter 2, was 228%. This translates to explaining that for every cost dollar invested in inventory, the company generated $2.28 or over a 100% return on inventory investment.

---

* "Building Health and More Sustainable Communities: Boots UK Corporate Social Responsibility Update," 2013/2014.

Boots supports the idea that CSR is strategic and that initiatives need to be integrated with business goals. They point to five "strategic pillars" that drive company efficiency. Figure 5.2 shows each pillar along with a brief description. The company motto, "Trust Boots," also signals commitment to CSR. The company identifies 21 CSR issues in four categories: *our marketplace, our communities, our people,* and *our environment.* The company uses this structure to report its CSR initiatives.

The purpose of the list in Table 5.5 is to provide readers with content examples of a company's robust program progress report and to demonstrate the recommended CSR portfolio profiling tool. To that end, the authors populated Table 5.4

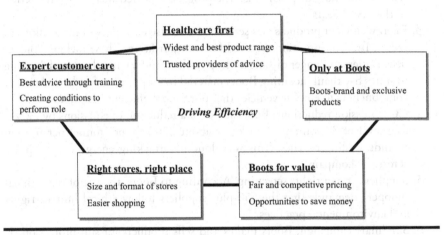

**Figure 5.2  Boots' five strategic pillars.**

**Table 5.5  Boots CSR Issues**

| Our Marketplace | Our Communities |
| --- | --- |
| Ethical investment<br>Corporate governance<br>Supplier verification<br>Customer safety/access<br>Cause-related marketing | Community healthcare<br>Charitable giving<br>Education<br>Employee fund-raising<br>Employee volunteering |
| *Our People* | *Our Environment* |
| Women in the workplace<br>Diversity<br>Training and development<br>Health and safety<br>Employee forums | Chemicals<br>Sustainable products<br>Energy<br>Biodiversity<br>Waste and recycling<br>Transportation |

based on information provided in the Boots CSR report. The following paragraphs describe each CSR item briefly:

1. Pension plan obligations. The sale of a business allowed Boots to more fully fund by £85 million its pension plan for employees. This signaled a "commitment to ensuring the long-term financial health of our people." Although noble, this is a basic obligation.

2. Total materials used. The initiative seeks to cut landfill waste from product packaging, in-transit packaging, and store waste by 20% in 5 years. Use of recyclable material for displays is also promoted. Boots also challenges store requests for more disposal bins. The progress reported was a 7.5% reduction in the first 3 years.

3. Energy-efficient products and services. Boots used a variety of innovations to reduce fuel consumption required for transportation. These include double-deck trailers for longer distances, drop trailers, and having the fleet delivering to stores backhaul incoming Boots material by stopping at suppliers. Another component is to employ vehicles that burn more efficient fuel mixes.

4. $CO_2$ emission reductions. Boots achieved a reduction of emissions by 22.9% to a level of 37 tonnes (1000 kg or about 2200 lb. per tonne) per million pounds sterling of sales. This was done by attacking energy consumption across the company.

5. Supplier human rights screening. According to Boots, the rise of the "ethical shopper" demands that the 550-plus suppliers follow ethical human rights and environmental practices.

6. SunSmart campaign. Boots makes and sells products for sun protection. It delivered advice for safe sun exposure to virtually all the schools in the United Kingdom.

7. Change One Thing antismoking campaign. This program was launched in early 2006 to increase store traffic after the holidays. It was based on the premise that many had New Year's resolutions to quit smoking. Two million participated, leading to 500,000 committing to giving up smoking.

The examples demonstrate one company's effort to put its sustainability reporting on the same level as its financial reporting. Of particular note are the last two, which are most likely to change the competitive context or the way customers view the company, sun protection and antismoking. Such efforts are increasingly essential for customer-facing retailers.

## 5.5 Summary

Many of the CSR examples in this chapter are not limited to a single company. But the retailer is often the target of organizations agitating for a better society through sustainability and other CSR dimensions. That force will be felt up the chain; being capable of controlling the negotiation between society and private industry requires more attention to the situation. This means having an inside-out plan rather than reacting to outside-in mandates.

# References

1. Sloan Foundation Workshop Series, Marketing, "Merchandising, and Retailing: The Role of Intermediaries in Global Value Chains," June 7–9, 2004. Sponsored by the University of Washington Business School.
2. Smith, Hedrick and Young, Rick, "Is Wal-Mart Good for America?" Frontline program available at http://www.pbs.org/wgbh/pages/frontline/shows/walmart/, Hedrick Smith Productions, 2004.
3. Nattrass, Brian and Altomare, Mary, *Dancing with the Tiger, Learning Sustainability Step by Natural Step*, Gabriola, British Columbia: New Society Publishers, 2002.
4. Chu, Kathy and Emmerentze Jervell, Ellen, "As Costs Rise, Factories Move Closer to Customers," *Wall Street Journal*, June 9, 2016, p. B1.
5. Wal-Mart, *Global Responsibility Report*, 2016, p. 8.
6. *An Introduction to G4, the Next Generation of Sustainability Reporting*, Global Reporting Initiative, 2013, 8 pp.
7. Porter, Michael E. and Kramer, Mark R., "Strategy and Society; The Link Between Competitive Advantage and Corporate Social Responsibility," *Harvard Business Review*, Volume 8, Number 6 December 2006, pp. 78–92.
8. Bonini, Sheila M.J., Mendonca, Lenny T., and Oppenheim, Jeremy M., "When Social Issues Become Strategic: Executives Ignore Sociopolitical Debates at Their Own Peril," *The McKinsey Quarterly* (online journal of McKinsey & Co.,) 2006, Number 2, pp. 20–32.

# FORCES SHAPING THE RETAIL SUPPLY CHAIN ENVIRONMENT

The five chapters in Section II cover topics that play a role in the design of retail supply chains.

| # | Chapter Name |
|---|---|
| 6 | Drivers of Retail Supply Chain Change |
| 7 | Paths to the Customer |
| 8 | Supply Chain Risk |
| 9 | Retail Supply Chain Metrics |
| 10 | Meeting the Needs of Supply Chain Decision Makers |

A model that joins together seven major drivers of supply chain change is outlined in Chapter 6. These drivers are not unique to retail supply chains, but apply to all types and include the following:

1. New product/process technology—an external driver
2. The innovation cycle from internal or external sources
3. Extended product design—base products and associated services
4. Globalization of sourcing and markets
5. Flexibility—the ultimate supply chain capability
6. Process-centered management
7. Collaboration among trading partners along the supply chain

Chapter 7 extends the simple supply chain model introduced in Chapter 1 and reflects the complexity where many manufacturers supply many points of sale. Emerging markets and far-flung merchandise sources increase the level of risk in supply chain operations, the topic covered in Chapter 8.

Responses to the changes include the growth of new metrics covered in Chapter 9 and the development of complex information systems and software solutions addressed in Chapter 10. The chapters also inventory available measurement models and describe methods to select appropriate metrics and information technology solutions to fit varying business requirements.

# Chapter 6

# Drivers of Retail Supply Chain Change

This chapter describes drivers fueling change in retail supply chains. Most of the transformations witnessed today can be traced to one or more of these drivers. In marketing, these are referred to as *uncontrollable variables*. They can take many forms: competition, regulation, economy, society or social evolution, and technology. This list forms an acronym—CREST.

Supply chain management has its own particular set of change drivers. Table 6.1 presents a working definition of the drivers the authors consider important; Figure 6.1 models the connections among them.

The chapter also illustrates a framework for defining requirements for the flexibility driver, a cornerstone of supply chain design. Supply chain features needed to achieve flexibility are pervasive, making demands on product offerings and design, logistics network channels, workforce capabilities, and financial resources.

## 6.1 Drivers Are Important

Many drivers are beyond the power of individuals or companies to influence. People embedded in supply chain operations may not even connect change drivers to their daily tasks. However, the need to adjust to changing conditions is always present, even if unseen. This section describes these drivers and explains how they might compel changes in the retail supply chain. Those formulating projects to improve retail supply chains should understand and acknowledge their projects' "roots" in the form of these drivers.

**Table 6.1  Supply Chain Change Drivers Defined**

|   | *SCM Drivers* | *Definitions* |
|---|---|---|
| 1. | Innovation | Technical advances in products and processes. Examples include material technology, production equipment, software, and artistic input. |
| 2. | Extended product design | The necessity for features and services beyond the base, or physical, product. Often driven by commoditization of the base product. |
| 3. | Globalization | Having to source or sell across international borders. Includes trade for raw materials, manufacturing, distribution, and marketing/sales. |
| 4. | Flexibility imperative | The advantage gained from effective responses to market and technology changes. Examples include product mix, volume, base product design, choice of channels, and extended product features. |
| 5. | Process-centered management | A focus on multicompany business processes for designing or improving organizations and systems. |
| 6. | Collaboration | Using intra- and intercompany cooperative efforts to meet mutual goals. Exchanging transaction information between partners. Joint development and improvement of supply chain capabilities. |

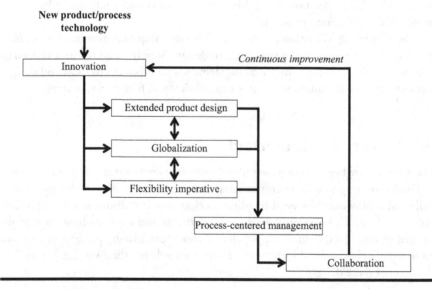

**Figure 6.1  Drivers of SCM change.**

*Innovation*, in Figure 6.1, pushes the change process forward, so we place it first in the sequence of drivers. Innovation is affected by changes in product and process technology and may be external to companies in the supply chain. The fruits of collaboration among supply chain trading partners also promote innovation and serve as an internal source driving adjustments over time.

The three drivers, *extended product design*, *globalization*, and *flexibility imperative*, shape the direction, scope, and form of products and services and their supply chains. Two-headed arrows connecting these three drivers signify simultaneous, coordinated responses. In effect, the output of innovation is "digested" and transformed into requirements for retail supply chain process designs and the collaboration required to implement and sustain them.

The next driver is what we call *process-centered management*, encompassing the requirements for new supply chain processes—processes that inevitably cross both internal department and intercompany boundaries. Crossing these boundaries challenges the traditional organization-centric or budget-centric paradigm in most companies. The process design is enabled by organization designs and technology. These, in turn, define needs for *collaboration*, the last driver. Collaboration among supply chain partners sets in motion more innovations in the form of continuous improvements and more far-reaching changes.

"Where are the company boundaries?" is a question asked about Figure 6.1. In other words, "Are the drivers internal or external to a single company?" The answer is, "Both." The drivers act on industry supply chains. However, the need for any one company to react will depend on the driver and its impact on the industry and the company. For example, *new product/process technology* innovation often originates outside the company and its immediate trading partners. *Collaboration*, on the other hand, is between one's own company and its trading partners, so it's contained within the supply chain. The following sections discuss the drivers and how each plays a role in motivating supply chain change.

## 6.2 Innovation Driver

The model in Figure 6.1 shows innovation as the "engine" of change, affecting products, extended product services, and the processes needed to meet customer requirements. An innovation in product technology, such as nanotechnology, improvements in diesel engines for automobiles, or the development of self-driving cars, will act on current supply chains for related products and services. Tesla, a primary pioneer in the latter industry, is facing opposition to its desire to sell cars directly to consumers in the state of Michigan. Tradition in the historically dominant home of major auto brands defines the supply chain to include a licensed distributor, a practice that Tesla is trying to avoid. However, the company is facing political opposition in the state to making such a change. A totally new product could require new suppliers as well as redesigned distribution models.

Process innovations such as RFID, shipping containers, or supermarket shopping carts alter the way the product is produced or distributed, making it better or lowering the cost of shipping, handling, and storing it.

Product, process, and supply chain innovations interact. The interactions can overlap or be sequential in their timing. Unfortunately, development of new products, changes in process technology, and the pursuit of new markets are often the responsibility of different departments in a company. This division of responsibility is a barrier to coordinated implementation. Those responsible for the innovations may come together only by happenstance or when things are obviously "broken." Some companies have developed innovation teams where all parties are brought together concurrently so that development and supply chains are planned almost simultaneously. In the case of General Motors, this sped up model development considerably and in the apparel industry has led to the ability to develop multiple product lines rapidly for very quick shipping.

Without innovation, the push for supply chain change would be much more limited than it is. Product innovation will increase the value of products to customers. The reward is more than a minimal profit over cost—the kind of profit enjoyed by product innovators such as those in the pharmaceutical (new drugs) and technology industries. Clothing retailer Zara, a "fast fashion" women's clothing chain, has also honed its process for adopting new styles quickly and can produce new apparel lines within weeks; Au Bon Pain and Jimmy Johns have had similar results with sandwiches. The Indian Company, offering motorcycles, profits from the stream of new products and uses these earnings in order to fund new investment, enrich producers, and fuel more innovation.

On April 15, 2015, two companies with unique supply chains, Etsy and Party City, went public in the United States. Etsy, established in 2005, is a peer-to-peer e-commerce website. That is, it connects buyers and usually small sellers in markets for handmade or vintage merchandise and some selected manufactured items. Its mission is to "to reimagine commerce in ways that build a more fulfilling and lasting world." Practically speaking, Etsy provides small sellers with a much broader audience than could be had formerly.

Wikipedia reports the firm had 54 million users, 685 employees, and 29 million items on its website as of December 31, 2014. Etsy product categories include home and living, jewelry, clothing, craft supplies and tools, wedding, and toys and games.

Party City is a more traditional chain focused on party supplies founded in 1986. They have 900 company-owned and franchised outlets operating under Party City, Halloween City, and Party Outlet store names. The company's size is evidence of market focus effectiveness. In 2014 Party City had $2.27 billion in revenue and $56.1 million in profit.

The innovation driver is powerful because low-cost supply chain companies in markets set the competitive standard. Also, as process innovations decrease costs and improve service, products become more affordable, increasing customer accessibility to the product and expanding the target market. New products often allow companies early into markets to reap higher margins in the Introductory and Growth Stages of the Product Life Cycle.

The consulting firm McKinsey captured the effects of process innovation by examining U.S. retail sales leader Wal-Mart.[1] The author of the study, Bradford Johnson, notes that in 1987, Wal-Mart had only a 9% market share, but was 40% more productive than competitors as measured by sales per employee. By 1995, through "big box" stores, electronic communication with suppliers, low prices, and central distribution centers, Wal-Mart had a 27% share and a productivity advantage of 48%.

From 1995 to 1999, competitors played catch-up, but Wal-Mart maintained its edge. McKinsey's study summarized how Wal-Mart achieved the gains through changes in both product and process.

- *Managerial innovations* that did not involve information technology. An example is cross-training employees to increase flexibility in their assignment and the hours they work.
- *Focused IT investments* that enhanced Wal-Mart's low-price objective and did not include more recent investments in real-time sales data collection and dissemination.
- *Higher-value goods* matched to market desire for upscale products. For example, the $30 shirt costs as much to handle and sell as the $20 shirt, but is far more profitable.

In the early years of the twenty-first century, Wal-Mart illustrated the innovation driver for supply chain projects. The company used its supply chain capability to identify products that yielded the highest profit. For a retailer bringing thousands of products to market, pegging profitability at the product level is a vital, and often daunting, task. Relying on data, not buyer intuition, is key. Chapter 19 recommends a process using activity-based costing to achieve this objective.

In recent years, Wal-Mart using its cost minimization strategy has lagged behind other very successful mass merchandisers such as Costco. Wal-Mart's failure to pay adequate salaries to its store staff has resulted in a deterioration of customer service and growing dissatisfaction with the shopping experience. Their workers were paid at about the 25th percentile nationwide, and the company employed 1.4 million of the nation's 16 million retail workers.[2] Declining sales increases and employer turnover began to reflect the lackluster store experience. In October 2015, Wal-Mart announced a program to increase wages to $9 per hour, an action emulated by TJX (TJMaxx, Marshalls, and Home Goods) and Target. In addition, staff members will receive extensive training in a strategy designed to give workers more creative freedom, make stores more pleasant, and appeal to customers of affluence. In order to survive, companies cannot rely on former innovations; they must innovate to meet changing conditions.

What about a company with only a few products where there's no confusion as to where profitability lies? This is often the case when the product is based on intellectual property (IP) that provides a monopoly of sorts. A *Wall Street Journal* article described the implications of this product category.[3] The article notes that the products based on IP are fundamentally different. Almost all the cost is in development, and almost 100% of every sales dollar is pure profit after the initial investment in development is paid off.

Is SCM important in cases where the incremental cost of the base product is close to zero? There are at least three ways supply chain considerations support such products.

1. *The introduction of "killer" products.* Effective supply chain processes speed moneymaking products to market. Delay glitches are tantamount to leaving money on the table. Also, such software products require, according to Bill Gates of Microsoft as quoted in the *Wall Street Journal* article, "monopoly power." This results only if you become an industry standard by being first to market. Without that dominating position, up-front investments may become total losses, not total profits.
2. *Reduction of unseen lost sales.* Reducing lost sales requires adequate supplies to meet demand. Products produce no profit if the sale is lost due to a stock-out. This is important to retailers who maintain processes dedicated to handling high-volume staple products.
3. *Extensions of product life.* The innovative product is not innovative forever. If costs are not reduced as it matures, it may die a sudden death. Squeezing out cost is a duty of supply chain managers.

Steven Wheelwright and Kim Clark have defined different types of product and process change.[4] Table 6.2 shows types *A* through *D* from Clark and Wheelwright; *E* is this book's authors' addition to recognize "partnership" projects, each of which contains its own issues. The table recognizes that each situation varies in terms of the product and process changes involved. For example, an *A*-type project involves minor changes in both dimensions. The companies' flows of new products are routine events, and the product introduction process is repeated over and over.

Next Generation *B* projects are more ambitious. Continual upgrading in computers and phones is an example. Product changes in the *B* category could result in the same effect on the process dimension, or needed processes could remain the same.

The *C* project is the "breakthrough" in either product or process. In retailing, the growth of Internet sales crowding out store sales is a *C* situation on the process side.

**Table 6.2  Types of Product/Process Development Projects**

| Type | Examples | Extent of Product Change | Extent of Supply Chain Change |
|------|----------|--------------------------|-------------------------------|
| A | Existing product enhancements Derivative products Variations on similar products | Minor changes Different content/ same form Few, if any, supplier changes | Incremental or no change Single department involved Requires material management changes |
| B | Next-generation product New product "platform" | Major changes likely Supplier changes more likely | Next-generation process Multiple departments involved Probable supply chain impact |
| C | Radical breakthrough | New core product Probable new suppliers and chain | New core processes New supply chain very likely |
| D | Research/advanced development | Leads to new core product New suppliers/chain likely | Design requires new core processes New supply chain more likely |
| E | Partnership projects | Likely to require a new supply chain if product is new | Supply chain change involving partners likely |

*D* projects represent the "fuzzy front end" of product and process development. Managers may choose how much supply chain planning is required. *E* projects are efforts with multicompany participation. These raise issues discussed in Section IV of this book.

Table 6.2 describes the impact on the retail supply chain from either new products or new processes. A next-generation process resulting from a *B* effort can happen even if there is not a great deal of change in the product itself. Likewise, a next-generation product may require only incremental process or supply chain changes.

Manufacturing companies may use the term "concurrent engineering," CE for short, to describe simultaneous development of manufacturing processes and products. Note that many efforts are confined to manufacturing at a company and do not address broader supply chain issues. CE speeds up product introduction. It is the opposite of the "over-the-wall" approach of engineering departments handing product designs to the production department or to suppliers.

The need to consider the capabilities of supply chain partners adds another dimension to the CE concept. In many cases, delays are just as long when handing a design to the procurement department charged with finding suppliers. Now it is not only tooling and material that have to be considered, but also other issues such as distribution channels and inventory policy. CE for the entire supply chain particularly fits in the case of *B, C*, and *E* products. In these cases, a new product is more likely to be accompanied by a new supply chain.

## 6.3 Extended Product Design

Figure 6.1 illustrates how product or process innovations feed the next SCM driver, *extended product design*. Our definition in Chapter 1, Section 1.2, describes the supply chain as "product life cycle processes comprising physical, information, financial, and knowledge flows whose purpose is to satisfy end-user requirements with physical products *and services* from multiple, linked suppliers." For many products, there are a lot of services, usually a source of differentiation.

Figure 6.2 depicts the base and extended products, and lists the supply chain links—retailer, distributor, original equipment manufacturer (OEM), or supplier—that might provide each service. In Figure 6.2, the physical product is labeled "base product," and with it are the services that make up the "extended product." For several services, such as *product availability* and *warranties*, more than one link along the chain will play a role. For example, the retailer or the distributor or both could be responsible for product availability.

A *Wall Street Journal* article confirmed the trend by stating that "manufacturers find themselves increasingly in the service sector."[5] The article attributes the trend to manufacturers having to provide services because that is "where the money is." Few products and services are commodities in the strictest sense. However, for many, extended product features may outweigh the importance of the base product, which customers may view as indistinguishable from competing brands. General Electric's former CEO, Jack Welch, portrayed service development associated with hardware production as fundamental to his success as the CEO.[6]

In an ideal world, supply chain managers methodically monitor the product and process innovations coming their way. They then design supply chains to incorporate each innovation. Or, in a slightly less ideal world, the managers slot each innovation into the "best-fit" supply chain already in place. However, in many instances, managers fall short of achieving either of these states. In fact, base product and extended product management, like other related functions, are often in separate departments. For example, base products may be the responsibility of R&D, engineering, and manufacturing departments, whereas marketing and sales shape extended products.

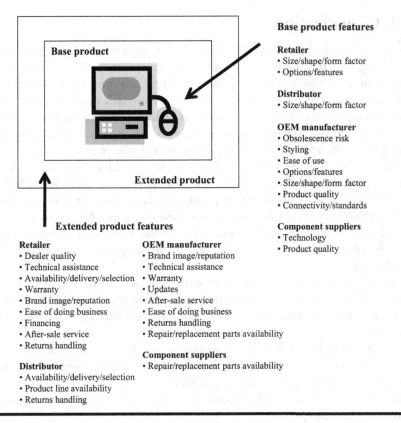

**Base product features**

**Retailer**
• Size/shape/form factor
• Options/features

**Distributor**
• Size/shape/form factor

**OEM manufacturer**
• Obsolescence risk
• Styling
• Ease of use
• Options/features
• Size/shape/form factor
• Product quality
• Connectivity/standards

**Component suppliers**
• Technology
• Product quality

**Extended product features**

**Retailer**
• Dealer quality
• Technical assistance
• Availability/delivery/selection
• Warranty
• Brand image/reputation
• Ease of doing business
• Financing
• After-sale service
• Returns handling

**OEM manufacturer**
• Brand image/reputation
• Technical assistance
• Warranty
• Updates
• After-sale service
• Ease of doing business
• Returns handling
• Repair/replacement parts availability

**Distributor**
• Availability/delivery/selection
• Product line availability
• Returns handling

**Component suppliers**
• Repair/replacement parts availability

**Figure 6.2    Base and extended products.**

Managers may assume that every product innovation must fit an existing supply chain instead of recognizing that the supply chain result, the service aspect, is fundamental to the extended product and must be carefully planned. Sometimes outside conditions precipitate major supply chain revisions. For example, a few years ago, apparel manufacturers met with an unexpected situation. With the manufacture of large quantities of clothing in China, shippers were originally delighted with the new volumes and would send partially full ships to the United States in order to keep the deliveries on schedule for retailers. Suddenly as competition sharpened, this was no longer practical; only full ships were allowed to sail and deliveries were held up. Supply chains, manufacturing calendars, and other distribution considerations became subject to immediate review and revision.

Inertia, hard-to-change information systems, required behaviors, and functional barriers make it hard to change current practices. Additionally, expensive investments in systems, staff, and facilities may be needed for the new product. Ignoring this driver will put the company at risk. Chapter 13 explains the activity system approach to developing extended product processes.

## 6.4 Globalization

Chapter 4 described the economics of comparative advantage behind globalization. By adding jobs and payrolls, social good also results from globalization through growth in multicountry supply chains. For supply chain managers, globalization influences range from upstream suppliers to downstream customers. For smaller manufacturers who export to other countries, their executives must not only ensure that the production lines are running but also that currency risks are hedged.[7] Changing tariffs and customs requirements also complicate the process.

The shift to "offshore" sourcing, often to cut material and/or labor costs, provides opportunities for jobs and investment in developing countries. When this occurs, globalization puts money in people's pockets, widening markets for company products. Narayana Murthy echoes these thoughts.[8] Murthy is the retired chairman of Indian technology services firm, Infosys Technologies Limited. Infosys recently reported sales of U.S. $9.5 billion, 194,000 employees, and service delivery in 50 countries.

Murthy reports that the company started on the premise that globalization would make the world "as wired and open as a trading floor." The founders' premise was that this globalization would bring a competitive advantage to low-cost skilled workers.

He describes how India, at the beginning, was bogged down in a culture of bureaucracy. His startup faced obstacles like a 2-year delay to buy a computer and 2 to 3 years to get a telephone line. His advice was to pursue fresh ideas with vigor, maintain a meritocracy, and continuously benchmark operations and products against the best competitors.

Global supply chains also bring government intervention in market forces. Calestous Jumas at Harvard observes that "the EU starves Africa" in the way it sets tariffs on coffee.* Africa is an important source of coffee including significant exports to Europe. The continent exported $2.4 billion of the crop in 2014. One country, Germany, earned $3.8 billion from coffee re-exports. The European Union levies a tariff on roasted coffee in the name of consumer safety. The effect is that African producers are cut out of the more lucrative re-export business where they can add more value to their product. This has the effect of discouraging African agricultural innovation and impedes improvement in living standards as well as depriving consumers of attractive product.

---

* The author is a professor of the practice of international development at the Harvard Kennedy School of Government. His article was published October 25, 2016 for the website for CapX Partners, a capital provider to middle market clients. The article was republished in the *Wall Street Journal*.

# 6.5 Flexibility Imperative—The Ultimate Capability

The last driver arising from innovation is retail supply chain flexibility imperative. Absence of flexibility infers a static supply chain that is unable to "flex" as changes in the environment require. Product designs, competitive responses, sales levels, and customer requirements rarely stay the same for long. Although the environment has many moving parts, many companies try to fulfill customer requirements with a "one size fits all" approach. They fail to take into account the needs of different customer segments, the necessity of providing extended product features, and the ever-changing base products.

Flexibility is a term with different meanings to different people. However, its importance raises the need to define the word and what it requires in supply chain design. For this to happen, management must be prepared to respond in three ways:

1. *Mindset.* The company must recognize the need for defining flexibility formally, and what kinds of flexibility are needed for the business.
2. *Long term.* Management must be skilled enough to match supply chain design, including supply chain capacity, with customer expectations. If it is not willing or can't do so, management must be prepared to drop low value customers.
3. *Short term.* Management must understand the markets they choose to serve well enough to define requirements for response time and production flexibility and to anticipate profit/loss outcomes.

The needed responses are interdependent. That is, a company must have #1 to get #2; and it must have #2 to get #3. The next sections explain each of these transitions further and their implication for retail SCM.

## 6.5.1 Management Mindset

If one believes that change in variables such as product demand and product mix will occur in the marketplace, then one must accept that flexibility is "imperative" in the supply chain, as well as in product characteristics. The flexibility imperative is the foundation for achieving objectives in the other supply chain metrics like cost, quality, and lead time. Being flexible brings the ability to move to where the supply chain needs to be with regard to reliability, responsiveness, cost, and asset utilization.

Describing the absence of the correct mindset is easier than defining its presence. Symptoms of such an absence include the following:

1. Company strategies are silent on the topic of flexibility.
2. Departments in the supply chain are frozen and unlinked. Separate budgets exist for functions—marketing, sales, purchasing, manufacturing, and distribution—without regard to the processes they share.

3. "Supply chain" is defined as warehousing, transportation, and other physical handling of products. Manufacturing, product design, marketing, and inventory management are not included in the definition.

4. The primary measure for supply chain managers is cost. An example is "supply chain cost per dollar of sales." This completely overlooks the impact on sales of slowing down the chain to save money.

5. Management pursues inventory reduction programs. Inventory is an effect, not a cause. It is the consequence of supply chain processes and cannot be reduced unless these are changed.

6. The company measures buyers on unit costs of purchased material, omitting other factors like margins, returns, and quality.

7. Lost sales due to out-of-stock and returns situations are not estimated and tracked. No one is accountable for them.

8. Inventory and other assets are considered "free" because their costs are not weighed in performance measures.

The presence of any of these conditions should raise alarms. However, absence of any of the symptoms is not sufficient for achieving a management mindset. Management should also articulate the types of flexibility needed for the business as described in the following section.

## 6.5.2 Defining Needed Flexibility

David Upton has recommended a methodology for incorporating flexibility into manufacturing systems.[9] His definition is

> Flexibility is the ability to change or react with little penalty in time, effort, cost, or performance.

This framework for flexibility can be translated from the manufacturing level, where he proposed it, to trading partners—suppliers, distributors, and retailers. Upton recognizes the problems that go with defining flexibility. Just saying, "We need to be flexible," is inadequate due to the many possible interpretations. To fill this gap, Upton defines flexibility as having three "dimensions" defined by answers to questions. Table 6.3 summarizes the framework and provides examples.

*Question 1* asks what parameter requires flexibility. APICS, a standard setting organization, identifies candidates that apply to manufacturers and other types of businesses, even those providing services:

■ Product mix
■ Design changeover
■ Product modification

**Table 6.3  Characterization of Flexibility**

|   | Component | Description | Examples |
|---|-----------|-------------|----------|
| 1. | Dimension | What is it that requires flexibility? | Different input materials<br>Mixes of product<br>Volume range |
| 2. | Time horizon | What is the period over which flexibility is required?<br>• Operational—seconds to days<br>• Tactical—days to months<br>• Strategic—months to years | Operational—schedule changes, daily shipments, order response time<br>Tactical—quarterly changes in mix, use of materials, number of SKUs to carry to support a product line<br>Strategic—longer-range changes requiring capital, new processes, or new systems |
| 3. | Element | In what way should we be flexible?<br>• Range—by how much the dimension (#1 above) must be able to change<br>• Mobility—transition costs (low or high) for moving within a range<br>• Uniformity—the ability to be consistent over a range | Range—volumes of output or deliveries, sizes of product, SKUs breadth, merchandise models<br>Mobility—having low setup costs to change product mix or to add or discontinue merchandise SKUs<br>Uniformity—the ability to maintain a certain standard such as delivery time, cost, or merchandise availability |

■ Volume
■ Rerouting, and
■ Material usage in the product

Most of these dimensions exist for retailers and distributors. Other common dimensions include delivery lead time, various extended product services, and product-line breadth and depth.

*Question 2* identifies the "time horizon." Upton uses operational, tactical, and strategic for short (seconds, minutes, and hours), medium (hours, days, and weeks), and longtime horizons (weeks, months, and years). Whether short means seconds or hours depends on the product, industry, and the company's position in the supply chain.

*Question 3* addresses "elements" of flexibility. Upton describes three elements under which most flexibility requirements fall. They are *range, mobility,* and *uniformity.* A *range* element specifies the limits of performance. For example, if volume flexibility, a common dimension, over a short period is sought (time horizon), the range will specify the high and low operating volumes. *Mobility* refers to the penalty in moving from one state in the range to another. For example, if there is little cost in moving from 100 units per hour to 150, then mobility is high. On the other hand, if it is very difficult to make this change, mobility is low. *Uniformity* refers to the performance over a range. For example, if the move from 100 to 150 units causes little change in the quality of the product, then flexibility is high with respect to quality.

Figure 6.3 illustrates a flexibility specification. Sandwich shops operate in the demanding build-to-order situation. The shops need to provide quick, consistent responses to customers. This requires supply chain flexibility in multiple dimensions including product mix, volume, and customer response time.

Product mix changes are required over an operational timeframe that, in this case, is daily. The element of flexibility is mobility. Any product mix can be made each day with the supply chain moving quickly to produce one unique product after another. A sandwich shop exemplifies this type of flexibility in a short timeframe measured in minutes, because the staff would like to assemble any menu sandwich as soon as the customer enters the store.

"Product volume" in our example is the ability to change overall volume up or down in a tactical, or intermediate, timeframe. For the sandwich shop, this period could be monthly. So, the sandwich shop, like other retailers, adjusts its schedule up or down across a range of expected business levels. If the shop is across the street from a college, then the capacity (number of workers) would be higher during the school year and lower during summer vacation.

"Response time" provides a strategic standard that is competitive in the market served by the organization. This dimension is likely to be as important to manufacturers and distributors as it is to retailers. It is a uniformity element, meaning

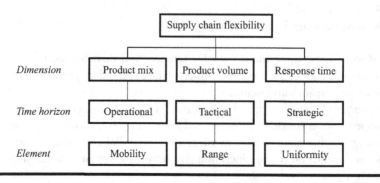

**Figure 6.3  Elements that define flexibility—an example.**

that customer response time must be uniform over the range of volumes in which the supply chain must operate. Jimmy John's, a sub sandwich shop opened in 1983, features homemade bread, locally sourced meats and produce, and high-quality branded condiments. The franchise chain now has 2522 outlets and, in addition to featuring high-quality ingredients, emphasizes top speed in producing custom-order products—and they will even deliver them 20 minutes from order time within a prespecified delivery area, a service that differentiates their service from the competition.

So, a sandwich shop must provide uniform service, building each sandwich within minutes at both high- and low-volume levels. In fact, McDonald's and other fast-food retailers track the time it takes to serve each customer and hold employees responsible for achieving targeted rapid customer service. If a particular order is delayed slightly in the drive-in lane, the customer is asked to pull to a special parking place to await order delivery to the car by a staff member. This allows the restaurant to keep other cars moving through the lane.

A sandwich vendor who doesn't make to order but stocks retailer shelves with prepackaged sandwich varieties has a different problem. He or she relies on forecasts to get the mix right and the quantity appropriate to minimize spoilage. A risk is that customers won't settle for a second or third choice if their first is sold out.

Contrasts in product mix flexibility requirements can be seen in the strategies of major retailers. Nordstrom, the clothing retailer, presents a broad fashion forward product mix to its customers, with individual departments targeting slightly different customers. Retailer Costco, a discounter, buys in bulk whenever product is available but limits the number of SKUs available at any time to 3750.[10] Consistency in offering low-cost merchandise that generates rapid turnover, rather than a wide range of goods, is the flexibility goal for this wholesale club format retailer.

Flexibility specifications are needed to design supply chain processes and shape collaboration with supply chain partners. Design parameters include capacity, inventory, and merchandising decisions along the retail supply chain. Static specifications are not acceptable. The Upton method guides the definition of ranges of operations and expectations for customer service. Also, many senior managers will seek a visual "cockpit" to monitor their operations. One based on defined flexibility parameters such as those in the example should be included in the cockpit.

# 6.6 Process-Centered Management

Examining end-to-end processes without taking on too much at once has gained currency. Awareness of the importance of processes is not new. Reengineering, Total Quality Management (TQM), Lean, and Six Sigma are mature initiatives aimed at process improvement. Yet there is often tension between those wanting to focus on end-to-end processes and functional managers focused on local improvements in their departments. These managers do this because their own performance measurements encourage local improvements, and changes here are easier because they control the departments and their direction.

Jack Welch, in the previously cited interview, talks about "world peace" projects requiring complex information technology.[6] In his first decade as General Electric's CEO, he approved many of these projects. His term, *world peace,* refers to over-hyped promises made to sell the projects. When promised results never materialized, Welch became far more skeptical. In his second decade as CEO, only projects that produced tangible with fast results moved forward.

What is the implication for SCM? Is top-down, top down end-to-end, or bottom-up the right model for retail SCM projects? Table 6.4 describes three scenarios framing how projects for supply chain improvement should be formulated, justified, and managed. Scenario 1 in Table 6.4 is bottom-up, originating in the department. A project might be the purchase of a machine tool in the manufacturing department. "We will cut our labor by 20%," is a claim that might describe expected results from such a project. It is likely a local savings, involving that portion of the process where the machine is used. It is not necessarily true that overall process cost will be reduced at all, especially when the cost of capital for the machine is taken into account.

Scenario 2 is top-down at the business unit level, with projects that cross department boundaries. A customer relationship management (CRM) system is an example. This technology could be deployed at the retailer, distributor, or manufacturer level. "We shall increase our sales 5%," might be a claim of success for the

**Table 6.4  Scenarios for Developing Supply Chain Projects**

|   | Level | Sponsorship | Examples | Goal | Justifications |
|---|-------|-------------|----------|------|----------------|
| 1. | Function | Department head | Machine tools, new production equipment | Department improvement | Return on investment, savings |
| 2. | Business unit | CEO | Enterprise systems, expansions/ contractions | Business unit improvement | Revenue increase or cost reduction |
| 3. | Supply chain | CEO, customer, supplier, alliance | Information sharing, investment sharing | Multicompany competitiveness | Market share, revenue increase or cost reduction |

system. However, an auditor might have difficulty tracing any "hard" return revenue increases to the system. Scenario 3 is "beyond" top-down because it extends past company boundaries. Projects in this category seek to reduce multicompany process cost across trading partners.

To be effective at the supply chain level, a process focus, i.e., top-down end-to-end, is a necessity. Reasons include avoiding local optimums at the expense of the overall process, the interdependence of departments and businesses in the supply chain, and the advantages of shared knowledge to solve problems. But there are also many obstacles to such performance that include physical separation, suspicion of other participants, inadequate cost accounting, counterproductive performance measures, and lack of skills or numbers. So, collaboration to improve processes is not easy. But the beginning is a process-centered focus that includes supply chain partners. Sections IV and V of this book recommend methods to bring about a supply chain process-centered focus.

# 6.7 Collaboration

The end-to-end process approach leads to the need for collaboration across internal departments and company boundaries. Few dispute the need for collaboration in improving supply chains. Like *flexibility*, the term *collaboration* can mean different things to different people. Certainly, both companies on either side of a supply chain link must agree to the form of collaboration.

## 6.7.1 Definitions of Collaboration

A big push for collaboration is technology based. To many practitioners, the term *collaboration* is a code word for *information sharing*, which in turn becomes a call for new systems. To meet the need, many supply chain information software applications have emerged to support collaboration. These products enable sharing of production and inventory data, online auctions, market places for buying and selling, and production planning along the supply chain.

It should be no surprise, then, that definitions of collaboration have an information technology tone. Table 6.5 contains definitions of collaboration by industry analysts who, at the time of the presentation, represented three prominent research organizations.[11] All three analysts described collaboration as a three-stage process. The levels begin with simpler forms of information sharing that are relatively easy to automate. They proceed to higher levels that involve joint decision making. These may be aided by technology, but are essentially powered by management decision-making processes that are difficult to automate.

Of the three, the version from Navi Radjou (right column) captures the widest range of decision-making activity. It also covers collaboration processes such

**Table 6.5  Definitions of Collaboration**

| Company | Company Represented | | |
|---|---|---|---|
| | Yankee Group | AMR Research | Forester Research |
| Analyst | Jon Derome | Larry Lapide | Navi Radjou |
| Level 1 | Exchange of structured data | Execution (routine documents such as purchase orders) | Monitor. Watch the process together |
| Level 2 | Free-form interactive sharing (Web tools, chats, online) | Information sharing, mostly one way | Manage. Coordinate activities |
| Level 3 | Process collaboration (structured, mix of human and automated exchange) | Collaborative relationship (joint planning and scheduling, coordinated execution) | Optimize. Joint decision making. Win-win partnerships across network |

as strategy setting and cost sharing of investments needed to compete on a supply chain basis.

## 6.7.2  Stage 3 (Multicompany) SCM

What general structure might collaboration take between two or more trading partners? An earlier article outlined a vision for *stage 3* supply chain collaboration efforts.[12] The term *stage 3* comes from the third, supply chain level as shown in Table 6.4. Multicompany collaboration features include the following:

1. Shared goals including strategic and tactical improvements. An example of the former is increased market share; an example of the latter is lower product cost or reduced inventory.
2. A team effort that includes representatives from participating companies on a full-time or part-time basis.
3. As needed, an honest broker to facilitate the effort. This can be a trusted team member or third party such as a consultant.
4. A multicompany CEO or senior management steering committee. This group would be responsible for the results.
5. Contracting that distributes costs and rewards based on contributions. Negotiations over costs and profits shouldn't fall back on standard buyer–seller

price negotiations but be guided by a model of supply chain costs using techniques such as those described in Chapter 19.

6. Process integration using appropriate technology and continuous improvement. An important component could be synchronizing the supply chain replenishment cycle.

Item 6 on the list also closes the loop as shown in Figure 6.1, taking collaboration back to further supply chain innovation—with ideas coming from inside the supply chain.

A stage 3 effort should not be a one-shot affair. After the initial effort, improvements should continue. Once established, the supply chain partnership becomes a source of innovations.

## 6.8 Know Your Drivers

This chapter addresses the elements that enable making supply chain change a way of life. Some companies will be slow in comprehending which of these drivers affect them most. However, the drivers will be there, exerting a force for change whether it's recognized in the organization or not.

Supply chain partners delivering functional, low-technology products seek innovations in processes. These could result in globalization of sourcing and innovations in tracking and transportation.

A technology product supply chain, on the other hand, must react to innovations coming from manufacturers in the supply chain. In any change, retailers in contact with customers and end-users should transmit market preferences back through the chain.

## References

1. Johnson, Bradford C., "Retail: The Wal-Mart Effect," *The McKinsey Quarterly*, 2002, Number 1.
2. "Wal-Mart and low-wage America: High expectations," *The Economist*, January 30, 2016.
3. Murray, Alan, "Intellectual Property: Old Rules Don't Apply," *The Wall Street Journal*, August 23, 2001, p. A1.
4. Wheelwright, Steven C. and Clark, Kim B., *Revolutionizing Product Development*, New York: Free Press, 1992, p. 49.
5. Ansberry, Clare, "Manufacturers Find Themselves Increasingly in the Service Sector," *The Wall Street Journal*, February 10, 2003, p. A2.
6. Welch, Jack, A conversation with Jack Welch, *MSI Executive Series* (Internet broadcast), April 16, 2002.

7. Phillips, Michael M., "Ship Those Boxes; Check the Euro!" *The Wall Street Journal*, February 7, 2003, p. C1.

8. Murthy, Narayana N.R., "Clear Conscious-Clear Profit," *The Wall Street Journal*, September 29, 2006, p. A16.

9. Upton, David M., "The Management of Manufacturing Flexibility," *California Business Review*, Winter 1994, pp. 72–89.

10. "Q2 2014 Earnings Call Transcript," Morningstar, Stocks Costco Wholesale Corp, Richard Galanti, March 6, 2014.

11. Lapide, Larry, Derome, Jon, and Radjou, Navi, Analysts' panel discussion, *Supply Chain World North America: Extending Collaboration to End-to-End Synchronization*, April 2002.

12. Ayers, James B., Gustin, Craig, and Stephens, Scott, "Reengineering the Supply Chain," *Information Strategy: The Executive's Journal*, Fall, 1997 (14/1), pp. 13–18.

# Chapter 7

# Paths to the Customer

Recently, Joe Skorupa, editorial director of Retail Information Systems, wrote on the website *Retail Leader*:

> Survival of tradition-bound brick-and-mortar retailing requires more than just hitting quarterly numbers and making incremental enhancements. Survival requires mercilessly assessing existing business processes, identifying weaknesses, sharply improving consumer convenience, and merging innovative technologies with new capabilities.[1]

True digital transformation is coming and Skorupa goes on to describe his vision of it.

> This Wi Fi 2.0 environment will drive a host of enterprise applications on associates' mobile devices, run self-help kiosks and digital displays in the aisles, and deliver location-based sensing and messaging to customers' smartphones wherever they are in the store. Shoppers will get personalized messages, both promotional and friendly, to build engagement. Associates will be fully empowered to deliver high-touch experiences, such as recognizing the status of high-value shoppers, possessing deep product information to become passionate advocates, and performing such store tasks as sales audits, inventory counts, and changing merchandise sets in a faster, more efficient way to help reduce in-store labor.

Chapter 6 described the drivers of supply chain change. New markets, new products, and shifts in end-user needs, in the face of anticipated technology-driven revisions to the basic retail business, demand innovation in supply chain process

**Table 7.1  Meeting Market Needs—SCM Dimensions**

| # | Market-Need Dimensions | Timeframe | SCM Relevance |
|---|---|---|---|
| 1. | Product portfolio | Long | Mix, technology employed, breadth and depth of line |
| 2. | Product design | Long | Configuration, reliability, usability, options |
| 3. | Capabilities and capacity | Long | How to source material, produce, and move the product |
| 4. | Competitive responses | Intermediate | Competitors, capabilities, strengths, and weaknesses |
| 5. | Product channels | Intermediate | Customer preferences, need for omnichannel options |
| 6. | Customer risk concerns | Intermediate | Returns, service and repair, technical support, durability |
| 7. | Matching supply and demand | Short | Channels, required flexibility, information sharing |

design. Responding to these drivers in a timely way entails attention to the seven dimensions of supply chain planning and design listed in Table 7.1. The list applies to all supply chain roles—retailers, distributors, suppliers, logistics companies, original equipment manufacturers (OEMs), and other service providers.

The importance of any one dimension will vary for any combination of supply chain role, product, and market. For example, *product design* and *capabilities and capacity* are likely to be more important for manufacturers than distributors. Companies with a narrow view of SCM too often overlook any or all of these. This chapter explores each dimension and describes methods for addressing each.

# 7.1  Meeting Market Needs—Dimensions

A SCM function with "deep roots" will contain processes that address dimensions listed in Table 7.1 in ways that meet their need to be competitive. The timeframes, in the second column of Table 7.1, will depend on the role–product–market combination. A *long* timeframe will normally exceed 1 year and could be as long as 5 years. For example, longer terms are characteristic of the anticipated new technology product developments, while an *intermediate* timeframe might apply to product upgrades.

A long-term timeframe could also apply to a middleman distributor who offers extended product services to manufacturers and retailers like carrying inventory and spare parts. Intermediate timeframes are generally measured in months. For a retailer, planning for holiday seasons could have an intermediate planning horizon. *Short* term is hourly, daily, or weekly and is often the domain of conventional, narrowly defined SCM.

The *product portfolio* (#1), a long timeframe dimension, includes decisions by the manufacturer for both the base product and extended product services. For a logistics service provider such as UPS and FedEx, it includes pursuit of those services that retailers and manufacturers outsource and that are increasingly time dependent. For retailers, it involves merchandising decisions regarding products and brands their stores and other outlets will carry, including new products heading to market from manufacturers.

*Product design* (#2) will obviously concern the OEM. New designs bring the need for adjustments in manufacturing processes and the supplier base, important supply chain features. Product design may also affect distributors and retailers if the product can be assembled, labeled, or otherwise processed along the path to the end user or by the end user.

Collaboration between a retailer and a manufacturer is necessary for private label brands. The retailer, not the manufacturer, oversees product design; and manufacturers produce to these specifications. Certainly, the rollout of new products brings the need for collaboration in the design process and marketing plan including forecasts.

Responses in the *capabilities and capacity* (#3) dimension range from no change to radical change in the case of new products and are increasingly important with the current technological revolution. This dimension also applies in planning regional expansions to new markets and countries as part of manufacturer or retailer growth plans. Because technology is evolving quickly, significant supply chain changes are expected over the next few years. For example, a June 2016 *Wall Street Journal* article cited in Chapter 5 reported on the movement of factories closer to customers.*

At the 2007 National Retail Federation Annual Conference, Steve Ballmer, then the CEO of Microsoft, stated

> The young generation has grown up in a connected world which will continue to revolutionize how people shop. Any time they walk in your store, they will expect you to be able to deal with all their gadgets. They will expect to be the center of attention of any business that tries to serve them.†

---

* Op. cit. As costs rise factories move closer to customers.
† 2007 National Retail Federation Address, Ballmer, Steve.

That prediction has come to fruition. In an online article in *Forbes*, Micah Solomon, a noted customer experience consultant and author, emphasizes that in order to build superior customer service in new era of retailing, millennials should be the focus. The largest generation ever, millennials born between 1980 and 2000 will also have the most money to spend of any previous generation including the Baby Boomers.[2]

Solomon goes on to say that millennials have been "connected" by technology since their birth and do not have memories of the old ways often held by older consumers. For example, millennials have little experience with snail mail, rarely go in person to the bank, and have had the opportunity to apply values such as humane, green, fair-trade, and organic production to their purchases. Targeting this generation makes sense also because the expectations of these young people are also becoming the norm in older generations, partly because more than previous generations they get along with their parents, facilitating the transfer of information to older consumers.

Any planning, including that for the supply chain, should consider *competitive responses* (#4). This is particularly true if management seeks, or needs to seek, competitive advantage from its supply chain design. This book, in Section III and Chapter 13 in particular, recommends activity systems to establish unique, hard-to-copy processes.

Decisions regarding which *product channels* (#5) are needed to reach end users arise from customer preferences and market standards established by competitive responses. A growing expectation among customers is for omni-channel supply chains that include bricks-and-mortar stores, mobile and computer applications, and the arrival of many new types of digital media gadgets, both in and out of retail environments. These bring conveniences to customers like preselecting clothes to try on prior to going to a store, ordering the clothing online, and/or having it delivered just about anywhere.

This dimension may or may not be associated with the company's supply chain function. For many manufacturers, for example, decisions on channels are often the responsibility of the marketing department. However, supply chain professionals must implement these decisions and do so in an economical manner and can find themselves at odds with marketing's established plans.

*Customer risk concerns* (#6) have ramifications for supply chain design. Risks exist all along the chain. The ease of returning a purchase—to a store in the case of an Internet purchase, for example—may be a factor in the purchase decision. Many retailers have observed that online customers return a much larger percentage of their purchases than occurs with the traditional in-store customer. With generous return policies, the customer perceives less risk in making the purchase. For complex, large-price-tag purchases, such as automobiles or computers, customer service and repair support are a concern and likely play a big role in brand selection by the customer. Poor SCM of repair parts can result in greatly dissatisfied customers. This brings into the customer's consideration of the supply chain the need for repair and replacement parts and the service facilities to install them. For example, one of the authors purchased a vehicle that was involved in a major accident 6 days after purchase. The insurance company decided that it should be repaired rather than replaced. Because it was a brand new model and a somewhat specialized version, it took more than 6 months for the repair parts to reach the United States and another month for the repairs. This presented serious inconvenience to the consumer!

Chapter 22 describes the repair and replacement parts and services environment. If product use requires new ways of working or new skills, then the quality and accessibility of product support and training will be an SCM issue. The risk dimension also includes the vulnerability to security threats and the risk of substandard working conditions in offshore factories.

The final dimension, *matching supply and demand* (#7), encompasses operational activities all along the chain. Few would doubt this is an SCM domain. It applies to short, intermediate, and long time frames. The discussion of supply and demand is addressed in Section 7.4 and other chapters, particularly those in Section IV.

## 7.2  Procter & Gamble Case Study

This section describes the experience of manufacturer Procter & Gamble (P&G). The discussion refers to the P&G situation in the first edition (2008) and its more recent situation as described in its 2015 annual report.* The company *Fiscal 2015 Highlights* stated that the P&G has "continued the biggest transformation in the company history." The 2015 report describes a number of adverse conditions that affected results and the need for supply chain transformation. The CEO then and now is A.G. Lafley. A new CEO will have assumed the reins in late 2016.

### 7.2.1  P&G in 2006

P&G's 2006 annual report[3] and an earlier article from consultants McKinsey & Company describe the company's financial performance in the 5-year period from 2002 through 2006.[4]

- Sales, including acquisitions, grew from $40 to $68 billion, net earnings from $3.9 to $8.7 billion, and earnings per share from $1.46 to $2.79.
- By 2006, P&G had 22 brands selling over $1 billion annually in a variety of categories.
- Growth came from internal, organic growth and through acquisitions. The largest acquisition was Gillette, a U.S. consumer products company.
- The company emphasized fast integration of acquisitions into P&G processes. Much of this integration included information systems capabilities.

---

* P&G 2015 Annual Report, 88 pages.

- Sales for existing businesses, without the Gillette acquisition, grew 6% in fiscal 2006.
- A strategy that wasn't working was spending large amounts on "skunk works" product development that "pushed" products at consumers rather than "pulling" them based on user needs.

P&G identified what they consider their strengths. These are listed as follows and mapped to the applicable SCM dimensions from Table 7.1:

- Shopper and consumer understanding (dimensions 1, 2, 5, and 6 in Table 7.1)
- Branding (dimensions 4, 5, and 6)
- Innovation (dimensions 1 and 2)
- Go-to-market capability (dimensions 3, 5, 6, and 7)
- Global scale (dimensions 3, 5, and 7)

## 7.2.2 P&G in 2015

Results for 2015 were adverse and have motivated significant initiatives for change. Financial highlights included the following:

- Sales were down by 5% from 2014 (to about $71 billion) including the impact of foreign exchange losses.
- Organic sales growth of 1%; 2% growth in 10 core product categories.
- Strong cash flow with $11.6 billion returned to shareholders in dividends and share repurchase. Cash returns over the last 5 years had averaged $12 billion per year.

Mr. Lafley committed to "putting the strategies and capabilities in place to transform P&G into a faster-growing, more profitable and far simpler company." The following paragraphs profile strategic themes. They have value for companies of any size facing similar conditions.

**"A More Focused Business Portfolio."** This includes a focus on 10 business categories* with over 60 brands where P&G has a leading position, strong brands, differentiated products, and proven business models. This will require the "biggest supply chain redesign in the company's history."

**"Committed to Growth and Value Creation."** Progress toward this objective will be measured by *Operating Total Shareholder Return* (TSR). This measures cash flow to shareholders. Every employee will be aware of their contribution

---

* P&G's 10 product categories are baby care, family care, feminine care, fabric care, home care, hair care, skin and personal care, oral care, personal health care, and shave care.

to achieving this metric. A second metric is operating margins enabled by the company's innovation and productivity programs.

**"More Innovative and More Productive."** This calls for a product development strategy to offer the best-performing products in a category at a modest premium price. Gaining this objective requires efficient supply chains.

**"Better Execution."** The enabler is "a more agile, flexible, and faster distribution network to reduce out-of-stocks and optimize inventory." Execution also includes renewal of manufacturing operations that require lower cash and inventory levels, capital investment, and operating cost.

**"Better Balance."** P&G has underperformed when the company becomes "unbalanced." Balance includes sales and profit growth rising from innovation and productivity improvements. This requires balancing initiatives to achieve short, intermediate, and long-term objectives.

**"Stronger Ownership."** Simplification of the organization structure will enable accountability for results. They have linked Operating TSR at every company level in order to engage all employees.

# 7.3 Specifications for Supply Chain Design

A start toward the environment described above is to specify the roles that supply chain design must play. This process should address the seven dimensions. Vague higher-level but immeasurable goals such as "excellent customer service" may exist in any company, but these are seldom translated into consistent specifications for operations. The Operating TSR is the tool P&G uses.

Specifications for supply chain design play the same role they do in designing a product. Designers or users begin the design of an automobile or a computer with such a specification. For totally new products, there may be little customer experience to guide the effort, so the designer must create a specification based on common sense, customer inputs, and a formal statement of requirements. The QFD process described later in this chapter is a proven tool to generate specifications.

Table 7.2 lists examples of applying the template to three principal supply chain roles—manufacturers, distributors, and retailers. Items on the list suggest candidates for consideration as shared SCM functions, not just a marketing, a manufacturing, or a technology function. Often a brainstorming session by a team representing these stakeholders is used for deciding how to meet market needs.

Each of the principal links—the manufacturer, the distributor, and the retailer—has different concerns, examples of which are shown in the column headings of Table 7.2. Some decision categories will be common to different roles. Certainly, a manufacturer must pay close attention to the base products they design. The distributor, being a midchain service provider, has similar concerns with the service needs of upstream and downstream trading partners. Without these, the "plain vanilla" distributor that limits itself to physical handling of merchandise could disappear.

**Table 7.2 Supply Chain Specification Template Decision Categories**

| # | Market Need Dimensions | Manufacturer (concerns: base product success, ROI, operating TSR) | Supply Chain–Related Decision Categories | | |
|---|---|---|---|---|---|
| | | | Distributor (concerns: service offering success, GMROI) | Retailer (concerns: profit per square foot, GMROI) | |
| 1. | Product portfolio | Technology expertise to maintain New products/purging existing products Replacement parts strategy | Attractive markets/customers Base and extended products to offer Regions/customers to serve | Fit with marketing strategy Expected demand/shelf space Profitability/pricing In-house brands to carry | |
| 2. | Product design | Product base features Models/options needed Extended product features | Organization capabilities/skills/ facilities Customer expectations Opportunities for premium pricing | Potential for customer dissatisfaction Need for technical support Return policies and support | |
| 3. | Capabilities and capacity | Make or buy Processes/technologies required Capacity planning Collaboration strategy/trading partner links | Systems required Hardware investments Transportation requirements Supplier/customer links Vendor-managed inventory | Direct or through distributor Information sharing Schedule coordination Internal or external distribution centers | |
| 4. | Competitive responses | Basis for competing Technology leadership SWOT[a] analysis Activity system design | Competition from suppliers, retailers, other distributors Activity systems design | Strategy/activity system design Product line exclusivity Product turnover Supply chain integration | |

*(Continued)*

**Table 7.2 (Continued)  Supply Chain Specification Template Decision Categories**

| # | | Supply Chain–Related Decision Categories | | |
|---|---|---|---|---|
| | | Manufacturer *(concerns: base product success, ROI, operating TSR)* | Distributor *(concerns: service offering success, GMROI)* | Retailer *(concerns: profit per square foot, GMROI)* |
| | Market Need Dimensions | | | |
| 5. | Product channels | How to reach attractive markets Need for product customization Information technology requirements | Customers/regions to serve Channel-specific services to provide Plan for incoming/outgoing merchandise | Store and nonstore alternatives Direct to store delivery Needs for upstream customization |
| 6. | Customer risk concerns | Ability to return product Guarantees and warranties Part availability/obsolescence Retailer/dealer roles | Liability Handling of returns Requirements for lead time Requirements for delivery reliability | Availability planning/inventory policy Guarantees and warranties, recycling Factory working conditions |
| 7. | Matching supply and demand | Demand patterns Lead-time expectations/supplier capabilities Downstream information sharing Seasonal inefficiencies | Lead-time expectations Systems requirements Trading partner information sharing Seasonal inefficiencies | Product availability Manufacturer/distributor reliability Upstream information sharing Seasonal inefficiencies |

[a] Strengths, weaknesses, opportunities, threats. Applying the tool identifies issues related to the product introduction.

A common retailer concern is often the margin each product will generate for the corresponding investment in shelf space or store area. Gross margin return on investment (GMROI) as described in Chapter 2, Section 2.2, can measure this return. The annual reports of many retailers also report "revenues per square foot," a metric frequently used by merchant teams to choose between competitive products. Merchandise cost used in the calculation of gross margin includes the freight portion of supply chain costs.

The best use of the table for readers is to select the decision categories important to their own businesses. From these selections, they can specify requirements for their supply chains.

## 7.4 Nature of Demand

Meeting market needs, at the most fundamental level, requires an understanding of "demand." This is dimension 7 in Table 7.1. Figure 1.1 in Chapter 1 presents a "simplified" picture for physical and information flows in a supply chain. The illustration is a fairly common way to identify supply chain "players." These links in the chain are called *echelons*. In the example, there is a major supplier often referred to as an original equipment manufacturer, or OEM. Most retail supply chains are more like Figure 7.1, labeled "supply chain reality" and show physical flows.

In the retail supply chain, pathways are complex on both upstream (incoming) and downstream (outgoing) sides of the three OEMs competing in the market. Note that segments displace the single market view of customers shown in Figure 1.1. Each segment makes its own demands for product configuration, channels,

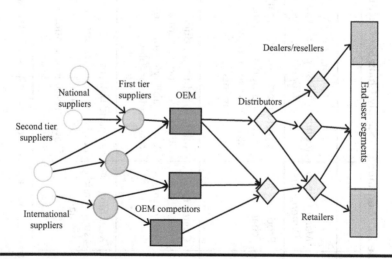

**Figure 7.1  Supply chain reality.**

technical support, delivery options, and other supply chain features. One message of Figure 7.1 is that many supply chain players may be far removed from end-user demand. Some barely see past their own upstream and downstream trading partners and are hampered in responding to change due to this blindness.

Research reported in *Supply Chain Management Review* points to the problems of defining demand in real supply chains.[5] The authors, John Mentzer and Mark Moon of the University of Tennessee in Knoxville, researched over 400 companies. They conclude, "Supply chain managers have only a hazy idea of what really drives demand." This reality is the consequence of the multi-echelon property of supply chains where raw materials and products follow convoluted paths similar to the ones shown in Figure 7.1.

Mentzer and Moon remind us that there are different types of demand. *Independent demand* is "the amount of product demanded (by time and location) by end-use customers of the supply chain." APICS, the Educational Society for Resource Management, defines independent demand as "that which is unrelated to the demand for other items." Examples include finished goods, parts for testing, and service parts. In Figure 7.1, independent demand from end users at the far right of the figure "sucks" product from the supply chain. The major suppliers, or OEMs, supply the channels that flow through distributors, go direct to retailers, or make direct sales to customers.

*Dependent demand* is directly related to the product and includes the components listed in the product bill of material (BOM). The OEM and its suppliers provide the production capability to support dependent demand. Sometimes a part will have both dependent demand as part of the final product and independent demand as a spare part.

To meet market needs, one theoretically need not forecast dependent demand if one has access to data on independent demand. A practical difficulty is the complexity involved in gathering information from points of consumption—both from trading partners and end users. This is particularly true in a retail supply chain with many points of sale to customers.

To demonstrate the level of waste this "fogginess" causes, Mentzer and Moon describe a hypothetical four-echelon supply chain—retailer, wholesaler, manufacturer, and supplier. To support these sales for a month, the retailer projects a sales forecast of 1000 units. However, the outlet then hedges its forecast by adding a 10% safety factor for its immediate supplier, the wholesaler. The authors assume that other echelons also hedge their forecasts by adding a 10% safety stock cushion to what they expect to sell.

In this case, the extra inventory that accumulates over the chain will exceed 100% of the needed supply. So, to support final sales of 1000, 1105 units of safety stock in excess of the 1000 actually needed will accumulate along the chain.

The authors recommend forsaking the traditional forecasting that assumes that each partner's demand is independent. In place of this, partners should utilize end-user sales for their production decisions by communicating this demand throughout the chain. This is an application of the demand-driven supply chain concept developed in detail in Chapter 17.

A barrier to sharing is that the source of the information, the retailer, has the least amount of safety stock—only 10%. So it has that much less motivation to participate. The upstream inventory, including its cost, is invisible to it. Another barrier is the inability by those upstream echelons to access and manipulate the data even if is they are available. Large computers may be part of the answer. An article reports the discussion of panelists at a conference on high-performance computing (HPC) sponsored by the Council on Competitiveness in September 2006. The Council pursues measures to increase the level of U.S. innovation. Panelists included representatives from both P&G and Wal-Mart.

Nancy Stewart, Wal-Mart's chief technology officer, stated, "It's an advantage if suppliers can link into Wal-Mart systems and perform their own analyses using Wal-Mart's complex tables." According to Tom Lange, P&G's director of corporate modeling and simulation, barriers to supplier use exist regarding software licenses, technical capabilities, and middleware that enable supply chain members to extract data to support decisions.[6]

The tidy model of computer links from all points of sale to the dozens of manufacturers involved in producing a product faces many hurdles. These range from formidable capital investments in computer gear to the necessity for sophisticated technical support infrastructure. This has been described as the "many-to-many" problem. Figure 7.1 supports these observations. By tracing the arrows, first- and second-tier suppliers find their components employed in the products of multiple OEMs. These in turn sell to different market segments with some going directly to end users, whereas others sell their products to distributors. Also, retailers must be depended upon to provide the information required. Some, like Wal-Mart, may do so willingly. Others are unable to by virtue of their own existing systems. Another group may consider the information to be competitively sensitive, not to be shared because competitors could gain access to it.

A phenomenon related to excesses in inventory along a supply chain is the "bullwhip effect." This occurs when a supply chain experiences wide swings in production and inventory despite a relatively steady level of final demand. The reasons include the just described tendency to hedge when making estimates of demand shared up the supply chain, time lags, lack of information sharing as discussed by the panel, poor information quality, and the planning systems and decision rules along the chain. Errors in forecasting are often the result of the participating party's desire to avoid stock-outs and the accompanying lost sales. Instead maintaining too large inventories ultimately resulting in markdowns and lowered margins occurs.

A third type of demand, *derived demand*, results from final product sales that are not linked directly through the BOM. For example, a second-tier steel supplier company may monitor auto sales to make its own production forecasts. Increases or decreases in auto sales say a lot about future demand for steel.

Mentzer and Moon recommend a "demand management" function based on an understanding of these types of demand. Recommended responsibilities for the position include the following:

- Internal and external information sharing including marketing function initiatives such as promotions.
- Assessment of customer and product profitability. The function would eliminate both products and customers who are not profitable.
- Supply chain relationship management in which performance improvement benefits are shared.
- A sales and operations planning (S&OP) process that includes sales forecasting, planning, and replanning. A multifunction group is charged with providing forecasts, rationalizing products and customers, capacity management, and production scheduling should execute the process. There is more on this in Chapter 15, Section 15.3.

These recommendations open the topic of possible roles for the supply chain manager, which could be broader than that of the "demand manager" recommended above. The broader role would entail inbound and outbound sides of the organization—as well as internal operations.

# 7.5 Quality Function Deployment Tool

Quality function deployment (QFD) is a technique to translates requirements—defined by customers and end users—into specifications for a product or service. The QFD application produces these specifications for the base product, the extended product, and process design. Design teams can use the Table 7.2 decision categories to set the boundaries for the QFD effort.

According to *The QFD Handbook*, the name—which often leaves English speakers scratching their heads—is a Japanese phrase with three characters.[7] The characters have the following meanings:

1. Qualities, features, attributes
2. Functions or mechanisms
3. Deployment, evolutions, diffusion, or development

The handbook summarizes, "QFD means deploying the attributes of a product or service desired by the customer throughout all the appropriate functional components of an organization." The QFD tool accomplishes this through a series of structured matrices that begin with the "voice of the customer" and translate that into product or service features. The supply chain is a service that delivers products and other services, so QFD can also be employed to specify supply chain processes to flesh out a strategy for serving customers.

## 7.5.1 QFD Overview

QFD "forces" designers to consider customer needs important to the product or service design. Customer requirements can be developed by survey or by assumptions made in the absence of formal research. The process lowers the risk of leaving something out and is particularly appropriate for very new products or services. According to *The QFD Handbook*, properly executed QFD offers the following benefits:

1. It transitions customers' jargon into technical specifics.
2. It links the customer with the design of the product, service, or process.
3. The QFD process enhances the productivity of a diverse Design Team by assuring no customer requirement is either overemphasized or omitted.

At the center of the QFD approach is the "house-of-quality" matrix shown in Figure 7.2. The analogy of the house arises from the shape—several square matrices topped by a triangular roof. The house encapsulates what is known about customer requirements, their importance, and the product or supply chain features needed to meet those requirements. Customer requirements (labeled #1 in Figure 7.2) are gathered from surveys, questionnaires, market research, or internal knowledge. They become the "what" of the house (#2). That is, the characteristics that the supply chain must

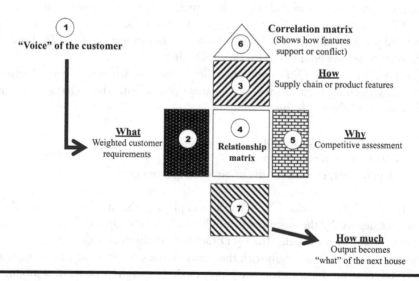

**Figure 7.2   QFD house of quality.**

include to satisfy the customer. Examples could include speed, variety, and product support. These requirements are weighted in terms of customer priorities.

An example used in QFD training sessions is a cup of coffee. Base product features include the shape and size of the cup, the temperature of the coffee, the insulating wrap around the cup, and the type of beans used to brew the coffee. The supply chain and extended features include options for serving size, variations in ingredients, promptness of service, and ambiance of the location. Starbucks is an often-cited example of a company using supply chain and extended features to turn a functional product (cup of coffee) into an innovative one (multiple options, ambiance, lounge chairs, Internet connections, music, and so forth). An example related to the base product is Starbucks' extra effort in buying coffee beans. Their coffee suppliers must be geographically located within certain latitudes (between the Tropic of Capricorn and Tropic of Cancer) and at specified altitudes (1300–1800 m) to meet their customer standards for taste. Recent sustainability concerns have also produced specifications for growing conditions and the treatment of labor in the coffee fields.

The team should weight the requirements in the order of importance (also performed in #2). A common approach is to assign percentages to each factor, with all factors adding to 100. For example, the most important feature might have a weight of 30, the second 20, and so on. An important contribution of this exercise is that it forces the Design Team to define who its customers are and to enumerate priorities of purchasers. The team might also prepare multiple matrices—one for each customer segment.

In the case of coffee, market research might find the customer values both product and supply chain features. For example, *taste* might be the first-ranked quality, earning a 40%, and *comfortable ambiance* the second-ranked with 20%.

The "why" (#5) is a competitive assessment on the right of the matrix in Figure 7.2. The evaluation displays the company position against competitors on each customer requirement. The information should show company product and supply chain positions in terms of the features most wanted by customers.

The "how" is a list of supply chain or product features listed along the top of the matrix (#3). If the purpose of QFD is to evaluate the current supply chain, then these *how's* could represent the existing (as-is) supply chain. In designing a new process or supply chain, the *how's* can be features in the "to-be" supply chain. A *how* in the coffee business could be product variety and aspects of the interior design of the stores. Another *how* might define flexibility requirements to assure service levels as described in Chapter 6, Section 6.5.2.

The relationship matrix (#4) links the customer requirements (the "what's," #2) with the design features (#3; the *how's*). Coffeehouse lounge chairs (a *how*), for example, will contribute strongly to *comfortable ambiance* (a *what*). In the case of responsiveness in product delivery (also a *what*), a customer requirement for 5-min service would provide an important specification for the staffing process (the *how*). The supply chain design must provide enough servers to limit line length.

In the relationship matrix (#4), design features are evaluated in terms of their contribution to each customer requirement. So a supply chain design feature that contributes significantly gets a higher weight than one that contributes to a lesser degree. There are many scales used to quantify the relationships. One calls for a 9-3-1-0, ranging from strong to weak to no support at all, for a customer requirement. The correlation matrix (#6, the roof of the house of quality) indicates reinforcing or conflicting supply chain features. An example might be the conflict between costly inventories to provide short turnarounds required to be responsive and the need for cost reductions required to be efficient.

The output of the house is the "how much" (#7). This quantifies what needs to be done and provides the team an incentive to rethink design features. For example, the coffeehouse may need to add varieties to its product lines and more lounge chairs. The preference here is for specificity. So the requirement for lounge chairs might be expressed in relation to customer traffic; thus, a rate of sales of 40 customers per hour requires at least eight lounge chairs.

## 7.5.2 Supply Chain QFD Example

Figure 7.3 displays a filled-in house of quality completed by a Design Team of a fictitious manufacturer, Delta Technology. Delta's product, a multifunction printer for small offices, is sold through a variety of channels—retail office stores, equipment resellers, and direct through the Internet. Delta has decided to upgrade its existing supply chain. In preparation for the redesign, it has queried the retailers and resellers it serves and gathered their inputs about what customers seek in the product. For the purpose of this example, there are no important differences between the weights for features provided by retailers and resellers; that means that all features are equally important in the example.

The first output of the survey is a list of seven customer requirements, or *what's*. In this case, these included both product—such as reliability in operation—and supply chain features. These are listed along the left side of the matrix in Figure 7.3. Based on interviews with users, the Design Team ranked the requirements in terms of importance to customers.

A second product of the survey enabled the team to assess where it stood with respect to its three largest competitors. This is displayed on the right. Delta, from the competitive assessment, ranks high in technical support (requirement 2) and reliability (#3). It is, however, seen as "expensive" (#1). Although customers believe Delta's product is worth more, it is considered "pricey" as indicated by a low rank for price parity on the competitive assessment.

Delta also ranks low in all the categories that would be considered as key supply chain elements. These include keeping customers supplied in a timely way (#4 and #5). This causes customers to keep more merchandise stock on hand than they think is necessary (#6); they would like to see these stocks reduced. Order tracking (#7), a low priority with a 5% weight, would be a nice feature, but not

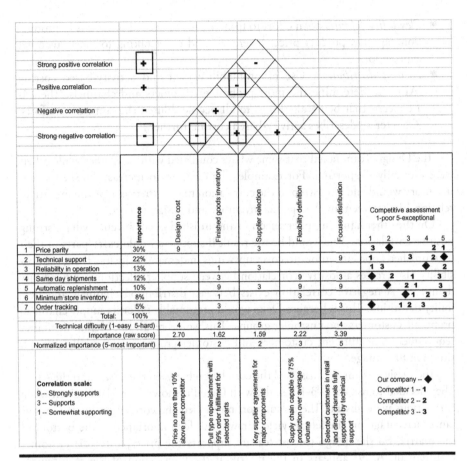

| | Importance | Design to cost | Finished goods inventory | Supplier selection | Flexibility definition | Focused distribution | Competitive assessment 1-poor 5-exceptional |
|---|---|---|---|---|---|---|---|
| 1 Price parity | 30% | 9 | | 3 | | | 3 ◆ ... 2 1 |
| 2 Technical support | 22% | | | | | 9 | 1 ... 3 ... 2 ◆ |
| 3 Reliability in operation | 13% | | 1 | 3 | | | 1 3 ... ◆ ... 2 |
| 4 Same day shipments | 12% | | 3 | | 9 | 3 | ◆ ... 2 1 ... 3 |
| 5 Automatic replenishment | 10% | | 9 | 3 | 9 | 9 | ◆ ... 2 1 ... 3 |
| 6 Minimum store inventory | 8% | | 1 | | 3 | | ◆1 2 ... 3 |
| 7 Order tracking | 5% | | 3 | | | 3 | ◆ ... 1 2 3 |
| Total: | 100% | | | | | | |
| Technical difficulty (1-easy 5-hard) | | 4 | 2 | 5 | 1 | 4 | |
| Importance (raw score) | | 2.70 | 1.62 | 1.59 | 2.22 | 3.39 | |
| Normalized importance (5-most important) | | 4 | 2 | 2 | 3 | 5 | |

Correlation scale:
9 -- Strongly supports
3 -- Supports
1 -- Somewhat supporting

Column descriptions:
- Price no more than 10% above next competitor
- Pull type replenishment with 99% order fulfillment for selected parts
- Key supplier agreements for major components
- Supply chain capable of 75% production over average volume
- Selected customers in retail and direct channels fully supported by technical support

Legend:
Our company -- ◆
Competitor 1 -- 1
Competitor 2 -- 2
Competitor 3 -- 3

Correlation key:
- Strong positive correlation ⊞ +
- Positive correlation +
- Negative correlation -
- Strong negative correlation ⊟ -

**Figure 7.3   QFD example.**

entirely necessary. It might be a "catch-up" action needed to stay in the game, but it would not add materially to overall competitiveness.

The Delta Design Team next devised five supply chain features as part of a strategy (*what's*) for dealing with the challenges presented by the survey. These are shown in columns along the top of the matrix.

- *Design to cost.* A product redesign that was constrained by the need to be more cost competitive. Success means product costs are closer to, not necessarily less than, competitors.
- *Finished goods inventory.* A decision to employ inventory buffers in the form of Delta finished goods in order to enable faster responses to orders.
- *Supplier selection.* Reassessment of existing suppliers and selection of fewer, more capable partners willing to cooperate in meeting new response goals.

- *Flexibility definition.* An effort to formally make needed trade-offs in production capacity, product price, inventory, and order taking to meet customer expectations.
- *Focused distribution.* Use of profitability data and activity-based costing (ABC) to determine the most profitable customers and channels. There is a concern that being all things to all people diluted the company's efforts. (Chapter 19 describes activity-based costing further.)

The Design Team noted that some what's conflicted with each other while others were mutually supporting. For example, the decision to increase finished goods inventory would add to cost, so in the correlation matrix there is a "strong negative" relationship between finished goods inventory and design to cost.

On the other hand, supplier selection and finished goods inventory have strong positive correlation. This would be the result if suppliers would carry parts in their own finished goods inventory to cover upswings in demand at Delta. The same possibility also creates a positive correlation between supplier selection and flexibility definition. A negative correlation exists between distribution channels and flexibility definition. This is because Delta would presumably tailor its supply chains to profitable customers and customer groups. This would result in different flexibility requirements for different customers and customer groups, a potentially difficult situation to manage.

The Design Team next assessed the correlation between the *what's* and the *how's.* They decided to use the 9-3-1-0 scale, with 0 credit, shown by a blank, given when correlations were absent. The calculation multiplied the correlation by the importance percentage on the left to yield a raw score for importance at the bottom of the matrix. So the design-to-cost feature supports the price parity (#1) customer requirement. A "9" appears in the matrix at the intersection of the requirement and the feature. At the bottom, the *importance* (raw score) sums the products of the combinations. This produces a rating of 2.7 (30% × 9) for the design-to-cost feature.

The team also assessed the degree of difficulty in implementing each element of the strategy on a scale of 1–5 with 5 being the most difficult. An importance rating on a scale of 1–5 with 5 the most important provides a normalized importance score. This importance level was awarded to the focused distribution feature. This insight should help the team to concentrate its attention on the most important elements of the strategy.

The final step produces the "how much" specification at the bottom of the matrix. This part of the matrix compiles conclusions about what has to be done to create an effective supply chain or product. It should be as specific as possible. For example, Delta's products were awarded a premium price in the marketplace, but there was a limit to how large this premium could be. So the team created a design-to-cost goal of no more than a 10% price premium compared to the next largest competitor. Prior to this decision, product development had no "price constraint" around which to design the product.

For finished goods inventory, the team set a "fill rate" specification of 99% for selected parts. These would be high-turnover, critical parts. Supplier selection would be guided by the willingness of suppliers to enter into agreements to support the strategy. Working together to lower unessential inventory through collaboration on ordering and response times would be key.

A cornerstone of flexibility definition would be setting a band for production. Delta, as a premium-priced offeror, decided to build in enough flexibility to handle peaks in volume. By examining historical data, the Design Team defined the upside capacity capability as 75% over average volume. The team could use any or all of the following to achieve this flexibility specification: extra shifts, overtime, added capacity, and work-in-process inventories.

The last specification was to develop custom extended product features tailored to large customers or large segments. These fulfillment centers would include order taking, order tracking, technical support, and customer billing.

## 7.6 Summary

Discovering paths to the customer is not simple. It involves all seven of the SCM dimensions listed in Table 7.1. Unfortunately, the responsibility for addressing these dimensions, if there is any at all, is vague if not totally absent in most companies. The chapter presents arguments for company strategies to consider the SCM function as a logical participant, or even "owner," of these dimensions. Understanding the basic nature of demand in various channels and how to turn customer requirements into product features and supply chain processes should be an essential SCM role.

## References

1. Skorupa, Joe, "It's the End of the Store as We Know It," *Retail Leader*, 2016.
2. Solomon, Micah, "Customer Service Secrets for Millennial Customers (That Improve Boomer Customer Service, Too)," *Forbes*, http://onforb.es/1OmGJkK, 2016.
3. Information in this section is from the P&G Annual Report for the fiscal year ending June 2006.
4. Gupta, Rajat and Wendler, Jim, "Leading change: An Interview with the CEO of P&G," *The McKinsey Quarterly*, Web exclusive July 2005.
5. Mentzer, John J. and Moon, Mark A., "Understanding Demand," *Supply Chain Management Review*, May/June 2004, pp. 38–43.
6. Conway, Steve, "HPC (High Performance Computing) and Supply Chain Management," *HPCwire*, September 15, 2006.
7. ReVelle, Jack B., Moran, John W., and Cox, Charles A., *The QFD Handbook*. New York: John Wiley & Sons, 1998.

# Chapter 8

# Supply Chain Risk

A primary risk category consists of threats external to the supply chain and includes events such as dock strikes, hurricanes, fires, earthquakes, and accidents. For example, products on the way to Louisiana retailers during the severe summer 2016 flooding could not be delivered, and were either destroyed in the floods on the way to delivery or diverted to other locations. Millions of dollars were lost as a result.

A second category of risk, project management risk, is encountered in managing efforts to develop or change the supply chain. Examples in this second risk category include missing requirements when setting up a distribution system, introducing a new product and neglecting needed supply chain capabilities, the perils of installing or upgrading an information system, or embarking on a relationship with an unknown trading partner. Such project risks are not covered here but are the subject of a related book in this series.[1]

Market criteria for products and delivery vary over a wide range. For example, a need for the lowest-cost product will encourage high-cost producers to outsource to low-cost producers—often in faraway places. Currently, this is the situation in much of the U.S apparel industry, where local wage rates make it feasible for clothing manufacturers in the United States to compete only in the highest-margin products. However, this industry is showing evidence of reemerging domestically. American manufacturers in various industries have begun to "reshore," return to manufacturing at home, and the apparel industry makes up about 12% of this activity.[2] An article cited in Chapters 6 and 7 describes efforts to bring more production closer to customers.

A decision to go to distant sources, in turn, adds risks such as those related to lengthy transportation links, delivery schedule uncertainties, theft of intellectual property, currency exchange, tariff uncertainty, and so forth. These risks require a conscious or unconscious trade-off that evaluates the benefits of the move against the risk of losing market share because of costs.

Supply chain risks often are hard-to-quantify factors faced in the seven market need dimensions listed in Table 7.1 (Chapter 7). These are product portfolio, product design, capabilities and capacity, competitive responses, product channels, customer risk concerns, and matching supply and demand. Supply chain risk is present in all the dimensions.

The Quality Function Deployment (QFD) tool, described in Section 7.5, provides a tool for identifying and weighing risk trade-offs. Often, avoiding a risk of one type, such as the loss of market share from a too-high product cost, brings on another; for example, the result could be having a lengthy (in terms of both distance and time) supply chain from a far-off low-cost contract manufacturer, thereby delaying delivery and requiring larger inventories to support the delivery schedule.

*Risk* is a term with multiple meanings; one can take his or her choice of definitions from a number of sources such as those on the following list:

■ *Thorndike–Barnhart dictionary.* A chance of harm or loss; the amount of possible loss.
■ *Wikipedia.* A concept that denotes a potential negative impact to an asset or some characteristic of value that may arise from some present process or future event.
■ *APICS.* The educational society for resource management. Uncertainty associated with the research, development, and production of a product, service, or project.
■ *Project Management Institute PMBOK*[3]: An uncertain event or condition that could have a positive or negative effect on a project's objectives.

The definitions use *chance, potential,* and *uncertainty* to describe risk. *Uncertainty,* the authors believe, best captures the concept of risk in a single word.

As the definitions indicate, uncertainty is not confined to negative outcomes; it also includes the possibility of things going better than expected—for example, a risk that sales will exceed forecasts. Although this is usually a positive event, the situation could result in negative consequences such as customer dissatisfaction, extra costs for expediting, and harm to the company's image and credibility.

APICS, the association for operations management, has also defined the term *risk pooling.* Pooling in this context is important in supply chain planning. Risk pooling refers to the collection of stock in a central location to protect against stockouts. This inventory supports multiple points of sale, not just one, as customers make purchases. This results in lower inventory than is required if the inventory were dispersed to points of sale, a practice common in the retail industry. For example, Target brings its imports from Pacific countries to a distribution center in Lacey, Washington, for shipment to points around the United States. Another example mentioned in an early chapter is the centralization of unusual shoe size inventories by Nordstrom, a practice adopted prior to the development of their main online store.

Forecasting becomes extremely important in such a system. A technique called *postponement* calls for not committing merchandise in terms of its final configuration or destination until the latest possible time. This saves money and reduces the risks of stockouts. Chapter 17 describes this technique as a fundamental tool of creating the demand-driven supply chain.

Editor Francis Quinn of the *Supply Chain Management Review* (*SCMR*) has summarized research on supply chain risk performed at Dartmouth College.[4] The article calls attention to the variety of risks faced by managers in retail supply chains, particularly those from disruptions in information flow. Table 8.1 lists risks cited in the article plus others associated with managing supply chains. In keeping with the idea that meeting market needs has several dimensions, we associate the risks with applicable supply chain management (SCM) market need dimensions described in Chapter 7, Table 7.1.

The list in Table 8.1 is a good start for establishing formal processes for considering risk for a manufacturer's supply chain. Readers may face risks that don't appear in the table, and these must be addressed in their particular supply chains and those of their partners.

1. *Location/trading partner selection risks.* Uncertainties that go with the decisions about where and with whom to partner. It includes the risks that go with adding partners in other countries to a supply chain.
2. *External supply chain production/logistics risks.* Risks that lie outside the ability of managers in the supply chain where it is difficult or impossible for a manager to intervene. Examples are disruptions due to weather-related emergencies, labor market instability, quality of infrastructure, foreign exchange fluctuations, adequacy of legal institutions, and material availability.
3. *Internal supply chain production/logistics risks.* Risks that managers can control. These are inherent in the company's and its trading partners' product portfolio, markets, processes, and infrastructure. This category should be susceptible to avoidance or mitigation if recognized in a timely way.

The following sections explain each of the three risk categories further.

# 8.1 Location/Trading Partner Selection Risks

The cited SCMR article argues that the best way of mitigating risk lies in trading partner selection. No doubt that is true, but what risks and trade-offs should one assess in selecting trading partners? The category lists several. Intellectual property violations (#1), counterfeiting (#2), and information leaks (#8) are associated with partner honesty and attention to security issues.

**Table 8.1 Supply Chain Risks**

| | | Market Need Dimensions[a] | | | | | | |
|---|---|---|---|---|---|---|---|---|
| | | Product Portfolio | Product Design | Capabilities and Capacity | Competitive Responses | Product Channels | Customer Risk Concerns | Matching Supply and Demand |
| **Location/Trading Partner Selection Risks** | | | | | | | | |
| 1 | Intellectual property violations[b] | • | • | | • | | | |
| 2 | Product counterfeiting | • | • | | • | | | |
| 3 | Contracting/legal issues | | | • | | | | |
| 4 | Insufficient oversight | | | • | | | | |
| 5 | Financial difficulty | | | • | | | • | |
| 6 | Technical capability weaknesses | • | • | • | | • | • | • |
| 7 | Unknown unaligned incentives[b] | | | | | • | • | • |
| 8 | Proprietary information leaks[b] | • | | | • | • | | • |

*(Continued)*

**Table 8.1 (Continued)  Supply Chain Risks**

| | | Market Need Dimensions[a] | | | | | | |
|---|---|---|---|---|---|---|---|---|
| | | Product Portfolio | Product Design | Capabilities and Capacity | Competitive Responses | Product Channels | Customer Risk Concerns | Matching Supply and Demand |
| **External Supply Chain Production/Logistics Risks** | | | | | | | | |
| 1 | Foreign exchange reverses | | | | | ● | | |
| 2 | Labor disruptions | | | | | ● | | ● |
| 3 | Weather consequences | | | | | ● | | ● |
| 4 | Information infrastructure weakness[b] | ● | | ● | | ● | | ● |
| 5 | Material availability | ● | ● | | | | | |
| 6 | Liability—labor related | | | ● | ● | ● | ● | |
| 7 | Liability—environmental | | | ● | ● | ● | ● | |

*(Continued)*

**Table 8.1 (Continued)  Supply Chain Risks**

| Supply Chain Risks | Market Need Dimensions[a] | | | | | | |
|---|---|---|---|---|---|---|---|
| | Product Portfolio | Product Design | Capabilities and Capacity | Competitive Responses | Product Channels | Customer Risk Concerns | Matching Supply and Demand |
| **Internal Supply Chain Production/Logistics Risks** | | | | | | | |
| 1  Market misses | • | • | | • | | | |
| 2  Insufficient production capabilities | | • | • | | | | • |
| 3  Quality performance weaknesses | | • | • | | | • | • |
| 4  Synchronization failures | | | | | • | | • |
| 5  Forecast error consequences | | | | | • | • | • |
| 6  Physical bottlenecks | | | • | | • | | • |
| 7  Delivery variation (lead time)[b] | | | • | | • | | • |
| 8  Returns handling capabilities missing | • | • | • | • | | • | • |

[a] See Chapter 7.
[b] Risks mentioned in *Supply Chain Management Review* article.[3]

One may also find a potential trading partner in a region where contracting and/or legal institutions (#3) are weak. Insufficient oversight (#4) addresses management weaknesses that lead to poor business practices, such as missing promised delivery dates. A partner may also have financial difficulty (#5) that could affect the delivery of vital parts or result in lost sales in attractive markets.

Internal management issues also include lack of technical capabilities (#6) and unaligned incentives (#7). The former may be critical to a new product in the case of a scarce production capability, or in terms of having the capacity to produce sufficient volumes for the designated market.

With regard to incentives, every company will have its distinct culture. That culture may, and very likely will, place different values on the same goals you put first. Mitigation of risks lies in the process of selecting partners and in the specifics of the partnership agreement. Section IV, Supply Chain Process Improvements, recommends methods. Chapter 16, Collaboration with Supply Chain Partners, is particularly relevant.

## 8.2 External Supply Chain Production/Logistics Risks

This category encompasses factors outside the company and its trading partners. Factors are geographic, social, legal, and financial. The presence of any risk in this category is likely to be embedded in the country or region. Labor and environmental liabilities may pose a customer relations risk. This occurs when news of a retailer's partners' poor labor practices and harmful chemical emissions is widely publicized. Situations such as this have triggered retailer audits of manufacturers to ensure compliance with the norms of the retailer's customer base. Chapter 5 described the challenges retailers face in fulfilling societal expectations. One path is to experiment by starting to produce or sell in a selected region or market and then expanding if successful. Sometimes called test marketing, the process allows the manufacturer to unearth problems with the product and/or strategy for selling it before exposing a very large market. The main negative associated with this strategy is that it gives early notice to competitors of both of these: product and strategy. This allows them to respond earlier to new competitive threats.

The risk of material availability (#5) is placed in this category. Often, shortages exist globally, so the risk will be a general one and will have an adverse impact on all industry participants. However, sometimes materials will be less available in a particular region or country than they are in a traditional supply chain. This risk applies to differences in availability, not general shortages, and can result in either a competitive advantage or a disadvantage. For retailers producing large amounts of private-label merchandise, such as GAP, Inc., and Old Navy, such risks can be substantial.

# 8.3 Internal Supply Chain Production/Logistics Risks

This category is the most controllable in terms of the decisions made in building a supply chain. The risks on this list should also be considered in the supplier selection process. Sections IV and V on supply chain process improvements and collaboration recommend mitigation measures for these risks.

Market misses (#1) relate to deviations from expectations for the success of new products or old products sold into new markets. The risk arises when too much or not enough is produced to meet market demand, and the supply chain cannot make the necessary adjustments in a timely way. This is different from forecast error consequences (#5), which refers to shorter-term differences in estimated and actual end-user demand.

Insufficient production capabilities (#2) can be shortfalls in capacity or the inability to perform an operation. Inadequate capacity is a physical constraint. A shortfall in the ability to perform could be a management inability to use the capacity that is available. Causes can be quality related, a lack of appropriately trained workers, or insufficient material where the capacity exists. Gaming companies address this by starting new products at high prices and managing demand over time by gradually lowering prices as experience curves result in lower costs so that new customers can afford to enter the market.

Physical bottlenecks (#6) have broader meaning because these bottlenecks can include production, logistics, and supplier limitations. Quality performance weaknesses (#3) add cost to cover process waste, limit capacity, and raise the risk of selling defective products to customers.

Synchronization failures (#4) and delivery variation (#7) will affect the smooth running of the supply chain, especially if the chain is tightly linked. The authors believe that these factors are rarely considered in building supply chains. The vision for addressing this situation is the subject of Chapter 17, describing demand-driven supply chains. The working of the demand-driven supply chain is abetted by having multiple partners synchronized in terms of the replenishment cycle. This creates a rhythm in the chain, whether the period used is daily, weekly, monthly, or quarterly. West Marine, described in some detail in Chapter 15, sought to synchronize its supply chain. Toyota parts operations, through fixed-interval milk runs, synchronize operations as described in Chapter 17.

Toyota also points to delivery time variability as a major obstacle to achieving efficiencies in the supply chain. The Toyota example cites variation in arrival times at its manufacturing plants and warehouses as detrimental to its goals for its "sell one, move one" approach to replenishment.

The lack of returns handling capabilities (#8) should be considered where such resources might be needed. Likely cases include critical, complex components and situations where the return loop needs to be fast. For example, a laptop computer made in Taiwan shouldn't have to go back to Taiwan for a warranty repair. In addition, returns handling is becoming both more important and more complex with the rapid growth of companies like Amazon that handle high volumes of products sold online where returns tend to be higher than in brick-and-mortar stores.

## 8.4 Supply Chain Risk—Summary

Risk management issues pervade SCM functions. Supply chain designs that address risks require an understanding of the hazards involved and feasible alternatives to minimizing their effect. For retailers, risk can result in late and unseasonable deliveries such as not receiving Christmas holiday inventory until February, long after the holidays are over, making the merchandise basically unsalable. Subsequent chapters will describe ways to manage risk through avoidance in partner selection and insurance policies that take the form of extra capacity or inventory.

## References

1. Ayers, James B., *Supply Chain Project Management: A Structured Collaborative and Measurable Approach*, Boca Raton: St. Lucie Press, 2004.
2. Pasquarelli, Adrianne, "Apparel Manufacturing Picks Up in the U.S.," *Crain's New York Business*, December 14, 2014.
3. *A Guide to the Project Management Body of Knowledge (PMBOK Guide)*, 5th Edition, January 2013, Project Management Institute.
4. Quinn, Francis J., "Ready for the Digital Future?" An interview with M. Eric Johnson, *Supply Chain Management Review*, July–August 2006, pp. 26–32.

# Chapter 9

# Retail Supply Chain Metrics

This chapter explores the definition of retail supply chain performance and its measurement. In particular, it points out how these differ among trading partners along the supply chain. For example, a retailer has different performance metrics than a manufacturer or distribution service provider. However, even if they are different, they must align with their downstream trading partners' priorities such that sales occur to the consumer.

The chapter also describes how supply chain managers in a company can connect performance measures to their organization's retail format and its strategies for competing. The Supply Chain Operations Reference Model[1] (SCOR) is a tool that synthesizes good practices for supply chain operations. Since its latest edition in 2014, this tool has come under the wing of a new organization, then APICS Supply Chain Council (APICS SCC).

SCOR, as a best practice in SCM, describes a process to enable aligning the supply chain plan and its execution with the financial plan. This chapter describes ways to accomplish this objective.

Retail *format* is the term commonly used to describe what business a retailer is in and who its competition is. Michael Levy and Barton Weitz define the term *retail format* as follows:

> The retailers' type of retail mix (nature of merchandise and services offered, pricing policy, advertising and promotion program, approach to store design and visual merchandising, and typical location).[2]

Earlier chapters noted the rise of omni-channel retailing in which the retailer interacts with customers and end users in many distribution channels including stores and online. Over recent years, the lines between standard retail formats such as department stores, drugstores, and stationers have blurred.

Stores with similar formats are seen as belonging to the same retail category. However, most stores now operate in multiple channels of distribution. For example, leading department store Macy's connects with customers through its stores, online presence, mobile applications, print catalogues, and newspaper inserts, to name a few. Costco, a discount mass merchandiser, connects through physical stores, an online store, print coupon catalogs, and others. Example general retail formats include convenience stores, department stores, big box retailers by merchandise category, supermarkets, and discount stores, but almost all of these today realize that they must somehow be available to customers at any time of day to provide information and access to ordering applications.

Also, stores with similar retail formats are often considered to be competitors, but in this era of "scrambled" merchandising, customers have choices of stores with different formats. For example, someone needing aspirin has format choices such as supermarket, chain drugstore, small pharmacy, convenience store, gas station, catalogs, or discount store, but they can also order from an online site or call in an order on the telephone, the latter in many cases also 24 hours a day.

Factors such as other concurrent product needs, distance to the store, severity of the pain, time spent in the store, and pricing may be more important store selection criteria for the aspirin decision. But for most retailers, the store format served as the original cornerstone of corporate strategy. As a result, format has served as the driver of appropriate metric selection, not only at retailers but also by upstream supply chain partners.

However, big changes are afoot. The success of many retailers who only have online presence is changing the face of retailing and therefore of the supporting supply chains. The dominant emergence of Amazon has shown that customers are now willing to order most anything online, a huge change from its beginning as a retailer of books online. Recently, Amazon has opened a physical store near its headquarters in Seattle, Washington, apparently to get a better understanding of its customers, but has not yet set establishing such stores as a major strategic objective for the company. The current physical store carries only books and Amazon's technology products such as the Kindle and the Echo.

Figure 1.1 in Chapter 1 shows the "echelons" in the typical retail supply chain. One immediately sees that there are large numbers and types of participants. With regard to types, the figure, starting on the left, shows second- and first-tier suppliers, original equipment manufacturers (OEMs), distributors, and retailers. In addition, there are numerous providers of transportation, customs brokerage, information technology, freight forwarding, and delivery services. Li & Fung Limited of Hong Kong, XPO Logistics in Greenwich Connecticut, Federal Express,

Expediters International of Washington, and UPS are prominent examples of service companies.

With so many different roles, strategies and measures of performance vary from echelon to echelon, retail format to retail format, and company to company.

# 9.1 Metrics Problems

Metrics are important because they define performance expectations and supply chain performance in terms of strategy fulfillment. However, these are accurate only as long as supply chain operations metrics are aligned with strategy. Debra Hofman, vice president and distinguished analyst at the research firm Gartner, formerly launched the AMR Benchmark Analytix service. She has described challenges for measuring supply chain performance.[3] She lists the following problems observed in companies surveyed by her firm:

- *Too many metrics.* This creates confusion, costs a lot to maintain, and in many cases inhibits taking action.
- *Metric debates.* Those being measured debate the metric's value, who should be measured, and how to calculate the metric.
- *Changing metrics.* New metrics are introduced to replace existing ones, but they cause confusion.
- *Old data.* Lags exist in gathering and acting on metrics, reducing their effectiveness in guiding interventions. Just because it's measured doesn't mean it's controlled.
- *Gaming.* "You get what you measure" is a repeated observation about metrics. Those being measured manipulate the system to improve their measures.

Tools like the SCOR model reinforce the theme of metric proliferation. SCOR consists of high-level process descriptions that users employ to evaluate the completeness of processes in their own companies. These include planning, executing, and enable processes. SCOR's generic "executing" processes include SOURCE, MAKE, DELIVER, and RETURN. Another category, ENABLE processes, includes performance measurement and alignment of metrics with company financials. Together, all the SCOR process descriptions contain hundreds of metrics that measure the health of individual processes. SCOR does not advocate using them all, but their existence is emblematic of the multitude of choices. Many users err on the side of inclusion when selecting metrics for processes, a fault noted by Ms. Hofman and resulting on overly complex analysis.

Ms. Hofman also observes that companies have different levels of performance measurement maturity. Mature companies that are effective at measurement know what to measure, have in place processes to measure those selected, and can access and act on the data in a timely way. Ms. Hofman defines supply chain metrics at three levels:

- *Ground level for correction* for assessing processes and addressing problems as they occur. The hundreds of process metrics in SCOR are options for this level.
- *Diagnostic mid-tier level* exemplified by the cash-to-cash cycle that applies to most businesses. Components are accounts payable, inventory, and accounts receivable.
- *Assessment top-tier level* for enterprise evaluation. Examples from Ms. Hofman's article are forecast accuracy, perfect order performance, and the cost of managing the supply chain.

The authors believe that the process of developing metrics should be "top down," beginning outside the supply chain realm with company strategy and then progressing to these three levels. The strategy should link with the highest level (assessment) in the hierarchy just described, and then deploy downward to the diagnostic and ground levels and should always reinforce the designated retail format or a service provider's supply chain role.

For example, Wal-Mart's main strategy targets the lower 25% of the population in income by emphasizing low prices and a lean supply chain. Their metrics must reflect this, and trading partners in Wal-Mart's supply chain are expected to support the retailer's goals. Some Wal-Mart suppliers will function well in this highly competitive environment, whereas others will not. The conclusion is that large participants, in this case the retailer, exert a lot of power on the supply chain at each echelon.

The following section describes a framework for matching top-tier supply chain assessment level measures with company strategies for competing.

## 9.2 Alignment with Strategy

A framework, utilizing a concept called the "driving force," will help explain alignment of metrics and strategy. Michel (Mike) Robert is the founding partner of Decision Processes International (DPI), a firm that consults on strategic planning. Mr. Robert's observation is that strategic planning is often not done at all or, where it is done, is done poorly. As a solution, he proposes a "strategic thinking" process described in his book, *Strategy Pure & Simple II*.[4]

According to his work, companies fall into one of four categories based on having operations that support or don't support strategies. From worst to best the categories are

1. Operationally incompetent. Uncertain strategic vision
2. Operationally incompetent. Explicit strategic vision
3. Operationally competent. Uncertain strategic vision
4. Operationally competent. Explicit strategic vision

Robert goes on to state that having a strategic vision does not include exercises that do little more than produce strategic planning paperwork. The operations dimension refers to the execution of daily tasks, the operating processes that execute the strategy. The best-run companies, Type #4 in the preceding list, are good at both visualizing a strategy and executing it. Others are good at neither task (Type #1); in the absence of a coherent strategic vision, it's obvious that operations can't be shaped to fulfill that vision.

Operations in some companies can actually be quite efficient (Type #3). However, they may not be effective in strategic terms. Robert believes this is the case for most businesses. The first reason is that many executives come through company ranks and lack a strategic perspective. A second reason may be that measures focus excessively on ground-level or mid-tier processes without links to strategy. A coherent strategy suitable for linking with ground-level processes is missing.

Land's End experienced the consequences of attempting to make a strategic change without the underlying processes to support it, a Type #2 error. The company brought in Federica Marchionni, a former executive with both Ferrari and Dolce & Gabbana who "sought to inject more style into the maker of outdoorsy, casual clothes by adding slimmer-fits, stiletto heels and a new line of activewear."[5] Ms. Marchionni chose to run the company primarily from New York City, rather than from its home in Dodgeville, Wisconsin. The result was that the changes needed in the corporate culture in Dodgeville to achieve such drastic strategic alteration were ignored, and the employees were not prepared, sales and profits declined before the strategy could really be tested, and Ms. Marchionni was asked to depart.

A third reason applies to U.S. markets. Robert notes that domestic markets may be too familiar and homogeneous.* A manager in a smaller country, who must operate in multiple, varied markets, will likely have superior strategic skills. Going after new, unfamiliar markets forces deep strategic thinking. As a fourth reason, the company may blindly pursue growth and market share as ends. Necessary strategic choices don't get made. Chapter 13 describes the activity system approach to making such choices and embedding them in operations.

Robert observes that additions to global capacity have transformed many world economies from relative scarcity to surplus capacity. He terms these the old push (scarcity) and the new pull (excess capacity) economies. The pull economy with its increased competition requires supply chain innovation. The customer is king, not the producer. Product life cycles are short. Market segmentation and the growth

---

* Not all agree with Robert's assessment of U.S. regional differences. In "The Influence of Geographic Subcultures in the United States," authors Hawkins, Roupe, and Coney demonstrate that there are regional differences that affect purchasing behavior. Within the United States, supply chain strategies must take these into account. "The Influence of Geographic Subcultures in the United States," Hawkins, Del I.; Roupe, Don; and Coney, Kenneth A.; *Advances in Consumer Research*, Volume 8, 1981, pp. 713–717.

of omni-channel distribution have resulted in market fragmentation. The need for efficient manufacturing supply chains has given way to the need for flexible supply chains focused on satisfaction of consumer demand.

Robert's insight is that one single *driving force* is the "strategic heartbeat" of the business. It is the determinant of company products, market segments, customers, and geographic focus. Robert identifies 10 strategic drivers listed in Table 9.1. One of these 10, and only one, is central to the way a company operates, according to Robert. People in the company may or may not be aware of their own driving force. In fact, they may believe they actually pursue, and have to be good at, all 10!

According to Robert, underlying factors such as quality, customer service, and profitability are "givens." This is #11 in Table 9.1. This means that all companies serving the market must perform to some threshold to survive; and most of the improvement activity in a company is in the given category.

These companies are likely operationally competent but lack strategic vision. SCOR metrics provide measures for these essential processes. Achieving competitive levels as measured by SCOR metrics is necessary, but not sufficient, for measuring success in retail supply chains.

Competitive advantage centers on managing activities associated with the driving force—what Robert refers to as "areas of excellence." Within this framework, potency in the marketplace is measured by the contribution to "areas of excellence" where the company excels over competitors beyond the "givens." For example, a project to automate product configuration processes between the customer and company's salesperson could be strategic in one company and not strategic in another. In a company with a technology-driven (Type #5) or a natural-resource-driven (Type #8) strategy, it would not be strategic even though it might lower costs or improve customer service in the "givens" group. But the project in a product concept (#1) or sales/marketing-driven (#6) company would likely be strategic.

Managers in a company with ongoing projects and with options for new ones can apply the driving-force framework to rank the potency of their projects in terms of supporting strategy. A simplified categorization is shown below:

| Potency Rating | Contribution |
|---|---|
| High | Supports an area of excellence |
| Medium | Supports a "given" area of improvement |
| Low | Maintains a basic capability |

We can estimate the potency of reengineered supply chain processes on organizations with different driving forces. Table 9.1 does this with example project objectives listed in the right-hand column. These serve as a test for candidate projects. If an existing project fulfills the listed objective, it is likely to support the company's

**Table 9.1   Driving Forces for Strategy**

| # | Driving Force | Examples | Areas of Excellence | Supply Chain Improvement Objective |
|---|---|---|---|---|
| 1. | Product/service concept | General Motors/cars, IBM/computers, Boeing/aircraft | Product development<br>Sales/service | Assure material support for improvements and service |
| 2. | User/customer class | *Playboy* for men, Johnson & Johnson for doctors, families | User research<br>Customer loyalty | Design chains for tailored product offerings to the targeted users |
| 3. | Market type/category | American Hospital Supply for hospitals, Disney for families | Market research<br>Customer loyalty | Design chains to deliver product categories to the target markets |
| 4. | Production capacity and capability | Capacity: hotels, airlines, paper mills<br>Capability: job shops, specialty printers | Operating efficiency<br>Substitute marketing[a] | Find integration and cost reduction opportunities throughout the chain |
| 5. | Technology know-how | DuPont in chemicals, 3M, Sony | Technology research<br>Application marketing | Design supply chain concurrently with technology development. Bring products to market fast |
| 6. | Sales/marketing method | Avon for door-to-door selling,<br>QVC Home Shopping Network | Sales recruitment<br>Selling effectiveness | Assure the sales department has reliable material supply |

*(Continued)*

**Table 9.1 (Continued)   Driving Forces for Strategy**

| # | Driving Force | Examples | Areas of Excellence | Supply Chain Improvement Objective |
|---|---|---|---|---|
| 7. | Distribution method | Telephone companies, department stores, food wholesalers, FedEx | System effectiveness System organization | Support sales force and product delivery. Assure all requirements, like cold chain, are in offerings |
| 8. | Natural resources | Oil and mining companies | Exploration Conversion | Improve logistics between source and conversion points |
| 9. | Size/growth | Companies driven by growth for growth's sake | Volume maximization Asset management | Consolidate and improve resource utilization. Seek economies of scale |
| 10. | Return/profit | Conglomerates, leveraged buyout companies, hedge fund companies | Portfolio management Information systems | Increase asset/working capital utilization. Support new services |
| 11. | "Givens" | Product quality Low-cost manufacturing Basic levels of customer service Growth and profit | Pursuit of operating efficiencies to maintain parity with competitors | Maintain state-of-the-art processes |

a   Refers to increasing the share of one's own product over substitutes. An example is printed corrugated containers over adhesive labels.

driving force. If a company has no supply chain project that supports its driving force, management should reconsider the strategy or look for new projects.

Most supply chain literature, including Ms. Hofman's article, describes production-driven companies (#4). This reinforces the view that supply chain design is really not strategic but is in the realm of the "givens." Certainly, ground-level metrics in models such as SCOR support this, calling to mind the manufacturer with its networks of suppliers, distribution, and retail customers. As Table 9.1 indicates, however, there are many ways in which supply chain design enables companies with other driving forces. The next section describes how the driving force in a cross section of companies will vary.

## 9.3 Definitions of Supply Chain Success

The most intensely sought-after performance goals for supply chain companies are likely to be visible in reports to shareholders. Table 9.2 summarizes plans and reported performance from eight companies, many of them market leaders, across the retail supply chain spectrum. The same companies were profiled in the first edition.

This list of eight provides examples for those searching for better ways to measure supply chain operating performance. Also, several are used elsewhere in this book as case studies for various supply chain management dimensions. Also included is a reference by number to the driving force in Table 9.1. Identifying the driving force provides a necessary foundation for designing supply chain performance metrics.

The first two examples are from manufacturers that provide products ultimately destined for the consumer through retail outlets. Procter & Gamble (P&G, Example #1) seeks growth in a variety of ways, one of which is "organic" or internal growth. This is growth in the current business and excludes that added by takeovers, divestitures, and foreign exchange gains. A reading of P&G's reports indicates that growth is an important, if not the foremost, measure of business health. (See Chapter 7, Section 7.2.) Herman Miller (#2), on the other hand, redesigned its supply chain to speed product to customers while minimizing its capital requirements. It did this by fundamentally altering its financial measures to account for capital, particularly inventory and receivables. This redirection forced a new focus on shortening process cycle times for order taking through installation of its office furniture systems on customer sites. (See Chapter 10, Section 10.1.)

Examples #3 and #4 are both supply chain service providers—to shippers in the case of Expeditors (#3), and to retailers in the case of Li & Fung (#4). The two companies have succeeded in attracting customers who seek "one-stop shops" for supply chain services. Expeditors (#3) provide air and ocean shipping along with customs brokerage and other services. A determinant of profitability is filling the cargo space they purchase. Li & Fung offers an array of supply chain services for soft goods such as apparel. These services include all the activities needed to deliver finished products to retail outlets. Li & Fung positions itself to its largest market, retailers

**Table 9.2   Plans, Initiatives, and Performance by Selected Supply Chain Companies**

| # | Company Driving Force | Supply Chain Echelon Report Year | Recent Plans and Initiatives | Reported Goals and Performance |
|---|---|---|---|---|
| 1. | Procter & Gamble #9 | OEM manufacturer (2015) | Tough year, adverse foreign exchange conditions<br>Shifted strategy to 10 focused product lines | Declining sales/profits<br>Organic sales growth 1%<br>Maintained strong cash flow and shareholder return |
| 2. | Herman Miller #10 | OEM manufacturer (2015) | 100-year company serving international commercial markets with high-end office furnishings<br>Through 2014 acquisition, moved toward consumer markets<br>Maintains e-commerce website | Employs lean manufacturing in the Herman Miller Performance System<br>Minimizes inventory with a pull system and 10–20 day lead times, extended to overhead functions and business partners |
| 3. | Expeditors International of Washington #4 | Logistics service provider (2015) | Provides "supply chain solutions" tailored to clients<br>Focused on customer cost reduction through supply chain services labeled as Plan, Source/Make, Book/Move, and Deliver | Changed management team<br>Shifted emphasis to strategy execution away from planning<br>Record year for income, operating income, and earnings |
| 4. | Li & Fung Limited #3 | Consumer supply chain company (2015) | Themes are a sustainable enterprise, keeping things simple, and organic growth in the business of end-to-end supply chain management | "Muted" performance including the impact of e-commerce on retailers seeking to differentiation. |

*(Continued)*

**Table 9.2 (Continued)   Plans, Initiatives, and Performance by Selected Supply Chain Companies**

| # | *Company Driving Force* | *Supply Chain Echelon Report Year* | *Recent Plans and Initiatives* | *Reported Goals and Performance* |
|---|---|---|---|---|
| 5. | McKesson Corporation #2 | Healthcare and related products distributor (2016) | International expansion through acquisitions. Renewed customer agreements with existing customers. | $190.9 billion sales, up 9%, with earnings up 10% |
| 6. | Foot Locker, Inc. #4 | Athletic footwear and apparel retailer (2015) | Vision: "to be the leading global retailer of athletically inspired shoes and apparel." European expansion Build apparel penetration/profitability Build digital business with channels | Record year. Increases in store and direct-to-customer channels. Sales: $10 billion Gross margin: 33.8% Sales per sq. ft.: $600 Annual inventory turns: 3 |
| 7. | Wal-Mart Stores, Inc. #4 | Global Retailer (2016 Annual Report) | "New period of disruption." Big goals: zero waste, 100% renewable energy, and selling products that benefit people and environment. Committed to shareholder returns in dividends and stock purchases. | 107% in global e-commerce sales in four years. Additions of online grocery service with $2.7 billion investment. 10% earnings increase. |
| 8. | West Marine, Inc. #7 | Boating Supplier Retailer and Wholesaler (2015 Annual Report) | 2015 a turning point for sales growth strategies Moved from "boats part dealer" to a "Waterlife Outfitter" | 6% stores sales increase Pretax profit improved by 110% Enabled by upgraded e-commerce capability |

in the United States, as an alternative to having a captive sourcing department. *Forbes* magazine has referred to Li & Fung as a "vital bridge between East and West."[6]

McKesson (#5) follows a similar path. It operates in the supply chain for pharmaceuticals and health and beauty aids sold at retail. This supply chain is a many-to-many relationship with numerous manufacturers—over 2000 medical surgical suppliers and over 500 pharmaceutical manufacturers—on the supply side, and numerous points of sale—200,000 physicians and 25,000 pharmacies—on the demand side. McKesson offers physical distribution and many supporting "value-added offerings" for managing supply chain inventories for retail chains and individual stores. General pharmacy business consulting is one of their services: keeping their retail customers in business keeps McKesson in business!

Three retailers focus both on return on assets and on customer service. Foot Locker (#6) has a long-term goal against which it reports to shareholders. This is revenue generated for each gross square foot of store space. This measure, very common in retailing, meets the simple and actionable criteria discussed in Section 9.1. (Gross space includes both selling and nonselling areas of the store and usually equals total leased space.)

Wal-Mart (#7), in late 2006, had to cut back on its growth to increase its profitability. A strategy change that curtailed capital expenditures grew from investor fear that top-line sales growth would occur without corresponding profits. This could be interpreted as a shift in strategy from a #9 Size/growth focus to #4 Production capacity focus. In its recent report, Wal-Mart cites growth opportunities in international markets and in online grocery services. At the same time as discussed earlier, the company is focusing on increasing the productivity of its sales force to pull more product through the system. West Marine (#8), on the other hand, stresses service for the 50,000 items it carries in a retail chain of over 400 stores. It reports success in changing its image from a parts dealer to a broader "solution" provider. This transition, a response to declining boat sales, is to become the retailer of choice for cruisers, sailors, power boaters, anglers, and paddle sports enthusiasts. Chapters 15 and 16 use West Marine as a case study for multicompany collaboration.

## 9.4 Mid-Tier and Ground-Level Metrics

With awareness of the driving force, a company can select metrics that fit their strategies. This selection has two dimensions.

1. Selecting metrics that are needed in the business matched to the driving force
2. Deciding to what level in Ms. Hofman's hierarchy the metric belongs: top-level assessment, mid-tier diagnostic, or ground-level process problem correction

Column A in Table 9.3 displays common business level and supply chain metrics or metric families. Supply chain practitioners will recognize these metrics that

**Table 9.3 Metrics Use by Driving Force**

| | | | *Driving Forces (Table 9.1)* | | |
|---|---|---|---|---|---|
| | *A*<br>*Metric/Metric*<br>*Family* | *B*<br>*Echelons*<br>*Employing*<br>*the Metric*<br>*Family*[a] | *C*<br>*Assessment*<br>*Level* | *D*<br>*Diagnostic*<br>*Level* | *E*<br>*Process*<br>*Level* |
| **Service Metrics** | | | | | |
| 1. | Market share (%) | S, O, D, R, SP | All | | |
| 2. | Perfect order (%) | O, D | #7 | #2, #3 | All others |
| 3. | Order fill rate (%) | O, D | #2 | All others | |
| 4. | On-time delivery | S, O, D, SP | #2, #3, #6 | All others | |
| 5. | Delivery lead time | S, O, D, R, SP | #2, #3, #5 | All others | |
| 6. | Return rate (%) | O, R | #2, #3 | All others | |
| 7. | Backorders (#) | O, D, R | | All | |
| 8. | Backorder frequency | O, D | #1, #2, #3 | All others | |
| 9. | Volume flexibility | S, O, D | #4 | All others | |
| 10. | Mix flexibility | S, O, D, R, SP | #1, #3 | All others | |
| 11. | Product-line breadth | O, D, R | #1, #2, #3 | All others | |
| **Operational Metrics** | | | | | |
| 12. | Product quality | S, O, SP | #1 | All others | |
| 13. | First-pass quality | S, O | #1, #4 | | All others |
| 14. | Process capability | S, O | #4 | | All others |
| 15. | Labor productivity | S, O, D, R | #4 | | All others |
| 16. | Retail floor space productivity | R | #6, #7, #10 | All others | |

*(Continued)*

**Table 9.3 (Continued)   Metrics Use by Driving Force**

| | | | Driving Forces (Table 9.1) | | |
|---|---|---|---|---|---|
| | A Metric/Metric Family | B Echelons Used for Assessment[a] | C Assessment Level | D Diagnostic Level | E Process Level |
| **Financial Metrics** | | | | | |
| 17. | Total cost of ownership (TCO) | O, R | #1, #2 | All others | |
| 18. | Revenue growth (%) | O, R, SP | #3, #5, #6, #9 | All others | |
| 19. | $ New product revenue (%) | O, R | #1, #5 | All others | |
| 20. | Profit growth (%) | O, R, SP | #2, #6, #10 | All others | |
| 21. | Total operating cost | S, O, D, R, SP | #4, #8 | | All others |
| 22. | Cash-to-cash cycle | O | #3, #6, #7 | All others | |
| 23. | Inventory turns | O, D, R | #6, #7 | | All others |
| 24. | Return on investment (ROI) | O, D, R | #10 | All others | |
| 25. | Gross-margin ROI (GMROI) | D, R | #2, #3 | All others | |
| 26. | Residual income, EVA® | S, O, D, R, SP | #4, #7, #8 | All others | |

*Note:* EVA® is the registered trademark of Stern Stewart.

[a] Echelons: S—Second-Tier Plus Supplier, O—OEM Manufacturer, D—Distributor, R—Retailer, SP—Service Provider.

are divided into service, operational, and financial categories. Also included are metrics associated with the overall business—such as *market share* and *total cost of ownership*. The rationale for their inclusion is that supply chains must support their retailers' objectives reflected in these metrics as well as their own. Shown in Column B are the echelons—Supplier (S), OEM (O), Distributor (D), Retailer (R), and Service Provider (SP)—most likely to deploy the metric as an assessment level gauge of business success, the top level of the metric hierarchy.

Selecting the "vital few" metrics for the assessment level will trim the number of metrics tracked, addressing the problem of proliferating measures. Column C associates driving forces with appropriate assessment level metrics. This does not mean that other metrics shouldn't be put to work at the diagnostic level (column D) or process level (column E). If metrics are broader and have multiple determinants, they should be diagnostic-level metrics. When a diagnostic metric falls below the desired level, the root cause may not be associated with a single process failing. Many metrics can and should be associated with individual processes at the process level (column E).

## 9.4.1 Service Metrics

Many consultants encourage their clients to start reengineering projects by understanding and documenting customer requirements. So the service category is first in Table 9.3 with 11 metrics. *Market share* (#1) is the broadest metric. Its inclusion is justified by the fact that high market shares likely go to companies that provide the best value to the market, broadly defined as products, service, and price. All the echelons, regardless of the driving force, might deploy this as an assessment level metric for the supply chain. Of course, other factors beyond the scope of supply chain operations will affect market share—particularly if the company has a lead position in offering innovative products as described in Chapter 11. As a general statement, however, either a slippage in market share or a goal of increased market share calls for an examination of how supply chain design should support that goal.

The *Perfect order* (#2) has its origins in the logistics field. "Perfect" means all items ordered are delivered on time, and order-related paperwork is also perfectly executed. This metric is usually associated with OEMs and distributors, although the metric can travel to other echelons. An enterprise focused on distribution channels should pay close attention to execution. Enterprises focusing on customer classes or market categories would also strive for perfect orders as a high-level goal.

*Order fill rate* (#3) and *On-time delivery* (#4) are components of the perfect order. But their importance will be elevated in the case of some companies with certain driving forces. Having predictable lead times is also mandatory for many suppliers to retail stores and distribution centers. Reliable delivery within defined windows reduces customer disruptions at the store or warehouse. The enormous success of fast fashion retailers like Zara and H&M has increased the pressure on older, more slow-moving institutions to speed up and increase the number of fashion cycles during the year, thereby exerting more pressure on the supply chain. Other formats should use these metrics at the diagnostic level because there are usually multiple causes of shortfalls. *Delivery lead time* (#5) measures responsiveness in addressing customer requirements. For many products, the shortest lead time may win a competitive battle.

*Return rate* (#6), *Backorders* (#7), and *Backorder frequency* (#8) indicate mismatches in demand and supply. They also might reflect problems in collaboration along the chain for sharing information about end-user demand. *Return rate* exceptions might be due to defects, over-ordering, salesperson errors, or the lack of penalties for returning merchandise. If a retailer is heavily involved in online selling, increased returns are to be expected and planned. The return system must return merchandise to for-sale inventory quickly so that it can be sold to the next customer. The number or percentage of *Backorders* in certain products should lead to reviews of forecasting and production plans. *Backorder frequency* in total or by merchandise category indicates systemic problems, supplier bottlenecks, or forecasting shortfalls.

*Volume flexibility* (#9), *Mix flexibility* (#10), and *Product-line breadth* (#11) are key in determining supply chain performance. Chapter 6, Section 6.5, described the "flexibility imperative," and these metrics measure how well flexibility needs are met. In constructing such metrics, managers should consider the tool described in Section 6.5. Certainly, shortfalls in other service category metrics may be traceable to insufficient supply chain flexibility.

## 9.4.2 Operating Metrics

There are many metrics in this family, particularly in tools such as SCOR. The list in Table 9.3 contains metric families related to quality and productivity. Service and flexibility are addressed in the previous section. *Product quality* (#12) is interpreted narrowly in terms of form and function and broadly in terms of features that "please" or "delight" end users. It is certainly vital to the manufacturing companies that design and produce the products, as well as to service providers along the chain. *First-pass quality* (#13) and *Process capability* (#14) are both indicators of the reliability of processes—whether they are deployed in producing the base physical product or providing extended product services. Chapters 19 and 20 describe these metrics in greater detail. *First-pass capability* finds application in manufacturing. It measures the percentage of products completed without any rework. *Process capability* is closely related, and the target of Six Sigma efforts. A process rated high in capability produces few defects. *Labor productivity* (#15) is a useful metric by all echelons.

*Floor-space productivity* (#16) is usually expressed in monetary terms, such as sales dollars per unit of area (square feet or square meter) or gross margin per unit of area. Foot Locker, in Table 9.2, reports this measure in its annual report. The metric captures the productivity of investments in real estate—the stores where products are carried. It does not address productivity through other channels such as e-commerce sales. However, different metrics can be used to measure e-commerce sales productivity based upon return on the operating expense and assets required. Other driving force examples in this chapter describe how supply chain participants, namely Expeditors International and Li & Fung in Table 9.2, seek higher-value product mixes. In these cases, a similar measure to retail floor space productivity could be adapted to substitute contribution or gross margin on sales that involve higher value product mixes.

## 9.4.3 Financial Metrics

As most readers likely know, financial measures rule decision making along the supply chain. There are many variations in this family of metrics, but for retailers these are often reported as total revenue figures for the company or for "same store" operations. The latter removes the impact of new store sales on the metrics and measures "organic" growth. The Financial Metrics section of Table 9.3 lists several. *Total cost of ownership (TCO)* (#17) is a popular metric for durable products that require supply chain support after the sale. This support includes technical advice, maintenance and repair, upgrades, and disposal. Many products are even sold on the expectation that the service provided after the sale will compensate for a low initial price. Supply chain managers should be involved in goal setting and measurement of the TCO. Electronics retailers such as Best Buy have developed a product replacement/repair program that operates much like "product insurance" in order to participate in this piece of the pie.

*Revenue growth* (#18), *$ New product revenue* (#19), *Profit growth* (#20), and *Total operating cost* (#21) are basic measures of profitability. Chapter 19 advocates a methodology for measuring growth and profits by product or product category using activity-based costing. Many metrics address the investment required to support sales. These include the remaining metrics #22 to #26. The following paragraphs describe each briefly. Chapters 2 and 3 introduced several as they apply to retailers.

The *Cash-to-cash Cycle* (#22) metric is the time, usually in days, between cash outflows to create a product to the time when customers' money is collected. It is calculated as work-in-process (WIP) inventory plus accounts receivable less accounts payable. Many supply chain efforts seek to reduce this period. Dell is known for being able to collect from the customer before acquiring the parts necessary to build the computer, resulting in an impressive cash-to-cash cycle. *Inventory turns* (#23) also captures the speed of processing through the supply chain. It is measured as cost-of-goods-sold (COGS) divided by average inventory valued at cost. Some use sales prices instead of COGS to make the calculation; in this instance, inventory is valued at assigned retail price.

*Return on investment (ROI)* (#24) measures gross margin or profit as a percent of the investment required. This investment can be total assets or equity investment. *Gross-margin ROI* (#25) is a tool for retailers that is calculated as gross margin divided by average inventory. This metric measure is under the control of the merchandise buyer at the retailer and was described in detail in Chapter 2. *Residual income*, EVA* (#26) captures asset cost by converting the value of an investment into an equivalent cash flow expense. *EVA* stands for economic value added and is discussed further in Chapter 10 in the Herman Miller case. The application uses

---

* EVA is a registered trademark of Stern Value Management incorporated as Stern Stewart & Co.

the enterprise cost of capital expressed as an interest rate and the lifetime of the assets involved. The effect is to convert working capital and fixed asset capital costs into equivalent period expenses. Chapter 19, Section 19.2.2, shows the impact of different assumptions when converting capital costs to equivalent uniform annual costs.

## 9.5 Supply Chain Metrics—Summary

Successful supply chain companies involved with retailers must monitor factors important to their success and relevant to their strategy. Recognizing the driving force is a major step in identifying the needed measures to monitor the business, including the expectation for supply chain performance. It's also an important step in reducing the number of metrics. There are as many variations as there are businesses. Few, however, use the concept of the driving force as the foundation for their performance measures. Doing so will clarify missions and simplify the management process. Clear definition of appropriate supplier metrics that reinforce the needs of the retail format will drive the success of all supply chain members.

## References

1. *Supply Chain Operations Reference Model*, Revision 11.0, Supply Chain Council, 2012, 976 pages.
2. Levy, Michael and Weitz, Barton A., *Retailing Management*, 6th ed., New York: McGraw-Hill Irwin, 2007, p. 612.
3. Hofman, Debra, "Getting to World-Class Supply Chain Measurement," *Supply Chain Management Review*, October 2006, pp. 18–24.
4. Robert, Michel, *Strategy Pure & Simple II*, New York: McGraw-Hill, 1998, pp. 58–72.
5. Meredith, Robyn, "Global Trading at the Crossroads," *Forbes*, April 17, 2006, pp. 45–47.
6. Kapner, Suzanne and Lublin, Joann, "Lands' End CEO Is Pushed Out after 9 Months"; *The Wall Street Journal*, September 27, 2016.

# Chapter 10

# Meeting the Needs of Supply Chain Decision Makers

This chapter closes Section II with a description of the needs of supply chain decision makers. Examples range from day-to-day placement of orders and scheduling of manufacturing operations to designing complex supply chain networks requiring longer-term decision making. These and the many other decisions are embedded in supply chain processes that require structure in the form of organizational assignments, information systems, collaboration with business partners, and customer research. Chapter 9 described supply chain metrics, which guide decision making. But there is a need for assuring that the data are effectively employed to make sound decisions. The journey is next described in the form of a case study.

## 10.1 New Decisions at Herman Miller

Herman Miller was introduced in the first edition (2008) and profiled briefly in Chapter 9. This section updates company efforts since that time. The case illustrates how achievement of financial objectives brought on an impressive supply chain transformation. Herman Miller, headquartered in Zeeland, Michigan, is a major manufacturer of office furniture that includes desks, filing cabinets, chairs, and panel systems found in offices, healthcare facilities, and homes throughout the world. Manufacturing facilities are in the United States, China, Italy, and the United Kingdom.

As reported in the first edition, Herman Miller had fiscal 2005 sales of about $1.5 billion. At that time, the operation carried the name of Miller SQA—for Simple, Quick, and Affordable. By fiscal year 2015, sales had grown to about $2.1 billion with a gross margin of $791 million, or 38%. Since the case implementation in the late 1990s, Herman Miller has dissolved the SQA division and adapted the streamlined approach described here for all its make-to-order business.

At the beginning of its supply chain overhaul described in the earlier edition, the office furniture industry commonly delivered orders in 4–6 weeks. In addition, the delay for installation at the customer's site, often by the local dealer who sold the system, could be 1–2 weeks. All this time was required for a product that could theoretically be manufactured and installed in hours, not days or weeks. The long waits also cut into revenues because some customers cancelled their orders, adding to Herman Miller's receivables.

The "old" Miller shipped from finished goods inventory or, when it had to build to order, from a large raw material inventory kept on hand. This make-to-stock approach, one that relies on forecasts and finished goods inventory, has been common among manufacturers in retail supply chains.

The improved performance is the product of an initiative it labels the Herman Miller Performance System (HMPS), a collection of Lean manufacturing approaches that speed order fulfillment (within 10–20 days) while maintaining low inventories. The May 30, 2015, annual report shows inventory level at about $130 million and the cost of sales that includes materials and other period costs of $1.3 billion. This is over 10 inventory turns per year.

The company further reports that it "has extended this lean process work to its non-manufacturing processes as well as externally to our manufacturing supply chain and distribution channel. The company believes these concepts hold significant promise for further gains in reliability, quality and efficiency."*

Of particular note, Miller was adopting a financial measurement tool called EVA[†] (Economic Value Added, which was introduced in Chapter 9). EVA takes into account the cost of assets such as inventory and receivables. So, the cost of capital required to support inventory, warehouses, and factory capacity would be captured and charged against SQA's profits. As a result of its supply chain reengineering, Herman Miller raised its return on investment considerably—tripling its EVA to $40 million, resulting in an increase in stock value from $11 to $36 per share.

---

* Herman Miller, Inc., and Subsidiaries 2015 Annual Report, p. 19.
[†] EVA is a registered trademark of Stern Stewart & Company.

Despite the improvements, the 2015 annual report shows the performance of Herman Miller stock against the S&P 500 and NASDAQ nonfinancial indexes in the 2010–2015 timeframe. Herman Miller lagged both of the other indices. This is seen to be due to external economic factors.

Working with suppliers, the project drastically cut the time Miller took to fill an order, making corresponding cuts in the inventory and receivables committed to support sales. The result was an inventory reduction of 24%.[1] These actions also have satisfied customers by quicker response to orders. Fast response also means that customer money is collected sooner, leading to a 22% receivables reduction. With the new method, the company assembles orders rather than makes to stock, eliminating finished goods and a wasteful raw material inventory.

The transition was not quick; the original project took about 2 years to complete. It required shifts in supply chain decision making and the systems to support them. The project manager, William Bundy, in discussing the impact of the supply chain project on Miller, compared his company with Dell, the seller of personal computers and other computer hardware.[2] "Dell succeeds not because it has the latest product technology but because it has built a 'service model' that builds to customer order and delivers with great speed and reliability."

Miller looked at the lead time it wanted to reduce and identified three major components or "zones," each with its own set of challenges:

1. Customer contact to order entry
2. Order entry to shipment (manufacture)
3. Shipment to installation

At Miller, manufacturing (component 2) consumed only 20% of the lead time. So, to make a dramatic improvement, the company had to reduce all three lead-time components, including sales and material supply as well.

An important component of the initial plan was to partner with a third-party logistics provider, Menlo Logistics. Menlo staffed a separate material-staging facility—called the Production Metering Center—where logistics into Miller's production facility could be handled. The logistics specialist, Menlo, also brought expertise in transportation and warehousing to the supply chain. By cutting raw materials to the bone, bringing them into the Metering Center only in response to actual customer demand, Miller could produce an order in 8–10 hours and place it in the schedule up to 2 hours before production started. Because orders consisted of a variety of color-matched products that used different production lines, coordination was not simple. An enabling goal was drastically reducing the number of parts needed in its products.

To become what it wanted to be, Miller had to make choices about its financial and customer service–related goals. It had to stop being a follower and become a leader by being different from its competitors. The result has been a hard-to-copy set of distinctive supply chain activities like those developed using a strategic planning tool called activity systems, described in Chapter 13. Components of an activity system include the following:

- *Conduct business with the customer through an "easy" customer interface.* Help the customer visualize the new office layout. Have software configure the bill of material (BOM) for the order in real time.
- *Build to order.* Carry minimal amounts of raw material by paying only for what is used, standardizing parts, and having no raw material or finished goods inventory at all.
- *Deliver direct to the user's site.* Provide visibility on progress of the shipment to the dealer who will install the furniture. Have everything in the customer's order arrive in one shipment, helping the local dealer install the furniture quickly.

A key to Miller's achievement was its relationship with its suppliers. Just about every aspect of this relationship was redesigned. This required a dramatic reduction in the number of suppliers along with the parts reduction. Daily deliveries were also instituted. This was made possible by the closeness of suppliers to the Herman Miller factories in the furniture-making center in southwest Michigan. The delivered stock of raw materials was on consignment, meaning it was paid for only after it was used for production.

Technology proved to be a vital enabler of new processes. Among the computer tools used were the following:

- An application called SupplyNet to track inventory at SQA and the suppliers, and to plan replenishment and production schedules.
- An order entry tool called SQA 1:1, plus a visualization tool for the new layouts called Z-Axis.
- An enterprise resource planning (ERP) system to capture and maintain correct bills of material. Achieving bill of material accuracy was a major challenge.
- A manufacturing execution system (MES) for maintaining material requirements and planning production.
- An internally developed tool called Expert Scheduling that checks for material availability and manufacturing capacity and automatically schedules about 50% of production. In situations where automated scheduling was not possible, a human scheduler would intervene.

The following are typical measures of supply chain performance and indicate how much Miller SQA performance improved.

- Throughput, or capacity, up 25% with no additional investment.
- On-time shipments: more than 99% compared to an industry average of 75%.
- Order lead time of 2 days; the industry standard was 5 weeks.
- Inventory turns increased from 21 to over 100.
- Staff productivity up 20%.

The Herman Miller case is an important example of the opportunities to compete better at the retail level through improved supply chain management. It illustrates the impact of better processes enabled by technology. However, the work of conversion to the new supply chain was not just technology focused. It required accurate bills of material, collaboration with suppliers, process mapping across organizations, employer behavior change activities, and implementation of formal policies and procedures.

As a result, decision-making processes became more tightly orchestrated. Table 10.1 summarizes the *before* and *after* differences in the Herman Miller supply chain

**Table 10.1  Herman Miller Changes in Decision Making**

| Decision Category | Before | After |
|---|---|---|
| Supplier selection | Most suppliers chosen on traditional criteria such as price. | Had fewer suppliers, those willing to collaborate in implementing new processes. |
| Order configuration | Worked out by dealer. Forwarded to plant. | Translated into bill of materials as order is taken. Electronically transmitted. |
| Raw material replenishment | Forecast driven. Economic lot sizes ordered from suppliers. | Demand driven. Material pulled to staging areas as orders come in. |
| Production scheduling | Manual. Based on availability of a wide range of materials. Sequential production. Order components gathered as they are completed. | More automated. Fewer stock-keeping units (SKUs). Staged material moved quickly to production. Simultaneous production of order components. |
| Installation scheduling | Orders shipped to dealer sites. Installation scheduled by dealer. | Orders shipped to installation site. Scheduled arrival determines installation timing. |

design. The reader should note that new processes fundamentally changed the nature of the decisions being made, automating many of them and tightening the timeframe in which they were made.

## 10.2 Proactive Decision Making

Information technology solution providers have answered the need for speed exemplified by Herman Miller. Supply chain and information technology worlds are evolving toward managing exceptions rather than pushing data at decision makers for them to parse. Newer terms include *workflow, business rules,* and *supply chain event management* (SCEM). Workflow, according to Wikipedia, is "the movement of documents and/or tasks through a work process." Workflow is enabled, but not dependent on, information technology. It must also be a by-product of task definition and assignment of responsibilities. These elements also include *business rules,* which define exceptional situations and predefined actions to respond. SCEM, according to the About Logistics website, is "an extension of process control" that defines a response to an unexpected event.[3] So, if the Herman Miller scheduling program, Expert Scheduling, could not schedule a particular order for some reason, a "proactive" SCEM software tool would automatically transfer it to the human scheduler.

What proactive systems add to conventional systems is a focus on decision-maker needs in those processes. Decision makers fulfill roles in the process based on the ultimate customer's needs. Thus, where decisions are required, such as when the Herman Miller scheduler could not schedule a job, the proactive system uses business rules to redirect the scheduling task for human intervention.

In Figure 10.1, the decision maker is at the center. Extending the Herman Miller example, this decision maker might be the production scheduler. Inputs from the external environment of suppliers, customers, and other departments either pass through existing applications such as the order entry system or go directly—to our decision maker. Example inputs to the scheduler could come from any or all of the following:

- From the retailer or dealer at a customer location with order changes
- From customers via retailers regarding convenient times to install their orders
- From transportation companies with shipping schedules to the point of installation
- From the Metering Center confirming the completeness of the BOM
- From suppliers notifying the scheduler of a delayed shipment
- From accounting reporting that a customer's check has bounced, requiring communication with various parties and a delay in shipping

The arrows symbolize the many potential data transactions within a proactive system. What makes the environment proactive is the *rules server* that processes

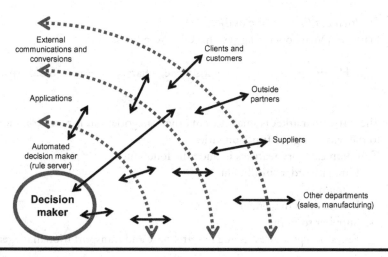

**Figure 10.1  The proactive system model.**

and delivers the inputs to our decision maker. The rules guide the information flow and the conditions that make the communication necessary. The delivery matches the needs of the individual decision maker, reflecting the authority vested in that individual.

Rules are a product of management practice on empowerment, continuous improvement, and organization philosophy. Values, philosophy of delegation, and decision analysis—not technology—dictate rules. These rules will be unique to any particular organization and, quite possibly, a source of competitive advantage due to better-executed, cheaper, and faster processes. In many cases, the critical examination of required decisions finds all sorts of alternative solutions. Individual practice, a result of training and habit, gives way to a best practice by design.

# 10.3  Applications for Information Technology

Many information systems applications are on the market to support supply chain decision makers. The website Software Advice lists software applications in many categories including SCM applications. Its business model is to provide those seeking solutions links to providers who pay a fee for referrals.

The SCM category returns 155 applications. These can be screened based on the following parameters:

- Industry (aerospace/defense, automotive, food and beverage, and pharmaceuticals)
- Size of the organization (# of employees)
- Relative price of the software (four levels)
- User ratings (five levels)

■ Deployment (on-site or cloud)
■ Platform [MAC operating system (OS), Windows, Linux]

Daniel Harris, market research associate, characterizes the SCM space as follows:

■ The software market is smaller than other categories but is more complex due to the wide range of functionalities.
■ Common category features include the following:
    − Purchase order fulfillment
    − Shipping
    − Inventory management
    − Supplier sourcing
    − Execution processes related to warehouse and transportation management

Table 10.2 lists nine features that are common to the applications in the SCM category. The website also contains links to other software categories. The *retail point of sale* category identifies 214 systems. Common features include

■ Point of sale
■ Inventory control
■ Retail accounting
■ Retail customer relationship management

Figure 10.2, borrowed from William T. Walker, depicts the supply chain as zones.[4] This is useful because it recognizes that there are natural "breaks" as the product flows through supply chains. For example, Herman Miller identified three zones when it embarked on its program.

Each zone has individual issues that are not always shared with other zones. The task of selecting software can benefit by a model proposed by William T. Walker. He depicts the supply chain as zones.[4] This useful method recognizes that there are natural breaks as the product flows through the supply chain. The Software Advice website enables retrieving lists focused on each zone.

When we talk about procurement, manufacturing, distribution, and retailing, we demonstrate that these zones exist. Figure 10.2 depicts common zones. The *upstream value-added transformation* zone produces raw materials and components. The *midstream value-added transformation* zone produces a finished product inventory ready for customization (final configuration, packaging, etc.) to retailer or customer requirements.

Many in this zone are manufacturers producing products to a BOM with components from upstream trading partners. The *downstream value-added fulfillment* zone delivers products to end users. A *reverse-stream value-added transformation* zone contains processes for repair, customer returns, recycling, or disposal. *Quality defect reverse streams* handle defective products.

**Table 10.2 Software Features**

| # | General Functional Areas | Number of Specific Functionalities |
|---|---|---|
| 1 | Supply chain planning | Forecasts demand; adjusts the flow of production accordingly |
| 2 | Demand planning | Software designed to improve the accuracy of demand forecasts |
| 3 | Vendor-managed inventory | Provides vendor capability to monitor and replenish inventory automatically |
| 4 | Supplier management | Used to monitor supplier performance and risk |
| 5 | Procurement | Executes purchases and reports the financial relationship with suppliers |
| 6 | Strategic sourcing | Used to set goals and screen potential suppliers |
| 7 | Warehouse management | Monitors and controls warehouse transactions; assists in warehouse design |
| 8 | Transportation management | Tracks movements to and from the warehouse |
| 9 | Order fulfillment | Helps to reduce lead times in fulfilling orders |

*Source:* http://www.softwareadvisor.com.

Within any zone, there are likely to be several echelons, each representing a step in the supply chain process. For example, product inventory in the original equipment manufacturer's (OEM's) warehouse may be a part of the *downstream value-added transformation* zone and include processing by multiple echelons such as a distributor, a retailer's distribution center, and a store before it reaches the end user (Table 10.3).

This framework is useful because each zone will call on different decision-making application types. For example, in Ford Motor Company's early years, Henry Ford ran a vertically integrated operation—from ore mining to steel production to manufacture and to delivery to the customer. Thus, Ford operated in all the zones. Today, companies are increasingly dependent on trading partners, so they look to others to provide raw materials, products, and services.

To the degree that zones operate independently of each other in a particular supply chain, the more likely the zone might be a bottleneck in the supply chain. This would be the case for a small manufacturer whose products are distributed by intermediary distributors to a large number of retailers. The distance between that manufacturer and the end user is great. For example, the produce in a grocery store has, in many cases, traveled quickly down a long channel of distribution. End-user loyalty in this case will likely accrue to the retailer.

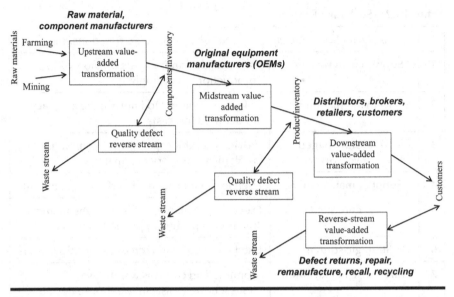

**Figure 10.2 Supply chain zones. (From Walker, William T., *Supply Chain Architecture: A Blueprint for Networking the Flow of Material, Information, and Cash*, Boca Raton, FL: CRC Press, 2005. p. 15.)**

At the other end, an automobile manufacturer will be tightly linked with both its suppliers and dealers. End-user loyalty will likely be to the manufacturer, although dealer quality also plays a role in determining loyalty. A distributor like McKesson that caters to pharmacies, large and small, and takes on supply chain services, such as vendor-managed inventory (VMI), for its retailer customers will need more systems capability. It can be seen as expanding the scope of its services back into the midstream value-added transformation zone.

## 10.4 Assessing the Need for Information

With a major share of company expense consumed by or affected by manual and automated information processors, reviewing information needs along the supply chain will pay handsome dividends. Table 10.4 outlines a method for assessing what information is needed and what can be done away with using methods in other chapters and the checklist in Table 10.3. The purpose is to identify gaps and excesses in decision making. The methodology builds on tools and techniques from other chapters.

The columns in Table 10.4 are the following:

1. *Activity.* For the company using the activity system methodology described in Chapter 13, identify the activity with which the information exchange is associated.

**Table 10.3  Functional Areas and Zones**

| # | General Functional Areas | Upstream Transformation | Midstream Manufacturing | Downstream Fulfillment | Reverse Streams |
|---|---|---|---|---|---|
| 1 | Customer relationship management | | | • | |
| 2 | Forecasting | • | • | • | |
| 3 | Inventory planning/management | | • | • | |
| 4 | Manufacturing | | • | | |
| 5 | Order processing | | • | • | |
| 6 | Other advanced planning | • | • | | |
| 7 | Procurement | | • | • | |
| 8 | Transportation management | | | • | |
| 9 | Warehouse management | | | • | • |

**Table 10.4  Assessing Information Requirements**

| | | | As Is | | | To Be |
|---|---|---|---|---|---|---|
| 1. Activity | 2. Process | 3. Type | 4. Done/Not Done | 5. How Done | 6. Meets Needs | 7. Future Vision |
| Make-to-order manufacturing | Raw materials ordering | Type II Two-way data exchange | Not done | Forecast replenishment | No | Demand-driven replenishment Type III |

2. *Process.* Each activity consists of processes. Identify the process with which the information exchange is associated.
3. *Type.* List the information exchange type using the methodology described in Chapter 16, Section 16.1.2.
   a. One-way data exchange (transactional)
   b. Two-way data exchange (transactional/coordinative)
   c. Cooperative collaboration with simultaneous access to information
   d. Cognitive collaboration in cases of joint decision making where risk to both is high
4. *Done/not done.* State whether the information exchange is occurring or not.
5. *How done.* If it is done, describe the method of exchange—data exchange, meetings, reports, etc.
6. *Meets needs?* If done, is the current method satisfactory?
7. *Future vision.* How should this exchange be done in the future? Solutions should not be limited to technology fixes.

Using this approach, a company can assess whether their information systems are aligned with their strategy, whether important information exchange tasks meet participant needs and needs for future information exchanges. The purpose is to assure that money spent on developing information resources for decision making is money well spent.

The example in Table 10.4 represents Herman Miller's desire to shift from forecast-driven to demand-driven replenishment of materials. The activity, in this case, was *make-to-order manufacturing* (column 1). The process, which could be one of many for this activity, is *raw material ordering* (column 2). This was a traditional type II collaboration with two-way data exchange (column 3). Column 4 indicates that this was not done at the time the strategy was devised. Column 6 ("no") indicates that the process must be changed. The future vision is for demand-driven replenishment, a type III form of collaboration.

# 10.5 Meeting Decision-Maker Needs—Summary

Changing supply chains, such as the effort undertaken by Herman Miller, will bring radical shifts in the roles of decision makers and their needs for information. Decision making is not often an item on the income statement, but it accounts for much of the cost and time incurred in executing processes plus the harm done when wrong decisions are made. This chapter seeks to make that point and to guide the reader toward a methodology for achieving the benefits of decision making in a Lean environment. Lean practices apply to any processes and are not limited to manufacturing.

# References

1. Information on the Herman Miller case is available at http://www.sternstewart.com/action/miller.php.
2. Bundy, Bill, Brown, Art, and Dean, Steve, Changing the rules of the game, Presentation Council of Logistics Management Annual Meeting, October 1999.
3. http://logistics.about.com/library/weekly/uc083002a.htm
4. Walker, William T., *Supply Chain Architecture: A Blueprint for Networking the Flow of Material, Information, and Cash*, Boca Raton, FL: CRC Press, 2005. p. 15.

# RETAIL STRATEGY AND SUPPLY CHAINS

The four chapters in Section III address formulating strategies for building and managing strategies for retail supply chain companies.

| # | Chapter Name |
|---|---|
| 11 | Product Types—Value to the Customer |
| 12 | Businesses Inside the Business |
| 13 | Activity Systems and Process Definition |
| 14 | Retail Supply Chain Management—Skills Required |

Chapter 11 calls attention to the need to consider different product types when developing supply chains. Often, these differences require individually designed supply chains for each product type. Thus, most companies need more than one supply chain to be competitive. Chapter 12 describes how to "carve out" multiple supply chains from existing functionally based supply chains. The one-size-fits-all approach is insufficient.

The activity system tool from strategy guru Michael Porter is the subject of Chapter 13 and suggests the first step in achieving supply chain change. This chapter also provides a framework for using supply chains to support strategies for competing.

Management skills for executing supply chain change are identified in Chapter 14. A tool is presented that can aid an organization in assessing under the present structure the existence of the human resources required to bring about desired changes.

# Chapter 11

# Product Types—Value to the Customer

This chapter describes concepts and models that apply to products sold through retail channels, and these call attention to the fact that each individual customer will evaluate products differently, assigning different values on product features. Chapter 2 introduced this concept when it described staple and fashion merchandise. Greater customer value for one product over another takes form in a higher profit margin somewhere in the supply chain—at the retailer, at an original equipment manufacturer (OEM), or perhaps at a supplier of a key component. Even though one partner may enjoy the premium margin, all trading partners benefit to the extent that sales of the product are stronger than its competitors. The key lesson of this chapter is that *supply chain design must be consistent with customer and end-user perceptions of product value.*

Although Chapter 2 described processes used by retail and distribution organizations, this chapter focuses more on the producers of retail merchandise. These are the OEMs and their suppliers shown Figure 1.1 in Chapter 1.

The strategy of adding more value to a product is the path of choice for manufacturers beset by the consequences of globalization. One example is what is called the *Nagoya boom*, reported in the *Wall Street Journal.*[1] The boom refers to a group of manufacturers supplying traditional smokestack industries such as steel that have moved production of their staples to low-cost regions and focused on high-value goods produced at home. Examples include research and development (R & D)–intensive products such as engines for electric vehicles cars and robots for industrial use.

Another industry on a distant side of the world reported a similar strategy. The privately owned Italian company Finanziaria Arnoldo Caprai has moved up the value curve for decades.[2] In the 1980s, the owner, Mr. Caprai, transformed his sweater line from lambs' wool to cashmere in response to competition from Hong Kong. He then shifted his sources for raw material and manufacturing to China but retained design control to protect his hard-to-copy products. Back in Italy, the company also found profitable niches in high-value linens, tablecloths, and lingerie.

An example of invasion from the low side is "Two Buck Chuck," a popular product from Bronco Wine Company. Varietals under the Charles Shaw brand are priced around $3 (up from its earlier price that earned it the nickname "two-buck chuck") retail in California and only slightly higher in states having higher liquor taxes. Having mastered the art of cost cutting, Bronco has been "driving down costs and prices in a way that is shaking up the entire (wine) industry."[3] Bronco's partner, retailer Trader Joe's, has successfully exploited the Charles Shaw brand as a traffic builder for its globally sourced, successful grocery stores.

Traditionally, apparel and department store retailers have moved to carrying significant percentages of private label merchandise designed in-house for the company's own particular target segments. At Macy's, efforts have been made to establish many of these brands to appear to be national brands. Private label brand names like Style & Co., Charter Club, Tools of the Trade, and many others sit side by side with highly advertised brands like Ralph Lauren, Keurig, and Fieldcrest.

A principle of this book is that supply chain design must reflect the value and profitability of the product to end users. That is, a supply chain for a lower-value product should be different from one for a higher-value product. This difference is ignored in companies that employ a one-size-fits-all supply chain for all their products. In the highly competitive and growing domestic wine industry, Bronco Wine Company carved a low-end niche by taking a cost-cutting knife to the wine supply chain.

To capture more value, some business models use vertically integrated supply chains. In this way, the retailer maintains control of product design and manufacture. Like the Caprai company discussed earlier, retailers Inditex, through its Zara chain (fast fashion clothing) and IKEA (knockdown furniture), retain design control over their products, communicating the brands' understanding of their customers' taste and capturing the value customers place on those designs. Au Bon Pan and Jack in the Box, which run fast-food stores, promote new sandwiches and other menu items to entice their customers to return. Software companies, motion pictures, and music producers also survive on a steady flow of new versions of their product lines.

Other retailers market diverse sets of products designed and made by others. These retailers sift through the offerings of many designers and manufacturers to find the high-value gems. Made in Washington, a store and online retailer, carries only products made within the state and searches for particularly unique products. Department stores, discount stores, grocers, and most small retailers fit a similar model with greatly expanded geographic borders. Wal-Mart promotes its lowest-priced item in its stores with focused displays and keeps higher-priced (and profit) alternatives nearby. Wherever a company is located in the supply chain—as a retailer, a distributor, or a supplier—supply chain designers should be aware of the concepts described in the following sections.

## 11.1 The Product Life Cycle

An important concept for supply chain designers is one long used by marketers, called the *product life cycle*. Figure 11.1 illustrates the product life cycle showing the four stages in a product's life cycle—inception (also called the introductory stage), growth, maturity, and decline. The model helps to define the role of supply chain management (SCM) at different stages in the life cycle. This becomes complicated in a company where there are many different products at different stages in the life cycle. To the harm of many companies serving retail markets, a consequence is a one-size-fits-all supply chain many should avoid, not individualized procedures, ones tailored to products at different stages in the life cycle. Employing an omnichannel strategy that offers customers alternative ways to purchase a product is a strong response, one that will vary by product features and requirements as well as life cycle stage. For example, grocery stores selling a staple produce product like lettuce through an online grocery delivery service will have a different supply chain than the one for in-store-shopping lettuce purchases.

Another complication related to the retail industry is the concept of a *product*. Retailers often think of *categories* rather than individual products. Categories, according to Levy and Weitz, can be any grouping that makes sense to the retailer.[4] Each category will have many individual products accompanied by even more stock-keeping units (SKUs), as discussed in the merchandise budgeting sections, Sections 2.2 and 2.3, in Chapter 2. So, product, in discussing the product life cycle, also applies to product categories.

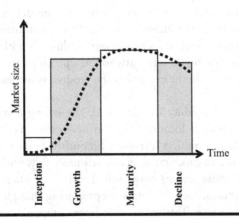

**Figure 11.1   The product life cycle.**

In retailing, a category consists of items that are substitutable and/or complementary for each other. An apparel retailer might have categories for men's sportswear or girls' swimwear. An automobile dealer may use categories such as sport utility vehicles (SUVs), sedans, or minivans. For maximum effectiveness, supply chain trading partners must agree on category definitions and respond to the needs of the customer by providing the products that match their choice criteria.

Levy and Weitz identify four types of "category life cycle" in terms of the longevity of the category product line:

1. Fad—a one-shot wonder with a very short life cycle, perhaps one season.
2. Fashion—a multiseason product with many individual products and SKUs during its life cycle.
3. Staple—a basic product that achieves considerable longevity but eventually goes into decline.
4. Seasonal—a product whose sales fluctuate over the course of a year. This type includes both fashion and staple items.

The authors note that "forecasting and inventory management systems used for fads and fashion merchandise are very different than those used for staples" (see Ref. 4, p. 380). One of these differences is the approach used to planning inventories. Fashion buyers often use merchandise budget planning as described in Chapter 2, Section 2.3, while staple-product buyers use historically based forecasting procedures.

In the inception stage, the product or category is at center stage. Originally, the product life cycle was used to describe the appropriate strategies for introducing and maximizing the potential profitability of a unique, previously unknown product. However, in practice, it is often used to apply to new versions of existing products. If the product is not a new version of an existing product line (such as a new movie, CD, software program, apparel style, sandwich, or automobile), a new supply chain will be needed. Often, even when it is needed, supply chain design is a secondary priority in the inception stage. This is definitely the case in many high-tech companies in electronics or software industries with hot new products. Ideally, these companies should start early to line up customers and suppliers—that is to say, a supply chain—in the event that the product is successful and moves into the growth stage.

When a new retail product is introduced, the selling company is faced with trying to find distribution locations for the newcomer. Traditionally, there are thousands of new food products introduced monthly. Food retailers only want to give space in the store to products that will sell profitably, with high margins and significant volume. These grocers have limited real estate (shelf space) upon which to display these products. New ones must be promising enough to replace products already holding that space. This means that large companies with big budgets for promotion like Procter & Gamble have an advantage in gaining new space. As part of a launch, they may even share in the risk with the retailer, whereas a young company starting up does not have the marketing budget to do so.

The shelf or display space issue exists for all types of products, although the competition for space in-store space is most significant in the food category. With omnichannel retailing, it has become easier for smaller introductory products to get before audiences since online and mobile channels have much lower barriers to entry than physical stores.

Growth products—whether they are fad, fashion, or new technology—in the next stage are climbing to the top of the sales curve. Successful products become profitable for industry leaders; improved versions of the product better match customer needs, and supply chain trading partners enjoy profits from higher margins and volume. Supply chain processes are geared to keep up with demand, which is ample for all but the worst competitors.

The maturity stage represents the situation where growth of the product category has leveled off. Often, these consumer products are bought routinely and without much variation. These products were previously defined as staples. These are also referred to as *frequently purchased consumer goods* or FPCGs. Some would say the growth product has been *commoditized*. Competition stiffens; the supply chain mission migrates toward cost reduction as higher-cost industry participants are squeezed out of the market. Competitors target segments with extended product features to maintain their volume. Although mature products must have efficient supply chains, the base products themselves are no longer exceptional compared to competitors. Extended product features such as service, financing, and a reputation for reliability play an increased role. An example of a product in maturity is the TV show or movie repackaged as a DVD or delivered in online streaming services like Netflix.

Products in decline, former staples, hang on for dear life. Unless they move backward to another phase by rejuvenating their product or supply chain, they will not survive. For example, Arm & Hammer successfully revived their product by finding numerous new applications for baking soda, combining it with other products or brands (toothpaste, laundry detergent, and various types of deodorizers). In many cases, the supply chain task is to identify and winnow out products in the decline stage from the portfolio before they become unprofitable. Fad products with short product life cycles die quickly and are characterized by very short or nonexistent mature stages. These are more easily extinguished than staple merchandise goods that may have a staunchly loyal following even as total sales of that product decline.

Long-lived legacy products such as automobiles, computers, and appliances must be supported after they are no longer sold. Maintaining long-term commitments requires moving the product support function into a different supply chain altogether. This product aftermarket support may regenerate the product or its components as fashion or staple merchandise. An example is the vintage car collection. New challenges arise, e.g., finding parts, warranty and nonwarranty service and repairs, software maintenance, providing manuals and parts lists, and readily accessible technical support. Recently, old-fashioned major kitchen appliances have remerged in new form, playing on the popularity of vintage design but with improved operation, thereby further diversifying this need to source repair parts and add-ons.

A shortfall in some retail trading partner strategies is treating the aftermarket as an afterthought. Other industries such as cell phones and computer printers actually focus on the aftermarket as part of their basic strategy, realizing that phone minutes and ink cartridges will generate far more profit than the initial sale. Accordingly, these companies rely on a penetration pricing strategy for the original product when they anticipate a strong aftermarket.

## 11.2 Innovative and Functional Products

Marshall Fisher describes a similar framework for ensuring that supply chain design is appropriate for two different product types.[5] His two types, *functional* and *innovative*, are different by virtue of the nature of product demand. Functional products, as the name implies, are the staples described above. Although competition is fierce for these products and margins along the supply chain are thin, large volumes insure adequate profitability, and demand is constant and relatively easy to forecast. In the life cycle model, these products would be in the mature or decline phase.

Innovative products are differentiated in the market; they are fads or fashions and are likely in the inception and growth stages in the product life cycle. Seasonal products also frequently fit this mode, although some like Christmas trees become mature and have long lives. Innovative products have advanced technological features or styling, or both. They carry higher margins, but demand can be hard to forecast, and their life cycles may be short, especially if associated technology is rapidly changing. A product that is now mature and replaced by many new devices is the iPod.

Fisher characterizes the features of each type of supply chain summarized in Table 11.1. Functional products generally will have longer lives than innovative products. Their demand will be easier to forecast with corresponding lower chances of stockouts or markdowns. Lead times should be determined by cost trade-offs that take into account production and distribution economics, the cost of inventory, and other such factors. Innovative products have short lives, their very innovation suggesting that improvements will be coming along quickly. The benefits of high profitability are offset by market risks that take the form of forecast misses and corresponding markdown threats from overproduction or overpurchasing. Ideally, lead time would be the result of a supply chain design that maximizes flexibility within forecast ranges.

Fisher, like Levy and Weitz, asserts that these two product types require fundamentally different supply chains. Functional products require an *efficient* supply

**Table 11.1  Differences between Innovative and Functional Products**

|  | *Functional Products (staples, everyday purchases)* | *Innovative Products (technology, fads, fashion items)* |
|---|---|---|
| Length of product life cycle | Long | Short |
| Profitability per unit | Low | Initially high |
| Forecast errors | Low, always a market | High, accurate forecasting difficult |
| Stockout rates | Low risk | Higher risk |
| Markdown on prices | Unlikely | Likely for excess merchandise |
| Lead time | Set by economics/competition | Set by supply chain flexibility |

*Source:* From Ayers, James B., *Handbook of Supply Chain Management*, 2nd ed., Boca Raton: CRC Press, 2006.

chain; innovative products require *responsive* supply chains. For example, vertically integrated American Apparel, headquartered in Los Angeles, specializes in fast turnaround in its product lines for screen-printed apparel. For the Fourth of July holiday in 2016, the company offered a wide line of flagged apparel for men and women. Proper delivery times are critical for its seasonally based merchandise. The firm prides itself in being the highest-paying apparel company in the United States and not being dependent on low-cost, out-of-country suppliers.[6]

# 11.3 Market Mediation Costs

Fisher also advises recognition of what he calls "market mediation" costs. The mission of the supply chain is to match supply and demand, resulting in the satisfaction of marketplace needs. These costs result from mismatches in demand and supply, essentially underperforming the basic SCM mission. Forecasting demand for innovative and fashion products is often particularly difficult and results in higher business risk and can signal impending financial losses.

Recently, the *Wall Street Journal*, in a response to an article written by Nicole Hong, ran a number of letters to the editor written by wives of men who insist on continuing to wear carpenter shorts even though design gurus say that they are passé. This style represents a product that was designed as a fashion or innovative item but has now transitioned into a staple in the mature stage of the product life cycle. Although fashion experts find them distasteful, men have embraced the convenience and comfort of the carpenter shorts and enjoy the loose fit. This classification change results in greater order predictability and solidifying supply chain procedures, thereby lowering financial risk.

Disconnects between supply and demand result in market mediation costs. If there is too much product, the price must be marked down. If there is too little product available for sale, the company incurs the opportunity costs from lost sales. These include the loss of anticipated revenue and profits from the sale, as well as customer disappointment and possible devaluing of the store itself as a product source for future purchases.

In some cases, prices can be raised in times of short supply but, more generally, only in markets that are relatively inelastic in terms of supply and demand. It is hard to get far away from the customers' reference price, a price established by their previous experience purchasing the product. For example, in 2014, beef herds in the United States were small, and prices rose above the expected price.[7] Spurred by higher margins in 2016, beef prices have declined. Also, chicken prices have declined, while pork prices have risen, changing the trade-offs consumers might make when choosing between the two types of white meat. When market mediation costs are taken into account, the added cost of an inflexible supply chain can be substantial compared to the budgeted logistics costs of getting the product to market. Many measurement systems ignore this reality.

For products such as automobiles, both functional and innovative products can be assembled on the same production line. Fisher notes that a functional car like a four-door sedan should use an efficient supply chain with as much cost squeezed out as possible. But a high-margin convertible or electric vehicles that is popular with customers could earn more profit with a flexible supply chain that is more responsive to demand. This point is significant because some managers may think that a tailored supply chain will involve duplicate facilities. Note that this can be done without changing the physical process flows for the base product involving assembly and distribution but by modifying the business rules for production scheduling, finished goods, and work-in-process inventory levels. So, the convertible and the sedan could be assembled on the same production line, but the line's scheduling is governed by different parameters.

Applying Fisher's model, supply chain design has two branches. For the functional product, it means advances that reduce the cost of sourcing, manufacturing, inventory, distribution, and sales. For the innovative product, it means reducing the physical costs of the product where appropriate, while recognizing potential market mediation costs.

This is a more complex equation because most companies do not, and, in fact, cannot, track these costs with precision. However, any attempt to reduce lost sales will certainly require as much flexibility in the supply chain design as possible and argues for applying the SCM postponement strategy when possible. This supports the *flexibility imperative* driver of supply chain change described in Chapter 6. Too few organizations pursue this goal, seeking instead to focus excessively on cost reduction as they design supply chain processes and business rules.

Table 11.2 illustrates the two market mediation costs—the situation when actual demand falls short of forecast and when actual demand exceeds the forecast. The table assumes that the company produces or orders the forecast number of units (100,000). It also assumes that the supply chain lead time and flexibility make it impossible to adjust as actual sales become apparent.

The left-hand column calculates the market mediation cost from a shortfall in demand. The company is paid full price ($100) for 70,000 units, whereas 30,000 units must be sold at a discount ($30). Because the unit cost is $40, the result is a loss of $10 on each discounted unit. The total market mediation cost would be $300,000. The right-hand column calculates market mediation cost in the case of lost sales of 30,000 units. In this case, the market mediation cost is the gross margin ($60) times the number of units of lost sales (30,000), or $1,800,000. For this example, the cost of lost sales is far greater than that of overproduction, suggesting that overforecasting is less serious than underforecasting.

Two obstacles retard applying this concept to work in the retail industry. First, accounting systems do a fair job of capturing the markdowns that go with shortfalls in demand, but altogether ignore lost opportunities from underforecasting demand. So, extra analysis based on estimates of lost sales must be done. The second obstacle is the paradigm that supply chains represent only cost and need to be measured on cost alone. Actions that increase flexibility but add cost are discouraged. Examples include extra capacity, buffer inventories, and airfreight over ocean freight.

## 11.4  Customer Value and Product Types—Summary

Figure 11.2 summarizes concepts described in this chapter in a product life cycle grid. The grid shows the inception, or introductory, stage in the upper right-hand corner. The supply chain challenge, for an entirely new product, is to develop trading partners in advance of higher levels of production. This could be the domain of the fad products that are "here today and gone tomorrow." The supply chain should maximize profit over the brief product life.

The next quadrant (upper left) is the growth stage. It contains longer-lived fad products and fashion-type products that have higher profit margins. The supply chain challenge is meeting the demand. The maturity stage is at the lower left-hand quadrant. This is the home of staples requiring efficient supply chains. Some of these staples may be moving into the decline stage. Products in the decline stage are candidates for either aftermarket innovations or elimination.

This chapter has presented the case that retail supply chains must be designed with the perception of customer value and product competition in mind. This will

**Table 11.2  Illustration of Market Mediation Costs**

| Forecast ($) | | Sales More Than Forecast | |
|---|---|---|---|
| Forecast (units) | 100,000 | | |
| Unit price | 100 | | |
| Unit cost | 40 | | |
| Gross margin | 60 | | |
| | | Actual demand | 130,000 |
| Forecast Error (units) | | Lost sales (units) | 30,000 |
| | | Gross margin per unit | $60 |
| Market mediation cost | | Lost profit | $1,800,000 |

| Sales Less Than Forecast | |
|---|---|
| Actual sales (units) | 70,000 |
| # units marked down | 30,000 |
| Markdown price | $30 |
| Loss per unit | $(10) |
| Markdown cost | $(300,000) |

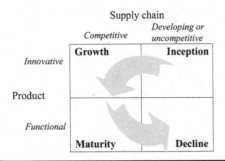

**Figure 11.2   Product life cycle grid.**

maximize returns to the retailer and its trading partners in terms of customer loyalty and profit, and to the customer in terms of met needs. The implications are important to the retail enterprise and the manufacturers and distributors that support them. Creativity and collaboration by trading partners is the surest route to achieving winning supply chain designs. The next two chapters describe how they might go about the task.

# References

1. Sapsford, Jathon, "Japan's Economy Gains Steam from Manufacturing Heartland," *The Wall Street Journal*, October 11, 2005, p. A1.
2. Di Leo, Luca and Stock, Jenny, "Trying to Stay a Cut above Chinese Textiles," *The Wall Street Journal*, July 25, 2005, p. A13.
3. Hirsch, Jerry, "Wal-Mart of Wine," *Los Angeles Times*, April 30, 2006, p. C1.
4. Levy, Michael and Weitz, Barton A., *Retailing Management*, 5th ed., New Delhi: Tata McGraw-Hill, 2004, chap. 12.
5. Fisher, Marshall L., "What Is the Right Supply Chain for Your Product?" *Harvard Business Review*, (75/2), March–April 1997, 105–116.
6. Hong, Nicole, "What Happened after I Wrote the Cargo Pants Story," *Wall Street Journal*, August 6, 2016.
7. "Food Price Outlook, 2016–2017 Summary Findings," US Department of Agriculture Economic Research Service, July 22, 2016.

# Chapter 12

# Businesses Inside the Business

This chapter extends the discussion of product types and customer value described in Chapter 11 and builds on the argument that delivering value to retail customers and end users is best done with specifically tailored supply chains.

## 12.1 The Conventional Supply Chain Meets Omnichannel Retailing

The retailer, distributor, or manufacturer will likely need more than one supply chain to be successful. Proof of this is the deployment of omnichannel supply chains with parallel processes for physical, information, and financial flows.

There is ample evidence of the move toward this concept; the often-used example of Wal-Mart is one. In mid-2006, Wal-Mart decided to drop their one-size-fits-all approach to store design and stocking. Its new approach created six store models with different merchandise, staff, and logistics support for differing market types. The company admitted that by serving all customers with the same store type, they were also underserving everyone.[1]

An update article since the first edition of this book described the extension of the multiformat store that complements other channels like online ordering.[2] The article reports that the intent is to extend the range of stores Wal-Mart needs to serve its customers. The author noted that current stores range from 260,000 sq. ft. Supercenters down to 15,000 sq. ft. Wal-Mart Express stores. In January of 2016, Wal-Mart pulled the plug on its small Express stores in favor of the larger 30,000–40,000 sq. ft. Neighborhood Markets. Competition for the very low price customer with Dollar General's more than 12,000 stores was cited as one of the reasons for this strategic change.

"Growth of this format will allow Wal-Mart to better address competition from traditional grocers such as Kroger, Publix, Ahold and Delhaize, which have been out-comping Wal-Mart in Grocery for some time."[3]

The Supercenter stores had a 25% market share by targeting the needs of those making the weekly restocking trip. At the other end of the spectrum, the Wal-Mart share of the one-at-a-time convenience store business was only 10% of a $415 billion market.

Standing in the way of multiple customer-serving supply chains is the conventional functional organization present in many companies. The organizational structure often consists of specialized departments with narrow missions measured on how that part of the mission is accomplished, rather than the company's overall strategic goals. For example, the functions of a manufacturer serving retail markets may include purchasing, manufacturing, marketing, distribution, design engineering, finance, and human resources.

Distributors and retailers may also be organized in a similar way, creating internal walls, or "silos," which results in internal organizational barriers that impede the flow of products and information. Also, department-level measures of success will produce unintended consequences. For example, a transportation manager at a retailer or distributor might not employ expensive airfreight to rush a delivery to a valued customer, because that supply chain individual is measured on the cost of transportation rather than on the sales or profitability of the transaction, not to mention its impact on long-term customer value.

The driver of supply chain change, process-centered management, described in Chapter 6, Section 6.6, is the antidote to situations like these. The recommended view is of end-to-end processes, not the separate missions of collections of individual departments. Before embarking on an end-to-end supply chain design effort, there's a need to define the boundaries of that supply chain. In effect, the supply chain will be "carved out" of the overall operation, creating "businesses inside the business." This will enable the addressing of barriers and developing ways to increase customer value. The method described here builds on the principle of market *segmentation*. Segmentation calls for dividing markets according to differences in customer and user needs and purchasing propensities and then designing supply chain processes to satisfy those needs.

## 12.2 Market Segments

The supply chain model in Chapter 1 (Figure 1.1) showed customers and end users as the consumers of retail goods and services. The Wal-Mart store types described above cater to different markets—the weekly shopper at major Supercenters and the grocery convenience shopper patronizing Neighborhood Markets. A single customer may fall into both segments. The weekly customer fills the refrigerator in a single shopping trip. With more dollars at stake, these customers are likely to value low prices. During the week, the same customer may make several short trips for needed items and enjoys the convenience of a smaller store, possibly paying a little more for the ease of shopping. The Wal-Mart strategy seeks to close the gap in the market share in these two markets.

Therefore, customers are not monolithic; that is, they fall into groups based on purchasing proclivities and can be described by any number of factors. Figure 7.1 represents the "supply chain reality." Marketers define customer groups with similar purchasing propensities as segments and tailor their marketing strategies to the needs of these segments. These needs are explicitly identified through company experience, sales analysis, or market research.

Levy and Weitz, in *Retailing Management*,[4] identify the three components of a successful retail strategy:

- Identification of the target market (segments served)
- Retail offerings of products and services
- Source of the competitive advantage (positioning)

For example, Nordstrom targets middle- to upper-income customers using a fashionable specialty department store format providing superior customer service. An appropriate supply chain design will define all three market strategy components.

Segmentation assumes that within-segment customers use the same purchasing models. Realistically, companies use more visible factors of a market for this process. Most segmentation is based on a number of factors, including the following:

- Geography or location
- Income level
- Demographics such as age and gender
- Frequency of usage
- Benefits of value to the customer or end user, such as convenience, cost, and prestige
- Preference for distribution channels
- Family life-cycle stage
- The relative importance of various product attributes but only when they can be identified

Although useful for designing retail strategies, this type of segmentation may or may not be helpful in designing the supply chain to serve the segment. In fact, different supply chains may not be needed for each customer segment. A different approach, beyond market segmentation, is needed to aid those identifying the need for and designing successful supply chain processes.

## 12.3 Spheres—Modules for Supply Chain Design

The recommended tool to identify the boundaries of supply chains is a *sphere*, introduced in a previous book in this series, the *Handbook of Supply Chain Management*.[5] A sphere is defined as a *market–product–operation* combination that provides a way to "divide and conquer" in developing and implementing supply chain processes. The term *sphere* comes from the three dimensions that comprise a sphere—markets, products, and operations—summarized in Table 12.1. Sphere identification draws supply chain boundaries, helps decide an appropriate organization model, and identifies requirements for customer service processes. All three elements are vital to successful supply chain management (SCM) that supports retail strategies for competing in the current marketplace.

The dimensions, in the left-hand column in Table 12.1, are markets, products, and operations. The *market* portion of the sphere definition can include multiple segments as long as a common supply chain can serve those segments. *Products* are those sold to the identified retail market; they include both physical products and value-adding services. They can be expressed as categories or as other groupings used in that particular retail sector.

This section describes the Wal-Mart Remix program that set up a supply chain for high-volume products. For a complex product with many components, the products could be major component groups such as high-value custom components or low-value commodity components. The product includes not only the base physical product but also extended product features that are delivered by the supply chain processes.

*Operations* is the supply chain machinery used to source, make, and deliver the products to the customers. These include hard assets such as the supplier base, manufacturing, distribution networks, vehicles and equipment, and facilities of

**Table 12.1  Sphere Dimensions**

| Dimension | Definition |
| --- | --- |
| Markets | Defined by customer groups or segments where end users have common characteristics and buying behavior. Does not have to match segments identified for marketing strategies. |
| Products | Includes the physical, or base, product, major components, or extended product features such as customer service, inventory and scheduling policies, warranties and aftermarket support, financing, technical support, and other features. |
| Operations | Suppliers, manufacturing/production capabilities, distribution organizations/channels, equipment, and facilities. Can be either inside the company or at upstream or downstream external trading partner operations. |

all types. Operations also includes "soft" assets and capabilities that support the sphere. Examples are information systems, customer service centers, the sourcing organization, and vendor agreements.

Figure 12.1 is a supply chain model that provides examples of the sphere concept. The customers/end users are on the right; the different patterns in the vertical bar represent different customer groups—#1, #2, and #3. An option is to have *market-centric* supply chains serving each of the three groups. This is appropriate if there need to be separate supply chains based on different customer/end-user requirements.

Moving to the middle of Figure 12.1, there are three products, A, B, and C. Each of the three products might also justify a separate focused supply chain. These would be *product-centric* supply chains. Often, capital intensiveness or the need for specialized production or distribution capabilities will dictate product-centric supply chains. Car companies might use this approach, with the products being the platforms producing similar cars under different brand names.

There are also *operations-centric* supply chains, where some operating capabilities are important to all products and markets. In these cases, competitive advantage comes from supply chain processes within a company or is shared among trading partners. These are referred to as *enabling* processes. Examples include transportation networks, information systems, performance measures, and research and development capability.

Defining spheres is an intuitive right-brained exercise that should build on the company's strategic planning process and, ideally, be part of that process. The syntax for defining a sphere simply puts the market–product–operations combination together with a divider between each part of the definition. Table 12.2 lists examples based on the supply chains displayed in Figure 12.2.

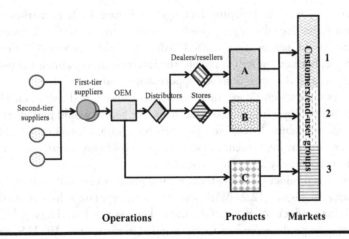

**Figure 12.1  Sphere concept OEM original equipment manufacturer.**

**Table 12.2  Sphere Examples**

| # | Type | Markets | Products | Operations |
|---|------|---------|----------|------------|
| 1 | Market-centric | Market 1 | All (A, B, and C) | All |
| 2 | Product-centric | All markets (1, 2, and 3) | Product C | All |
| 3 | Operations-centric (enabling) | All markets | All products | Sourcing, buying, quality assurance |

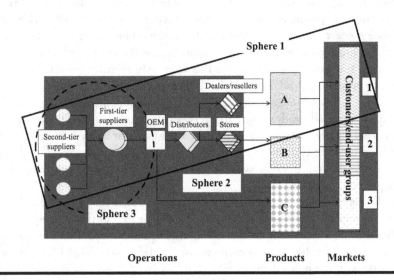

**Figure 12.2  Example spheres.**

Sphere 1, shown as a slanted rectangle in Figure 12.2, is market-centric. It focuses on delivering all company products to one market, market 1. Operations in this sphere would include those needed to deliver all three products to that market. For example, market 1 might carve out the Internet sales channel, the products to be sold there, and the operations to support that channel.

Another market-centric example would focus on tailored services for high-net-worth individuals by a financial services firm. The sphere would provide specialized products (investments, loans, etc.) just for this group. Operations could include account executives, investment advice, special reports on investments, travel services, and user-friendly access to account data.

Sphere 2 is product-centric—built around product C—and is shown as a large shaded area in Figure 12.2. With this concept, separate self-contained spheres (one each for products A, B, and C) handle their assigned products. All the operations needed to produce product C are included in the sphere. The U.S. automaker Chrysler employed this concept with platform teams that designed and produce the various brands that make up the platform: Jeep; Dodge trucks, cars and minivans, and future midsize products; and high-performance vehicles under Chrysler's SRT (Street and Racing Technology) brand.[6]

In another product-centric example, Wal-Mart has separated its products into fast selling and regular as part of the previously mentioned Remix program. The company operates six major types of warehouses, those for

1. Regional general merchandise centers
2. Full-line grocery, grocery, and perishables food distribution centers
3. Import/redistribution centers
4. Fashion distribution centers
5. Sam's club distribution centers
6. Specialty distribution centers:
   a. Export
   b. Optical labs
   c. Pharmacy—locations highly classified
   d. Returns processing
   e. Tires
   f. Print and mail
   g. E-commerce*

The purpose is to move high-volume products direct to store shelves expeditiously to limit stockouts.[7] The effort resides in its almost 150 highly automated distribution centers, processing an average of 600,000 cases daily, and separates rapid selling merchandise (paper towels, toilet paper, seasonal items, and some foods) from regular deliveries. This saves time when the goods arrive at the store, where employees no longer need to sift through the incoming shipment to find the fast movers. To make sure that no shelves are empty, selected warehouses are designated for "high-velocity" handling. They are designed accordingly to save time at the store and increase sales per square foot by preventing stockouts. With the sphere idea applied to Wal-Mart's Remix program, the new product-centric sphere could be defined as follows: all markets/fast-moving products/selected high-velocity warehouses and their supporting processes.

The operations piece of the sphere would include facilities, equipment, and transportation resources needed to keep fast movers rolling off the shelves quickly. Component candidates are purchasing, cross-docking, supplier collaboration, and special arrangements with transportation companies.

Sphere 3, shown on the left in Figure 12.2 as an oval, is operations-centric. Such spheres are *enabling spheres*, whereas market-centric and product-centric spheres are *product-producing* spheres. The Wal-Mart buying organization that finds sources (meaning it approves suppliers but does not make purchases) for both high-speed

---

* "The Walmart Distribution Center Network in the United States," MWVPL International, 2016.

and low-speed products for all stores could be such a sphere (all markets/all products/sourcing organization). If the high-speed and low-speed spheres do the actual buying, the buying organization would be included in those spheres—enabled by the sourcing organization that finds the vendors they buy from.

Chrysler, mentioned earlier, also has an enabling platform operation for power train components (engines, transmissions). This capability serves all the platform teams (all products, all markets, power train design and manufacture). Amazon, pressed to deliver a wide variety of products to massive numbers of locations on a timely basis, has probably the most complex fulfillment operation in the world, further complicated by the fact that each shipment contains a relatively small number of items. Such a system is highly *operations-centric*.

## 12.4 Businesses Inside the Business—Summary

The sphere approach puts forward a method to align the supply chain to the needs of customers and end users. The choice of spheres will guide process design, the organization structure needed to run them, needed systems to support the processes, and metrics to manage the supply chain.

The company that views the supply chain as a strategic asset needs a way to begin the design process. Focused supply chain designs produce competitive advantage, adding more value to customers and end users. The spheres framework provides a way. Chapter 13 describes the next step in this process after spheres have been defined.

## References

1. Zimmerman, Ann, "Thinking Local: To Boost Sales, Wal-Mart Drops One-Size-Fits-All Approach," *The Wall Street Journal*, September 7, 2006, p. A1.
2. Ausick, Paul, "Walmart Now Has Six Types of Store," http://247wallst.com/retail/2014/03/22/walmart-now-has-six-types-of-stores/, March 22, 2014.
3. Mahone, Sarah, "Wal-Mart Changes Small-Store Strategy," *Marketing Daily Media Post*, January 18, 2016.
4. Levy, Michael and Weitz, Barton A., *Retailing Management*, 5th ed., New Delhi: Tata McGraw-Hill, 2004, chap. 12.
5. Ayers, James B., *Handbook of Supply Chain Management*, 2nd ed., Boca Raton: CRC Press, 2006, chap. 18.
6. Mayne, Eric, "5 Product Teams for Chrysler," http://wardsauto.com/news-analysis/5-product-teams-chrysler, February 1, 2008.
7. Hudson, Kris, "Wal-Mart's Need for Speed," *The Wall Street Journal*, September 26, 2005, p. B4.

# Chapter 13

# Activity Systems and Process Definition

This chapter describes the application of spheres, or "businesses inside the business," discussed in Chapter 12. The path described here is from sphere definition (Chapter 11) to supply chain processes that add value for customers or end users and erect barriers to competitors. This would also be the case for companies seeking a "blue ocean strategy," with the intention of making competitors irrelevant in a particular market.[1] Such strategies seek monopolies in uncontested market "space."

The recommended tool for process development is the *activity system*, an approach developed by Michael Porter of the Harvard Business School. In 2001, Harvard University and the Harvard Business School created the Institute for Strategy and Competitiveness to further Professor Porter's prolific work. Activity systems are suitable for application no matter where a company is located in the retail supply chain—retailer, distributor, original equipment manufacturer (OEM), or supplier to an OEM.

The authors' experiences with clients demonstrate the value of activity systems. The approach fits well with facilitated team sessions since client managers serving on design teams readily grasp the process. Subsequent use increases understanding and willingness and capability to think strategically.

This chapter turns to retailer Inter IKEA Systems B.V., the Swedish knockdown furniture retailer, as an illustration of activity systems. Dr. Porter used this company case in an article describing the methodology.[2] The case study here contains insights from that article and additions based on IKEA's communications through their website, other articles, and information about the company. Another example later in this chapter refers to the Wal-Mart Remix effort described in Chapter 12.

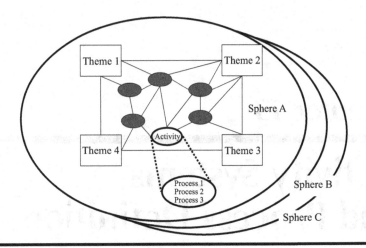

**Figure 13.1  Spheres, themes, activities, and processes.**

Figure 13.1 depicts the relationship between components in the supply chain planning process. The figure assumes that the planning task described in Chapter 12 has identified spheres that are "businesses inside the business." These "carved-out" supply chains are suitable for focused strategies leading to custom supply chains. In Figure 13.1, the spheres are labeled sphere A, sphere B, and sphere C. Inside sphere A, there's a picture of an activity system with strategic themes anchoring the activity system. Smaller, shaded activities support the themes. Within each activity, there are implementing processes.

The case study company, IKEA, built its business model over a long period beginning in the late 1940s. Over time, it has become a leader in its niche by the choices made in that process. Activity systems are a more recent planning innovation, so IKEA did not employ the tool while building the business. Nevertheless, the IKEA uniqueness presents a formidable barrier to competitors—one that supply chain planners can look to in creating their own business models.

## 13.1  Activity System—The IKEA Example

IKEA uses low-cost methods to make purchases of private-label home furnishings, mostly furniture, available to the widest possible market. IKEA began to design its own furniture in 1955 and opened its first store in Sweden in 1958. In 1959, it began to produce self-assembly furniture to lower freight charges and other costs to retail customers. This approach continues today. IKEA now has over 200 stores in 30 countries. Each store has about 9500 different items for sale. Its 2015 sales are over €31.9 billion (over U.S. $35.7 billion), total sales increased by 8.9%, and same-store sales were up by 5.1%. Total retail sales in the United States that year were up by only 2.1%.

The IKEA Concept guides the company. On their website, they beckon customers, "Refresh your homes for less!" Their concept is to make "well-designed, functional home furnishing products" at low, affordable prices. In fact, the design process for a new product begins by setting the retail price for an item the company sees demand for in the marketplace. It then proceeds to design production processes that meet the cost objective. Finally, the product is designed to IKEA's style standard. This standard omits cost-adding frills that add no value in terms of functionality. The following sections use IKEA to describe the process of creating an activity system.

### 13.1.1 Make Choices, Develop Themes

A first step in developing an activity system is to make choices based on trade-offs between strategic options. According to Porter, there is no strategy if choices are not made. It is choices that lead to a unique strategy capable of repelling competitive assaults. In particular, operating effectiveness or low-cost production is not a strategy. Any competitor can probably copy cost-cutting strategies.

The strategic choices, in the form of themes, anchor the strategy as shown in Figure 13.2. The themes reflect the thrifty philosophy of IKEA founder Ingvar Kamprad, who came from a region of Sweden where people, mostly farmers, worked hard to support themselves. Their customers sought and continue to seek value for their money. In applying the process to IKEA, Porter identifies four themes to illustrate the power of activity systems:

1. Low manufacturing cost—for control of cost and style
2. Modular furniture design—for minimizing shipping and storage cost
3. Limited customer service—to assure store labor efficiency
4. Self-selection by customers—to involve the customer and further reduce cost

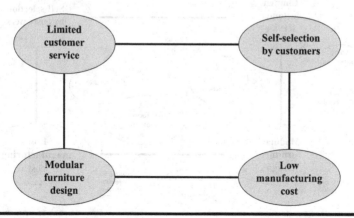

**Figure 13.2   Strategic themes for IKEA.**

Themes are shown as large shaded ovals in Figure 13.2. They can be viewed as features or objectives of the IKEA interaction between its stores and customers. A traditional furniture store is just the opposite of the IKEA model. Traditional stores will likely have high-end furniture on the floor, ample sales staff, and longer lead times for delivery unless the customer buys store stock. Products usually come preassembled and incur significant freight charges.

Chapter 11 introduced the idea of functional and innovative products. IKEA blends the virtues of both types. It stresses low cost by purging design frills and supply chain steps out of its processes, a strategy for functional products. On the other hand, it offers modern product designs that satisfy even high-end buyers as long as they are handy with a screwdriver and appreciate IKEA value. The best choice for IKEA products is to call them "innovative" in terms of the base, physical product while being extremely "functional" in the delivery of the product.

### 13.1.2 Define Activities

The next step makes the activity system approach valuable to supply chain planning. It requires definition of the activities that are needed to support the strategic choices. These activities constitute enterprise operations from high-level strategy to day-to-day working processes. Figure 13.3 shows some of the activities needed to implement IKEA's themes.

The activities support the low-cost theme using modular furniture packaged in unassembled knockdown form. This minimizes shipping cost and storage space at warehouse-like stores sized to hold inventory. To facilitate transactions, stores are

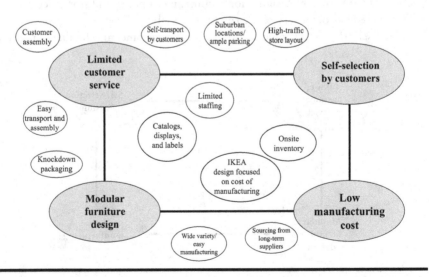

**Figure 13.3 Activities and links.**

located where there is ample parking. This enables transport of bulky merchandise by customers. The low-cost theme also applies to the store sales staff. IKEA calls this "customer involvement" in the sales process. This includes picking out merchandise (IKEA provides tape measures), transporting them home, and assembling them for use. For those who can't or won't perform these tasks, IKEA will provide the services for a fee.

### 13.1.3 Draw Links

The final step shows how activities support each of the themes and other activities. Figure 13.4 shows these linkages. IKEA suppliers have long-term relationships with the company. They work with product designers to ensure that the retail price target for the product is achievable. The *catalogs, displays, and labels* activity supports the themes of *limited customer service* and *self-selection by customers*. It also supports the *limited staffing* activity, replacing personnel with printed information on products.

Porter holds that the links between activities and choices lead to strategic "fit." This fit creates and sustains competitive advantage. Consistency between numerous complementary activities is harder to duplicate than copying a single activity, making competitive copies difficult to implement given IKEA's long head start.

There are three types of fit. First-order strategic fit means direct support or *simple consistency*. Eliminating design frills is an example of first-order fit in meeting IKEA's cost objectives. Strategic fit of the second order is demonstrated when activities reinforce each other. *Suburban locations/ample parking* supports *high-traffic store layout* and *self-transport by customers* because both of these activities require ample

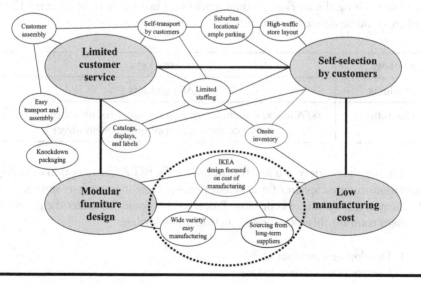

**Figure 13.4  Activities and links.**

parking space. IKEA's low costs draw many customers; they will require parking spaces while shopping. Additionally, the same customers use their vehicles to haul away their purchases.

Third-order fit is what Porter calls "optimization of effort." Establishing long-term relationships with manufacturing suppliers is an example. With the building of a relationship, IKEA creates the environment for the collaboration needed to make product functionality and design trade-offs. This harmonizes the product and manufacturing strategies along the supply chain and results in the best-designed products for the customer at retail. Achieving this third-order fit is particularly important to supply chain designers because optimization of effort among trading partners is an ultimate supply chain management objective.

## 13.2 Enabling Spheres and Supply Chain Processes

This section extends the activity system methodology to support processes needed to implement company goals at the retail level. Figure 13.1 shows that the activity system should be supported by needed processes under each activity. These will likely exist in a mature company but need to be created in a startup. The processes may be perfectly fine as they exist. More likely, they will have to be modified to fit with a new strategy.

At this point, it may be useful to set up operations-centric, or enabling, spheres for process improvement. A dotted line in Figure 13.4 encircles a group of activities in the IKEA activity system suitable for combined implementation. This sphere would be especially important as a multicompany effort involving IKEA and its suppliers. Using the market–product–operations taxonomy from Chapter 12, the sphere could be defined as follows:

| Markets | All markets |
|---|---|
| Products | All products |
| Operations | IKEA marketing, new product design, procurement, product cost accounting; supplier representatives |

For the wide variety of home furnishing it sells, IKEA has an option of multiple operations-focused spheres for different product categories, such as storage items, kitchenware, or furniture collection. Processes that could fall under the purview of a design team for this sphere could include the following:

1. Develop new product ideas
2. Prepare new product designs
3. Perform market research

4. Source materials from suppliers
5. Gather process costs from suppliers
6. Prepare design templates for product categories
7. Work with suppliers to implement new production processes
8. Coordinate packaging development
9. Prepare catalog, display, and label information
10. Forecast sales; suggest inventory levels

Note that this would be a cross-functional team, one designed to speed new product introductions to retail markets. Should this construct take on a "category manager" flavor, the product portion of the sphere definition would be one of the categories. For furniture maker IKEA, one product-centric sphere definition scheme could address living room, bedroom, kitchen, and so forth. Another could be table, chairs, desks, utensils, and so forth, or the types of categories previously cited.

## 13.3 Defining Processes

To define processes in a traditional supply chain setting, we return to the Wal-Mart example in Chapter 12. That example is the Remix program that splits Wal-Mart distribution between warehouses for standard fare and those for fast-moving items. The purpose is to ensure that fast-moving products are always on store shelves, reduce stockouts, and avoid wasted time of store workers who must sort through fast-moving and slow-moving merchandise as shipments arrive. This product-centric sphere was defined in Chapter 12 as follows: all markets/fast-moving products/selected high-velocity warehouses and supporting organization, systems, and processes.

Creating this sphere reflects the fact that Wal-Mart, and other retailers no doubt, must handle at least two types of products, if not more. The first business handles the routine medium- and low-volume products. For most retailers, legacy processes are built to satisfy the needs of the average product—an example of a one-size-fits-all supply chain. Wal-Mart has achieved distribution success and volume growth in the past by streamlining these procedures. However, such supply chains are too slow for fast-moving products, as Wal-Mart has come to understand. Its reaction was not to tinker with existing slow processes but to supplant those processes entirely for its high-volume products.

Note that Remix is not only for high-value items. Many of these products may indeed be low-price, low-margin items, but customers buy them in large quantities. Toilet paper, detergent, and paper towels are examples; customers buy one or more of these items every time they go to the store. The absence of these items from shelves causes shoppers who want these items to go to competitors for satisfaction of these needs, taking their other business with them. Therefore, avoiding stockouts in these high-volume categories is exceedingly important.

Figure 13.5 depicts a possible Remix activity system. This example could apply to Wal-Mart or others seeking to develop a sphere for high-velocity retail products. In fact, the fundamental choice is to abandon the one-size-fits-all approach in favor of one that addresses distribution for the high-volume product group in a fundamentally different way. This activity system also employs four choices, or themes:

1. Dedicated warehouses (distribution centers or DCs)—for a selected subset of high-volume products that need to be in stock at all times.
2. Frequent replenishment—to ensure cost-effective supply. This requires OEM suppliers to deliver frequently to lower inventory, quickly adjust to demand fluctuations, ensure supply, and facilitate cross-dock handling. It also encompasses frequent store replenishment through continuous fixed-interval replenishment schedules.
3. Coordinated delivery scheduling—to synchronize store, DC, and transportation schedules so that high-volume items arrive at stores at the most convenient and feasible time.
4. Expedited shelf stocking—by removing the work required to handle selected stock-keeping units (SKUs) and separate delivery of high-volume items.

Figure 13.5 shows 11 supporting activities. Table 13.1 groups these, identifies the fit order (first, second, third) of the activity, and provides descriptions or processes associated with each activity. Table 13.1's grouping points to the multifunctional nature of activities in this sphere. Not only must several internal departments be involved, but also, the contracting activity, in particular, must draw in OEM and transportation providers to collaborate on implementation. In Wal-Mart's case, transportation providers can include Wal-Mart's own fleet as well as those of contracted companies.

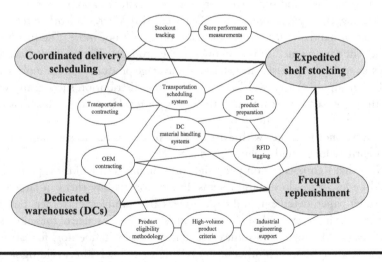

**Figure 13.5   Remix activity system.**

**Table 13.1  Wal-Mart Remix Activities and Processes**

| # | Activity | Fit Order[a] | Description/Processes |
|---|----------|-----------|----------------------|
| **Contracting Functions** | | | |
| 1 | OEM contracting | Third | Write contracts to coordinate operations. Provide RFID tags at item, pallet, or container level. Establish transportation interface. Purchase high-volume items from OEM suppliers. |
| 2 | Transportation contracting | Third | Contract for frequency/cost of deliveries. Establish scheduling methods for store delivery that minimizes disruptions. |
| **Product Selection Functions** | | | |
| 3 | Industrial engineering support | Third | Minimize total cost. Adjust product eligibility criteria. Perform warehousing, transportation network design. |
| 4 | Fast-product criteria | First | Provide yardsticks/tests for selecting SKUs for fast-track inclusion. |
| 5 | Product eligibility methodology | Second | Maintain product list by store. Include assignment of store–SKU combinations to selected high-volume DCs. |
| **Operating Functions** | | | |
| 6 | DC material-handling systems | Second | Design and equip DCs with racks, conveyors, docks, and equipment to move stock quickly. |
| 7 | DC product preparation | First | Get agreement on SKU-specific configurations for products to be delivered to stores. |
| 8 | RFID tagging | First | Define SKU-specific requirements for RFID to speed processing along the supply chain. |
| 9 | Transportation scheduling system | Third | Coordinate OEM, DC, and store schedules. Optimize to the extent possible. |

*(Continued)*

**Table 13.1 (Continued)   Wal-Mart Remix Activities and Processes**

| # | Activity | Fit Order[a] | Description/Processes |
|---|----------|-----------|----------------------|
| **Control Functions** | | | |
| 10 | Stockout tracking | Second | Flag candidate SKUs. Test criteria; maintain list of high-volume items. |
| 11 | Store measurements | First | Design and measure parameters that confirm effectiveness such as store profitability, market share, stockout history, and sales of high-volume SKUs. |

*Note:* DC = distribution center; OEM = original equipment manufacturer; RFID = radio-frequency identification; SKU = stock-keeping unit.

[a] First-order fit is *simple consistence*, second-order fit is *reinforcing* other activities, and third-order fit is *optimization of effort*.

The fit column indicates the nature of the fit: first order is simple consistency; second order is reinforcing of other activities, and third order is overall optimization of effort. Certainly, both contracting activities (#1 and #2 in Table 13.1) seek to set ground rules for trading partner coordination. Industrial engineering support (#3) is a service for all the processes. Its most visible impact is felt in determining which SKU–store combinations should be included in the Remix program. The transportation scheduling system (#9) orchestrates the activities of the various parties (DC, store, and transportation provider).

## 13.4 Activity Systems and Process Definition—Summary

Many supply chain improvement projects fall short of expectations because participants have no road map. Such a road map will identify the need and set criteria for operating processes. The activity system structure provides such a road map. This will improve the chances that the linkages between strategy and operations are strong, with no needed supply chain process omitted from the design.

## References

1. W. Chan Kim and Renée Mauborgne, *Blue Ocean Strategy*, Boston: Harvard Business School Press, 2005.
2. Porter, Michael E., "What is Strategy?" *Harvard Business Review*, (74/6) November–December, 1996. pp. 61–78.

# Chapter 14

# Retail Supply Chain Management— Skills Required

Management skills are key to implementing changes to retail supply chains. Effective retail supply chain management (SCM) requires abilities ranging from strategy making to operating processes improvement. This is counter to the mindset in many organizations that retail SCM is limited in scope, confined to either procurement or physical distribution. That limited view sees SCM having a role in controlling costs but no role in improving strategic position. Therefore, a retailer's merchants and store management are left to plan and implement strategy without input from those managing the supply chain for products.

The examples in Chapters 12 and 13 illustrate the challenges to including SCM as an important contributor to successful strategy. For example, IKEA built its current business model over decades and, in so doing, refined its supply chain operations as a part of long-term processes. But companies in today's fast-moving competitive environments do not have the luxury of extended schedules. Competitive forces and the globalization of markets make strategic change a continuous necessity.

The Retail Industry Leaders Association 2016 sixth annual study, "The State of the Retail Supply Chain," details the burning SCM management issues of the day.[1] Although 2015 sales growth was unexciting, online retailing and the continuing pressure to move to omnichannel retailing and distribution was responsible for the need for significant changes in retail SCM.

In the past year, "Amazon captured 51 cents of every additional dollar spent online during 2015 and is reportedly taking steps to build its own delivery capabilities. Walmart poured an estimated $900 million into e-commerce technology and fulfillment centers. And India is quickly becoming the new e-commerce battleground for global retailers."[2] Further complicating the flat sales scene were rising delivery costs and festering online competition. Interestingly, omnichannel selling appears to require a fast-enlarging set of deliver-from locations.

Previously, decision making around SCM moved at a leisurely pace, but current strategizing requires real-time, hands-on rapid decision making by managers, complicated by the ever-growing Amazon behemoth. The goal is to support consumer demand from anywhere in the supply chain rapidly and economically. For many, this infrastructure–demand alignment calls for building out fulfillment networks, improving infrastructure utilization through increased automation, and leveraging brick-and-mortar stores as distribution points in numerous ways. Emphasis is on four major omnichannel SCM initiatives:

1. Improving the speed of fulfillment while holding down costs.
2. Utilizing the supply chain as a revenue driver through home order delivery, reducing order cycle time, and utilizing returns processes as a sales driver. Objectives include improving the customer experience and providing faster deliveries.
3. Synchronizing stock-keeping unit (SKU) placement around demand or making sure inventories are placed in such a way that delivery to the customer is optimized at lowest cost.
4. Managing change by encouraging creative process development and obtaining buy-in from employees previously steeped in outdated processes. In other words, planned changes are only as effective as they are implemented by human beings.

Defining and building activity systems requires the management capabilities described in this chapter. These are broad skills calling for both right-brain, or aesthetic, intuitive capabilities and left-brain, or logical, analytical capabilities. Although using some left-brain input, right-brain skills are heavily brought to bear in merchandise selection, store decoration, advertising, and the sales process. Left-brain skills are needed in the back office—to move the product around, locate stores, stock the shelves, and track money. In developing and implementing retail supply chain strategies, both are needed.

According to the *Wall Street Journal*, the retail industry has been long on the right-brain skills, coming up short on the left-brain side.[3] The article notes that many retail executives have made decisions based on instinct rather than analysis. The advent of computers has brought about significant movement toward analytical management. A traditional hiring solution for companies such as Coach and Limited Brands, Ltd., and many retailers has been to look for candidates with highly developed analytical skills graduating from business schools.

# 14.1 Five Tasks for SCM Excellence

Although the need for skills is recognized, the right- and the left-brain perspectives often conflict. There is a need for tools and processes to bring them together, such as those described in this book. The work of implementing effective supply chain change is carried out by way of five management tasks. Table 14.1 defines the five tasks and lists retail supply chain functions involved in each.

No matter where a company is along the supply chain, a strategy to compete is needed, whether it be for retailers that sell to consumers, distributors, service providers, original equipment manufacturers (OEMs), or second-tier suppliers. Each of these supply chain players must have access to strategy-making skills to remain competitive. Figure 14.1 shows the relationships between the retail SCM tasks. The format is a phased-project Gantt chart displaying the sequence in which the tasks are performed. Task 1 strategy development begins the process in phase 1. Deliverables include sphere definitions and activity systems for each sphere as described in Chapters 12 and 13. These also produce the requirements for collaboration to achieve internal alignment and collaborative partnerships with principal trading partners.

Phases 2 and 3 bring internal alignment (task 2) followed by alignment with trading partners (task 3). Tasks 4 and 5 address process development or improvements to existing processes.

These tasks will likely rely on new information technology (task 4) and other process development approaches (task 5). An important goal is to achieve the benefits of the *demand-driven supply chain*, which uses actual demand rather than forecasts to manage production. Tasks 4 and 5 must be tied together to avoid implementing technology for its own sake. Investments in technology must be justified in terms of process changes that result in better customer service or a greater return on investment or both. Once a strategy is in place, the feedback loops shown in Figure 14.1 trigger continuous improvement to upgrade the strategy and the processes.

**Table 14.1  Five Retail SCM Tasks**

| | Task | Description | Retail Functions Involved |
|---|---|---|---|
| 1 | Designing supply chains for strategic advantage | Competitive success requires supply chain innovation. Supply chain designs must support company and business partner strategies for competing. | Senior management functions, merchandise management groups, marketing, sales, category managers, senior financial executives |
| 2 | Implementing collaborative relationships | Internal organization structure, responsibilities, and measures enable supply chain innovation. The task covers relationships and communication inside the organization that are needed to implement processes that cross department boundaries. | Functional managers from operations, marketing, and sales; direct reports to chief executive; financial management; information systems |
| 3 | Forging supply chain partnerships | Outside partners are needed to be successful. Old paradigms must be discarded. Implementation requires an organized, multicompany project approach. | Merchandising, procurement, sourcing, and operations |
| 4 | Managing supply chain information | Opportunities to succeed wildly or fail miserably abound. Information systems must support supply chain processes that are embedded in activity systems. | Process teams from affected departments, information technology, finance staff |
| 5 | Removing cost from the supply chain | Effective change initiatives to improve service and reduce cost require understanding and managing root causes of cost in supply chain processes. | |

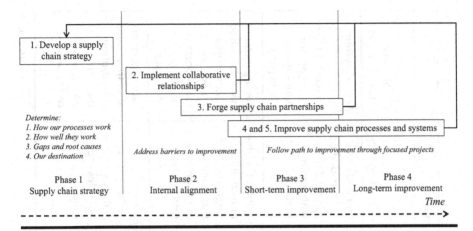

**Figure 14.1    Project plan for executing retail SCM tasks.**

## 14.2  Assessing Retail SCM Skills

Before embarking on the design and implementation of a supply chain strategy, a management team should understand its competence and capabilities to perform the five SCM tasks. Because retailers stand at the end of the supply chain, it is particularly important that they take a look at not only their own company abilities but also those of its supply chain partners. The maturity matrix in Table 14.2 describes a tool for this purpose. It shows levels of management capability with respect to the five tasks. The team can readily identify a position on the matrix from the descriptions in each cell.

An assessment using the matrix should be a two-step process. First, it should address the current state of practice in the company. This effort addresses the question of whether current supply chain processes support existing strategies. It can be called the "as-is" level of maturity. The assessment may also show that little in the way of SCM practice even exists.

Second, the matrix can assess company capability. Dimensions of capability include the capabilities of management team members, the willingness to change, the urgency for action, and the presence of the resources needed to implement change. The resources include capital and the time required to make changes. For example, current practice for *task 1: designing supply chains for strategic advantage* may be level I: dysfunctional. But a newly hired management team may be capable of achieving level III or level IV practice.

Chapter 13 developed two activity systems—one for IKEA and the other for the Wal-Mart Remix program. Table 14.3 illustrates the importance of having a "full quiver" of capabilities in implementing a new, or refining an existing, activity system. The table lists some of the elements of the IKEA and Remix activity

**Table 14.2  Levels of Retail SCM Capability**

| | | | Stages of Retail SCM Capability | | | |
|---|---|---|---|---|---|---|
| Task | Name | I Dysfunctional | II Infrastructure | III Cost Reduction | IV Collaboration | V Strategic Contribution |
| 1 | Designing supply chains for strategic advantage | No strategy exists to guide the implementation of supply chain designs. | Some supply chain awareness. Managers view the company as stand-alone. | Supply chain processes viewed as a nonstrategic, one-size-fits-all supply chain. | Joint initiatives are pursued on a limited basis with trading partners. | Activity systems are implemented in collaboration with supply chain partners. |
| 2 | Implementing collaborative relationships | Internal measures, goals, and objectives don't acknowledge the need for supply chain excellence. | Organization is functionally focused. Initiatives are departmental and limited to the company. | Internal cross-functional initiatives that focus on cost reduction are chartered. | Supply chain has moved into a single function that manages multicompany relationships. | The organization has established multicompany infrastructure for important supply chain processes. |
| 3 | Forging supply chain partnerships | Relationships with suppliers and customers are arm's length at best, antagonistic at worst. | Collaboration up and down the supply chain is limited to transaction data. | Efforts are limited to supplier initiatives focused on cost reduction, not revenue increases. | Partners collaborate on activity systems, but roles are static. | Trading partners alter their value contributions through transfers of responsibility. |

*(Continued)*

**Table 14.2 (Continued)   Levels of Retail SCM Capability**

|  | | Stages of Retail SCM Capability | | | | |
|---|---|---|---|---|---|---|
| Task | Name | *I* *Dysfunctional* | *II* *Infrastructure* | *III* *Cost Reduction* | *IV* *Collaboration* | *V* *Strategic Contribution* |
| 4 | Managing supply chain information | Information needed for decision making is missing, not timely, or inaccurate. | Technology improvements focus on individual departments. | Systems efforts support cost reduction within the organization. | Two-way information exchange supports transactions and mutual decision making. | Appropriate level of technology is integrated into supply chain activity systems and processes. |
| 5 | Removing cost from the supply chain | Cost reduction and process improvement is a hit-and-miss affair. Efforts may hurt more than help. | Reductions are internal and tracked by department budgets. Customer service not addressed. | Cost reduction efforts cross departments but are limited to internal efforts. | Multicompany cost reduction is limited to logistics, purchasing, and other operating costs. | Cost reduction across the supply chain is the target. Benefits are shared among key trading partners. |

**Table 14.3 Implementing Case Study Activity Systems—Retail SCM Skills Required**

| | Retail SCM Management Tasks | | | | | |
|---|---|---|---|---|---|---|
| 1 | Designing supply chains for strategic advantage | | | | | |
| 2 | Implementing collaborative relationships | | | | | |
| 3 | Forging supply chain partnerships | | | | | |
| 4 | Managing supply chain information | | | | | |
| 5 | Removing cost from the supply chain | | | | | |
| *Activities Requiring Retail SCM Skills* | *1* | *2* | *3* | *4* | *5* | *Likely Barriers* |
| **IKEA Activity System** | | | | | | |
| IKEA design focused on cost of manufacturing | • | • | • | | • | Trade-offs between design and cost. Need to cooperate with suppliers. |
| Sourcing from long-term suppliers | • | | • | | | Developing and maintaining lasting relationships. Building trust. |
| On-site inventory | | | | | • | Forecasting correct amounts. Providing timely replenishment. |
| Knockdown packaging | | | • | | • | Product configuration and packaging design. |
| Suburban locations/ ample parking | | • | | | | Agreement on attractive sites. |
| Limited staffing | | | | | • | Developing substitutes for staff while providing adequate service. |
| **Wal-Mart Remix Activity System** | | | | | | |
| Industrial engineering support | • | | | • | • | Finding skilled people to execute strategy who understand operations. |
| Product eligibility methodology | | • | | | • | Agreeing to criteria/items selected for high-volume distribution process. |

*(Continued)*

**Table 14.3 (Continued)   Implementing Case Study Activity Systems—Retail SCM Skills Required**

| Activities Requiring Retail SCM Skills | 1 | 2 | 3 | 4 | 5 | Likely Barriers |
|---|---|---|---|---|---|---|
| OEM contracting | | | • | | • | Coordinating deliveries and format with suppliers. |
| Transportation contracting | | | • | | • | Coordinating operations and making trade-offs with transporters. |
| Transportation scheduling system | | | | • | • | Developing and maintaining system. Contingency planning. |
| Distribution center material handling system | | | | • | • | Equipment decisions. Technical design. Use of technology. |
| Radio-frequency identification (RFID) tagging | | | | • | • | Cost to suppliers. Benefit identification. How deployed—item, pallet, etc. |
| Stockout tracking | | | | • | | Definitions. Accuracy of information. |
| Store performance measurements | | • | | • | • | Store/management agreement. Data collection and presentation. |

systems and their requirements for retail SCM skills. The table also describes barriers to success that might be encountered during implementation. Skill at the retail SCM task will help navigate the barriers.

Retail enterprise planners should evaluate their strategic plans by listing the barriers to implementation. This effort could also lead to an introspective review of enterprise talents. Hiring people with new skills or commissioning consultants can fill gaps.

The RILA Supply Chain Report identified for 2017 three major areas that are expected to lead to best-in-class performance.[4]

1. Demand planning finesse: includes forecast accuracy, peak period demand prediction, promotional demand anticipation, omnichannel plans by channel, and SCM execution.
2. Store-based fulfillment consistency
   a. Options for online order fulfillment
      i. Store pickup by customer
      ii. Shipped from store

        iii. Integrated fulfillment center

        iv. Drop-shipped from vendor

   b. Balance online against needs of in-store customer; avoid in-store stock-outs or oversupply

3. Customer returns dexterity

   a. Often treated like poor stepchild and not planned.

   b. Return costs include both time and money. Timeliness affects the resalability of returned products.

   c. Major returns activities to be managed include authorization, in-store handling, decisions and execution relating to disposal, moving goods out of the store, returns to vendors, and utilizing returns metrics to improve performance.

## 14.3 SCM Skills—Summary

This chapter is meant to link supply chain design with the need for skills to implement the design. Too often, functions with the "supply chain" are relegated to narrow functions—procurement, merchandising, and distribution are examples. But the retail SCM discipline of today calls for far broader perspectives. The success stories in retail SCM are founded on unique hard-to-copy processes that are well designed and executed and reflect the changing conditions of the industry. This is no simple task in the competitive omnichannel retail market place; acquiring new skills is essential.

## References

1. Gibson, Brian J., Defee, C. Clifford, and Ishfaq, Rafay, "The State of the Retail Supply Chain: Essential Findings of the Sixth Annual Study," Auburn University Center for Supply Chain Motivation in Conjunction with Retail Industry Leaders Association, 2016.
2. Ibid.
3. Clark, "Monica, More Retailers Shop Business Schools for Talent," *The Wall Street Journal*, September 18, 2006, p. B4.
4. Ibid.

# RETAIL SUPPLY CHAIN PROCESS IMPROVEMENT

Section IV describes initiatives to improve supply chain processes, utilizing both right- and left-brained techniques for tracking products along the retail supply chain.

| # | Chapter Name |
|---|---|
| 15 | Organizing to Improve Retail Supply Chain Performance |
| 16 | Collaboration with Supply Chain Partners |
| 17 | Demand-Driven Supply Chain |
| 18 | Product Tracking along Retail Supply Chains |

The West Marine case in Chapter 15 describes one retailer's effort at collaborating with its trading partners. The company based their change process on Collaborative Planning, Forecasting, and Replenishment (CPFR), an industry blueprint for collaboration. CPFR and other collaboration models are described in this chapter.

Chapter 16 illustrates trends toward fewer but better trading partners. One step in this direction is classifying partnership types, whether the combination takes the form of an informal agreement, written contracts, or an outright merger. Core competencies of the potential partners are addressed because the decision to partner requires definition of what core competencies need protection for the partnership to survive.

Chapter 17 addresses the need for sales estimates to be more demand driven than customary forecasting employs and explains why "pull" from sales generates more precise inventory planning data. The chapter makes suggestions about how to achieve conversion to demand-driven decision making and using actual demand, not forecasts, as the basis for replenishment decisions.

Transformative technology has vastly expanded retailers' strategy options. Chapter 18 describes some of the technologies that have driven this revolution in capability and practice. Technologies used to track goods along the supply chain, including bar codes and radio-frequency identification (RFID), are discussed.

# Chapter 15

# Organizing to Improve Retail Supply Chain Performance

Chapter 14 described the implications of activity system design for acquiring management skills to improve competitive position. The current chapter describes the issues faced in aligning those skills to design and implement needed changes in a retailer's supply chain. Many of the activities described in this chapter will occur in phase 2 (internal alignment) of our project management timeline shown in Figure 14.1. These activities call for skills in task 2 of our SCM skill set (implement collaborative relationships). The collaborative relationships discussed here are those inside the organization—particularly across departments. Chapter 16 describes issues related to extending the strategy *across* company boundaries to trading partners. Trading partners in the retail supply chain include retailers themselves, distributors, transportation and other service companies, product manufacturers, or original equipment manufacturers (OEMs), and the OEMs' second-tier manufacturing suppliers.

Figure 15.1 is a framework for designing a supply chain strategy as part of phase 1 (develop a supply chain strategy) of Figure 14.1. The model starts with the *as-is* in the lower left-hand corner. Once the as-is documentation is complete, an improvement team can produce an evaluation of the as-is and develop a vision for the future, the *to-be* destination. *Barriers* are inevitable along the *pathway* to the destination. Pathway projects, in circles, are of two types—internal (gray circles) and external (white circles). Internal projects are those the company undertakes independently; the external projects are those requiring the cooperation of trading partners. Performing such an analysis is an important step in achieving internal alignment for implementing change.

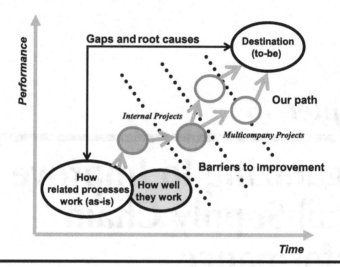

**Figure 15.1 Model for implementing supply chain change.**

Some reengineering practitioners may reject the idea of working from the as-is. This philosophy rejects the as-is-existing situation in favor of a "start-from-scratch" approach. The authors and others argue for documenting the as-is for many reasons. One article, in describing tools for Lean manufacturing, states the case well.[1]

- You will understand not only "what" but also "why"—the root causes—processes need improving. Documenting only the results of the current situation does not provide these insights.
- Mapping processes collectively leads to shared insights.
- Direct observation is a valuable skill that is embellished by the process.
- The current state is a "gold mine" in terms of insights about past experiments and failures.
- You identify and gain understanding of mistakes you are currently making.
- You must be doing something right, or you wouldn't be in business. You'll want to retain process features that are working.
- You need an understanding of the existing situation to create the necessary "tension" to move the change process forward.

This list should be kept in mind if there is a temptation to shortcut the processes recommended in Figure 15.1 by passing the as-is step.

## 15.1 West Marine Case

This chapter relies on a case study of retailer West Marine to illustrate approaches to working with trading partners and achieving internal alignments.[2] This is one of the companies that illustrates the range of retailer types in Chapter 3. The use of the case here is not intended to promote the West Marine solution for every retailer. Even though the case describes a retailer's perspective, it will help manufacturers, distributors, and third-party service providers understand issues faced by their retail customers. Other retailers are likely to take steps similar to those adopted by West Marine. Also, many retailers, including West Marine, are in a strong position with regard to their suppliers and can effectively dictate the direction suppliers must take if they want to retain the retailer's business.

Business schools work with companies in developing case studies for teaching purposes. Lyn Denend authored the West Marine case, published in April 2005, under the supervision of Dr. Hau Lee of the Stanford Business School, an authority on supply chain management. The case illustrates challenges in a marine supply retail business and describes one retailer's path toward solving these problems. Through Larry Smith, Senior Vice President, Planning and Replenishment, West Marine has also been active in the VICS CPFR (Collaborative Planning, Forecasting, and Replenishment) Committee, which sponsors the CPFR®* initiative. West Marine implemented CPFR as part of its solution. Smith also updated the West Marine story in a related article, which was also a source for this chapter.[3]

Figure 15.2 is a West Marine timeline annotated with data available from the case and the company. West Marine was founded in 1968 with a narrow product line and first-year sales by mail order of $32,000; it went public with sales of $123 million in 1993. The company has marketed its products through its stores, via the Internet and catalogs, and through wholesale channels. According to the study, West Marine considered itself a "specialty retailer" and benchmarked itself against companies such as Brookstone and Cost Plus.

The company grew steadily until it acquired a rival, E&B Marine, in 1996—the starting date for our case period (1996—2002) as shown on the timeline. Just prior to the acquisition, West Marine had about $224 million in sales and about 50,000 products. Acquiring E&B, a financially troubled retailer with 63 stores, opened a new market in the powerboat segment. West Marine, with 161 stores, was better known in the sailboat segment.

West Marine runs three types of stores: *standard*, or traditional, stores (8000 sq. ft., 8000–10,000 SKUs [stock keeping units], about $1.5 million in annual sales), *express* stores (2800 sq. ft., 2500 SKUs, $600,000–$800,000), and *megastores* (24,000–30,000 sq. ft., 30,000 SKUs, $10–$15 million). West Marine relies on its own distribution network to stock its stores. Its 250,000-sq.-ft. western distribution center (DC) is in Hollister, California, and was opened in 1996. The 472,000-sq.-ft. Rock Hill, South Carolina, facility was opened in 1998. Today, most merchandise flows through DCs, although the company seeks to increase direct-to-store shipments from its suppliers.

---

* CPFR (Collaborative Planning, Forecasting, and Replenishment) is the registered trademark of the Voluntary Interindustry Commerce Solutions Association, or VICS.

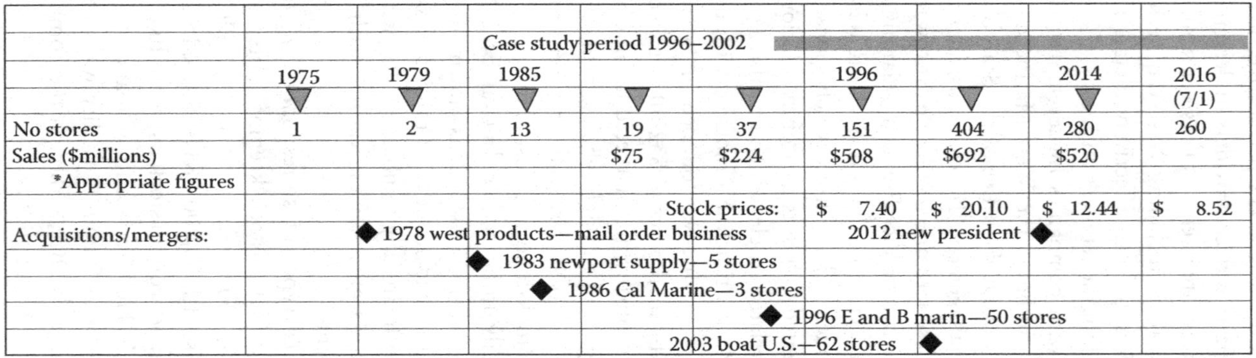

| | 1975 | 1979 | 1985 | Case study period 1996–2002 | | 1996 | | 2014 | 2016 (7/1) |
|---|---|---|---|---|---|---|---|---|---|
| No stores | 1 | 2 | 13 | 19 | 37 | 151 | 404 | 280 | 260 |
| Sales ($millions) | | | | $75 | $224 | $508 | $692 | $520 | |
| *Appropriate figures | | | | | | | | | |
| Stock prices: | | | | | | $ 7.40 | $ 20.10 | $ 12.44 | $ 8.52 |
| Acquisitions/mergers: | | | | | | | | | |

◆ 1978 west products—mail order business

◆ 1983 newport supply—5 stores

◆ 1986 Cal Marine—3 stores

◆ 2003 boat U.S.—62 stores

◆ 1996 E and B marin—50 stores

◆ 2012 new president

**Figure 15.2 West Marine history.**

After the 1996 merger, the company stumbled badly and a turnaround began in 1998 with the hiring of a new CEO, who pursued a strategy that relied heavily on changes to the supply chain. The sections that follow organize data from the case, company reports, and an interview with vice president Larry Smith into tables illustrating the steps in the Figure 15.1 model for implementing change.

## 15.1.1 West Marine As-Is

Table 15.1 describes the supply chain situation that, although not readily apparent at the time of the merger, contributed to West Marine's troubles. These factors were the result of many forces. Industry consolidation, with West Marine fast becoming the leading player, was a symptom of a mature or even declining market. The E&B powerboat business brought new products, suppliers, and customer buying behaviors into the West Marine environment. In particular, the powerboat customer was more price sensitive than the sailing customer. Also, West Marine practices gave customers what they wanted when and where they wanted it, with little sensitivity to the costs of that service. Management mindset reinforced this attitude, and lack of supply chain awareness dulled management senses to the coming crisis.

The last six items (#7 to #12) on the as-is list are symptomatic of operations on the point of breakdown. Many companies in retail supply chains take operations for granted. But when they break for any reason, the penalties are serious. West Marine wanted top-level service and was willing to pay the price in terms of low inventory turnover. So, it was particularly painful when stock availability suffered and lost sales penalties occurred in spite of high inventories. The growth before the E&B merger had been slow enough to be manageable. The size of the E&B operation was more than West Marine could absorb.

In many new companies, the management team comes out of the industry. In the West Marine case, the company served a recreation industry in which many on the management team were active boating enthusiasts and drew their experience from their market space. However, they lacked broader skills. At a larger size, such enthusiasm is not sufficient to ably manage the myriad transactions necessary to serve customers efficiently. The introduction to Chapter 14 describes recent efforts to build managerial skills in retail companies.

## 15.1.2 Evaluation of the As-Is

The evaluation process for the as-is situation of a retailer should use data analysis, benchmarking comparisons, and team sessions to draw conclusions about the current situation. Such conclusions should call attention to the needs for change that should be addressed in designing the to-be destination. One way to format this evaluation is around processes, organization, and systems as shown in Table 15.2. Note the evaluation points to problems in each of the three areas, and some evaluations could apply to more than one category. For example, inbound processing (#4)

**Table 15.1  West Marine As-Is**

| | Supply Chain Features | As-Is Situation Post Merger (1996) |
|---|---|---|
| 1. | Industry trends | Its growth had made West Marine an industry leader. Consolidation was ongoing in the industry, which was also shrinking as boaters left the sport. Among other factors, supply chain problems (cost and availability of supplies) contributed to the decline in boaters. |
| 2. | Customer linkages | The most profitable customers used multiple channels (store, Internet, catalog) to purchase West Marine products. |
| 3. | Service philosophy | West Marine adhered to a high customer service philosophy requiring higher inventories than other retailers. |
| 4. | Seasonality | Large seasonal swings in business levels and product mix were common. West Marine used tailored mailings for warm and cold climates and each customer segment. |
| 5. | Management mindset | At the time of the E&B acquisition, West Marine managers thought of themselves as "boaters first and businessmen second." The consequence was "chaos" and poor financial performance. |
| 6. | Supply chain awareness | There were many supply chain problems, but few managers were aware of the impact of their operating practices on the business. This created a reactive fire-fighting environment. The E&B acquisition aggravated the situation when the number of suppliers increased from 1000 to 1400. |
| 7. | Supplier base | The supplier base was fragmented. Most suppliers were not sophisticated or well capitalized. For example, there were often multiple deliveries for one order, doubling or tripling the handling involved. |
| 8. | Merger impact | The 1996 merger with E&B Marine went smoothly financially. However, infrastructure implementation was rocky. Systems and processes were inadequate to keep all stores stocked. The results were "disastrous" with an 8% sales drop in the first year after the acquisition. |

*(Continued)*

**Table 15.1 (Continued)   West Marine As-Is**

|   | *Supply Chain Features* | *As-Is Situation Post Merger (1996)* |
|---|---|---|
| 9. | Data infrastructure | After the E&B acquisition, data integrity was suspect. Back-end databases were not interfaced between the companies. There was no way to gain an accurate end-to-end understanding of supply chain performance. |
| 10. | Distribution center changes | At about the same time as the acquisition, West Marine shifted from a 70,000-sq.-ft. distribution center (DC) to the nearby, automated 500,000-sq.-ft. facility at Rock Hill to serve its Eastern customers. Employees didn't have the skills to operate the technically advanced facility. |
| 11. | Staff turnover | Turnover at Rock Hill increased to where 1200 people were hired to fill 280 peak-season positions. |
| 12. | Supply chain bottlenecks | Sales levels were increasing at the time of the acquisition. Distribution bottlenecks occurred as incoming and outgoing volumes overwhelmed employees at the Rock Hill DC. Peak season out-of-stocks reached 25%. |

could be interpreted as a process problem as shown or as an organization problem with a gap in internal communications. It would be an organization problem to the extent that performance measures for purchasing encourage overbuying. It is a process problem if the DCs aren't prepared to receive the merchandise.

Some assessments are broad, such as leadership (#5). The evaluation calls for a wide-ranging change in management team skills. On the other hand, internal collaboration (#6) is more specific. It calls for the need for better forecasting methods. In addition, the implication is that, when the forecasts could be improved, they should be shared with the suppliers who need to act on them (#8). Such forecast sharing could improve merchandise availability and lower the supplier's cost by reducing "surprises." The systems group notes the general lack of company ability, not of software, to make it work properly (#9 and #10). This gap includes problems with data accuracy and insufficient technical capabilities.

## 15.1.3  Destination (To-Be)

The West Marine *strategic framework*, or "to-be," included three important components: a vision, strategic performance indicators, and critical success factors. Chief

**Table 15.2 West Marine Evaluation**

|  | Supply Chain Success Factor | As-Is Assessments and Conclusions |
|---|---|---|
| **Processes** | | |
| 1. | Supply chain processes | The company had outgrown its infrastructure. No formal processes existed. New supply chain processes were needed. |
| 2. | Operations planning | The merger was botched from a customer-service viewpoint. West Marine overlooked the advantages of preserving the E&B brand by changing the storefronts. |
| 3. | Supply base | The supply chain was "complex, difficult, and broken" and needed fixing. There were too many vendors for a company with seasonal influx of inventory. Some boating industry vendors in larger companies were "second-class" citizens due to the industry's lower priority. |
| 4. | Inbound processing | Merchandising did not consider supply chain issues in deal-buys with suppliers. This caused unexpected surprises at DCs and disrupted in-process replenishment activities. |
| **Organization** | | |
| 5. | Leadership | A need existed for more business experience on the management team. Going to the next level—from $500 million to $1 billion in sales—required new skills. |
| 6. | Internal collaboration | Supply chain planning and replenishment were disconnected in the merchandising team. Forecasts were considered inaccurate and generally useless. |
| 7. | Cost consciousness | West Marine needed to address culture. Some would "take care of the customer" at any cost. No rules/guidelines existed for day-to-day decision making to implement the principle. |

*(Continued)*

**Table 15.2 (Continued)   West Marine Evaluation**

|    | Supply Chain Success Factor | As-Is Assessments and Conclusions |
|----|------------------------------|-----------------------------------|
| 8. | Supplier communications | There was substandard communication and collaboration with suppliers. Relationships were conducted on a purchase-order-to-purchase-order basis. For example, a product would be added to West Marine's assortment, but no quantity forecasts were given to the supplier, causing shortages, including those associated with promotions. |
| **Systems** | | |
| 9. | Information systems | Although information systems were modern by most standards, they were not being utilized properly, nor could they be reliable without accurate data. |
| 10. | Technical capabilities | West Marine had a "Ferrari" of SCM software but no one who could drive it. Software complexity was beyond organizational capabilities. |

features of the to-be, listed in Table 15.3, provide high-level direction toward improvement. These begin (#1, #2, and #3) with goals setting and establishing accountability for supply chain results. These three reflect a need to restrain West Marine's growth to stem the effect of lost sales that had cut profits from $15 million to $1 million.

The direction relied on processes from the CPFR® initiative, described later in this chapter. CEO Larry Smith had become familiar with CPFR while at Kmart, and turned to the model to help West Marine. At the time of the case, CPFR encompassed nine model processes shown in Table 15.4. These processes guided CPFR users in redesigning their operations. Today's CPFR model, summarized in Figure 15.4, is a circular process that depicts a continuum of processes that build on each other. Process categories include strategy and planning, demand and supply management, execution, and analysis. For additional information, see http://www.vics.org/committees/cpfr/.

One emphasis during this time at West Marine was on improving forecasts. This included defining responsibility for the forecasts, improving their accuracy and relevance, and making the commitment to act upon them. An early West Marine decision was to assume sole and independent responsibility for forecasts and replenishment at the retail level rather than sharing that responsibility with suppliers. In CPFR terms, this is referred to as conventional order management. Other options include sharing the responsibility for order planning/forecasting and

**Table 15.3  West Marine Destination (To-Be)**

|  | Category | To-Be Features |
|---|---|---|
| 1. | Supply chain objectives | Goals, defined by "strategic performance indicators," were set for return on equity (ROE), cash flow, comparative year-to-year sales, earnings, service levels, market share, customer satisfaction, and employee satisfaction. |
| 2. | Critical success factors (CSF) | CSF emphasized efficient execution, best of class SCM, right product assortments at the right place at the right time, strong customer relationship culture to maximize sales and profits, effective marketing strategy, and motivated professional associates. |
| 3. | Responsibilities | Individual leaders defined tactics for their functions to deliver the results. Formal reports tracked progress toward goals. |
| 4. | Phased growth | To avert crisis, West Marine halted store expansion in order to stabilize the supply chain. |
| 5. | Visibility | To get relief from firefighting, the company focused on achieving end-to-end visibility and increased collaboration between inside functions and with suppliers. |
| 6. | Shared forecast role | West Marine adopted CPFR processes to align internally and with suppliers. The heart of CPFR was the shared forecast. Features included exception management, performance measures, monetized risk, and incentives to collaborate. |
| 7. | Supply chain synchronization | West Marine synchronized its purchasing cycle with the manufacturers' production cycles. This enabled "make-to-demand" or demand-driven decision making. It also reduced the need for manufacturer finished goods inventories. |

order generation with suppliers. The conventional choice was based on the belief that the buyer was best suited to generate and own the forecast.[3]

## 15.1.4 Barriers to Success

Realism about barriers and addressing them improves the chances of success. *Barriers* are defined in this book as environmental factors. A *constraint* is a limitation on actions that can be taken. An example of a constraint could be a decision

**Table 15.4   CPFR Processes (at Time of Case)**

| Planning | Develop front-end agreements |
|---|---|
| | Create joint business plan |
| Forecasting | Create sales forecast |
| | Identify exceptions for sales forecast |
| | Resolve/collaborate on exception items |
| | Create order forecast |
| | Identify exceptions for order forecast |
| | Resolve/collaborate on exception items |
| Replenishment | Generate orders |

to stay in a location because of a long-term lease or a limit on money available to implement a plan. For example, one constraint enacted by West Marine management was that internal transfers of personnel should satisfy new organization roles, not headcount increases.

As West Marine progressed, it encountered barriers. Table 15.5 lists several. The first three are internal to the firm and are likely to exist in any organization. They are defensiveness, cross-department cooperation, and internal opposition. West

**Table 15.5   Barriers to Success**

| | *Barrier Type* | *Barrier Description* |
|---|---|---|
| 1. | Defensiveness | As West Marine struggled, improvement teams were less inclined to share issues, challenges, and needs across organizational boundaries. |
| 2. | Cross-department cooperation | The changes required four executives to collaborate to make improvements, including merchandising, planning and replenishment, distribution, and information systems. |
| 3. | Internal opposition | A CPFR pilot met with mixed enthusiasm internally. Results won many over, but others chafed at the rules and structure. |
| 4. | Supplier reluctance | West Marine had to continuously sell CPFR to suppliers. Many suppliers didn't believe the benefits were worth the price. Some vendors argued over performance metric relevancy and accuracy. |

Marine was challenged to restore its financial vitality, and the pressures that arose caused the team to collaborate less when the need existed to collaborate more. This could have been the result of increased requirements for accountability and the accompanying performance measures that were implemented.

Success also depended upon the cooperation of four departments that needed to cooperate—merchandising, planning and replenishment, distribution, and information systems. Lack of coordination was an obstacle to success. Because applying CPFR processes changed the way people had to work, "push back" occurred in the early stages. However, successes begat enthusiasm among those who could see the results.

The last barrier listed (#4) was supplier reluctance to collaborate with West Marine. The CPFR processes included regular communications and updates between entities. Also, information technology solutions encouraged suppliers to make their systems compatible with the West Marine forecast formats. As with any measurements, those individuals being measured disputed the relevancy and accuracy of the metrics, resulting in additional communications challenges.

## 15.1.5 Pathway to Change

Table 15.6 details important components of the West Marine solution to the situation generated by the E&B merger. Larry Smith summarized the collective impact of the changes.

- The West Marine supply chain was converted from supplier-driven push to demand-driven pull.
- Forecast accuracy increased to 85%; on-time shipments to 80%.
- CPFR has extended to 200 suppliers and 20,000 items, representing 90% of the procurement spend.
- West Marine was able to effectively incorporate another purchase—of rival BoatU.S.—in 2003. The BoatU.S. DC was integrated in 30 days, and in-store systems in 60 days.

Internal collaboration, the subject of this chapter, was the key to West Marine's successful recovery. Figure 15.3 displays departmental accountabilities that resulted from the implementation (#9 in Table 15.6). The figure is an example of a tool for presenting as-is and to-be organization responsibilities. Across the top are the supply chain processes West Marine relies on. Down the left are the positions that participate in each process. One enhancement is, when applicable, to show how, not just whether, the position participates in the process. Common modes of participation include *accountable* (has decision-making authority), *responsible* (completes certain processes), *consulted* (provides input), and *informed* (receives progress reports).

Chapter 17 describes the migration from the forecast-driven to the demand-driven supply chain. In the demand-driven supply chain, decisions are based on actual end-user demand rather than forecasts. West Marine claims to have displaced

**Table 15.6  Pathway**

|  | Project Type | Implementation Subprojects |
|---|---|---|
| **Internally Focused Changes** | | |
| 1. | Departmental alignment | The CEO addressed multidepartment processes to plan the transition and demanded joint accountability. He did not tolerate silo mentalities. |
| 2. | Culture change | West Marine brought in an expert in culture change who redefined roles and refocused employees on their jobs. |
| 3. | Communication | The company sought to open lines of communication with cross-functional meetings and project teams. It encouraged mutual responsibility among departments for cross-functional metrics. |
| 4. | Supply chain role | West Marine assumed responsibility for the forecasting process, including order planning and order generating. It also committed to buy any order they forecasted seeking to eliminate bullwhips along the supply chain. The initiative required one scalable systems platform, not multiple incompatible ones. |
| 5. | Technology choices | West Marine adopted a suite of applications from JDA Software Group Ltd.—Merchandise Management System, POS, and Warehouse Management System. |
| 6. | Integration | The company started to codevelop a multi-echelon solution with JDA that integrated store and warehouse replenishment. This would free time to work with suppliers rather than reconciling data. The company ended up developing a custom solution. It claims it is one of the first in the retail industry. |
| 7. | Forecast methodology | West Marine forecast components included base annual forecasts, seasonal selling curves (profiles), ranking or service level for items by importance, and demand from DCs for items that West Marine did not stock. These changes enabled accurate 52-week forecasts of supplier orders with little manual intervention. Other factors were seasonal geographic profiles, product rank, and scheduled promotions. The forecasts were updated every 24 hours as timeliness was a key to accuracy. |

*(Continued)*

**Table 15.6 (Continued)  Pathway**

|   | *Project Type* | *Implementation Subprojects* |
|---|---|---|
| 8. | Data integrity and consistency | Data cleanup effort included shipping quantities, case pack quantities, and other data needed for reducing errors. The effort matched store quantities with DC quantities and set rules on authorizing changes. |
| 9. | Merchandising, planning, and replenishment | Organization changes included reorganization and definition of roles of between merchandising and planning and replenishment. The company deployed a category management approach for 24 distinct product clusters. There is a category manager (CM) and assistant category manager for each. A collocated merchandise planner and a replenishment analyst were added to each team. CMs decided what to sell in which channels and negotiated vendor agreements. Merchandise planners acted as "supply chain captains" cutting POs, monitoring shipments and fill rates, and coordinating from the supplier to the DC. The replenishment analyst worked to get the merchandise from the DC to the store—monitoring forecasts, ensuring stores received products, and managing special requests. |
| 10. | Store operations | Teams worked with assortment planning (part of the planning and replenishment department), visual merchandising, and marketing. Assortment planning assured that each store had the right mix. Visual Merchandising used planograms to locate each store's assortment and provide consistency between stores. |
| 11. | DC labor | West Marine developed work standards in the warehouse to improve labor productivity. |
| 12. | Space and shipping efficiencies | The warehouses used technology to document the dimensions and weight to manage storage space in the warehouse. This also enabled filling cartons to fully utilize shipping space through standard packaging. |

*(Continued)*

**Table 15.6 (Continued)   Pathway**

|  | *Project Type* | *Implementation Subprojects* |
|---|---|---|
| **Externally Focused Changes** | | |
| 13. | EDI (electronic data interchange) | West Marine implemented EDI to standardize electronic transfer of information. EDI coverage included purchase orders, invoices, and shipment notifications. Use of EDI by suppliers was requested, not demanded. The EDI increased visibility of inbound inventory liability and suppliers' performance. |
| 14. | CPFR pilot test | The company initiated CPFR pilot following structural, process, and information system changes, picking 12 suppliers. West Marine spelled out goals and expected performance levels and required no investments by the vendors. Each had to designate someone in the organization to deal with supply chain captains. |
| 15. | Supply base deployment | The deployment consisted of weekly forecast sharing. It also required vendors to provide weekly performance updates and participate in monthly status meetings with team and vendor representatives. |
| 16. | Commitment to orders | West Marine guaranteed no hassle to suppliers and promised to commit to purchase 100% of forecast orders. West Marine became responsible for any mistakes. |
| 17. | Inbound transportation | West Marine picked up shipments from vendors to decrease freight costs and control the flow of material into the DCs. |

its push methods with pull. But it still relies on what it calls "forecasts." There is no inconsistency here for the following reasons:

■ West Marine updates its forecasts daily (#7). So, what it calls forecasts are in reality tracking actual demand.
■ West Marine has synchronized its ordering and promotions in collaboration with its suppliers, recognizing that each supplier has a different lead time depending on its products.
■ West Marine has also created multi-echelon systems (#6) so that there are no disconnects between transferring the data on customer purchases and how replacement merchandise is planned by stores and DCs.

| Positions/entities | Department | Concept: Source product | Concept: Negotiate vendor agreement | Concept: Determine pricing and margin | Concept: Determine promotability | Plan: Define assortment | Plan: Formalize pricing | Plan: Incorporate into planograms | Plan: Create initial forecast | Plan: Prepare for rollout | Plan: Plan specific promotions | Action: Load forecasts | Action: Share forecast with vendor | Action: Purchase initial fill | Action: Implement product rollouts | Action: Execute collaborative processes | Action: Execute scheduled promotions |
|---|---|---|---|---|---|---|---|---|---|---|---|---|---|---|---|---|---|
| Category management | Merch | ● | ● | ● | ● | ● | ● | ● | ● | ● | ● | | | | | ● | ● |
| Assortment planning | P&R | | | | | ● | | ● | | | | ● | | | | | |
| Merchandise planning | P&R | | | | | | | | ● | | ● | | ● | ● | | ● | ● |
| Replenishment analysis | P&R | | | | | | | | | ● | | ● | | | | ● | |
| Marketing | Mrktg | | | | | | | | | | ● | | | | | | ● |
| Visual merchandising | Merch | | | | | | | ● | | | | | | | | | |
| Stores | | | | | | | | | | | | | | | ● | | ● |
| Vendors | | | ● | | ● | ● | | | | ● | ● | | | | | | |

*Merch* *Merchandising*
*P&R* *Planning and Replenishment*
*Mrktg* *Marketing*

**Figure 15.3 Functional responsibilities (to-be).**

## 15.2 Continuous Improvement Cycles

Once a strategy is in place, such as the one West Marine developed in a period of distress, a company needs to continuously improve its processes. This process is often presented as a continuous cycle. The total quality, or TQM, approach calls for the Shewhart, or Deming cycle: Plan-Do-Check-Act (PDCA). Six Sigma adds a step to reach DMAIC: Define, Measure, Analyze, Improve, Control. CPFR, as mentioned earlier, has adopted a more complex cycle that also depicts a continuous process for improvement. In fact, West Marine used that approach in moving beyond its short-term turnaround objectives described earlier in the case study.

Although continuous improvement cycles are deceptively simple, they are often hard to maintain. This is not true in "crisis" situations similar to that faced by West Marine where adversity produced urgency. However, continuous improvement is probably the best insurance against falling into a situation that requires crisis management. Of these methods, only CPFR focuses on multicompany efforts. However, PDCA and DMAIC can be applied at the multicompany level.

### 15.2.1  PDCA in a Retail Supply Chain

The *Plan* step requires an overall strategy for the organization along with a list of priorities for process improvements. In addition to supply chain considerations, this could include a vision for future processes, financial objectives, and product development plans. The plan can identify ways a reconstituted supply chain should support the firm's retail strategy. A plan might also divide the supply chain into processes. Examples include order fulfillment, payments, inbound material, physical distribution, production control, and new product introduction. The planning often includes a definition of the new method that is to be tried. The activity system tool described in Chapter 13 can fill this role.

The *Do* step includes further design of the proposed change in organization and its implementation. It tests a wider range of solutions in pilot implementations. The *Do* step should also implement the organizational structure and measurements needed for success. It also implements facility and information technology modifications to support the redesigned processes.

In the *Check* step, a management team might change the solution based on objectives for improvement. This is done in an appropriate amount of time, depending on the changes being made. *Act* evaluates the change and confirms that it is to be retained or it is to be discarded. *Act* also extends proven solutions as appropriate, thereby restarting the *Plan* step.

### 15.2.2  DMAIC

DMAIC is also a cyclical process like PDCA. *Define* encompasses retail customer definition, critical issues, and processes to be covered. *Measure* collects data relevant to the processes from available sources. This includes information from external and internal customers of the processes. Because processes are there to benefit customers, this information should point to areas for improvement.

*Analyze* dissects the data and often creates what are called process or value stream maps. Their purpose is to understand reasons for the shortfalls as seen by customers. *Improve* means implementing solutions, and is a creative process. *Control* means locking in the changes. This includes implementing supporting systems and facilities. It also requires monitoring to avoid backsliding.

### 15.2.3  CPFR Model

The updated CPFR model as published by VICS is complex. Figure 15.4 is a simplified version. The CPFR model also displays the processes as a cycle that is continuously upgraded. Within it are eight core supply chain processes that are jointly executed between retailers and the manufacturers that supply them. Figure 15.4 shows the eight processes in four groups, reflecting different phases of a continuous improvement process. An examination of the CPFR model correlates strongly with

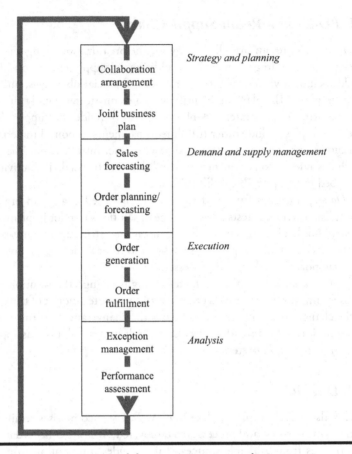

**Figure 15.4   Current CPFR model (summary presentation).**

the PDCA and DMAIC processes. However, the principal difference is that CPFR processes require an ongoing collaboration between trading partners: retailers, distributors, suppliers, and, ideally, raw material producers.

## 15.3  S&OP Process and Functional Roles

One of the barriers West Marine had to overcome was the need for internal departments to collaborate through information exchange and cross-department process design. Perhaps this is because the goals and measures of the departments were different. Operations departments seek from sales or, in a retail setting, the merchandising function, "iron clad" forecasts around which to build production and purchasing schedules. However, in many industries, accurate forecasts are hard to come by. In other words, the forecast is either wrong or, in the rare incidents when it is correct, it was just plain lucky. This was the as-is situation at West Marine and led to calls for a sales and operations planning process, also called S&OP. As the name implies, S&OP calls for collaboration between the sales and operations functions and is increasingly common in manufacturing companies.

Defining S&OP is difficult because it has different meanings in different companies and industries. The APICS dictionary, an authority on related terminology, defines S&OP as the following:

> A planning process with a 2–5 year horizon that develops tactical plans to support the organization's business plan. The objective is to balance supply and demand.[4]

According to APICS, the input is a 5- to 10-year business plan; the output is a 12- to 18-month master production schedule. The product of the S&OP process produces "tactical plans to balance supply and demand." S&OP is not necessarily conducted with trading partners. However, corresponding CPFR processes certainly are.

Benefits of the S&OP process include a common set of numbers and assumptions, added business visibility for both departments, and team building. The process of getting the merchandising and operations departments together is complicated. In a large organization, there may be a "many-to-many" relationship between merchandising organization and the functions that serve them. This means there are a lot of products and entities contributing to forecasts. To address this problem, West Marine collocated its merchandising and replenishment functions into category teams. It also orchestrated a disciplined schedule of meetings with other functions and suppliers.

Table 15.7 lists topics for the S&OP dialog. Each company will differ in terms of the forum for the dialog. Simpler organizations where the functions are colocated have an easier job than the global organization with the many-to-many relationship between functions.

The table contains two categories for the S&OP agenda: general requirements and supply chain requirements. The former apply to all products, whereas the latter apply to individual products or product categories. A general requirement deals with responsibility for supply chain performance metrics. This can be a "hot potato." If operations stocks to a merchandising forecast, can it be responsible if inventory is too high? Is anyone going to call a high-producing salesperson on the carpet for a faulty forecast? This is doubtful. Is an accurate forecast even possible? Sometimes they are, and sometimes they are not. Can supply chain design immunize against the consequences of poor forecasts? Tools for the demand-driven supply chain described in Chapter 17 will help. Our case in this chapter showed how West Marine made its supply chain more demand-driven through a variety of measures.

**Table 15.7  S&OP Functional Contributions**

|  | Merchandising/Sales Contributions | Operations Contributions |
|---|---|---|
| General requirements | Market trends<br>Sales plan by product category<br>Customer segments and corresponding needs<br>Pricing, profit, and cost objectives<br>Competitive response times<br>New product plans and requirements<br>Metrics for customer service<br>Metrics for supply chain performance | Production locations and third-party sources<br>Capacity constraints and plans for addressing them<br>Inventory policies<br>Supply chain problems (raw materials, manufacturing, distribution)<br>Methods for information exchange<br>Plans to ensure data integrity<br>Metrics for supply chain performance |
| Supply chain requirements | Desired paths to end-users<br>Seasonal patterns<br>Promotions<br>Price increases<br>Direct shipment to customers<br>Favored configurations (size, dosages, packaging)<br>Plans for adding/dropping SKUs, new products | Cost reductions leading to better margins and lower prices<br>Past consumption, trends, forecasts<br>Replenishment policy<br>Supplier lead times<br>Direct shipment selections<br>Stocking strategy by echelon<br>Resource requirement plans<br>New product supply chain setup |

*Note:* S&OP = sales and operations planning, SKU = stockkeeping unit.

# 15.4  Organizing to Improve Performance—Summary

This chapter has focused on achieving internal alignment to execute a supply chain strategy. The West Marine case describes how a company team might document the problems and opportunities and prepare a plan for implementation. Retailers and their manufacturing suppliers are mutually dependent. So, their support must be forthcoming. Chapter 16 returns to the West Marine case to further discuss issues related to this kind of collaboration.

# References

1. Pawley, Dennis and Flinchbaugh, Jamie, The current state: Progress starts here, *Manufacturing Engineering*, October 2006, pp. 71–81.
2. Denend, Lyn, West Marine: Driving Growth through Shipshape Supply Chain management, Stanford Graduate School of Business Case Study GS-34, 2005.
3. Smith, Larry, "A CPFR Success Story," *Supply Chain Management Review*, March 2006, pp. 29–36.
4. Leimanis, Eriks, *APICS Illustrated Dictionary*, 11th ed., APICS—The Educational Society for Resource Management, 2004.

# Chapter 16

# Collaboration with Supply Chain Partners

Chapter 15 focused on alignment of a supply chain strategy among functions within a company. This chapter describes issues related to multicompany efforts, those that take place between trading partners. Chapter 15 describes how West Marine sought to improve its supplier-related processes. Examples are listed in Table 15.6. To make life easier for its suppliers, West Marine accommodated the inevitable, varying lead times of suppliers due to product manufacturing and delivery differences. To *synchronize* their replenishments, they accommodated needs of their suppliers to be productive. West Marine also committed to buy any item it had placed in its forecasts and presented to suppliers in advance.

West Marine continues to operate in a consolidating industry, having grown through acquisitions of others in its industry. The result is that suppliers in the industry are in a weak position in terms of bargaining power with West Marine. Without West Marine, most would have lower sales, giving the retailer considerable power in the supply chain. This is a compelling motivation to play ball by adapting one's systems to fit with the larger partner, attending frequent meetings, and cooperating in continuous improvement initiatives as directed by the large retailer. Naturally, the power relationship will vary in various supply chains. In some instances, key suppliers may hold stronger positions than the retailers they serve.

This chapter describes issues faced by trading partners seeking to change the basis for doing business together through structured partnerships. In our case study, West Marine went from a purchase order–to–purchase order relationship with its suppliers to being an active collaborator over the longer term. Survival as manufacturers and retailers will necessitate similar partnerships in the future, with the sharing of data, decision making, product design, and logistics being an important foundation for collaborative relationships.

## 16.1 Supply Chain Roles

The growing awareness of the term *supply chain* in place of the older concept of logistics has resulted in an increase in external partnerships as companies link operations. A single manufacturing company that delivers retail merchandise will have an *upstream* supply chain for raw materials and will serve a *downstream* demand chain to customers and end users.

However, it is important to realize that a company does not have to have partnerships with either the upstream or the downstream trading partners. Some may intentionally avoid them. Retailers also may operate from purchase order to purchase order rather than collaborating with its suppliers, continuing to operate in the traditional manner. The awareness that more collaborative relationships can prove cost effective for all partners has been growing and provides an alternative worth considering strategically.

### 16.1.1 Fewer but Broader

Figure 16.1 models traditional relationships among suppliers, their customers, and end users. The model reflects a transaction-based relationship similar to what West Marine had before its changes. In this model, the buyer–seller linkage is likely to be driven by price and other conditions such as quality and delivery. Customers and ultimate end users, on the right, also have their choices of supplier. In logistics circles, these supply chain levels are called *echelons*.

Procurement policies and practices perpetuate the traditional model. For example, this takes the form of requiring several suppliers for each material category, as shown by multiple participants at the retailer and manufacturing echelons. West Marine may carry life jackets from a number of different suppliers. This ensures that the company will offer the customer a selection of items from which to choose,

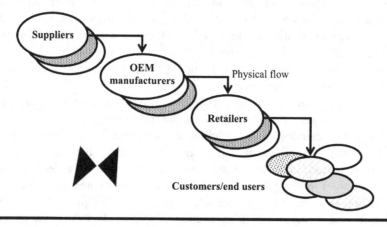

**Figure 16.1   Traditional partnership model. OEM, original equipment manufacturer.**

and it will be protected from stockouts or dependence on a supplier whose quality deteriorates. The figure also shows spaces between the players, reflecting the arm's-length nature of the relationships. There is little sharing in terms of technology, data, capital spending, promotion plans, or facilities. Some use the "bow tie" to represent this "single-point-of-contact" model.

Managers with traditional logistics and procurement mindsets find comfort in this arrangement. Having multiple suppliers, they feel, provides the "best value," often equated to the lowest price. In fact, decisions over source selection are simplified by having fewer factors to consider beyond price. Having multiple suppliers also is seen as reassurance to the retailer of adequate supplies of important merchandise. If one vendor has a problem, another will cover the shortfall, often a necessity if a firm does business with shaky suppliers who owe their position to their low prices. Traditional managers also equate low price with the most cost-effective solution. Indeed, their performance measures may support that paradigm. Earlier chapters point out that low prices alone do not provide an effective long-term strategy since the approach is easily copied by competitors.

In traditional companies, the procurement function processes the transactions necessary to buy and stock needed materials and merchandise. Most procurement functionaries have skill levels sufficient to execute these tasks. Unfortunately, there is too little talent available for strategic thinking and for managing partnerships. The lack of skill and resistance to change are bottlenecks for partnering in supply chains and the adoption of more modern management methods.

Figure 16.2 models the emerging relationship. The figure shows that there are fewer echelons, thereby simplifying the supply chain. It also shows that manufacturers and retailers have expanded their roles—symbolized by overlapping circles. There is more communication among the companies, symbolized by the "diamond" shown in the box.

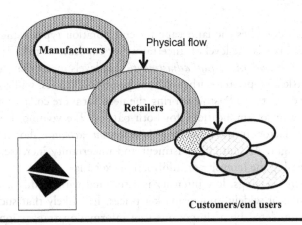

**Figure 16.2    Emerging partnership model.**

Chapter 7, Section 7.5, describes quality function deployment (QFD), a tool to capture this voice. West Marine reached back to its suppliers by taking over the transportation of merchandise into its distribution centers. This gave the company greater control over schedules and transportation costs. It also enabled its manufacturers to bypass its distribution centers with direct shipments to West Marine's stores. This creativity is needed for supply chain partners to fill in the open space between trading partners. One fruitful area is trying to establish higher forms of collaboration described in the model that follows.

## 16.1.2 Collaboration Landscape

When the supply chain concept first emerged, the Supply Chain Council, now APICS Supply Chain Council (SCC), commissioned a team to explore the theme of collaboration. The effort identified a useful multilevel collaboration model for relationships between trading partners. The model remains relevant. The following descriptions range from lower to higher levels of collaboration:

■ *Data exchange* where partners *exchange transaction-related information* to complete day-to-day transactions. Data exchanges can have two forms: one-way or two-way.
■ *Cooperative collaboration,* where partners *share systems and tools so each has simultaneous access to information needed for decision making.* However, the decisions made are independent. Examples range from sales and forecasting data to interpersonal planning.
■ *Cognitive collaboration,* involving "joint, concurrent intellectual and cognitive activity between partners." This *level embraces information sharing to jointly gain and weigh knowledge to make joint decisions.* This level includes the knowledge exchanges in our definition of supply chain flows in Chapter 1, Section 1.2.

Figure 16.3 describes the landscape for collaboration types using this model. On the vertical axis is the level of uncertainty, or exposure to risk. The horizontal axis measures the level of *mutual adjustment.* Low levels mean that outcomes will likely bring little disruption to either party's operation. Business will go on as usual. Higher levels of mutual adjustment bring the need for more collaboration because outcomes have major implications for both parties. The volume, frequency, and complexity are factors in the *intensity of information exchange,* shown by a sloping arrow on the right. As mutual adjustment and uncertainty increase, so does the need for increasing the intensity of information exchange.

In *transaction* settings, low intensity is associated with readily available commodity products at widely known market prices. It is likely that such a transaction can be completed by a simple one-way information transaction—box A in

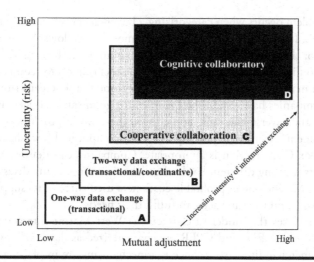

**Figure 16.3    Collaboration levels.**

Figure 16.3. For example, a buyer goes to a retail bookstore, Barnes & Noble, to buy a book for its marked price. The book is in stock; the buyer purchases the book and leaves the store. Communication is *one-way* from the book's retail customer to the bookstore.

To the extent that any of these three conditions grows more uncertain, the need for communication increases. In box B, the book buyer goes online and orders the book. The seller confirms the order by e-mail and notifies the buyer when the book is shipped. In this setting, there is *two-way* communication between buyer and seller.

High levels of mutual adjustment go with potentially disruptive outcomes. The *cognitive collaboratory* in box D anticipates these outcomes and the appropriate adjustments. The auto assembly plant receiving just-in-time components shuts down if a single part is missing. The resulting cognitive collaboratory assures capacity at the supplier, qualifies new parts, constructs supplier plants close to assembly plants (or even inside the plant), requires buffer stocks, sets up real-time communications, and continuously monitors the supplier's health and performance.

Box C, cooperative collaboration, holds an interesting position in the collaboration spectrum. Examples include insurance agents selling a range of policies that vary by individual need, real-estate agents providing buyers information on houses and prices, and companies that must configure their products—think car dealers or computer sellers who deliver customer service along the supply chain. These organizations must provide technically capable salespeople to counsel customers on complex product choices, particularly for high-priced purchases. The Geek Squad that advises customers at retailer Best Buy plays such a role.

One problem occurs when categorizing a buyer–seller relationship as a B when it is really a C. In fact, the "clicks-and-bricks" movement allows the buyer to choose whether he or she wants to deal in a B or C environment. The B model often takes the form of online linked help screens. The C model is likely to require much more expensive human interaction once the clicking through the screens runs its course.

Also, companies have established *markets* for goods and services through brokerage sites and reverse auctions. Sometimes, these work, providing execution in a B environment. At other times, especially for complicated, technical goods and services, a box C interaction is appropriate. Companies can define supply chains for customers wanting different levels of collaboration in making decisions on purchases. West Marine's most profitable customers used three of its supply chains—stores, catalogs, and the Internet—to fulfill their needs.

Table 16.1 uses the model to characterize West Marine interactions with its suppliers. Note that EDI and CPFR are characterized as data exchanges. Picking up supplier merchandise is seen, once the mechanisms are in place, as a two-way exchange to arrange the pickups. Higher levels of collaboration characterize deployment of forecasts to the supplier base. The West Marine commitment to purchase what it forecasted and its promotion planning required one-on-one collaborations with key suppliers.

**Table 16.1   West Marine Supplier Collaboration Types**

| External Focused Changes | A One-Way Data Exchange | B Two-Way Data Exchange | C Cooperative Collaboration | D Cognitive Collaboration |
|---|---|---|---|---|
| EDI | | • | | |
| CPFR | • | • | | |
| Supply base deployment | | | • | |
| Commitment to orders | | | • | |
| Inbound transportation | | • | | |
| Breakthroughs | | | | • |
| Promotion planning | | | | • |

*Note:* CPFR = Collaborative Planning, Forecasting, and Replenishment; EDI = electronic data interchange.

## 16.2 Core Competency

Another motivator for partnerships, and a deeper strategic one, is the need to focus on *core competencies*. In other words, "We do what we do best; partners do the rest." Assumptions about core competency underlie many decisions about the need for partnerships. A decision to perform or not perform an activity or produce or not produce some component of a good or service is a strategic decision. In fact, the emerging model in Figure 16.2 calls for shuffling workloads up and down the supply chain. West Marine's taking over inbound merchandise transportation is an example. In this case, it was "insourcing" rather than outsourcing that function. The net result will often be fewer echelons and individual participants adding value to the chain. Deciding which capabilities to retain and cultivate and finding the right partners can be daunting. Typical candidates for outsourcing non-competencies include manufacturing, facilities management, information systems, transportation, and inventory management. For many retailers with strong private label lines, various parts of the supply chain activities are outsourced, including the actual manufacture of goods.

Gary Hamel and C. K. Prahalad introduced the concept of core competency.[1] Core competency holds that competitive success requires nurturing distinctive skills, the *competencies*. Other activities outside the core may contribute little to competitive position. In the worst case, noncore activity diverts management attention from activities that create real value. Hamel and Prahalad define competitiveness on three levels. These are (1) core competence, (2) core products, and (3) end products. Their analogy is a tree, as shown in Figure 16.4, with core competencies as the roots and end products as leaves.

In the figure, one or more competencies support a *core product*. Core products are the heart of products that go to market. So Honda's core products, engines and power trains, produce multiple motorized products including automobiles, all-terrain vehicles, outboard motors, personal watercraft, generators, and engines.

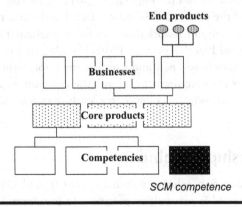

**Figure 16.4   Competencies: the roots of competitiveness.**

The *businesses* promote and sell end products that have their roots as core products based on core competencies.

The authors illustrate the point with Canon, a manufacturer of high-technology products. Canon has three core competencies—in precision mechanics, fine optics, and microelectronics. Similar to Honda, Canon applies combinations of these to a score of products ranging from cameras to copiers.

In their article, Hamel and Prahalad point to the important role of partnerships in nurturing core competencies. They believe that partnerships are an inexpensive way to advance a competence. They also decry the tendency of many companies to organize around strategic business units (SBUs) at the business level (the leaves), perhaps the least important level in the long run. For example, Gap focuses on the relative performances of their major SBUs: Gap, Old Navy, Banana Republic, and the newer Athleta. SBU performance measures are immediate, focusing on profits generated from the sale of end products. Unfortunately, no single SBU is a custodian of core competencies or perhaps even core products. Gap's core competencies include apparel design and manufacture for a particular range of target markets. The root competencies should be nurtured across SBU boundaries. They can wither because of management focus on SBU performance.

Because core products rely on multiple competencies, a competence can also be integration of diverse technologies. This integration requires movement of technology across SBUs and partnership companies. Another competency might also be found in building partnerships. If partnerships become vital to success in the business, it is reasonable to treat partnership-building skills as a competency. West Marine would be a good example of a retail chain that decided to cultivate this competency.

The shaded competence on the lower right in Figure 16.4 represents a competency in the five tasks that constitute supply chain management (SCM). One could also argue that any successful retailer needs to cultivate similar competencies, and any manufacturer of merchandise would also do so to profitably serve retailers.

For example, Amazon has demonstrated potent SCM core competencies and continues to expand the number of these. Amazon has decided to establish its own delivery and transportation network designed for its particular and unique needs. FedEx and the United Parcel Service (UPS) are finding that in spite of their own core competencies, they have a new and strong competitor in the market. The very volume of Amazon's own requirements allows the company to enter new markets with enough volume to compete at lower cost levels than most startups.

## 16.3 Partnership Vocabulary

A structured classification scheme will help identify and describe partnership opportunities. The need is particularly pertinent to businesses for which partnering is a novelty. Many have muddled along for years doing everything themselves, bargaining at arm's length with trading partners and, in many cases, cultivating a "not-invented-here" syndrome. The recommended classification has three dimensions. These are *purpose, direction*, and *choice*. If you characterize your need for a partner in each dimension, you are off to a good start in making the right choice of partners.

## 16.3.1 Partnership Purpose

The most important factor is whether the partnership will create new "space" along the supply chain. Creating space does not necessarily create cost reductions, which has been a motivator of many partnerships and mergers. Creating new space is similar to the concept behind the Blue Ocean strategy. In this approach, a company gains in a monopoly in an unserved marketplace (for more reading, see Ref. 2).

With respect to mergers, consultants from McKinsey & Co. have documented what they call the "habits" of the busiest acquirers.[3] The authors note that mergers and acquisitions (M & A) should be a tool, not a strategy in and of itself. Companies trying to promote their top lines have often turned to acquisitions as a strategy for growth. In the 1980s, many large conglomerates acquired retailers to "grow" their organizations and to increase their markets. However, there was no real strategic base for these acquisitions, and because these conglomerates did not understand the retail business, divestitures and bankruptcies occurred with regularity. Later research found that investment bankers and lawyers brought no competitive advantage to acquirers. The best acquirers sought to fill a hole or, as we describe it, space in their strategy that could not be filled internally.

Of course, creating new space is more complex than refining existing roles. Most partnerships are intended to refine current positions with lower cost or better service rather than to define new space. In many cases, the potential to define new space is not even considered. In Figure 16.2, the expanded shaded circles around those of the manufacturers and retailers symbolize new space.

West Marine, as described in Chapter 15, ran into trouble when it merged with a large competitor, E&B Marine. West Marine had focused on the sailing segment, and E&B on power boaters. This example did not create new space. In fact, when West Marine started converting E&B stores to its own brand, assortment, and pricing, it lost customers and destroyed value.

Figure 16.5 shows the options for defining partnership purpose in terms of creating space. The shaded square (quadrant IV) represents the as-is situation with respect to partnering. The decision process includes two steps: first, identifying whether new space is created, and second, deciding how to fill that space in the supply chain—either organically (internally) or by merger. Moves from quadrant IV to either quadrant I or quadrant II positions represent this decision. The second decision is whether a company can do this on its own (quadrant II), or it can choose to partner (quadrant I). Few partnerships create new space. At least initially, the West Marine merger with E&B was a quadrant III transaction.

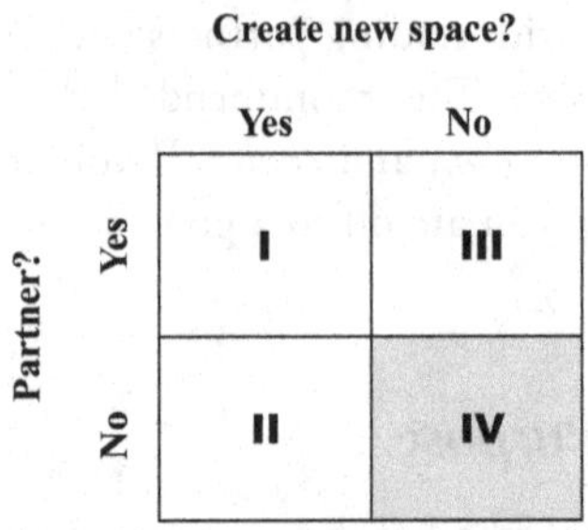

**Create new space?**

|  | Yes | No |
|---|---|---|
| **Yes** | I | III |
| **No** | II | IV |

**Partner?**

**Figure 16.5   Potential for new supply chain space.**

Examples of creating space occur in technology products when each partner brings a critical technical capability not possessed by the other partner. Pharmaceutical distributor McKesson follows this model with its large and small retail customers—as described in Chapter 3, Section 3.3. Distributors and third-party logistics providers create space when they take responsibility for stocking or customizing merchandise. Another example is manufacturers making merchandise floor-ready by providing it pretagged and on hangers, moving that preparation function out of the store.

## 16.3.2 Partnership Direction

Direction, the second classification category, is the term we give to the relative positions of the partnering companies along the supply chain. Figure 16.6 shows different directions. A *horizontal* combination, similar to the retailer combination between West Marine and E&B, means each partner is at the same echelon, and partner activity systems, as described in Chapter 13, will overlap. Another example is two wholesale distributors partnering to offer increased geographical coverage. Code sharing by airlines is another.

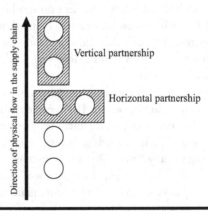

**Figure 16.6   Partnership directions.**

Partners in different echelons, whose capabilities do not overlap, represent a *vertical* partnership. An example is Wal-Mart, a retailer, providing point-of-sale information to McKesson to establish vendor-managed inventory. McKesson, as an upstream partner in the supply chain, is then able to provide timely delivery direct to Wal-Mart stores. McKesson's new space is the vendor-managed inventory service.

Figure 16.6 illustrates horizontal and vertical partnerships. Vertical partnerships reflect the trend toward supply chain consolidation for process simplification, reduced handling and transportation, and increased flexibility. For example, Chapter 17, Section 17.1.4, describes *disintermediation* of a distributor to simplify a supply chain. The emerging model of the supply chain described in Figure 16.2 indicates the growth of partnerships in the vertical direction. In these cases, fewer players perform more supply chain functions, capturing a greater share of the delivered value.

## 16.3.3 Partnership Choice

This category captures the relative strength of each partner. It is called "choice" because it reflects the availability of options for partnering. High choice means there are many options for partnering and trading partners; low choice means there are few options. Manufacturers of functional products have few choices when it comes to supplying a channel master such as Wal-Mart. If they want to sell to the world's largest retailer, they must follow Wal-Mart's rules. West Marine in fact has become the Wal-Mart of the marine aftermarket industry. Its suppliers have low choice of *whether* and *who* when it comes to partnering. On the other hand, in less concentrated industries and with growing innovative products, there are more choices for partnering. Current consolidation and the growth of very large chains such as Target and Best Buy have either reduced partnership opportunities for manufacturers or made them more of a necessity.

To establish a classification representing choice, we rely on a data management paradigm. Table 16.2 explains forms of partnership relationships. In the relationship characterization in column 1, your company is first. The options you have are second. For example, in retail, Wal-Mart would be a "one-to-many" company. It is the largest customer for most of the products it buys. Presumably, Wal-Mart, as a channel master, has many partners/suppliers eager for its business from which to choose. Likewise, a supplier to Wal-Mart would be a "many-to-one" if there were several choices for Wal-Mart for the product it sells. A manufacturing company or a distributor in a many-to-one situation may have a tough time standing out from the crowd. However, Chapters 12 and 13 describe how to be a viable partner to a channel master. Having a distinctive ability could enable a leader to consolidate an industry, acquiring its former competitors, or gain market share from those who fail to recognize or are unable to make needed changes.

**Table 16.2 Partnership Relationships Permission**

| Relationship | Description | Application |
|---|---|---|
| Many to many | Your company, one of many serving your market, has many partner candidates from which to choose. Neither partner is currently a dominant company. | Two companies form a partnership to separate themselves from the crowd. They may do so to target a particular segment neither could approach alone. An industry rollup or consolidation is an example in which a dominant company buys others offering similar services. In the marine aftermarket, West Marine played the consolidator role. |
| One to many | Your company is large, and you have many options for selecting partners. | You select the "best of breed" for partnering, or working alone, you develop capabilities appealing to many customers. Dell is a vertical example partnering with its suppliers. |
| Many to one | Your company has a low market share and must compete with others for the business of the strong partner. | You develop strategies for distinguishing yourself so you become the chosen one. You may ignore other segments to focus on the needs of the targeted strong partner. Successful West Marine suppliers of commodity-type products could do this by participating in the CPFR initiative. |
| One to one | This is a peer arrangement with dominant partners on each side. There is little choice in partner selection. | Because the size of the market and the scale of operations required, there are few choices. The Wal-Mart/ McKesson VMI effort was a vertical example. |

*Note:* CPFR, Collaborative Planning, Forecasting, and Replenishment; VMI = vendor-managed inventory.

# 16.4 Organizing a Partnership

Organization design is an art form. New contributions occur frequently, but the topic of multicompany structures has barely been touched. Perhaps there are good reasons for this, because it is hard to impose conditions on trading partners. On the other hand, those entrusted with establishing partnerships should consider what kind of structure is needed. Table 16.3 outlines components of such a partnership agreement.[4]

**Table 16.3  Partnership Agreement Articles**

| Partnership Article | Description |
| --- | --- |
| Purpose | Establishes the need for the partnership. |
| Parties to the agreement | Provides the legal names involved in the partnership. This is important because larger companies have many legal entities. |
| Basis of the agreement | The shared value proposition. Partnership expectations. |
| Organizational process boundaries | Areas of primary supply chain process responsibility. |
| Interface response time | Response expectations over time and space (geography). |
| Decision escalation | Hierarchy of individuals or positions on both sides of the partnership who will resolve issues. |
| Face-to-face meetings | The parties involved in the meetings (including senior management) and the frequency. |
| Performance measurement | Shared performance measures with which to track the effectiveness of the partnership. |
| Intellectual property | Each partner's rights to trade secrets, trademarks, copyrights, and patents arising from the partnership. |
| Investment decision making | Expectations for each party's share of investments and returns. |
| Mediation and conflict resolution | Defined process for conflict resolution. |
| Nonexclusive provision | Acknowledgement of the right of either party to participate in other supply chain networks, even if they compete. |
| Renewal | Term of the partnership. Whether renewal is automatic or not. |
| Signatures | Senior executive commitment from each organization. |

Surprisingly, companies overlook the role of contract incentives in motivating improvements. Consultants from McKinsey & Co. documented this lapse in a study of 12 European food and consumer products manufacturers.[5] In retail industries in major European countries, most of which were consolidating, the researchers found that there are few manufacturers offering "bracket prices."

Such prices provide unit price discounts for ordering larger volumes. For example, it becomes cheaper for the retailer to order truckloads of a product rather than single pallets.

The authors note that the logistics costs are from 5–20% of net sales. So they believe that having such discounts could reduce retailer costs by 2–3% of retail price. They also point out that salespeople have little experience or expertise in negotiating cost-efficient terms. They also note that lowering barriers in the United States is increasing the use of pricing that recognizes supply chain efficiencies.

Once agreements are in place, overseeing a complicated effort requires new ways to organize and control the effort. A previous article describes "stage 3" SCM, referring to the participation of multiple companies.[6] Chapter 6, Section 6.7.2, introduced the structure of a stage 3 SCM effort. In this model, stage 1 is the department level; stage 2 is the company or business-unit level. West Marine was at stage 1 or 2 when it was purchasing merchandise on an order-by-order basis. New stage 3 practices produce a cooperative effort that includes trading partners in supply chain improvement. The following features will characterize stage 3 supply chain improvement and should be considered in implementing each partnership:

■ A focused and measurable goal for the effort with objectives such as strategic positioning, market share increase, and financial improvement. The West Marine program described these as "breakthroughs." Ideally, these initiatives should consider the partnership as the enterprise, rather than as individual companies.

■ Multicompany funding and staffing. Joint projects reflect a commitment to effective supply chain design. Such participation will shorten implementation lead time. A challenge will be to balance contributions among partners through win–win contracting.

■ As necessary, a third-party *honest broker* to facilitate the effort and provide an outside, neutral perspective. The third party can be a team member or a jointly funded outside organization.

■ A CEO (or senior-management-level) steering committee from partner enterprises. The steering committee should meet frequently while establishing the partnership, and as necessary during its operation.

■ Multiyear projects with self-funding short-term wins. The model for implementing supply chain change described in Chapters 15 and 17 is useful for structuring this effort. This allows the program to be sustained by cash flow benefits.

■ Process integration. This means deployment of appropriate technology solutions. A plan for systems to share information should accompany the design of partnership processes.

The initiative for supply chain improvement will come from a *sponsor's* firm. The sponsor is an executive who champions the multicompany partnering effort. The sponsor's firm may be a dominant player in the supply chain or one with a major stake in the project's success. The sponsor should have completed the partnership preparation steps described earlier in this chapter and will likely be somewhere in the process of developing and implementing its supply chain strategy. A project timeline similar to that introduced in Figure 14.1 is appropriate. Indeed, the sponsor's firm may have already completed internal restructuring tasks.

## 16.5 Partner Collaboration—Summary

The emerging model of collaboration calls for new capabilities in building partnerships. These capabilities include developing partnership strategies during the planning processes, deciding what types of partnerships should be pursued, and implementing the partnerships through multicompany projects.

## References

1. Hamel, Gary and Prahalad, C.K., "The Core Competency of the Corporation," *Harvard Business Review*, (68/3) May–June, 1990, pp. 79–90.
2. Chan Kim, W. and Mauborgne, Renée, *Blue Ocean Strategy*, Boston: Harvard Business School Press, 2005.
3. Palter, Robert N. and Srinivasan, Dev, "Habits of the Busiest Acquirers," *The McKinsey Quarterly: The Online Journal of McKinsey & Co.*, July 2006.
4. Walker, William T., *Supply Chain Architecture: A Blueprint for Networking the Flow of Material, Information, and Cash*, Boca Raton: CRC Press, 2005.
5. Sänger, Frank and Tochtermann, Thomas C.A., "Better Logistics in European Consumer Goods," *The McKinsey Quarterly: Web exclusive*, January 2007.
6. Ayers, James B., Gustin, Craig and Stephens, Scott, "Reengineering the supply chain," *Information Strategy: The Executive's Journal*, Fall, 1997 (14/1), pp. 13–18.

# Chapter 17

---

# Demand-Driven
# Supply Chain

---

Chapters 15 and 16 focused on ways to enlist internal departments and trading partners in collaborative improvement efforts. This chapter describes how to exploit these relationships to improve supply chain planning and production processes. As described in the West Marine case, these efforts should include pursuit of the *demand-driven supply chain*. In this vision, *demand* displaces *forecasts* in making replenishment decisions. Implementation is not an overnight process; it calls for a program with multiple projects to reach objectives.

The chapter begins by defining what it means to be demand-driven; following that are tools and techniques for achieving demand-driven objectives. Finally, the chapter addresses the subject of sponsorship—which supply chain participants—retailers, distributors, and original equipment manufacturers (OEMs)—are best positioned to lead the transition from forecast-driven to demand-driven.

## 17.1 Vision for the Demand-Driven Supply Chain

Most supply chain practitioners are well aware of the virtues of being "demand-driven" and particularly those advantages related to Inventory control. In fact, the quest to be demand-driven is behind many innovations in SCM. One example is RFID mandates such as those described later in Chapter 18. RFID stands for radio frequency identification. RFID technology is not instituted for its own sake but as a means to achieve increased visibility over product location. Visibility, in turn, enables the efficiencies and customer service improvements that support being demand-driven. Since RFID-tracked merchandise provides accurate location data required for better decisions, inventories can be planned and managed with greater precision and economic efficiency.

Another motivating trend is the growth of "scan-based trading." With this practice, the manufacturer or distributor retains ownership of merchandise until it is purchased (scanned). This shifts inventory costs upstream in the supply chain. However, it provides a competitive advantage to the seller along with tighter information links with customers that deliver visibility over final demand.

Just what the term *demand-driven* means is less widely accepted. This chapter defines it as follows:

> *Basing supply chain decisions on actual end-user consumption rather than forecasts.*

*Decisions*, in this definition, are those required to plan and schedule operations along the supply chain. Decisions are driven by the need to replenish stocks as customer demand "pulls" merchandise out of the end of the supply chain path. These operating decisions turn factories on and off, approve accumulation or burn-off of inventory, introduce new products, generate markdowns when necessary, and plan capacity at various links.

Longer-term decisions such as how much capacity to have will always depend, to some extent, on planning forecasts; these are not included in this definition. Note also that the demand-driven supply chain will be driven by *end-user consumption*. This might not be the same as actual *sales* because a purchase may not coincide with consumption, particularly far upstream in supply chains with long lead times. Another supply chain classification, *push* or *pull*, may be familiar to readers. Forecasts are associated with *push* strategies that force merchandise to the next-in-line participant in the supply chain without understanding what the end user is actually consuming. *Pull* approaches utilize end-user demand for making decisions, thereby "pulling" merchandise through the supply chain.

Why is being demand-driven important? Basically, forecasts for many products are unreliable. Cynics say forecasts are either "wrong" or "lucky." Even though companies automate the forecasting process and continuously search for better algorithms, the time and effort required to produce and apply forecasts often creates paperwork and teeth gnashing. Management behavior factors also play a role. What if the production forecast falls below sales commitments? The forecast gets boosted whether the business is there or not. Another problem is that sales departments provide forecasts in currency terms or product categories. These don't align with the needed operating decisions on what stockkeeping unit (SKU) to make, in what quantities, and when to make it.

The result is the unfortunate consequence of inventory accumulation along the supply chain, as described in Chapter 7, Section 7.4, along the chain. This also produces "bullwhips," wide fluctuations in production without commensurate changes in end-user consumption. These inventories stretch the "cash-to-cash" cycle, requiring more working capital to support the business. The Dell approach provides a "build-to-order" (BTO) model that is a frequently cited example of shortening this cycle. Dell assembles final products from vendor parts after orders are received and paid for by the end user. Its cash-to-cash cycle is thus negative—the customer pays Dell before Dell pays the suppliers. The Toyota Production System, the foundation of "Lean" approaches, also has a "make one move one" philosophy. West Marine, described in Chapters 15 and 16, approached this ideal with its daily updates and multi-echelon planning systems in which each user refers to the same data.

Other retailers and their suppliers would like a similar model. Although this is not always possible, companies can move in the Toyota and Dell direction if they try. There are many examples of retailers exploiting demand-driven techniques. The retail grocery store is one. The store merely captures what merchandise is popular with customers who register their votes at the cash register. The empty shelf also signals a need for replenishment, a "visual" signal. The shelf may be filled, in the case of the retail store, by an order to the distribution center (DC) or manufacturer. The "Breadman" or jobber may do the same for the grocery store on frequent fixed-schedule visits, an arrangement called *vendor-managed inventory*, or VMI. In these cases, demand "pulls" the product along the supply chain as consumption occurs. The advent of scanners in the late 1970s and early 1980s has further streamlined the process and has made possible electronic replenishment systems for many items.

Benetton, whose brand is "United Colors of Benetton," has delayed dyeing its sweaters until the market signals the current season's most popular colors. This technique is called *postponement*. Once consumers register their preferences, Benetton can plan its color assortment to minimize dead stock and write-downs on unpopular colors. Another example is in-store paint matching using spectrometers that blend a few basic colors into an infinite number of combinations. Pharmacists also employ a demand-driven process when they dispense labeled prescriptions of a specified number of tablets from larger containers.

Weighing against becoming demand-driven are complications inherent in retail marketing strategies. These strategies rely on fashion items, seasonal product sales, and frequent product promotions. This book does not contend that forecasts should or can be abolished, especially in these categories. However, increasing the role of actual demand in supply chain decisions for all categories of goods will improve both financial performance and customer service.

As a general principle, retail supply chains, as they operate today, can be *more* demand-driven, if not totally so. This includes the supply chains for fashion, seasonal, and promotional sales. So, the property we call demand-driven is not absolute. Its pursuit can be approached using the continuous improvement models described in Chapter 15, Section 15.2, taken as far as possible within constraints imposed by the products sold and the markets served. This chapter describes how to undertake such a journey.

Figure 17.1 repeats our model for supply chain change and the elements of the model addressed in this chapter, which is necessarily lengthy. The figure indicates which chapter sections describe each model element. At the lower left is the "as-is" representing the existing processes for decision-making in the supply chain. A separate evaluation of those processes (how well they work) utilizes benchmarks, analysis, the perception of employees and participants, and inputs from trading partners. This evaluation takes into account product types, barriers, and business goals. This part of the model is the subject of Subsections 17.1.1 and 17.1.2.

*Constraints* that cannot be changed may limit what can be done to reach the desired situation. An example is a decision to use an existing system or to produce merchandise in a particular plant. *Barriers* must be navigated to arrive at the destination. The "path" is shown in the form of sequenced "projects" (in smaller circles) designed to close the gaps between the as-is and to-be. Some of these are likely to be multicompany projects; others may be internal. This topic is covered in Subsection 17.1.3.

A destination (upper right) for becoming demand-driven is defined next. This enables identification of gaps between the as-is and to-be. The gap analysis includes metrics, benchmarks, process design, governance along the supply chain, organizational structure, measurements, and systems. Subsection 17.1.4 covers this part of the model. Section 17.2 describes the pathway to the demand-driven supply chain.

This section uses the model in Figure 17.1 to describe how a company might develop a vision and project a plan for implementing the demand-driven supply chain. It begins with understanding the starting environment. Chapter 15 used the West Marine case as an example of the types of findings and conclusions that could

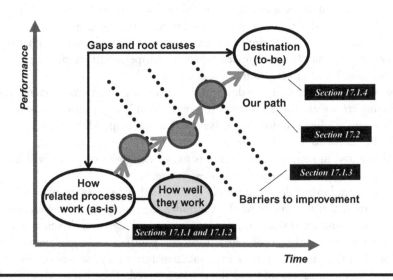

**Figure 17.1   Model for implementing supply chain change.**

result from applying the process. Refer to Chapter 15, Tables 15.1 through 15.6, for details of the case.

### 17.1.1 Documenting the Current Situation

To establish a vision for a demand-driven supply chain of the future, one should start with the current situation. Figure 17.2 illustrates a simple supply chain delivering a product to an end-user market segment. Supply chain decision points are shown as numbers along the bottom of Figure 17.2 beginning at level 1 (the retailer) and extend back to level 8 (a first-tier supplier). Table 17.1 documents each of the decisions. For practitioners, the data for Table 17.1 can come from industry knowledge, direct from collaborating trading partners, or as educated assumptions about how the chain works.

The figure and table (column 2) show the supply chain participants. It describes the steps taken to order material/merchandise or produce that merchandise (column 3), the action or decision required (column 4), and their frequencies (column 5). Column 6 shows the lead time to complete each step. Capturing the output of an important process is referred to as *time mapping*. Note that this example requires 21 weeks of lead time from the point an item is purchased until that signal is recorded with the manufacturer's supplier. The last three columns describe tools and data used in each decision (column 7), responsible parties (column 8), and whether the decision is forecast-driven or demand-driven (column 9). Out of eight decisions in this example, only two are demand-driven. One way to characterize the supply chain is to measure the percentage of decisions that are demand-driven. In this case, it is 25% (two out of eight decisions).

At the bottom of Figure 17.2, there is a row of large arrows. These represent the decisions using the configuration model from SCOR, which stands for Supply Chain Operations Reference Model. The model is maintained by the APICS Supply

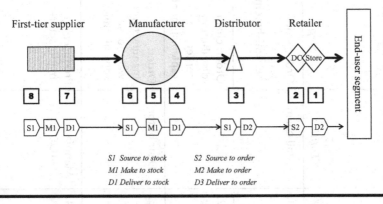

First-tier supplier     Manufacturer     Distributor     Retailer     End-user segment

| | |
|---|---|
| S1 Source to stock | S2 Source to order |
| M1 Make to stock | M2 Make to order |
| D1 Deliver to stock | D3 Deliver to order |

**Figure 17.2  Decision making along a supply chain.**

**Table 17.1  Documenting As-Is Supply Chain Decisions**

| # | 2 Entities | 3 Step | 4 Decision/Action Required | 5 Frequency | 6 Lead Time (weeks) | 7 Basis of Decision | 8 Responsibility | 9 Forecast or Demand Driven |
|---|---|---|---|---|---|---|---|---|
| 1. | Retail chain | Order: store-level replenishment | Refill stock to target levels | Daily | 1 | Point-of-sale system data | Automatic. Set by chain replenishment system | Demand driven |
| 2. | | Order: chain distribution center replenishment | Reorder predetermined batch quantity | Weekly | 2 | Reorder point set in system by SKU | Automated system. Buyer reviews by exception | Demand driven |
| 3. | Distributor | Order: manufacturer warehouse replenishment | Order predetermined batch quantity | Biweekly | 4 | Reorder point and forecast | Demand manager using forecast. Review by exceptions | Forecast driven |
| 4. | Manufacturer (OEM) | Produce: manufacturer | To make or not to make a batch on fixed schedule | Monthly | 2 | Orders from warehouse | Factory production planner Manufacturing manager | Forecast driven |

*(Continued)*

**Table 17.1 (Continued)  Documenting As-Is Supply Chain Decisions**

| # | *2 Entities* | *3 Step* | *4 Decision/Action Required* | *5 Frequency* | *6 Lead Time (weeks)* | *7 Basis of Decision* | *8 Responsibility* | *9 Forecast or Demand Driven* |
|---|---|---|---|---|---|---|---|---|
| 5. | Manufacturer (OEM) | Order: manufacturer raw material | Order predetermined batch quantity | Quarterly | 4 | Sales forecast | Commodity manager/buyer Sales department | Forecast driven |
| 6. | Manufacturer's supplier | Order: supplier warehouse replenishment | Batch size based on forecast | Quarterly | 4 | Manufacturer forecast | Commodity planner | Forecast driven |
| 7. | | Produce: supplier | Batch size based on forecast | Quarterly | 1 | Sales forecast and production plan | Factory production planner Manufacturing manager | Forecast driven |
| 8. | | Order: supplier material replenishment | Batch size based on forecast | Quarterly | 3 | Sales forecast | Commodity manager | Forecast driven |

*Note:*  OEM = original equipment manufacturer, SKU = stockkeeping unit.

Chain Council organization. The threads provide a user-friendly overview of a supply chain. The letters "S, M, D" stand for Source, Make, and Deliver, high-level supply chain processes in SCOR. The "1" and "2" designate whether the action is "to stock" or to "order"—essentially whether it is forecast-driven or demand-driven. A "3" covers engineer-to-order links in other chains but not in this one. The tool captures configurations of larger supply chains that spread over multiple companies.

Creating a vision for such a supply chain would assess whether any of these decisions can be converted from forecast-driven to demand-driven. This analysis, when aided by internal functions and trading partners, identifies improvement opportunities for early focus. These are often the points where the lead time is the greatest. The West Marine case in Chapter 15 sought to make decisions demand-driven by using common data at levels 1 and 2 and frequent sharing of up-to-date information at least on levels 3 through 5.

A fair question is "Can one part of the supply chain be forecast-driven and another demand-driven?" Of particular concern is when a demand-driven step is further upstream, feeding forecast-driven processes. The answer is "Yes," and the situation occurs frequently. For example, a manufacturer may consider the distributor as its "ultimate" customer. Yet the distributor orders from the manufacturer according to its own or retailer forecasts, while the manufacturer produces to the distributor's pull signals. So, the distributor is forecast-driven, whereas the manufacturer is demand-driven. This chapter next describes the implications of product types, how to address barriers, and the path to move from forecast-driven to demand-driven.

### 17.1.2 Product Types

Becoming more demand-driven will, in many cases, require both process and product changes. This section addresses the product design characteristics that support increasing the chain's demand-driven percentage. The most important product quality is commonality in components. Benetton sweaters in white all look alike, except for size. It is the color that makes them different. Delaying dyeing of the sweaters until the market has signaled demand levels for each color is an example of *postponement*. The final decision on configuration is made later (is postponed) in the supply chain process. Commonality, incidentally, also applies to services and software. Examples are standardized procedures for an attorney producing a client's will or individual software modules that developers can transport to new applications.

The demand-driven supply chain design must also consider product structures. The Theory of Constraints (TOC), developed by Eliyahu M. Goldratt and his colleagues, defines basic product structures and uses the letters V-A-T to distinguish them. A "V" product example is the Honda engine that goes to end-user markets in autos, watercraft, and snowmobiles. The core of each product is the Honda chassis, and the finished products are built around it. The V product also applies to many consumer goods such as food, consumer package goods, and pharmaceuticals. A food example is the orange, which goes to market as produce, juice, marmalade, sherbet, and other products. Consumer package goods and pharmaceuticals often originate in a single chemical formulation. In these cases, the formulation serves as a base for multiple products that differ in form (liquid, tablets, gels, lotions, etc.), dosages, size and quantity, and packaging. Packaging variations occur by virtue of several brands for consumer package goods, local legal requirements such as those for pharmaceuticals, or languages in local markets around the world.

An "A" structure product such as the automobile has many components that go into a single delivered product. The personal computer supply chain matches an A structure. The demand signal to Dell's component makers comes at final assembly after the customer orders a computer. Components are pulled up to Dell assembly lines as outgoing configured computers deplete the stock of supplier items. To support the model, Dell provides supplier visibility for these stock levels to better assure timely replenishment.

A "T" structure is also common in the consumer packaged goods, chemical, and pharmaceutical industries. Mix-to-order paint in the hardware store is an example. A few paint colors make a virtually infinite variety of colors and are configured at the point of sale. The ultimate product of a grocery store is the market basket. Each basket is a unique mix of individual products, with combinations that could never be forecast. The customer configures each basket from store shelves using a grocery list.

### 17.1.3 Barriers to the Demand-Driven Supply Chain

Given the variety of products and product types available, there are many reasons why retail supply chains rely so heavily on forecasts. We call these barriers rather than constraints because they can be managed, meaning we can adapt our demand-driven approach to accommodate the barrier. A "constraint," on the other hand, cannot be managed. Before embarking on a quest to become more demand-driven, a retailer, distributor, or manufacturer should understand and plan for constraints and barriers. Here are some of the common barriers:

1. *Unwillingness or unawareness of the value of operations.* Top management does not perceive operations as a source of strategic advantage. Like West Marine, the management team had little awareness of supply chain issues.
2. *Organizational boundaries.* There are internal boundaries between functions, particularly sales and operations and, often, marketing and sales, where collaboration is needed for the retailer and its supply chain partners to become demand-driven. Hard bargaining procurement departments may also restrain opportunities for collaboration.
3. *Training.* Many merchandise and production planners have been trained to use methods that utilize forecasts based on assumed lead times. These

processes are embedded in enterprise resource planning (ERP) systems. In time the computer calculates production orders based on out-of-date parameters that invalidate the plans.

4. *Lack of skills.* As described later, multiple disciplines are required for the transition to the demand-driven supply chain. Many companies do not have the knowhow to reform their processes. This book's mission is to address this situation.

5. *Inability to collaborate.* A consensus to proceed has to exist among supply chain partners, or one of the partners has to be strong enough to lead or guide the others down the path to a demand-driven supply chain. The fact that a manufacturer sells to multiple retailers also hampers collaboration because the manufacturer is serving multiple but competitive "masters" with different supply chain agendas.

6. *Choppy product flow.* Contributing factors include items mentioned earlier, such as seasonal sales with long lead times, sporadic promotions, short product life cycles, and fashion items with little sales history. Also included in this category are differences in replenishment cycle frequencies, too many participating companies, and component lead times throughout the chain.

A company or a group of trading partners must plan to circumvent these barriers. A next step on the path is to understand the potential to be demand-driven, taking these barriers into account.

### 17.1.4 To-Be and the Potential To-Be Demand-Driven

The physical structure of the product and the existence of barriers will affect how demand-driven a supply chain can be. Certainly, the decision of any one company to make changes is constrained by its influence in the chain. For example, Wal-Mart, a business to business customer with clout, is taking the lead when it requires its suppliers to put tracking tags or labelling on their products.

Measuring demand-driven potential begins with assessing the potential to convert decisions from forecast-driven to demand-driven. This could be a collaborative effort between a retailer and its larger manufacturing suppliers or distributors. Table 17.2 uses the Table 17.1 format to display one such vision. The principal changes include the following:

■ The to-be vision shows that the distributor is removed from the supply chain process for at least a portion of the product flow, an example of *disintermediation*. This cuts lead time and simplifies the chain.

■ The vision also synchronizes the factory with the weekly cycle at the retailer's distribution center DC. This has the effect of converting steps 4 and 5 from forecast-driven to demand-driven. Once implemented, this would

**Table 17.2  Vision for To-Be Supply Chain Decisions**

| 1 Level | 2 Entities | 3 Step | 4 Decision/Action Required | 5 Frequency | 6 Lead Time (weeks) | 7 Basis of Decision | 8 Responsibility | 9 Forecast or Demand Driven |
|---|---|---|---|---|---|---|---|---|
| 1 | Retail chain | Order: store-level replenishment | Refill stock to target levels | Daily | 1 | Point-of-sale (POS) system data | Automatic. Set by chain replenishment system | Demand driven |
| 2 | | Order: chain distribution center replenishment | Reorder predetermined batch quantity | Weekly | 1 | Reorder point set in system by SKU | Automated system. Buyer reviews by exception | Demand driven |
| 3 | Distributor | Remove the distributor from the supply chain. Institute direct delivery to the retail distribution center by the manufacturer | | | | | | |
| 4 | Manufacturer | Produce: manufacturer | To make or not to make a batch on fixed schedule | Weekly | 2 | POS data from the retail chain | Factory production planner | Demand driven |
| 5 | | Order: manufacturer raw material | Order predetermined batch quantity | Weekly | 2 | Factory consumption | Factory production planner | Demand driven |

*(Continued)*

**Table 17.2 (Continued)   Vision for To-Be Supply Chain Decisions**

| 1 Level | 2 Entities | 3 Step | 4 Decision/Action Required | 5 Frequency | 6 Lead Time (weeks) | 7 Basis of Decision | 8 Responsibility | 9 Forecast or Demand Driven |
|---|---|---|---|---|---|---|---|---|
| 6 | Manufacturer's supplier | Order: supplier warehouse replenishment | Batch size based on forecast | Quarterly | 4 | Manufacturer forecast | Commodity planner | Forecast driven |
| 7 | | Produce: supplier | Batch size based on forecast | Quarterly | 1 | Sales forecast and production plan | Factory production planner Manufacturing manage | Forecast driven |
| 8 | | Order: supplier material replenishment | Batch size based on forecast | Quarterly | 3 | Sales forecast | Commodity manager | Forecast driven |

increase the demand-driven percentage in the supply chain from 25 to 57. Also, lead time from the manufacturer to the end-user sale is reduced from 13 to 6 weeks. This change may face opposition from the distribution department that wants to fill trucks as full as possible, and from the manufacturing department that wants to produce larger batches because their performance is measured by the product weight they produce.

Note that the two principal changes are of different types, and both types are necessary to become more demand-driven. The first, disintermediation, removing an echelon from the supply chain, requires a multifunctional decision that includes senior management, distribution, sales and marketing, and operations. It is a "management improvement." The second, an "operating improvement," is more in line with traditional process-improvement approaches sponsored by operations managers.

The OEM's vision does not touch the processes for its own supplier. There could be a number of reasons. First, the manufacturer's business might not be significant enough to influence the supplier to collaborate. The decision could also be a question of priorities, and there might be insufficient benefits from inventory reduction and operating savings to justify the effort. Another factor will be the supply–demand situation for the supplier's product. If the supplier's product is in short supply, bargaining power may be limited. Large batches might be required to obtain access to the materials at a reasonable price. On the other hand, perhaps this effort to become more demand-driven could proceed in the future. That effort could establish a similar partnership with the supplier or could shift business to another, more flexible supplier or distributor.

## 17.2 Path from Forecast-Driven to Demand-Driven Supply Chain

This section describes the path to the demand-driven supply chain and describes tools for the journey. Tools include those from several approaches: Lean, Theory of Constraints, Six Sigma, and total quality management (TQM). Often these tools are applied to reduce inventory and operating costs; but their potency in creating a demand-driven supply chain should be understood.

### 17.2.1 Continuous Improvement Model for the Demand-Driven Supply Chain

Figure 17.3 describes a circular continuous improvement process for applying tools to create a demand-driven supply chain. This process will take time to complete; it is not one that happens quickly by fiat. At the core of the process is time-mapping, a

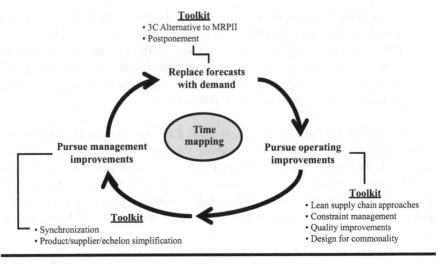

**Figure 17.3  Achieving the demand-driven supply chain.**

careful documentation of lead times throughout the supply chain as demonstrated in Table 17.1. Cutting lead time and cycle time is the core purpose of the journey.

Two important methodologies for becoming demand-driven rely on the virtues of *Commonality* discussed earlier. These are *postponement* and the *3C Alternative to MRPII*, shown at the top of the cycle in Figure 17.3. Examples of postponement include companies already noted in this chapter. Dell's build-to-order model for its A-type products "postpones" commitment of final product configurations until the order arrives. Mix-to-order paint technology at the point of sale enables blending colors to match other colors or paint chips provided by the customer. Apparel companies such as American Apparel and United Colors of Benetton delay dyeing garments until consumer demand for specific colors is determined by market performance, thereby avoiding costly overproduction of some colors.

A company implementing a demand-driven supply chain could start immediately to convert its decisions from forecast-driven to demand-driven. This should trigger efforts employing both operational and management tools to cut both process cycle time and overall supply chain lead time.

## 17.2.2  3C Alternative to MRPII

The 3C Alternative to MRPII deserves particular attention.* Although there are many ways to reach a demand-driven supply chain, this methodology has the elements one must address on such a journey. Similar to postponement, 3C capitalizes on the *Commonality* (one of the Cs) inherent in product structures. It is especially

---

* For further reading, see Refs. 1 and 2.

appropriate in products and market combinations where achieving forecast accuracy is difficult. This is likely in V and T products where products with a common base are sold in many forms and outlets. The fact that A-type products are sold through fewer channels means there are fewer sources for forecast data on which to base decisions. However, A-type products built on common modules such as Honda engines should also consider 3C.

The other Cs in 3C are *Consumption* and *Capacity*. Consumption comes from the demand-driven property in 3C wherein end-user consumption drives decisions along the chain. This is achieved by identifying "consumption centers" between links in the chain. The consumption centers trigger simultaneous replenishment orders from upstream sources. This feature addresses the common problem of lag due to differing replenishment lead times and serves to synchronize the chain.

Another example of a supply chain, shown in Figure 17.4, helps explain 3C. This is a V-type product example because it begins with a simple formulation that is reshaped into different configurations based on packaging and labels. Similar to the example in Figure 17.2, only retailers (1) and distributors (2) closest to the end user have visibility over actual consumption. If they base their decisions on demand, the percentage demand-driven for the supply chain is 22 (2/9). With consumption centers further back in the chain (3 upward), replenishment will be by demand rather than forecast, increasing the percentage of decisions that are demand-driven. For V-type products as in this example, the percentage should ultimately be high—90% to 100%.

*Capacity*, the last C, sets 3C replenishment rules. This is how much to replenish when the signal comes. These replenishments are on fixed intervals called the "time between pulls (or purchases)," or TBP. Note that 3C employs a fixed interval, variable quantity reordering cycle, rather than a fixed quantity, variable interval one used by those who rely on economic order quantity (EOQ). This ensures regular flow; one knows that product will move at every interval as long as there is consumption. If there is no end-user consumption, no production or other movement

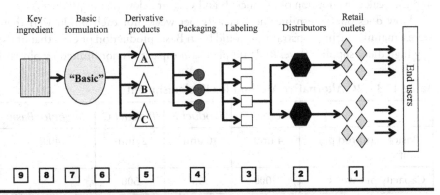

**Figure 17.4   Example supply chain for 3C application.**

will occur, limiting inventory additions in the absence of end-user demand. Also, by setting rules based on capacity, there can never—at least theoretically—be an out-of-stock condition.

The data in Table 17.3 illustrate how to derive a replenishment rule for manufacturing the Basic Formulation (level 6)—labeled "Basic" in Figure 17.4. This is the raw material for the three derivative products in Figure 17.4, products A, B, and C. With data from the bill of materials, or BOM, Table 17.3 shows how much Basic is required for each derivative product—4 units for each unit of product A, 10 units for product B, and 2 units for product C.

Conventional practice would have us forecasting all the end items for A, B, and C to decide how much Basic to produce. However, 3C takes a simpler approach. The rule is based on the frequency that Basic will be produced (the TBP), which is weekly in the example. The Capacity feature of 3C requires us to determine how much Basic could ever conceivably be consumed in the TBP period (a week). This capacity would assume that the largest user of Basic is 100% of product demand. In this case, this is product A that would require 4000 units. If nothing but product A were sold, 4000 units of Basic would be required. For product B this figure is 500 units; for product C it is 1000 units. This assumption is conservative because products B and C will likely also be sold in any given week.

So, the business rule is that Basic replenishment be sufficient to reach the target inventory of 4000 units. If downstream demand has "pulled," or consumed, 1500 units of Basic in the past week, then 1500 units would be ordered. If none were pulled, zero units would be ordered. No rule could be simpler. Note that the 3C method also builds in reserve stock of Basic to populate the chain with initial inventory and to account for Basic's lead time. But, essentially, the amount reordered equals the amount consumed, and customer demand is satisfied.

One reaction might be that targeting so conservatively will result in excess Basic inventory. The reality is that Basic will be consumed as it is produced, so that actual cycling inventory levels will never reach 4000 units. Also, the methodology allows for cutting back on the target inventory since the 100% assumption is probably unlikely, and the peak consumption of products B and C is far below that of product A.

How does one determine the "capacity per week" for each product? If there were a manufacturing constraint, it could be in Basic production or even that of the key ingredient supplier (level 8). If supply chain capacity is not limited by physical

**Table 17.3  3C Alternative Method for Replenishment**

|  | Product A | Product B | Product C | Target for Basic |
|---|---|---|---|---|
| "Basic" required per unit | 4 units | 10 units | 2 units | 4000[a] |
| Capacity per week | 1000 | 50 | 500 | |

[a] 4 Units A × 1000.

constraints, then the constraint is the maximum sales rate of all the products that use Basic. For most T- and V-type products, internal constraints are unlikely in downstream processes such as assembly, packaging, and labeling.

For a T-type product, the chief consumption center will be at the very end of the chain closest to the end user. A T-type product supplier seeking to provide VMI services to retailers with a broad customer base could use 3C to assure that enough inventory is on hand. For example, in Figure 17.4, the key ingredient supplier who serves many customers could manage its finished goods with 3C.

The supplier of a component to A-type assembly manufacturers such as Dell or General Motors could provide reliable, responsive VMI services to customers using 3C. Forecasts from the suppliers would establish initial inventories and be the basis for target inventories, providing a competitive advantage in selling to these customers.

Perhaps the greatest value of 3C is to V-type supply chains as in our example in Figure 17.4. Forecasting is very difficult because there are so many final product SKUs. Here, 3C offers an attractive alternative to synchronize the supply chain in the face of variable lead time and replenishment cycles, preventing inventory buildup and lost sales due to outages. Reducing lost sales addresses market mediation costs that arise from mismatches in supply and demand. These costs were the subject of Chapter 11, Section 11.3.

Mentioned earlier was the fact that retail supply chains must respond to goods in different parts of their life cycle, especially hard-to-predict fashion products. Some products may be "mature" with relatively consistency demand or declining and near the end of their economic lives; others may be "growth" products in great and growing demand because of their novelty. Other special situations arise from promotions, sales, and seasonal goods. All these factors are arguments for moving from a forecast-driven planning method to a demand-driven one that offers flexibility. The next section describes process improvement tools that complement postponement and 3C and make retail supply chains better able to handle seasonal and other special circumstances.

## 17.3 Demand-Driven Tools and Techniques

Figure 17.3 toolkit for initiatives that support the transition to the demand-driven supply chain shows both operations and management improvements. As we saw in Table 17.2, both types of improvement are required. The groups differ in the talents they call upon. Operating improvements require industrial and manufacturing engineering type skills. Management improvements are business-related actions, such as pruning products, reducing suppliers, and collaborating with trading partners.

Achievements in these efforts will show up in time mapping that reflects lead time and cycle time. Because there is some variability in how these terms are defined, the authors provide working definitions.

*Lead time* is defined as industry expectation, set by market forces, for the time required from order entry to delivery of the product. It can also include the time to totally close the transaction, including inspecting the product and making payment.

*Cycle time* is the amount of time it takes to produce the product if the velocity were 100% and there were no pauses or queues in the operation. That is, the product moves quickly from one step to another through the process. If a seller maintains a finished-goods inventory, the lead time will likely be less than the cycle time. Dell prospered early in its life because it, not necessarily its suppliers, has a cycle time less than the industry standard lead time for custom computers. For a major build-to-order purchase, for example an aircraft, the cycle time is less than the lead time because the customer is reserving a place in a future production schedule that could be years away.

Being able to claim the shortest lead time among competitors is a customer service advantage. Reducing cycle time to support the demand-driven supply chain also leads to competitive advantages through lower costs and better responses to market changes. This is possible because velocities—the percentage of lead time required by cycle time—in many supply chains can be less than 5%.

## 17.3.1 Operating Improvements

Many of the operating improvements listed here have been or are being adopted by companies. There will be few readers who will not have heard of "Lean" or "Six Sigma," for example. This section links them with the implementation of the demand-driven supply chain. Too often, they are only pursued for their own sake, not as part of an overall strategy to become demand-driven. Companies can enjoy higher returns if they blend these solutions. The obstacle to this is the reality that certain techniques come into fashion from time to time even though their underpinnings are not really new.

### 17.3.1.1 Lean Supply Chain Approaches

There are many techniques that arise from the Toyota Production System (TPS) that are collectively referred to as Lean manufacturing or, more recently, Lean supply chain. The two "pillars" of TPS are the following[6]:

- *Just-in-time* (JIT). This refers to the goal of producing the right products in the needed quantities at the right time, or being demand-driven. JIT in the TPS infiltrates the production process. JIT is also a goal of postponement and 3C.
- *Autonomation.* This is "autonomous defect control." This term refers to preventing the passing of defective units from one step to another, avoiding disruption.

Popular Lean approaches under the umbrella of these pillars include the following:

*Kanban systems to signal the need to move through the factory and supply chain.* The tool supports the demand-driven supply chain at the factory and work-center levels. Kanban is a fixed-quantity, variable-interval approach and can be used at intermediate processes between 3C variable-quantity, fixed-interval consumption centers. There are some operations that may require a minimum batch size to make production or shipping economical. If this is the case, 3C replenishment quantities should be expressed in "batches" rather than "units."

*Production smoothing (heijunka).* This is load leveling that establishes an operating band that avoids too rapid fluctuations in production. A major waste is uneven production where most of the production is at the end of fiscal periods, usually months or quarters. In 3C-regulated production, smoothing would assure that each item has a slot in production/shipping schedules during the time between pulls. Production leveling also includes the idea of "takt" time, also called the "drumbeat." Takt time can be long or short depending on the type of product. Boeing might produce seven aircraft a month, whereas GE produces 700 light bulbs a minute. The takt time in the first case is 4.2 days; in the latter it is 0.086 seconds.

*Standardized operations/standard work.* Documentation of individual operations as well as factorywide expectations for a process ensures that best practices will be employed. The standard way includes cycle time, the operations routine, work methods, skill definitions, and quantity of work in process.

*Setup reduction.* These efforts, referred to as SMED for *single minute exchange of dies*, involve advanced preparation of equipment needed for production in factories. The preparation enables a fast changeover from one operation to another. This is a foundation for attacking the batch mentality that squeezes as much production as possible out of a single setup. The result of SMED efforts is better utilization of capacity and fewer interruptions in the flow of product through the chain.

*Cells with improved layouts and flexible workers.* In manufacturing and DCs, a worker can operate several types of machines and is cross-trained in different operations. Multifunctional workers also enable the operation to work with fewer workers. All the resources needed to fulfill a customer need are clustered together in a cell. Increasingly, this includes not only production capabilities but also customer service, quality, engineering, and finance staff.

*Small group improvement efforts.* These efforts keep moving the organization toward continuous improvement in operations. *Kaizen* in Japanese means continuous improvement. Other sources of improvement are very intense projects that produce more radical, innovative change. In Lean circles, these are called *kaikaku*. Chapter 15 described several continuous improvement kaizen models. These included PDCA (Plan-Do-Check-Act) and Six Sigma's DMAIC (define–measure–analyze–improve–control). Undertaking the development of a supply chain strategy, using these models, is a kaikaku-type undertaking. Sometimes, such efforts seek to uncover "obstacles in the river." This is done by deliberately moving resources such as staff and inventory from a smoothly running process. When problems emerge, such as a rock or sandbar in the river, the company knows what to work on to improve the process.

*Visual controls.* These are easy-to-see displays of what is happening in operations. An example is prominent display of any conditions causing an interruption of flow so there is immediate awareness and understanding of deviations from normal processes. A worker can stop a production line if defects are being produced, thereby encouraging quick correction of the situation. With 3C, the tasks of monitoring consumption centers for shortfalls or excess inventory and calculating replenishment quantities are simplified.

## 17.3.1.2  Constraint Management

Figures 17.2 and 17.4 depict flow in the supply chain. TOC, referred to previously, observes that each process has a constraint and that these constraints need to be well managed. TOC calls the constraint the capacity constraint resource, or CCR. The CCR could be the same capacity constraint employed in setting replenishment levels with 3C. In our example in Subsection 17.2.2, the constraint was the sales rate, not a physical constraint. In Table 17.1, the 4-week lead time for the supplier finished goods replenishment (#6) might indicate a physical constraint in the supplier's production processes.

TOC calls for recognizing the constraint and adjusting inputs to the manufacturing enterprise or the supply chain so as not to exceed the constraint's capacity. Some companies, through lack of awareness of the constraint, may attempt to push too much product into the front end of their pipelines. This may be in response to previously mentioned new product introductions, sales campaigns, or promotions. It could also be from attempts to "stuff" channels with inventory to improve reported financial results.

TOC makes two other recommendations with regard to constraints. These are the following:

1. In seeking out investments to reduce costs, look for the CCR. Improvements there will return greater benefits because they improve the throughput, or capacity, of the entire supply chain. Savings at nonconstraints are minimal.
2. Use inventory to protect the CCR from upstream interruptions. So, in the event a nonconstraint operation ahead of the CCR is unavailable for a time, additional inventory will keep the CCR going until flow is restored. This is accommodated in the 3C methodology by considering upstream lead time when setting up initial inventories.

### 17.3.1.3 Quality Improvements

Quality improvements emphasize improving processes to minimize their variation. These occur at the "hands-on" operations that create value for the customer. They take the form of Six Sigma initiatives in many companies. Six Sigma initiatives often travel alongside Lean and TOC implementations as managers seek out opportunities for improvement.

Reducing process variability is even more critical as partners become more tightly bound by JIT replenishments in demand-driven supply chains. Slip-ups by partners are magnified several times. We address this in this section because poor processes lead to bad parts or no parts as downstream operations dry up, creating a scramble along the chain to fill in the gap. Indeed, many expeditors, purchasing people, ERP systems, and inventory-tracking methods are put in place to react to such foul-ups. At the retail level, the result can be costly stockouts. Taking away the root cause quality deficiencies enables costs to drop and revenues to increase.

Process capability measures how well a process can perform to the specification set for it. The metrics of process capability are statistical and measure how well a process conforms to these specifications. The specification in whatever form is an important part of the buyer–seller relationship. Too tight a specification means the seller must go to extraordinary means to meet the specification. It could also lead to scrap, lost sales, and profit erosion. Sometimes, specifications are set without consideration of the capabilities of the manufacturing or distribution processes. Too loose a specification, on the other hand, spells trouble when the seller's components go into the buyer's product, potentially resulting in poor-quality products and a negative reaction at the end-user level that creates a backlash aimed at the retailer. Any of these conditions will gum up a demand-driven supply chain.

The statistics for quality have been around for a long time. Common performance measures include $P_p$, $P_{pk}$, $C_p$, $C_{pk}$, first-time capability (FTC), line speed, and defective parts per million (ppm). This section provides an overview of common process capability terms and addresses their importance in the demand-driven supply chain.

The capability measures assume that outcomes of most processes will follow a normal distribution, known as the bell-shaped curve. Each normal distribution is specified by a *mean* (called X-bar) and a *standard deviation* symbolized by the Greek letter sigma, $\sigma$. The mean is the average of all the process outcomes; the standard deviation is a measure of the variation from the mean.

Both means and standard deviations can be calculated with spreadsheet programs. Adding all the outcomes and dividing by the number of observations gives the mean. For example, the mean of 1, 2, and 3 is $(1 + 2 + 3)/3 = 2$. The standard deviation takes the difference between each observation and the observation mean, squares it to remove plus and minus values, then divides by the number of observations, and finally takes the square root of the result. In the normal distribution,

68.3 percent of all outcomes are within one standard deviation of the mean, 95.4 percent are within two, and 99.7 percent are within three.

The three normal distributions in Figure 17.5 have the same mean but different standard deviations. "A" at the bottom has the highest standard deviation because it is the "fattest." "C" has the lowest because it is the narrowest. Because predictability is good when it comes to processes, a smaller sigma signals low variation from the specification, the sign of a reliable process.

However, reliability such as that in distributions A and B is not enough when you consider that there may be many processes required to produce a product. Even a "three-sigma" process capability will produce 3000 defects in a million tries. With many processes required to make a product, at three-sigma levels there will be many defective products unless expensive inspection steps are added to the process. A Six-Sigma capability close to what we see in B and certainly implicit in C means that only 3.4 outcomes in a million attempts are out of specification for a process. This low defect rate will lead to reliable, competitive products.

The concepts described in this section also apply to "attributes." Attribute measures are "yes, it passes" or "no, it doesn't pass" situations. The so-called "perfect order" in the distribution industry would be judged on attributes because it must possess predefined attributes (on time, complete, proper invoice, and so on). Certainly, a less-than-perfect order has the potential to generate unwanted transactions that

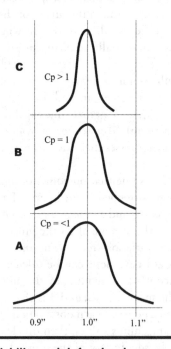

**Figure 17.5 Process reliability and defect levels.**

add cost and waste time. A benefit of 3C is that it sets up replenishment order rules among partners, reducing the chances of error ordering or quantities.

An example illustrates these concepts. A part is specified to be 1 inch long with a tolerance range of ± 0.1 inch. Thus, any part between 0.9 and 1.1 inch is acceptable under this specification, as shown in Figure 17.5. The performance measures for the process used to cut the part to that length are capable of repeatedly making parts within that range. After measuring a sample of actual parts, distributions similar to those shown in Figure 17.5 could result.

For example, we calculate a sigma value of 0.02 inch for a sample distribution of measured parts. The process sigma is then

$$\text{Process sigma} = \pm[\text{Process tolerance}/(2 \times \text{process sigma})]$$
$$= \pm[0.2/(2 \times 0.02)] = \pm 5$$

Another measure is called the process capability, or $C_p$, calculated by dividing the same process tolerance range by six times the standard deviation as follows:

$$C_p = 0.2/(6 \times 0.02) = 1.67$$

This value, which is greater than 1, most closely matches $C$ in Figure 17.5. It is well within the Six-Sigma capability and would produce fewer defects than 3.4 per million chances. A standard deviation of 0.033 would produce a curve like B in Figure 17.5 as long as the process was centered on the desired mean of 1.0 inch. This would also be a Six-Sigma process. Standard deviations greater than 0.033 produce $C_p$ values less than 1.0. These curves look similar to A in Figure 17.5. The process is not capable of meeting the Six-Sigma standard.

Despite the poor performance, the "A" situation has long been accepted practice in manufacturing, distribution, and retail. For manufacturing, this situation gave rise to "receiving inspection" where manufacturers head off suppliers' defective goods from reaching its product lines. Quality procedures now call for 100% inspection of parts if the processes that produced those parts fall below standards, creating a very visible cost of operations. To combat the situation, Jack Welch, the former CEO of General Electric, built a strategy around achieving Six-Sigma processes.

Figure 17.5 shows distributions centered on the specified mean—1 inch. What if they aren't centered? Figure 17.6 shows tight distributions, equivalent to acceptable values of $C_p$, but off the desired mean. The measure $C_{pk}$ corrects for shifts in the mean even though the spread is acceptable. "A" in this case is centered above the mean. "B" is below, whereas "C" is acceptable because it is centered. Both "A" and "B" would have $C_p$ ratings in the acceptable range, but $C_{pk}$ would be unacceptable for both. "C" has an acceptable $C_{pk}$ because it is centered.

Sometimes, only a small sample is available. This happens in the case of a new component or a new process. In these cases, the process is untested under high

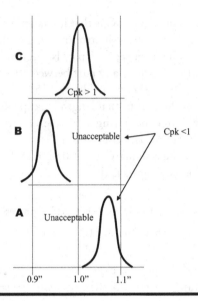

**Figure 17.6 Meaning of C$_{pk}$.**

volume conditions. So, managers will calculate $P_k$ and $P_{pk}$ using pilot production samples. A higher threshold is required. For example, a $C_{pk}$ threshold can be 1.33, while the $P_{pk}$ threshold is 1.67.

The measures we just discussed are likely found for individual operations. Other commonly used performance measures gauge the overall process. *First-time capability* (FTC) counts the number of acceptable products at each step in the process and at the end of the process. The constraint is that no rework can be done on the item at any point in the process. The picture provided is twofold. It shows how capable the collective process is, and it also points to possible bottlenecks that diminish capacity.

The equation for measuring FTC at the operation or process level is as follows:

FTC = (quantity attempted − quantity rejected)/quantity attempted

FTC is often combined with a line speed evaluation. In manufacturing, this evaluation will confirm that the capacity required by the buyer is available. Line capacity is an issue with high-volume, closely linked supply chains. Often, the supplier is dedicating capacity, including machines and tooling, to fulfill the buyer's requirements. Line speed verification means producing product using the facilities and equipment when full-scale production begins. FTC can be calculated simultaneously. Product can also be measured to calculate process capabilities.

With low tolerance for error becoming more prevalent, collaboration along the supply chain becomes more crucial. Here are some examples in which quality issues play a part in joint trading partner decision-making.

- *Designer versus doer.* The product designer, usually an engineer, must specify tolerances. Engineering is sometimes accused of "throwing the design over the wall" to manufacturing. SCM increasingly recognizes the need for the customer, designers, and operations people to work together to agree to and achieve process capabilities. Establishing collaborative relationships among trading partners to achieve the economies of the demand-driven supply chain will require the upstream partner to have capable processes.
- *Price versus quality.* The supplier selection decision may be driven by purchase price. However, the lowest purchase price may bring lower quality and bring on an abundance of hidden costs. Buying organizations must guard against this possibility. SCM practice will find new ways to reconcile conflicts between these two perspectives.
- *Old loyalties versus new blood.* There will be a time when the cord between the organization and a long-time supplier will have to be cut to assure the flow of quality components. When this should happen is often a gray area. Changing suppliers imposes a real cost on the buying organization. New sources have to be found; patterns of behavior have to be relearned.

The quality measures mentioned in this section emerged from manufacturing industry experience. They continue to find applications in the operations of nonmanufacturing supply chain partners such as transportation, warehousing, and consolidation and distribution centers.

## 17.3.1.4 Design for Commonality

The demand-driven supply chain strategies at the top of Figure 17.3, postponement, and 3C work best when there is commonality in product designs. Some organizations do not design their products with this in mind because there are design constraints, or they are ignorant of the advantages. Commonality benefits exist from modular structures for complex products down to using common fasteners and other small components. These reduce raw material cost and simplify aftermarket service. Interestingly, chain restaurants have for years recognized the efficiency in combining a limited number of inputs into a variety of menu combinations. For example, Mexican restaurants, employing postponement, use refried beans, tortillas, rice, guacamole, salsa fresca, various cheeses, and five or six preprepared meats in numerous menu offerings including tacos, tostadas, enchiladas, burritos, salads, and many other combinations.

Postponement is especially good at reducing the inventory needed to maintain a certain level of customer service. The savings in inventory can be calculated. If a company sells two items that can be configured after orders come in, then it can reduce the cycling inventory—which excludes safety and dead stock—by 39%. This benefit is because postponement has eliminated the end-item forecasts and substituted last-minute configuration. Likewise, a postponement of five items into one common item reduces the inventory required to maintain customer service by 55%. So, the economics are compelling as shown in the table.

| Consolidation from Postponement (Ratio) | Cycling Inventory Reduction (%) |
|:---:|:---:|
| 2:1 | 39 |
| 3:1 | 44 |
| 4:1 | 50 |
| 5:1 | 55 |

Achieving commonality requires collaboration between sales, marketing, operations, and design functions. Designing its products with this in mind can make a manufacturer a more attractive partner to downstream retailers and distributors.

Postponement provides benefits such as those in the preceding table even if physical configuration changes are not needed. This comes by delaying (postponing) distribution to endpoints in the supply chain, such as individual retail stores. This is also the 3C approach, and it is the role a distributor plays in serving multiple retail stores from a centralized facility. Assuming each store sells different amounts of an item, holding stock at the distributor, whether it's internal or external, reduces the chances of dead stock at slower-selling stores and stockouts at faster-selling ones. This was the basis for Sam Walton's original Wal-Mart distribution strategy, in which one DC served 10 or so stores within 250 miles, less than a day's drive away with the ability to return to the DC on the same day.

## 17.3.2 Management Improvements

Although operating improvements are most frequently assigned to technical staff, achieving management improvements requires managerial skills. Chapters 15 and 16 recommend frameworks for involving multiple functions and trading partners in initiatives to achieve the demand-driven supply chain. This involvement is important; some managers do not see operations as part of their job descriptions, yet their participation is necessary. The following subsections address issues using the demand-driven supply chain described in Tables 17.1 and 17.2. The decisions required are not technical in nature, but they do involve change, and must be understood and managed accordingly.

### 17.3.2.1 Synchronization and Fixed-Interval Planning

This category of management change could require widespread adjustments in many retailer and trading partner departments. For example, shifting to weekly, from monthly and quarterly, merchandise planning might require added staff and changes in systems, as well as changes in supplier behavior. It is also likely that synchronization would occur on a product-by-product or a customer-by-customer basis. This is because some product volumes are too low for such consideration, and some retail customers or suppliers may not want to participate. The result is tailored supply chains for individual "businesses within the business," such as those described in Chapter 12. In Chapter 15, West Marine tailored its replenishment schedules to correspond with the schedules of suppliers of different types of product.

Direct distribution from OEMs to selected retailer outlets will also strain some companies. This could require information links with the retailers and the ability to ship in smaller quantities—in this case, quantities similar to those distributed by former intermediaries. The reorder time for material is also shortened. This could require new procedures and relationships with suppliers. A company accustomed to a batch mentality must adjust to the fixed-interval discipline. This feature establishes a more continuous flow in the chain. It may also force a company to abandon department-level optimization. Costs such as transportation may increase with tighter control of inventory and the increased possibility of dispatching partially loaded delivery trucks or containers to customers.

### 17.3.2.2 Simplification

Many times, operating functions such as manufacturing and distribution must attempt to manufacture difficult products, manage complex distribution networks, or deal with poorly performing suppliers. The case from Table 17.2 shows that the demand-driven supply chain would bypass a distributor to create a direct path to the end user, increasing the speed of information flow about retail consumption. Depending on the situation, this could require support from marketing, sales, financial, and operations managers.

The case did not deal with the key suppliers for any of several reasons stated earlier. However, the potential for improvement looks attractive. Improvement could be seen if the materials supplier were to synchronize with the new, shorter periods required by the manufacturer, who will be moving to a weekly cycle to meet the needs of its customer, the retailer. This is especially true because the current cycle is quarterly. If this participation is not forthcoming, there will be a penalty in terms of excessive or insufficient raw material inventory for continuing to use this supplier.

## 17.4 Sponsoring the Demand-Driven Supply Chain

Leadership toward the goal of being demand-driven can come from any one of the links in the chain. This "leader" must enlist other echelons in the effort. Leadership will depend on motivation, the ability to collaborate, the product category, opportunities for profit improvement, and the amount of business at stake. Depending on these variables, there are three likely leaders representing different supply chain echelons:

1. Retailers seeking to lower merchandise costs while assuring availability. They may take a category-by-category approach or a focus centered on store brands.
2. Independent distributors seeking a competitive edge by virtue of the service while lowering their cost at the same time.
3. OEMs who seek to improve their position while lowering market mediation costs for themselves if they bear the brunt for returns or for the retailer.

An OEM will find implementing the demand-driven supply chain attractive if it can do more business with lower inventories while maintaining or achieving high levels of service. Some may employ the technique selectively with larger customers. Can each of these be a "business within the business" with a tailored demand-driven supply chain?

Retailers, probably the largest sector considered here, might take the leadership role with selected OEMs. Alternatively, the retailer might set up pull systems through their captive DCs, ordering merchandise from most or all its suppliers based on demand. This would require negotiations with a large number of suppliers.

Independent distributors may have the most to gain as intermediaries by injecting demand-driven techniques into decision-making process. Indeed, those providing vendor-managed inventory services already do. The distributor may also have the most to gain because their profitability is closely tied to their ability to manage inventory.

## 17.5 Demand-Driven Supply Chain—Summary

Achieving the demand-driven supply chain gives trading partners a reason for collaborating and provides mutual advantages. Depending on the priority and the complexity of the chain, the journey could be a lengthy one; so, the continuous improvement mentality is necessary. Also required are skills in working on multi-company improvement projects. It is likely that leadership for the demand-driven supply chain will lie with larger OEMs and distributors and include large retailers. Members of these echelons understand the problem better and can influence product design. All can utilize demand-driven delivery as a competitive weapon in the dynamic retail supply chain.

# References

1 Fernández-Rañada, Miguel, Gurrola-Gal, F. Xavier, and López-Tello, Enrique, 3C: A Proven Alternative to MRPII for Optimizing Supply Chain Performance, Boca Raton, FL: St. Lucie Press, 2000.

2. Ayers, James B, *Handbook of Supply Chain Management*, *2nd ed.*

3. Monden, Yasuhiro, *Toyota Production System*, Norcross, Georgia: Institute of Industrial Engineers, 1983.

# Chapter 18

# Product Tracking along Retail Supply Chains

This chapter describes retail supply chain tracking tools categorized as "automatic identification and data capture" (AIDC) technologies.* These technologies have enabled multichannel, or *omni-channel* supply chains. These offer consumers choices in ordering and receiving merchandise. For example, merchandise could be ordered online and mailed to the buyer. Or the buyer could call in the order and take delivery of the merchandise in a brick and mortar store.

Technical innovations, accompanied by an increasing number of solution providers, make this an area of "churn" in the roles of supply chain participants. For example, merchandise formerly bought in a store can be ordered online, diminishing the store role and the retailers' need for real estate.

The same technologies also create confusion among supply chain decision makers. The confusion arises in deciding which of the many proposed options is the "correct" one for a particular supply chain. Also, the economics of AIDC change continuously, with costs of implementation declining as technologies become more widespread.

Despite the confusion, channel masters such as Wal-Mart and the Department of Defense mandate increased use of radiofrequency identification, or RFID, by their suppliers. RFID is a prominent AIDC technology; therefore, managers along the retail supply chain, including manufacturers and distributors, must be informed about its applications.

The retail industry already relies heavily on technology. Each year a large retailer could easily have thousands of suppliers providing tens of thousands of stockkeeping

---

* The authors thank Mike Gerry for his review of this chapter.

units (SKUs) and hundreds of thousands of deliveries to hundreds of locations. The size of today's retailers such as Costco, Target, Best Buy, Walgreen's, and others has been enabled by electronic digital information processes. For any single company, these transactions generate millions—if not billions—of information exchanges in the form of forecasts, orders, shipping notices, receipt documentation, payments, and returns.

The need to track merchandise extends from the manufacturing process to the store shelf. In fact, according to Kerry Pauling, vice president of information systems at Wal-Mart, getting stock through the "last 90 feet" from the stockroom to the shelf is "where we often have breakdowns." An interesting example of potentially costly losses occurs in grocery stores. Customers often decide at the check stand against purchasing items they have previously selected. These may be perishables that, if not returned to refrigerators or freezers promptly, will spoil and become unsalable, yet the inventory tracking system has totally lost track of the whereabouts of these products. Keeping tabs on such complex, high-volume processes is daunting. Furthermore, in a global economy, trading partners in many countries are bolstering the need for standards that ensure efficient and timely information exchanges.

This chapter provides an overview of selected AIDC technologies, addressing technologies, and related standards. The contents include the following:

1. Standards for identification and tracking
2. RFID
3. The vision for integrated distribution and retail solutions

## 18.1 Low-Tech Retailing

Fred Abernathy is with the Center for Textile and Apparel Research at Harvard University. He has traced the growth of bar-code technology, an early AIDC technology. Bar codes, the most common of which are Universal Product Codes (UPCs), are the foundation standards for retail supply chain tracking. Abernathy describes the labor-intensive state of the retail supply chain before bar codes made their appearance.[1]

- Merchandise was spread around—on the store floor, in the backroom, or in the warehouse.
- Knowing what was actually selling was problematic.
- Orders were placed 6 to 9 months ahead of the selling season, well before trends in demand could be discerned.
- Assistant buyers tracked inventory manually, a labor-intensive process.
- Paper records reflected sales of categories, not individual SKUs, reducing the precision required for effective reordering.
- The retailer, detached by long lead time and information gaps from manufacturers, carried the risks that go with stockouts or surpluses.

Before bar codes, "Kimball tickets," a small form of the old punch card technology, was the only real mechanization that existed for inventory tracking. These tickets were processed by a form of unit record equipment and were prone to human error. The advent of bar codes began the shift to automated tracking. In 1973, IBM was awarded the contract by the Uniform Grocery Product Code (UGPCC) Ad Hoc Committee and the consulting firm McKinsey & Company to develop a bar-code technology usable across the industry. In June 1974, at a store in Ohio, a 10-pack of Wrigley's chewing gum was the first item to cross a bar-code scanner. Subsequently, the retailer Kmart introduced bar codes for apparel in 1983. Others like Wal-Mart followed, bringing the spread of what Abernathy describes as "Lean retailing." Improvements in computing technology aided and abetted the spread by translating captured bar-code data to support merchandising decisions.

The initial UPC specification had 12 digits, 11 required by UGPCC plus 1 check digit. The check digit protects against errors in reading the codes. This version is the first and is shown in Figure 18.1. Most current U.S. bar codes use this format, or *symbology*. After submittal, the IBM team was asked to add a 13th digit that could be read without modifying equipment already in the field. This is the second version in Figure 18.1. This addition provided country identification, in effect enabling the worldwide spread of the UPC. The additional digit also led to the European Article Numbering, or EAN, system administered by EAN International (now GS1). Their standards are called the EAN*UCC standard. They cover bar codes, electronic data interchange (EDI) transaction sets, XML schemas, and other supply chain requirements.

As noted later, they promote the standard under the auspices of another organization, EPCglobal. EPC stands for *electronic product code*. In the automated identification space, participating organizations, standards, and products have proliferated, a potential confusion factor to those who have not followed the evolution.

In Figure 18.1, there are 10 identifying digits plus "overhead" digits. These are for the check digit and identification functions. The EAN version has the two-digit

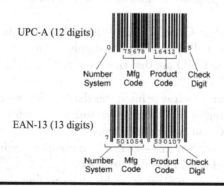

**Figure 18.1   Barcode formats.**

number system code plus a check digit, whereas the UCC version has one identifier and one check digit. A manufacturer (or distributor or retailer) can have 99,999 SKUs by virtue of the five-digit product code. Adding to the complexity of the standards, each of these symbology standards has variations for special circumstances. These variations use techniques to shrink the space required for the bar code, enabling bar coding of small items.

Once a manufacturer, distributor, or retailer is assigned an EPC manager code, the organization is free to assign codes to products. This can be for internal or external use. In fact, some retail merchandise such as an apparel item may have multiple bar-code identities as it passes along the supply chain. An example would be the product code for the original manufacturer and another for the retailer.

## 18.2  Beyond Basic Bar Codes

As older UCC and EAN formats have neared their capacities, standards for the 14-digit Global Trade Identification Number (GTIN) emerged. *GTIN* has become the umbrella term for all the bar-code data structures such as those in Figure 18.1 and others needed for other data carriers such as RFID. This number identifies the manufacturer, product, version, and serial number. Where a number uses fewer than 14 digits, it is padded with zeros, encouraging migration to a uniform bar-code length.

The voluntary nonprofit organization EPCglobal, Inc., is an independent body with a board of governors from leading supply chain "subscribers." The organization had its origin in the Auto-ID Center at MIT. GS1 and GS1 U.S., which set standards, are members. EPCglobal's mission is to support the deployment of radio-frequency technology. EPCglobal refers to this as the EPCglobal Network™. In 2005, the head of EPCglobal US, Mike Meranda, described the role of the organization.[2] Meranda stated, "Standards development is not the destination." He notes that technology is "a tool to achieve a business objective." His organization used five elements to promote its mission to the technical community:

1. Electronic Product Code™ (EPC)—the globally unique serial number that identifies items of all types along the supply chain
2. ID System—the RFID tag that stores the EPC and the hardware needed to read the EPC
3. EPC Middleware—software interfaces that manage supply chain read events and the handling of the information; interfaces with EPC information services (#4 below) and enterprise systems
4. EPC Information Services—enables information exchanges with trading partners through the EPCglobal network
5. Discovery Services—tools that enable users to find data related to specific EPCs

The core element, the EPC, includes items in the GTIN and adds extra digits for unique item identification, supporting what is called "item-level tracking" or ILT. ILT aids in combating counterfeits, providing product quality documentation, and better managing inventory. A report in the publication *DC Velocity* described emerging applications for ILT and the drivers behind them.[3]

- Tagging innovative products such as new CDs and DVDs so they are easy to locate during their short introduction windows.
- Documenting pharmaceutical movement through the supply chain. Example: Purdue Pharma shipping tagged bottles of OxyContin to Wal-Mart and a wholesaler.
- Cost-effectively locating hard-to-find sizes and colors of upscale apparel items before a customer leaves the store because an item can't be found.
- Theft reduction for high-value goods such as jewelry, rental skis, and electronics.
- Expiration date tracking for food items such as cream cheese.
- Monitoring temperatures along the supply chain.
- Automatically playing a promotional video about the product when a customer picks up a merchandise item in the store.

In early 2016, the GS1 website reported the continued momentum of item-level tagging. The report noted the need for increased supply chain efficiency and the desire "to reduce out-of-stock issues."*

Figure 18.2 shows components of the EPC. EPCglobal refers to this number as a "license plate." It can be assigned to "objects" in the supply chain such as individual items, cases, pallets, and locations. It is also compatible with existing numbering systems such as the GTIN. The "manager" number is assigned to companies wanting to use the bar-code system.

Although the basic 12- and 13-digit bar codes are familiar to most retail customers, other bar-code formats exist that enable greater returns from the technology. These include the following:

- Reduced space symbology (RSS), for placing bar codes on small items or adding needed information not available in regular bar codes while keeping a small footprint.
- Two-dimensional (2-D) bar codes that, used with or without one-dimensional (1-D) codes such as UCC*EAN bar codes, provide around 2000 characters depending on the format. Figure 18.3 shows examples of the many available formats.

---

* GS1 website FAQ (frequently asked questions).

---

016.48000.246890.100000000

| 1 | 2 | 3 | 4 |

1. Header: identifies the length, type, structure, version and
   generation of the EPC (3 digits)
2. Manager number: identifies the company or entity (5 digits)
3. Object class: SKU or other object identification (6 digits)
4. Serial number: tailored to the item being tagged (9 digits)

---

**Figure 18.2    Electronic product code (EPC).**

---

**Figure 18.3    2D Barcode examples.**

RSS formats include RSS-14, RSS Limited, and RSS Expanded, and find application on smaller items such as individual pieces of fruit, cosmetics, jewelry, and so forth. Their appearance is similar to regular bar codes. Some formats have "double deck" or two lines of code to conserve space. Sometimes, the retailer needs to add information to basic bar codes in the same space provided by UCC*EAN bar codes. SKUs with limited shelf life such as dairy products and pharmaceuticals are examples and need to include expiration dates. Other applications include SKUs sold by weight such as meat and produce, items that require tracing, and promotion products eligible for coupons.

As shown in Figure 18.3, 2-D bar codes resemble postage stamps with a variety of patterns imprinted on them. Some applications combine conventional 1-D with 2-D data. Such uses described by the 2-D bar code company Dataintro Software include income tax returns, mixed SKU packing lists, and patient medical records. In these situations, the 1-D bar code provides the license plate identifier. The 2-D bar code provides the details. Other versions are designed for data capacity or for reading on high-speed conveyor lines.

Designing systems to read bar codes can be an engineering challenge. Intermec, a firm offering supply chain automation solutions, recommends different technologies depending on the nature of the item read, the potential for dirt on the bar code, whether the location is inside or outside, whether the bar code is 1-D or 2-D, and the distance over which the read must occur. Such complexities, plus the frequent need for labor to use the technology, are motivators for supply chain managers to turn to RFID technology, although bar coding is considerably less expensive and, in some instances, can be used in conjunction with newer technologies.

## 18.3 Radio-Frequency Identification

RFID applications already appear around us in the form of automatic car locks, road and bridge toll collection, subway fare collection, library materials checkout and return, animal identification microchips, and human implants of various sorts. Successful RFID implementation depends on collaboration among supply chain trading partners. For the distribution center (DC) or the retail store to use RFID, the manufacturer must place tags on its pallets, cartons, or individual items. What level—pallet, carton, or item—will vary, depending on item value, the cost of implementation, the need for control, and other factors.

### 18.3.1 Retail Application

The most common RFID application in retail supply chains calls for placement of low-cost "passive" tags. These are part of open-loop systems. That is, the merchandise passes from company to company along the supply chain. The tag is passive if it has no energy source. "Active" tags, discussed later, have batteries or other power sources. These are often installed in closed-loop systems confined to a single company or small group of trading partners. The more expensive active tags are usually recycled for multiple trips through the process.

The energy required to transmit the passive tag's content is provided by the radio-frequency energy transmitted by the reader. The reader transmits enough energy to cause the tag to respond with identifying data stored on the tag. The tag antenna length is half the wavelength of the operating frequency, so lower frequencies have larger antennas, the most visible part of the tag. The chip, in fact, is about the size of the head of a pin that can be seen as small dots near the center of the tags. Figure 18.4 has examples of RFID tags.

The antennas on the passive tags have different sensitivity to the direction of the reader's signal. The tag signal is also affected by metal or liquids within and near the tagged product and the location of the tag on the product. Tags should be chosen with these factors in mind, as well as an understanding of how each tag will be scanned and where that will occur. For example, the four-dipole model (upper right in Figure 18.4) is less sensitive to orientation. With regard to capacity, a passive tag can hold up to hundreds of bits of data.

With RFID tags on each case on a pallet, a reader can identify all the cases without a person having to scan each case. Lower-frequency readers have a short range of a few inches. Higher-frequency readers have ranges up to about 30 feet.

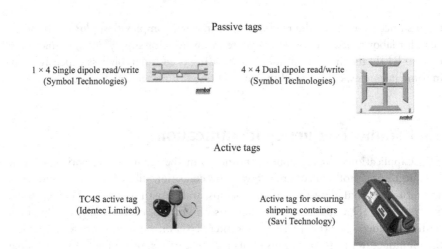

**Figure 18.4  Passive and active RFID tags.**

Like the bar-code system, designing an RFID application requires a number of considerations that depend on supply chain requirements and system costs. Some of these are listed later.

In a typical warehouse application, the reader will be placed at each dock door, or portal. The RFID data capture would take place as pallets are offloaded from the truck or railcar. Costs per portal can be in the thousands of dollars, so implementing RFID must be justified by savings in labor and improved tracking accuracy, particularly in large warehouses with 100 or more doors. To minimize this cost, warehouses frequently have separate RFID portals near a group of loading docks. Items are unloaded from trucks into a receiving area and then pushed through, or placed on a conveyor to pass through the RFID portal. Other applications call for handheld readers or readers on lift trucks. These provide added flexibility in exchange for a decreased investment.

The same economic hurdle exists at the store level—the need to lower the cost of tagging and reading enough so that improvements in labor cost and data utility can pay for the technology. Complicating matters is the fact that a company such as Wal-Mart dictates RFID to its manufacturers. However, the manufacturer may enjoy few direct benefits. However, the inclusion of RFID tags may result in large orders from large retail chains; most benefits accrue further down the supply chain. Section 18.4 describes an example of tracking stock as it moves from manufacturer to retail store shelf.

## 18.3.2 Active RFID

Active RFID tags include their own power supply. Two categories of these tags have internal power supplies in the form of batteries, an electric grid connection, or solar power. These are called active or semiactive (also called battery-assisted) tags. Active tags transmit to the reader unlike passive tags, which use energy from the reader to respond. The semiactive tag is triggered by the reader but uses onboard power to respond. This increases the range over which it can be read. The read is also faster because the delay involved in responding is lessened. A speedy response is important if the tag is moving at high speed. Active tags can be read at distances of about 300 feet.

Often, the best applications for active RFID are closed-loop supply chain processes. The closed-loop application takes place in a single facility or company or in linked processes shared by trading partners. An example is an auto parts supplier and its assembly plant customer. The active tag tracks material shipped to its supplier and is removed after the part is assembled onto an automobile. Another example would be a laptop computer repair facility serving a retailer such as Best Buy where active RFID tracks laptop location through the repair process. In closed-loop applications, the tag is attached when the item enters the process, and removed when it leaves.

Both passive and active tags support capabilities for rewriting data over the life of the tag. A read-only (RO) tag is programmed at the factory where it's manufactured; no rewriting is possible. So, this type of tag finds limited use. A write-once, read-many (WORM) is written by the user and read throughout the supply chain. This is the most common type of tag. A read-write (RW) tag can be rewritten practically indefinitely.

An alternative passive tag technology called the surface acoustic wave (SAW) has advantages over the microchips deployed in today's RFID tags. These chips are used on devices with touch screens and have a number of other applications. SAW chips utilize the piezoelectric effect, which relies on the fact that ceramic substances and some crystals generate voltage when mechanical stresses are applied to them. The transducer located on piezoelectric material generates a surface wave when excited by the reader's radio pulse. That surface wave is converted into acoustic wave pulses coded to the tag's data. The transducer then converts the waves back into a radio wave to send to the reader. The SAW technology has longer ranges, is more rugged, can be used around difficult materials such as metals and liquids, uses less power, and is more accurate.

### 18.3.3 RFID Applications

Engineering an RFID application must address a number of variables, including the following:

- The mission of the system—identification only, environmental sensing, or security
- The use for system data and interfacing systems that support data conversion
- The distance over which that must be read

- Antenna design to assure that tags can be read, and the orientation of containers to reader antennae
- The frequency to use for RF communication—generally, a choice between HF (3–30 MHz) and UHF (300 MHz–3 GHz)
- Materials in the environment and atmospheric conditions that might interfere with reception
- Economic factors such as the cost of tags and readers and the return on investment from the application (ROI)
- The need for rugged readers and tags in demanding locations such as warehouses
- The level of merchandise tagging (usually pallet, case, or individual item)
- Methods of attachment of tags to the pallets, cartons, or items to be read
- The frequency of data exchange, a determinant of battery life for active tags

Despite the complexity, RFID applications abound with usage application concepts seemingly limited only by the designer's imagination. The following are previously reported examples along the supply chain from manufacturers to end users. Note that the examples are not necessarily spread across the entire chain; finding a payoff from RFID often starts "bottom up" in a local application.

- International Paper uses passive RFID tags at its 300,000-sq. ft. paper mill warehouse in Texarkana, Arkansas. The system follows the location of its large paper rolls and manages the loading of the rolls onto railcars and truck trailers. The system locates paper rolls to a confidence of plus or minus 6 inches. A continuously updated picture of loading status for 50 truck and rail dock doors enhances visibility.
- Volkswagen in Germany uses active RFID to track new vehicles through the final stages of preparation for customer delivery. Tags are attached after a vehicle is assembled and tracked in a closed-loop application through washing, vacuuming, cleaning, and quality control until the customer picks up the car.
- A chemical company uses semiactive tags to track the bulk containers required to deliver its product to customers, another closed-loop application. Because the containers must be returned, the visibility provided by the system has lowered the company's investment by tracking the vessels and helped it recover the expensive containers that might not have returned.
- MTR Construction Ltd was contracted to build the portions of the Hong Kong rail system. It developed its RFID-based *octopus* card for riders on its trains. Now its Octopus card can buy merchandise at convenience stores, fast-food chains, supermarkets, and vending machines. It is an electronic payment system that uses a "contactless" smart card.
- Building on its experience, MTR added RFID tracking to construction material and construction equipment used in its rail-related and commercial development projects. Tagged items are principally concrete shapes where the

tags capture the results of quality testing to ensure the structural integrity of its buildings.

■ Intelligent Global Pooling Systems (iGPS) ordered several million Gen 2 passive RFID tags to attach to pallets. At 23 cents per tag, four will be placed at corners on each $55 pallet in the company's pool. The tags incorporate EPCglobal's Reusable Asset Identifier (GRAI) that uniquely identifies each pallet. The goal is real-time tracking of each pallet.

These examples serve to illustrate the creativity leading to the spread of RFID technology. They demonstrate that good returns are available if creativity is used to design the application. This particularly seems to be the case in closed-end approaches. The following sections focus on retail supply chain applications that are likely to find expanded deployment.

Two reports in early 2007 described the viability of RFID in open-loop retail applications.[4] A *Wall Street Journal* article provided another assessment with consistent conclusions.[5] Table 18.1 summarizes conclusions regarding the business case for RFID from these sources. The table shows benefits along the chain at retailer, distribution or transportation, and manufacturer echelons. The "most attractive" category refers to benefits that are most likely to justify RFID system costs at the time of the appraisal. The "emerging" category refers to benefits that are likely to justify RFID in the future.

Perhaps the most compelling case is prevention of out-of-stock incidents at retailers. This is the last 90 feet along the long supply chain and the reason Wal-Mart

**Table 18.1 RFID Justification**

| Justification | Retailer | Distribution/ Transportation | Manufacturer |
|---|---|---|---|
| Currently attractive | Prevents out of stocks/lost sales Automated processing/storage accuracy Promotions execution | Asset utilization | Promotional items |
| Emerging | Reduced shrinkage Inventory accuracy Product rotation Return tracking | Shipping/ receiving accuracy Faster pick and pack Electronic proof of delivery | Asset management Work-in-process tracking Recalls Shipping accuracy Cold-chain applications Chargebacks Maintenance/repair |

established its Remix supply chain described in Chapter 12, Section 12.3. Promotions execution, the subject of a case later in this chapter (Subsection 18.5.1), ensures that merchandise and displays are in place. These efforts often accompany expensive advertising and promotion campaigns. RFID helps protect that investment. Asset utilization refers to assets used in transportation; a couple of the examples mentioned earlier focused on this benefit. Faster pack and pick was a benefit sought by International Paper for its paper rolls. Many other benefits arise from automation of processes displacing bar-code reading.

## 18.4 Tracking in Transit

Total supply chain visibility requires knowledge of where the product is all along the chain, not just in controlled facilities. Visibility requires in-transit tracking, a capability provided by what are called real-time location systems (RTLS). This tracking is not always just for identification purposes. Security measures may seek to ensure that a container from a distant supplier poses no security threat. Monitoring the integrity of the container seal and monitoring for signs of hazardous materials provides assurance regarding a shipment. To this end, the U.S. government has elicited the cooperation of supply chain participants in C-TPAT, or Customs-Trade Partnership Against Terrorism. Those collaborating in this effort agree to take preventive measures to protect against container tampering.

Some products, and particularly those in the grocery environment, require a "cold chain." Chapter 21, Section 21.1, describes these demanding chains. Those responsible must be assured that temperature limits are met all along the chain. One way to ensure this is to monitor temperature in transit, at warehouses, and in the stores. This requires sensors attached to active RFID tags that keep track of temperature exposure as the product travels through its various intermediaries from manufacturer to retailer. Other types of sensors may monitor radioactivity, chemical environment, humidity, shocks, and vibration, as required.

Yoshibumi Kotsuka of Mitsui & Company in the United States describes a test implementation for RTLS.[6] Kotsuka's position at his company at the time of the report was Director, Transportation and Logistics. His company provided services and financing related to export, import, and offshore trading. The company has pioneered applications with RFID in manufacturing, logistics, and retailing. Mitsui offered a service called *SCM Live* for tracking material movements in global supply chains.

Kotsuka identified the following keys to success in implementing a supply chain visibility application:

- RFID tag data must be generated at the origin—where the goods are manufactured.
- Success requires cooperation among trading partners to avoid disruption and ensure ease of use.

- The solution must adhere to global standards and involve a blend of AIDC technologies. For example, his solutions include EDI, bar codes, active and passive RFID, and global positioning systems (GPS), among others.
- An infrastructure—such as Mitsui's *SCM Live*—must gather data generated by the system.
- Users must mine the data and put them to work to make decisions all along the supply chain.

Mitsui piloted the deployment of tracking technology. The test was from points of origin at manufacturing centers at Guangdong and Shenzhen in southern China across the ocean to U.S. ports at Long Beach and Los Angeles, and then on to inland DCs. This is a heavily traveled path for imports from China into the United States. Figure 18.5 depicts the path across several transportation links.

At the carton level, the manufacturer attached both bar codes and passive RFID. Each carton contained 16 individual items. Each pallet, which was also tracked with passive RFID, held 16 cartons, or 256 items. The pallets went into a container sealed with an active RFID tag and an "e-seal" security device from Savi Technology. The device included intrusion detection, environmental monitoring, and weapons of mass destruction (WMD) sensors monitoring radiological, chemical, and biological threats.

The container was read at the portals of the Chinese port of Yantian—this was the port's entry gate for the inbound container and the gantry crane for outbound containers. It was likewise read upon arrival in southern California. The GPS tracked the containers across the Pacific Ocean en route to the United States. RFID at the DC portals recorded the containers' arrival at the warehouse. During ship and truck transit, GPS also tracked the vehicle, making the system aware of which pallets were in which truck.

The trial report concluded that 100% of both passive and active reads were successful. Intrusion detection and real-time tracking was also sustained throughout

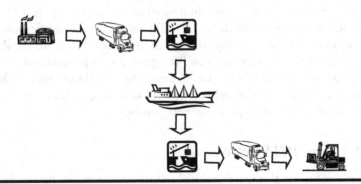

**Figure 18.5 Mitsui supply chain visibility tracking.**

the transit. When exceptions, or "events," occurred, the system dispatched notifications to supply chain decision makers.

## 18.5 Future of Product Tracking

This chapter began with a description of life before bar codes and the technologies deployed today. Bar codes economically contain individual, product-specific information, whereas RFID, at considerably more expense, allows for the tracking of inventories by supply chain participants on its path to the retailer. The chapter ends with a look into the not-so-distant future for retail locating systems.

### 18.5.1 Case Study for RFID Application

Procter & Gamble (P&G), through its Gillette subsidiary, has painted its picture of the future through experiments with RFID and the accompanying EPC.[7] The P&G EPC team has worked with retail partners to test RFID technology and to uncover the benefits that go with its implementation.

One test was the product launch of the Gillette Fusion razor. The test included two retail partners with over 400 stores. Tags were placed on Fusion cases, pallets, and displays. The displays were particularly critical to a successful product launch because they would be in prominent positions in the stores. The tagging also helped ensure that stores were adequately stocked to meet demand for the new product. Stores with RFID capability had considerably higher "display compliance rates" by day 3 of the launch. Compliance in this case was meeting the stores' commitments to deploy the displays and the adequacy of displays in terms of their numbers. The monitoring capability by RFID/EPC assured that the product was in place to support the demand generated by Fusion advertising and promotion.

Based on its experience, the P&G EPC team recommends RFID/EPC for certain "advantaged" merchandise. The best candidates are higher-value products with display modules to support time-sensitive product launches or promotions. Such display modules contain many individual units, and their proper placement in the store ensures higher levels of sales. The business case justification in this example lays not in internal savings at P&G or the retailer but in the collaborative space between them—making sure that P&G provides the product and the retailer deployed it on the store floor. These factors are not how RFID and other technology applications are justified. Most rely on internal operating savings ignoring wider benefits that are often a multiple of operating savings.

### 18.5.2 Future RTLS System

Like many solutions in this space, teams of technology companies have collaborated to prepare their visions of the end-to-end retail solution. One such team referred to their vision as the "agile" and "Lean" supply chain. The publication SCDigest summarized features of the "Leagile" supply chain strategy. This approach blends elements of "Lean" and "agile" supply chain strategies.* Some features of the supply chain included the following:

Use of make-to-order demand-driven supply chain techniques to pull merchandise through the chain

Use of different business rules for high running and less frequently ordered products

Passive RFID tags applied at both the item and case levels

"Intelligent shelf" technology, where RFID readers monitor the contents of storage locations in warehouses and stores

Automatic detection and reporting of out-of-stock items and shrinkage by monitoring the shelves

A warehouse management system (WMS) to oversee movement at warehouse and retail store levels

- Several applications to translate RFID data into updates for the WMS
- Cost-effective printing of RFID tags at the manufacturer
- Direct feedback to warehouse material handlers when errors in stock put away and picking are made
- Automated warehouse cycle counting for inventory
- A network inventory visibility system to monitor inventory within and between supply chain locations, creating notifications when exceptions occur

Figure 18.6 is an overview of the Lean/agile supply chain; Table 18.2 summarizes each step of the process. Once the commitment is made to item level tagging at the manufacturer, most of the downstream activities related to managing the inventory are automated. The agile supply chain also has the ability to sense shortages at the store or warehouse. This provides the benefit of maximizing revenue in the case of shortages at the retail level. It also signals to the supply chain when a product is not selling well, calling for cutbacks in production. However, the costs for RFID tagging are still high, so the use of this technology for lower-priced, lower-volume products still lies in the future.

On the operations side, incorrect picks or put-aways are also signaled. The system can also match actual inventory with what should be there, resulting in the automation of inventory taking, potentially a cost savings justification for using this technology. Differences between book inventories and actual quantities can be indicative of shrinkage, poor execution, or quality problems.

---

\* SCDigest, August 31, 2016, at scdigest.com.

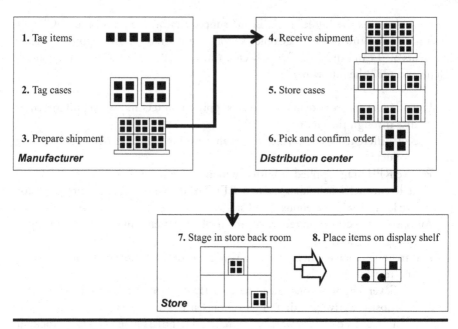

**Figure 18.6  Vision for the agile supply chain.**

**Table 18.2  Process Steps for the Agile Supply Chain**

| Step # | Step Name | Step Description |
|---|---|---|
| **At the Manufacturer** | | |
| 1. | Tag items | An operator scans the bar code to generate passive item tags on a printer. |
| 2. | Tag cases | An operator associates individual items with a case. |
| 3. | Prepare shipment | An incoming order for several cases is filled. Order documentation identifies the items included. |
| **At the Warehouse** | | |
| 4. | Receive shipment | The warehouse receives the shipment. |
| 5. | Store cases | The shipment is moved to intelligent shelves. Any errors in the shipment are detected. The WMS captures receipt of proper shipments. |

*(Continued)*

**Table 18.2 (Continued)  Process Steps for the Agile Supply Chain**

| Step # | Step Name | Step Description |
|--------|-----------|------------------|
| 6. | Pick and confirm order | An order for one case is received. The WMS authorizes picking. A picking error is detected, and material handlers are redirected to pick the correct item. The shipment is transported to the store. |
| **At the Store** | | |
| 7. | Stage in store back room | The item is staged for display shelves in the back room of the store on intelligent shelves. |
| 8. | Place items on display shelf | As sales occur, intelligent display shelves on the store floor are replenished from the staging shelves in the back room. |

## 18.6  Summary

The economic case for product tracking depends on the cost of tracking, paths to the customer, the value of the merchandise involved, and expected benefits. The visibility provided by using these technologies eases the work of matching supply and demand, particularly in reducing stockouts. This benefit is often subtle and unseen by potential users. Companies along the supply chain will continue to experiment with innovations in merchandise tracking. This chapter should heighten awareness of the alternatives and the challenges and opportunities that go with adapting tracking technology to one's supply chain.

## References

1. Abernathy, Fred, "Marketing, Merchandising, and Retailing: The Role of Intermediaries in Global Value Chains," Presentation at the University of Washington, June 6, 2004.
2. Quinn, Francis J. "Setting the Standards: An Interview with Mike Meranda," *Supply Chain Management Review*, October 2005, pp. 34–38.
3. Johnson, John R., "The Future is Now," *DC Velocity*, May 2006, pp. 57–60.
4. Lazo, Phillip, Keynote address at a Distribution Management Association (DMA) Conference "How Technology is Impacting Today's Global Supply Chain," February 22, 2007, Ontario, California.
5. Chopra, Sunil and Sodhi, ManMohan S., "In search of RFID's Sweet Spot," *The Wall Street Journal*, March 3–4, 2007, p. R10.
6. Kotsuka, Yoshibumi, "Case Study: Securing Cargo with E-Seals," Presentation to RFID Journal Live 2006 Conference, May 1–3, 2006.
7. Cantwell, Dick, "Procter & Gamble's EPC Advantage Strategy," Presentation to RFID Journal Live 2006 Conference, May 1–3, 2006.

# ACHIEVING FINANCIAL SUCCESS IN THE RETAIL SUPPLY CHAIN

# V

The complexities of managing costs in multicompany supply chains are addressed in Section V. Every link in the chain is affected with these efforts, sometimes with consequences compatible with other supply chain members' needs and sometimes incompatible with them. Strategies for coping are introduced.

| # | Chapter Name |
|----|--------------|
| 19 | Understanding Supply Chain Costs |
| 20 | Barriers to Addressing the Root Causes for Cost |
| 21 | Multicompany Collaboration to Reduce Costs—Who, What, and How |
| 22 | Retail Return Loops |
| 23 | Case Application: SeaBear/Made in Washington |

Chapter 19 addresses understanding where along the supply chain significant costs are. A methodology for profiling costs for targeted expense reduction efforts and for identifying product profitability is discussed. Root causes for cost are identified in Chapter 20.

Because costs in one part of the supply chain may be due to actions at a trading partner, the need for collaboration is especially important if common good is to be achieved. Chapter 21 provides direction for the identification of the best trading partners for this effort and how to structure mutually beneficial exchanges.

The next chapter in the book addresses what is often the final step in the retail supply chain process, understanding and planning for product returns and associated costs and revenue opportunities. Then Chapter 23 provides an example of an application of retail supply chain management principles applied to a company, SeaBear/Made in Washington.

# Chapter 19

# Understanding Supply Chain Costs

The subject of this chapter, costs, affects decisions all along the supply chain.* Profitability is the ultimate measure of business success for all echelons, and managing supply chain cost is essential in fulfilling that mission—probably about half the work. The other half is finding, marketing, and pricing profitable merchandise that is in demand by end users. Better cost numbers are more relevant in omnichannel environments to support decision-making related to merchandising and operations that contribute to success in implementing both tasks.

However, many forces hinder achieving control over costs. One is the rise of "virtual manufacturers" that rely on partners—often in faraway places—to produce the products they design. Another force is the rise of strategies that offer extended product services. An example is the distributor, Arrow Electronics, and its efforts to earn more from services such as financing, on-site inventory management, parts tracking, and chip programming.[1] Such services move beyond the traditional low margin role of distributors.

Another task is evaluating "make-or-buy" decisions. An example is the specialty retailer weighing a proposal from a logistics service provider such as Argix Logistics. Argix will execute four steps for specialty retailers—merchandise pickup at the source; sorting at the Argix distribution center (DC); transport to 40 store delivery terminals; and, finally, store delivery. If a company is doing these tasks in-house, it must understand the advantages and risks of outsourcing its work. For a smaller retailer, companies such as Argix offer an existing network, automated facilities, economies of scale in transportation, and up-to-date tracking systems.

---

* The authors thank Douglas T. Hicks for his review and comments on this chapter.

Unfortunately, companies offering such services or those considering buying them may get little help from their accounting departments. Their reporting formats are designed for financial reporting rather than managerial decision making. This chapter describes how to apply the technique called activity-based costing (ABC) to make any number of decisions that require an understanding of supply chain costs.

The reader can engage this chapter at two levels. The high-level alternative seeks knowledge of the role of activity-based costing in understanding costs, product profits, and partner contributions along supply chains. The alternative detail-level approach obliges the reader to examine the numbers presented in this chapter to better understand the mechanics of implementation. We've done our best in this chapter to make this detail examination as easy as possible.

## 19.1 Barriers to Cost Visibility

One would think that, being so important, the cost numbers that executives use when making supply chain decisions would be timely, accurate, and relevant. However, timely, accurate, and relevant data are more the exception than the rule. The next sections explain a few of the reasons.

### 19.1.1 Understanding Costs Is Complicated

The first reason is that most companies are locked into single-company accounting systems. As mentioned earlier, these use decades-old cost accounting methods designed for financial reporting. The focus is on precision, not on relevance. A primary reason for this situation is that accounting practices, in the United States in particular, are required to follow what are called Generally Accepted Accounting Principles, or GAAP. GAAP is designed to capture historical performance of the firm as a whole; it seldom accurately represents the current or future financial side at a process level. Firms, guided by their chief financial officers, are often adverse to duplication, so they steer away from creating additional numbers beyond those that are mandatory.

A second reason is that interactions between trading partners remain at arm's length. Partnerships, such as those described in Chapter 16, are unnatural, particularly in discussions about money. These discussions assume a "zero-sum" outcome where one party's financial gain is the other's loss. However, to make gains in customer service and cost effectiveness, decision makers need to understand not only their own costs but also the costs of their trading partners. Depending on the relationship, partners may provide these voluntarily, certainly the best of situations. If not, estimates based on industry knowledge of prices along the chain or by supplemental research can approach reality, even if not precise.

## 19.1.2 Partners Must Share Information

Sizable gains in service or cost reduction require collaboration to implement change among supply chain partners. The nature of the collaboration varies from case to case. Depending on the situation, collaboration examples could include design changes for the product or its packaging, removal of process bottlenecks, jointly financed capital investments, exchange of forecasts and sales data, modifying transportation and delivery methods, redesign of operating processes to achieve efficiencies, and other mutually advantageous measures.

However, there are real barriers to this collaboration beyond the willingness or ability to work together. Once sharing is agreed to, it can be difficult to decide what information is needed and how it should be applied to make decisions. This is compounded across company boundaries because of differences in accounting systems, industry practices, language, and geographical separation. This chapter describes a methodology for applying multicompany ABC for supply chain decision making. The following list identifies some of the applications for such information:

- Assessing the profitability of a product or product category
- Adjusting retail markups* for different types of merchandise
- Finding and prioritizing opportunities for cost reduction through process improvement
- Comparing the profitability of private-label versus major-label brands
- Comparing the cost of goods purchased offshore to that of domestic producers
- Working with partners to assess new technologies such as RFID
- Negotiating prices and cost sharing

The preceding list should signal the reader that ABC applications are numerous, so the effort to calculate activity-based costs should be worth the effort.

## 19.1.3 ABC Needs a "Makeover"

Note the use of the term "modest" in the previous section to describe the effort required to use ABC. Many organizations have pursued ABC efforts that required large investments in setting up and maintaining numbers that were ultimately little used to make decisions. Today's practitioners, including Robert S. Kaplan who introduced ABC in 1987, advise streamlined procedures.[2] Douglas Hicks, who reviewed this chapter, has long argued for what he calls the simplified *abc* approach.[3] This alternative approach, also called Time-Based ABC, moves away from the paper-intensive time reporting required by other approaches. In essence, the new method creates

---

* A *markup* is a factor added to the merchandise cost of an item to cover expenses and profit. Most retailers define markup as the percentage of the selling price consisting of margin. For example, if a retailer marked up an item that cost $2 by 50%, the selling price would be $4. Selling price – cost = markup. Markup $/Selling price $ = markup percentage.

*unit times* for each activity through direct measurement or other industrial engineering techniques. This facilitates measurement of capacity utilization. As an example, people in a work unit can produce one unit of output consuming one labor hour, the unit time. The capacity of the work unit is 60 hours a day—equivalent to about nine employees, considering downtime. If actual output is 45 units, there is extra capacity for growth, work additions, or staff cutbacks. This approach may call to mind older work measurement approaches that used stopwatches to browbeat employees into being more productive. That approach is not necessary; knowledge of work unit output and capacity is fundamental to managing workflow. Employee participation and agreement to unit times should be sought as well as their buy-in to the process.

This simpler approach is a "snapshot," not a movie. That is, cost data are assembled with a purpose—as part of an improvement project, for example. So, assembling ABC costs becomes part of the project; it is not an ongoing effort that has to be maintained alongside a conventional accounting system.

The methodology described here also recommends the use of both *top-down* and *bottom-up* cost numbers. Top down means all costs are included and are assigned to company processes. Bottom up turns to the *unit time* approach to understand the cost of individual processes.

In describing ABC, clarification of terminology is in order. Practitioners in strategic planning and project management use the word *activity* in different ways. It can mean an operation that is a step in a process or a set of processes. This view was described in Chapter 13 in relation to *activity systems*, a tool for developing strategies. There, activities were groups of operating processes that are designed as part of the company's strategy for competing.

In project management, an "activity" is an element of work performed during a project. The activity in activity-based costing is also an operating process that can cross department and company boundaries. Activities are expressed as verb phrases, such as *put away pallet*, in a warehouse, or *sell merchandise*, in a store. These activities produce a "deliverable" that defines the activity or process "driver."

In the case of a process called *pallet put away*, this deliverable and driver might be a pallet transfer from the loading dock to a storage space. For the *sell merchandise*, the driver might be *dollars sold* or *items sold*.

Other supply chain drivers include customer sales in a retail store, pallets, purchase orders, shipments, customer inquiries, and so forth. So, if a warehouse requires a unit time of *10 minutes per pallet* to perform the put-away activity, this time, in turn, can be translated into a unit cost. That cost could include labor, equipment in the form of the forklift, and facilities in the form of the warehouse itself.

## 19.2 Goal: Activity-Based Costing by Product

Creating activity-based costs requires development and manipulation of financial data. Figure 19.1 illustrates with an arrow the path from the current state using

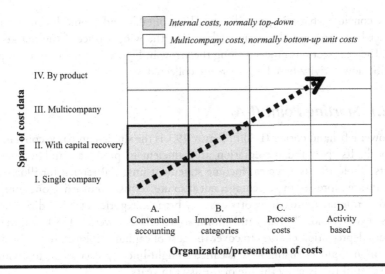

**Figure 19.1   Migration to activity-based cost by product.**

conventional accounting to the goal of activity-based cost by product. While there are other paths, the explanations in this chapter assume a team follows the diagonal arrow shown in the figure. The vertical axis, *span of cost data*, has four levels defining *what* cost data are collected. The horizontal axis has levels for *organizing and presenting* cost data. The improvement team, if its charter were focused on cost reduction, may decide that III-C (Multicompany process cost) is sufficient to achieve its objective. Another team, with a charter to purge unprofitable products, will need activity-based costs by product or product category (IV-D).

Numbers gathered in the shaded area in the lower left of the Figure 19.1 grid are top-down costs incurred inside the organization. "Top down," mentioned earlier, means all costs are collected, not just costs for selected processes or products targeted for improvement. These top-down costs point to opportunities for improvement because higher-cost activities signal areas of improvement potential. They are also suitable for assessing product profitability at the company level or to support make-or-buy decisions. The unshaded area is bottom up and moves outside the company on a process-by-process basis to explore well-defined process improvement (III-C) or product profitability (IV-D) opportunities.

An example of III-C ABC application is justifying a Collaborative Planning, Forecasting, and Replenishment (CPFR) initiative. In another example from Chapter 15, West Marine took over its inbound transportation function to better coordinate shipment arrival at stores. This reduced the hidden costs of interruptions in store working routines. At III-C, trading partners say, "This process cost $5,000,000; we can reduce that by 15%." At the IV-D level, the trading partners say, "Process A adds $123 to the cost of our widget. We aren't competitive in widgets. Here are ideas for reducing widget demands for Process A." Or, the team can jointly conclude that widgets will never be profitable and should be cut from the product line. Another alternative is boosting the widget price if the market permits. The next sections proceed along the arrow in Figure 19.1 using an example to describe how activity-based numbers are collected.

## 19.2.1 Starting Point (I-A)

The lower left-hand corner (I-A) in Figure 19.1 is the single-company, conventional approach. Its span and presentation are sufficient to produce standard financial reports. Table 19.1 is a typical income statement financial report; for illustration, cost data are expressed in percentage, not absolute, terms. Confined to one company, the conventional approach reports costs by broad categories such as "direct labor," "costs of goods sold," "general and administrative," and "overhead." Overhead often includes depreciation charges to cover the cost of capital employed in the business. A common approach, using what is called straight-line depreciation, is to divide the initial cost of the asset by the life of the asset in years.

The income statement follows accounting principles used by retail and industrial companies. In this model, many costs are allocated. A common example is the allocation of "overhead" to a "direct labor" base. This occurs despite the fact that direct labor in retailing, manufacturing, and other industries has shrunk. Also, direct labor costs may not cause, or "drive," the overhead costs. The failing in this method is that no costs are assigned to the "activities" that "consume" the

**Table 19.1  Conventional Accounting (I-A)**

| | | | |
|---|---|---|---|
| 1. | Gross revenue | 100 | |
| 2. | Returns and discounts | | 5 |
| 3. | Net revenue (#1 less #2) | 95 | |
| 4. | Direct labor expense | | 5 |
| 5. | Indirect labor expense | | 10 |
| 6. | Overhead expense | | 15 |
| 7. | Material/merchandise expense | | 50 |
| 8. | Cost of goods sold (#4 + #5 + #6 + #7) | 80 | |
| 9. | Gross margin (#3 less #8) | 15 | |
| 10. | General and administration expense | | 10 |
| 11. | Profit before tax (#8 less #10) | 5 | |

*Note:* Figures are percentages.

resources reported. This I-A approach has a number of shortcomings with respect to SCM:

- It is limited to *one company*, and supply chain processes, by definition, cross company boundaries.
- Cost accounts are built on reporting from individual budget centers— usually the organization's functional units (e.g., purchasing, receiving, planning, store), not the processes that generate the cost (e.g., purchase materials, put-away pallets, pick line items, or sell merchandise).
- The costs are not useful for analyzing the activities/processes that produce the cost.
- Current practices also underreport capital costs associated with the activity/ process by omitting the cost of capital. Capital costs include facilities, equipment, and working capital.

The following sections move along the path of the arrow in Figure 19.1. Each level—II-B, III-C, and IV-D—adds further insights to aid decision making.

## 19.2.2 Department Costs with Capital Recovery (II-B)

To move from conventional accounting, the initiating company should assemble all its own costs—the top-down approach. It should then sort them in a way to call attention to opportunities for cost reduction. Box II-B in Figure 19.1 represents this position. This step can best be accomplished by assigning internal costs, usually in the form of budget "cost centers," to improvement categories amenable to common cost-cutting approaches (B on the horizontal axis). This level also adds the cost of capital to fixed assets and working capital accounts (II on the vertical axis).

Table 19.2 lists cost categories that apply across the retail supply chain regardless of echelon—retailer, distributor, OEM, or second-tier supplier. The recommended list includes four workforce costs; recurring costs that include the cost of capital and three categories of purchased item costs. For retailers, most of the purchased item costs are for the merchandise they sell. In fact, these may dwarf the costs of internal operations. However, effectively managing internal operating processes makes the difference in customer service and profitability—particularly if one's competitors pay similar prices for the same merchandise.

Why separate costs into categories? We noted earlier that cost reduction techniques for each category are different. Table 19.2 describes the environmental characteristics of each cost category. In manufacturing, as an example, *direct labor* is often a target for cost reduction. Many manufacturers focus on this category using industrial engineering and operations research tools, even though this category may be a small proportion of total cost. For manufacturers and retailers, hard-to-measure administrative and technical groups offer more potential for increased efficiency and effectiveness, but making improvements in these groups requires a

**Table 19.2    Improvement Categories**

| Category | Description | Environment |
|---|---|---|
| **Workforce Costs** | | |
| Direct labor | Labor that "touches" the product. Examples: retail salespeople, purchasing, assembly workers, and material handling. | Customer-facing or product-producing. Easily measured. May be suitable for automation. Low level of decision making. Repetitive work. |
| Indirect labor | Direct support activity such as janitorial, transportation, and material handling. Often allocated. | Less easily measured support staff. Some activities may be outsourced. |
| Administrative/ clerical | Detached from direct activity. Often allocated. Managers, assistants, accounting staff, receptionists, and sales administration. | Overhead required to support customer-serving processes. Hard to control or evaluate. |
| Technical/ professional | Engineers, merchandising staff, information technology support, logistics planners, and other white-collar functions. | Requires decision-making. Involved in process- and product-related decisions. Hard to control or evaluate. |
| **Recurring costs** | Annualized costs of capacity— generally plant and equipment or working capital. Other fixed expenses such as corporate accounting or executive positions. | Normally not assigned to processes. Often in the General and Administrative category or allocated through overhead. |
| **Purchased Item Costs** | | |
| Services | Manufacturing, accounting, consulting, transportation, and engineering support. | Supplements or displaces staff by providing skills and services. |
| Specialized material/ merchandise | Material or merchandise made to company specification. Private label brands, unique components for products. | Few suppliers. Marked by a need for collaboration over product design and inventory replenishment. |
| Commodity material/ merchandise | Products or material bought by many companies. Low-technology, off-the-shelf design. | Provided by multiple sources, including distributors, where comparison is easy. |

wider skill set. This includes understanding not only the work content but also the effectiveness of the function, the role of incentives, the quality of decisions, the importance of work skills, and the potential for automation.

Box II-B also upgrades capital recovery reporting to account for the cost of money to acquire assets. These costs fit into the Recurring Costs category in Table 19.2. Capital items include plant and equipment as well as working capital such as inventory and accounts receivable. Calculating the cost of capital utilizes a rate of interest, or "discount rate." Many companies refer to this as the *hurdle rate* that any investment must meet to be approved. Companies often calculate the hurdle rate by averaging the rates of interest paid to those financing the enterprise—banks, leaseholders, shareholders, mortgage holders, franchisees, and bond holders.

Applying the discount rate, the resulting calculation is the *equivalent uniform annual cost* (EUAC) for the asset. This approach has variations including EVA®* (economic value added) and residual income. EUAC effectively converts the investment cost into an expense. Practitioners use tables or calculators because the equations that calculate EUAC are complex.

Table 19.3 provides examples of EUAC calculations for different assets. Example #1 is a $1,000,000 capital equipment item such as a production machine or warehouse conveyor. In this example, tax accounting rules allow writing the equipment off over 10 years. Current accounting doesn't allow the cost of capital to be added to the cost of operating equipment. But experience shows that, due to rapid obsolescence, this equipment has a likely "economic" life of only 3 years. Taking this and a 15% cost of capital into account, Example #1 shows an increase from $100,000 to $350,000 in the annual cost of the asset. Note that, for leased equipment, the lease payments may sufficiently reflect the EUAC because the leaser builds those costs into its lease rate.

The discount rate and asset life for dissimilar assets will vary in the same company. Example #2 in Table 19.3 shows comparable numbers for a building, which could be a store, a warehouse, corporate headquarters, or a factory. For example, a building asset may be less risky for the manufacturer or retailer because the building, but not the equipment, has a market value if the company sold the asset. For this reason, a lower cost of capital, in this case 10%, and a longer economic life, 10 years instead of 3 in Example 1, are appropriate. Again, rent paid for a leased facility may capture these costs.

Examples #3 and #4 are working capital assets that should also be converted to expenses. Example #3 is inventory that, with conventional accounting, is only recognized on the balance sheet. So, some managers may consider inventory to be "free." On the contrary, the cost of carrying inventory can be huge in retail supply chains. Despite its size, the cost of inventory is often not accurately calculated or assigned to the process steps that create it.

Sometimes, supply chain negotiations between trading partners center on transferring the cost of inventory to upstream companies. Dell, for example, has paid suppliers after the customer pays them for its direct sales. In Example #3, the

---

* EVA is a registered trademark of Stern Stewart & Co., a global consulting firm.

**Table 19.3  Calculation of Capital Cost (II-B)**

| # | Example | Conventional Annual Expense | Equivalent Uniform Annual Expense (EUAC) |
|---|---------|------------------------------|-------------------------------------------|
| **Fixed Assets** | | | |
| 1 | Equipment item cost: $1,000,000 | $100,000 based on a 10-year accounting life with straight-line depreciation | $350,000 based on a 3-year economic life and a 15% cost of capital |
| 2 | Building cost: $20,000,000 | $400,000 based on a 50–year accounting life | $3,200,000 based on a 10 year economic life and a 10% cost of capital |
| **Working Capital Assets** | | | |
| 3 | Inventory $50,000,000 | $0 in the income statement, displayed on the balance sheet | $12,500,000 recognizing interest, shrinkage, obsolescence, handling, and storage |
| 4 | Accounts receivable $25,000,000 | $0 in the income statement, displayed on the balance sheet | $5,000,000 based on interest, collection costs, potential returns, and bad debt history |

company has assigned a 25% per year cost to the inventory—a typical value that captures storage, financing, obsolescence, insurance, and other costs.

Example #4 in Table 19.3 is for the asset, *Accounts Receivable*. It is the money owed the company due to the delay between customer billing and customer payment, often a major item for retailers such as Macy's and Target that maintain house interest-paying charge accounts. This account also should be converted to a EUAC. Although it's an asset, high receivables may highlight unprofitable customers or lines of business. Some companies will use the cost of capital with an allowance for nonpaying customers added on. In Example #4, a 20% cost is assigned to the Accounts Receivable balance.

There is considerable latitude for presenting cost information at the II-B level. Table 19.4 presents a top-down example for a vertically integrated retail company. The table maps organization costs to improvement categories. Vertically integrated, in this case, means the company has merchandising, retail, distribution, and manufacturing operations. Because of its size, it has assembled numbers for each of its principal operations (columns 2–5). The data in the columns in Table 19.4 are summarized as follows:

1. Cost categories from Table 19.2 subdivided into workforce costs, recurring costs, and purchased items categories.
2. Costs for the merchandising department that selects and purchases merchandise. Note that merchandising is assigned the cost of merchandise and

**Table 19.4  Vertically Integrated Retailer Costs ($millions)**

| 1 | 2 | 3 | 4 | 5 | 6 |
|---|---|---|---|---|---|
| | Retailer Merchandising Department | Manufacturing Operation | Distribution Centers | Retail Outlets | Total Cost by Improvement Category |
| **Work Force Costs** | | | | | |
| 1. Direct labor | $1 | $8 | $12 | $35 | $56 |
| 2. Indirect labor | $1 | $15 | $2 | $5 | $23 |
| 3. Administration/clerical | $2 | $2 | $2 | $8 | $14 |
| 4. Technical/professional | $30 | $4 | $1 | $2 | $37 |
| **Recurring Costs** | | | | | |
| 5. Equipment | $1 | $10 | $15 | $2 | $28 |
| 6. Facilities | $1 | $6 | $30 | $80 | $117 |
| 7. Working capital | $350 | $4 | $10 | $0 | $364 |
| **Purchased Items** | | | | | |
| 8. Services | $5 | $3 | $20 | $3 | $31 |
| 9. Specialized material, merchandise | $300 | $80 | $5 | $3 | $388 |

*(Continued)*

**Table 19.4 (Continued)  Vertically Integrated Retailer Costs ($millions)**

| | 1 | 2<br>Retailer Merchandising Department | 3<br>Manufacturing Operation | 4<br>Distribution Centers | 5<br>Retail Outlets | 6<br>Total Cost by Improvement Category |
|---|---|---|---|---|---|---|
| 10. | Commodity material, merchandise | $500 | $20 | $3 | $5 | $528 |
| 11. | **Total:** | **$1,191** | **$152** | **$100** | **$143** | **$1,586** |
| 12. | Driver | Categories Managed | Units Produced | Pallets Handled | # Items Sold | |
| 13. | Quantity | 250 | 500,000 | 400,000 | 15,000,000 | |
| 14. | Cost per unit ($) | $4,764,000 | $304 | $250 | $10 | |
| 15. | Excluding merchandise ($) | $1,564,000 | | | | |

inventories as shown in the working capital line (#7). There is a division of merchandise cost into specialized and commodity material categories. The former represents fashion or innovative merchandise and the latter staples, or functional, merchandise.

3. Costs for internal manufacturing operation that makes an exclusive product line of merchandise, called the widget line.
4. Costs for internal DCs supplying the chain's stores.
5. Costs for the company's retail stores.

Table 19.4 shows the costs that are either incurred or controlled by each of the four functions. Note that the merchandising group (column 2) is responsible for merchandise expenditures because it selects the merchandise, negotiates with suppliers, in most cases arranges for shipping and delivery, and plans replenishment. The merchandise department is also assigned the cost of inventory ($350 million) because its source selection and replenishment decisions determine the amount of inventory in the company's DCs and stores.

The captive manufacturing operation (column 3) produces the widget line for sale only in company stores. The costs of production are included in the merchandise costs in column 2. This in effect treats the manufacturing operation as an independent supplier. The company DCs (column 4) are assigned only operating costs and are not charged for the merchandise that flows through the facility. Because the DC contracts for transportation, it is responsible for these costs under "services." The DCs also incur a modest working capital expense for packaging and displays. The retail outlets (column 5) handle stock at their locations and sell merchandise to customers. However, the merchandise department decides what the store will carry and generates the orders that dispatch merchandise from the DCs to those stores.

Table 19.4 also assigns "drivers" to the organization functions (lines #12 and #13). A driver is selected as a workload indicator because costs increase more or less directly as the driver volume increases. Precision in deciding what driver to use is secondary to finding a "mostly correct" parameter. As an example, the merchandising driver is *categories managed*. Each category increases the quantity of work, inventory, replenishment activity, and merchandise cost. Dividing the total assigned cost by the volume—in this case the number of categories managed is 250—produces the baseline activity cost of about $4.8 million per category. Internal costs that don't include merchandise purchases (lines #9 and #10) for operating the department are just under $1.6 million per category (line #15). Other driver candidates for the merchandise function could include *# SKUs*, *$ merchandise cost*, or *# of suppliers*.

If an analysis team were examining the workings of the merchandising department, they might use different drivers for different processes. For example, sourcing processes might use *# categories*, whereas inventory planning processes might use *# SKUs*.

For the manufacturing operation (column 3), the driver is the number of product units manufactured annually, in this case 500,000. The activity cost per unit is $304.

The DCs' cost is $250 per pallet handled. This includes both inbound and outbound pallets. Later, we develop separate figures for inbound and outbound pallets.

The retail operations of the company employ # *items sold* as a driver. This produces a cost of $10 per transaction, regardless of the value of the transaction or the product. The sales staff is considered "direct labor." Some retailers who employ a more consultative sale might assign the sales staff to the "technical/professional" category. Later, we'll show how to treat differences in selling time for different types of product—in this case, innovative, functional, and the widget line.

The presentation in Table 19.4 enables quick analysis to set baselines to measure improvement efforts or to make comparisons among alternatives. For example, a company such as Argix could supplant the internal DCs. So, these data would be helpful in evaluating a decision to outsource. Table 19.5 provides examples of such ratios. What emerges from the analysis is a higher-end specialty retailer with merchandise cost per item sold of $53 with a salesperson selling about 66 items a day.

A process flowchart is useful at the II-B level. Figures 19.2 and 19.3 provide a process view of the retailer's merchandising, distribution, and retail operations. The flowchart format is called $IDEF_0$—a modeling language supported in business process documentation tools. The node tree in Figure 19.2 summarizes the process. The detailed chart in Figure 19.3 shows inputs, outputs, mechanisms, and controls

**Table 19.5   Key Ratios—Vertically Integrated Retailer**

| # of sales people at $40K each | 875 |
|---|---|
| # of employees at $50K each | 2,600 |
| # Items sold/person/day | 65.9 |
| Merchandise cost per item | $53 |
| Merchandise cost per product category | $3,200,000 |
| Inbound/outbound pallets per category | 1600 |
| Purchases as percentage of cost | 60 |

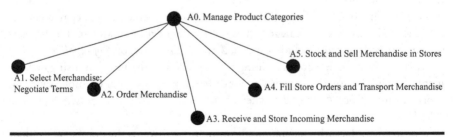

**Figure 19.2   $IDEF_0$ node tree process definition.**

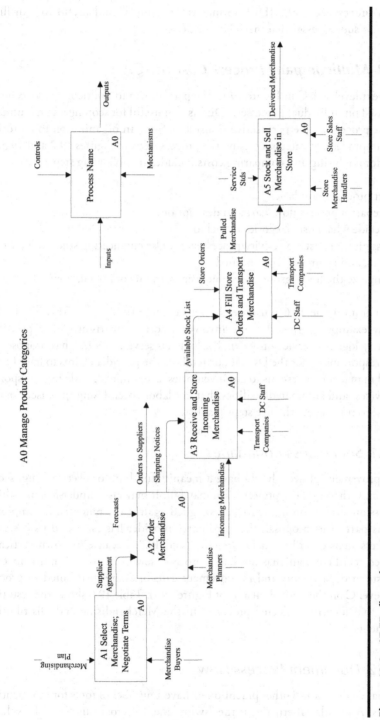

**Figure 19.3  IDEF₀ flow chart.**

for each process step. The IDEF format is "top down" and useful for "drilling down" into subprocesses that merit investigation.

### 19.2.3 Multicompany Process Cost (III-C)

At the next level (III-C in Figure 19.1), the path moves to multicompany accounting focused on individual processes. IDEF is also useful for scoping and documenting these processes. The perspective transitions from an organization to a process view of improvement categories using the process steps in Figures 19.2 and 19.3. A process for analyzing and comparing costs includes the following steps:

1. Set process boundaries.
2. Prepare a process flowchart and description.
3. Decide what cost categories to include.
4. Assign unit costs to activity/process steps. Use engineering studies, interview data, and estimates when needed.
5. Analyze the findings; prepare conclusions and recommendations.

Data from Table 19.6 illustrates how to execute these steps. This is a multicompany example in that the case involves a cost comparison with a potential third-party logistics service provider. The logistics service provider has proposed to assume responsibility for the DCs at our retailer. The provider claims to have better material management systems to cut inventories, economies of scale for transportation services, and automated facilities that cut labor costs. Using the case, the following sections execute the five steps just listed.

#### 19.2.3.1 Set Process Boundaries

Any improvement project should have a meaningful, but not overreaching, scope definition. Otherwise, the project team may fail. It may also "under-reach," taking on a mission that is too limited when weighed against the potential for improvement. As part of its proposal, the third-party provider has estimated its costs for the process steps described in Figures 19.2 and 19.3. Because our own vertically integrated retail company has not had a process view of its costs, it must uncover how costs in departments and improvement categories are distributed to process steps (Level C on the horizontal axis of Figure 19.1). Table 19.6 shows the resulting analysis that identifies affected processes in the Merchandising and Distribution departments.

#### 19.2.3.2 Document Process Flow

Industrial engineers and other practitioners have a number of tools for representing processes. A popular alternative is the "swim lane," or cross-functional flowchart,

**Table 19.6  Process Costs ($ Millions except per Pallet Figures)**

|  | A1 Select Merchandise; Negotiate Terms | A2 Order Merchandise | A3 Receive and Store Incoming Merchandise | A4 Fill Store Orders and Transport Merchandise | A5 Stock and Sell Merchandise in Stores | Total | Cost per Pallet ($)* |
|---|---|---|---|---|---|---|---|
| 1. External trading partner proposal | Not included in process | $3, Technical and professional | $10, Labor and transportation | $250, Labor, recurring inventory turns | Not included in process | $263 | $657 |
| 2. Internal: all departments | Not included in process | $10 | $38 | $394 |  | $442 | $1105 |
| 3. Merchandising department | — | $10, Technical and professional |  | $350, Working capital |  | $360 |  |
| 4. Distribution centers | — | — | $6, Direct labor; $10, transportation services; $22, Factory/equipment | $6, Direct labor; $10, transportation services; other labor, $5; $23, Factory/equipment |  | $82 |  |
| Comments: | Replenishment planner reductions |  | Covers inbound side of DC operations | Covers outbound side of DC operations |  |  |  |

*For 400,000 pallets per year

where flow is charted across organization groups. Another is the $IDEF_0$ format introduced earlier and used here to illustrate process documentation. The node tree in Figure 19.2 is "top down," meaning each level of activities can be decomposed into its components depending on the needs of the project. In Figure 19.2, there is one level of decomposition of the top-level process, *A0 Manage Product Categories*. The decomposition is into five subprocesses or activities that show how merchandise replenishment operates.

The second $IDEF_0$ representation is the flowchart in Figure 19.3. Each step in the process from the node tree is linked with other steps. The user-friendly documentation of process steps includes inputs, outputs, controls, and mechanisms. A team that understands how the company's processes really work can develop such a flowchart fairly quickly. This process should also evaluate which processes work and which do not. As the team prepares flowcharts, members should also explore why there are differences between the company's as-is cost and the third-party provider's proposed costs.

### 19.2.3.3 Decide What Cost Categories to Include

This step relies on the scope of the analysis. Because the team is chartered to look at operating processes, they decide to include the following categories:

- All the labor categories that employ people in the process—rows 1–4 from Table 19.4. This includes people who order merchandise and the DCs who handle merchandise.
- Recurring costs that apply to the process—rows 5–7 in Table 19.4. This would include equipment and facilities employed at the warehouses as well as inventory-carrying costs. In fact, the service provider is "promising" considerable inventory decreases in the order of $100 million annually.
- Services related to the process, particularly for transportation—row 8 in Table 19.4. The service provider expects that its existing transportation network enjoys economies of scale.

### 19.2.3.4 Assign Costs to Process Steps

Table 19.6 assigns internal costs to the process steps for comparison with the service provider's proposal. Using process steps provides a common ground for discussion across company boundaries. Row 1 shows process costs of $263 million for the service provider. Teams won't always have a neat comparison to make with an external entity. However, in similar situations, using a standard process like this one will enable responders to document their expected costs. An improvement team can also use row 1 to enter their cost estimates if best practices were utilized.

Row 2 lists costs of the process steps from the merchandising department and the internal DCs. Beneath these totals are the components from each department (rows 3 and 4). As indicated earlier, absolute accuracy is not essential, and probably not feasible. What is needed is certainty that the numbers are sufficiently accurate for decision making regarding sourcing or process improvements. The cost comparison on a per-pallet basis is $657 for the third-party provider and $1105 for the retail company, including planning, transportation, inventory-carrying costs, and material handling capital and labor.

### 19.2.3.5 Analyze Findings

The gap is certainly a great one. Much of the gap is due not to labor costs but to working capital and facilities/equipment utilization. Do the division of responsibility or department measures promote overinvestment in our company? Are the tools for planning and forecasting doing the job that is needed? The gap for planning staff as part of activity A2 is also great—$3 million for the service provider, $10 million for our company.

The questions posed to those evaluating the proposal include the following:

1. Does the service provider have better processes than we do?
2. Should we transfer our work to the service provider or should the company adapt the service provider's methods to its own business?

From the activity-based numbers, the answer to #1 is "most certainly." The answer to #2 is more complex. If the reasons for better performance can be adapted to the organization, it makes sense to implement the practices that produce the better result. Other alternatives include reassignment of process responsibilities and measures of performance. However, if the service provider is capable in terms of capacity, provides quality service, and is willing, the function is an excellent candidate for outsourcing some or all of the company's requirements.

## 19.3 Activity-Based Costs by Product (IV-D)

As noted earlier, the requirements for cost analysis are often fulfilled at the level (III-C) just described. This is particularly true if process improvement is the primary goal. Note that there has been little mention of prices or profits from the sale of merchandise. Adding these factors is the mission of level IV-D in Figure 19.1. At the IV-D level, merchandise costs are captured by activity and measured against market prices to assess profitability. Without such data, the actual profitability of specific products lines is likely to be cloudy.

Such data become useful in price negotiations with merchandise suppliers. The data also support efforts to rationalize the product line by purging unprofitable merchandise. Another application is price setting. As suggested at the beginning of this chapter, retailers may base their prices on across-the-board markups of their purchase costs. This method, although simple to apply, puts the retailer at risk of undercutting by competitors with a better knowledge of their costs. At best, the retailer's most profitable products subsidize the unseen laggards.

Accomplishing this requires some calculations because different processes, such as those shown in Figures 19.2 and 19.3, will have different cost drivers. Also, our product lines will differ in the amount of resources needed to support them. For example, selling specialized fashion or innovative merchandise usually takes more sales time than selling functional products. Our retail case in this section sold three product types: specialized merchandise, commodity merchandise, and the widget line that it manufactured itself. These will form the basis of our example in the next section, which describes a method for calculating activity costs by product.

### 19.3.1 Gather Product Line Information

With prices and profitability in the picture, data on the product lines selected for analysis provide a foundation. The example of needed data in Table 19.7 shows three product lines—innovative, functional, and the widget line. Lines #1 through #3 capture revenue and profitability figures. Lines #4 through #6 show the cost driver quantities for each product line. Those identified were *number of categories, # pallets handled*, and *# items sold*. Lines #7 through #10 show the profitability of the overall business; the ABC analysis will show the contribution of each product line, taking into account the merchandising, distribution, and the selling costs for each line.

### 19.3.2 Adjust Unit Costs and Volumes through Engineering Studies

Table 19.8 is another picture of the company cost structure. Rather than organizational units (Table 19.4), this presentation shows costs for process activities. Populating this table requires estimates or engineering studies that allocate organization costs to the processes. It is also a time to examine assumptions about unit volumes and the distribution of work. Table 19.8 shows two such adjustments— one for the workload in pallets handled that are now divided between incoming and outgoing pallets. The second is for the distribution of work among store staff.

In Table 19.8, the number of outgoing pallets (Process A4) is found to be three times the number of incoming pallets (Process A3). The numbers (100,000 and 300,000) are on line #13. This imbalance is due to smaller loads on each outgoing pallet and the requirements for sophisticated sorting systems to assemble those loads. Also, a salesforce analysis engineering study (lines 16–18) in the stores shows that salespeople spend about half their time selling innovative products. The rest of the time is divided between the widget line and functional products. The time cost required for each unit sold is $24, $9, and $4, respectively. These average to $10 on a volume-weighted basis.

**Table 19.7  Gathering Product Line Metrics**

| | | Product Type | | |
|---|---|---|---|---|
| | Innovative | Functional | Widget Line | Total/Average |
| 1. Retail sales (annual) | $750,000,000 | $714,285,714 | $608,000,000 | $2,072,285,714 |
| 2. $ Annual merchandise cost | $300,000,000 | $500,000,000 | $152,000,000 | $952,000,000 |
| 3. Profit margin (percent) | 60 | 30 | 75 | 46 |
| 4. Number of categories | 20 | 180 | 50 | $250 |
| 5. # Pallets handled | 60,000 | 240,000 | 100,000 | 400,000 |
| 6. # Items sold | 3,000,000 | 7,000,000 | 5,000,000 | 15,000,000 |
| 7. Average unit cost | $100 | $71 | $30 | $63 |
| 8. Average selling price | $250 | $102 | $122 | $138 |
| 9. Total operating expense | | $1,586,000,000 | | |
| 10. Pretax operating profit | | $486,285,714 | | |

**Table 19.8 Calculation of Cost Drivers**

| | A1 Select Merchandise; Negotiate Terms | A2 Order Merchandise | A3 Receive and Store Incoming Merchandise | A4 Fill Store Orders and Transport Merchandise | A5 Stock and Sell Merchandise in Stores | Total |
|---|---|---|---|---|---|---|
| **Workforce Costs** | | | | | | |
| 1. Direct labor | $0 | $1 | $6 | $6 | $35 | $48 |
| 2. Indirect labor | $1 | $0 | $1 | $1 | $5 | $8 |
| 3. Administration/clerical | $1 | $1 | $1 | $1 | $8 | $12 |
| 4. Technical/professional | $20 | $10 | $1 | $0 | $2 | $33 |
| **Recurring Costs** | | | | | | |
| 5. Equipment | $0 | $1 | $5 | $10 | $2 | $18 |
| 6. Facilities | $1 | $0 | $10 | $20 | $80 | $111 |
| 7. Working capital | $150 | $200 | $0 | $10 | $0 | $360 |
| **Purchased Items** | | | | | | |
| 8. Services | $4 | $1 | $8 | $12 | $3 | $28 |

*(Continued)*

**Table 19.8 (Continued)   Calculation of Cost Drivers**

| | A1 | A2 | A3 | A4 | A5 | Total |
|---|---|---|---|---|---|---|
| | Select Merchandise; Negotiate Terms | Order Merchandise | Receive and Store Incoming Merchandise | Fill Store Orders and Transport Merchandise | Stock and Sell Merchandise in Stores | Total |
| 9. Specialized material, merchandise | $300 | $0 | $0 | $5 | $3 | $308 |
| 10. Commodity material, merchandise | $500 | $0 | $0 | $3 | $5 | $508 |
| 11. Total: | $977 | $214 | $32 | $68 | $143 | $1,434 |
| 12. Cost driver | Categories Managed | | Pallets Handled | | # Items Sold | |
| 13. Quantity | | 250 | 100,000 | 300,000 | 15,000,000 | |
| 14. Cost per unit ($) | $3,908,000 | $856,000 | $320 | $227 | $10 | |
| 15. Excluding merchandise ($) | $708,000 | | | | | |
| 16. | | | | Innovative | $24 | |
| 17. | | | | Functional | $4 | |
| 18. | | | | Widget line | $9 | |
| | | | | Sales Force Analysis | | |

*Note:*  Costs are in $ millions.

For Process A1, which encompasses product selection and sourcing, there are two costs per unit (lines 14 and 15). The first includes the cost of the merchandise; the second excludes it, reflecting the process' operational cost without the merchandise cost included.

### 19.3.3 Calculate Product Line Profitability

The cost of the drivers can be used to calculate each product line cost. Table 19.9 performs this task using the driver unit costs (column #2) and the driver quantities associated with each product line from Table 19.7. This produces the total cost of each activity by product, shown in columns 6–8 of Table 19.9. The cost per unit is calculated by dividing by the volume of product sold in each category (line 6 in Table 19.7). The results are shown in columns 9–11 of Table 19.9.

Table 19.10 summarizes the unit costs for each activity by product line. The box outlines these costs. A profitability analysis by product line highlights costs and profitability. What the analysis shows is that two product lines (innovative and the widget line) are profitable. Functional products, as a whole, are not. Options based on the analysis include the following:

- Accept that some products are unprofitable but need to be carried to fill out the product line.
- Search the functional category further and drop the lowest-profit items.
- Cut internal costs for merchandising and ordering material. These are the highest-price activities.
- Transfer logistics for functional products to the third-party service provider. Retain control over innovative products and the widget line.

The last option recognizes that a focused provider might best handle the high volume of these products. The company might retain responsibility for the "crown jewels," at least until the service provider has proven its effectiveness.

## 19.4 Understanding Costs—Summary

This chapter describes a methodology for applying the activity-based costing tool to a vertically integrated retail enterprise. The growth of omnichannel paths to the customer makes ABC analysis potentially more valuable. Each organization will have to weigh the value of pursuing ABC for its own business. However, it is increasingly intractable to confine one's perspective to one's own organization. This is especially so as companies continue to outsource traditional operations. In a supply chain world, a broader view of cost is needed. Also, the use of across-the-board markups will inevitably overprice some and underprice other merchandise. This leaves a retailer susceptible to the competitor with better knowledge of costs, even if that retailer has no cost advantage. A sharper pencil is the solution; ABC is the tool.

**Table 19.9  Calculation of Unit Costs by Activity**

| Activity/Process Driver | | 1 Driver | 2 Cost per Driver Unit ($) (Table 19.8, Row 14) | 3 #Drivers—Innovative (Table 19.7, Rows 4–6) | 4 #Drivers—Functional (Table 19.7, Rows 4–6) | 5 #Drivers—Widget Line (Table 19.7, Rows 4–6) | 6 Activity Cost—Innovative ($millions) (#3×#1) | 7 Activity Cost—Functional ($millions) (#4×#1) | 8 Activity Costs—Widget Line ($millions) (#5×#1) | 9 Activity Cost per Unit—Innovative ($) | 10 Activity Cost per Unit—Functional ($) | 11 Activity Cost per Unit—Widget Line ($) |
|---|---|---|---|---|---|---|---|---|---|---|---|---|
| A1 | Select merchandise; negotiate terms (with merchandise cost) | # Categories | $3,908,000 | 20 | 180 | 50 | $78 | $703 | $195 | $26 | $100 | $39 |
| A1 | Select merchandise; negotiate terms (without merchandise cost) | # Categories | $708,000 | 20 | 180 | 50 | $14 | $127 | $35 | $5 | $18 | $7 |
| A2 | Order merchandise | # Categories | $856,000 | 20 | 180 | 50 | $17 | $154 | $43 | $6 | $22 | $9 |

(Continued)

**Table 19.9 (Continued)  Calculation of Unit Costs by Activity**

| | | 1 | 2 | 3 | 4 | 5 | 6 | 7 | 8 | 9 | 10 | 11 |
|---|---|---|---|---|---|---|---|---|---|---|---|---|
| Activity/Process Driver | | Driver | Cost per Driver Unit ($) (Table 19.8, Row 14) | # Drivers—Innovative (Table 19.7, Rows 4–6) | # Drivers—Functional (Table 19.7, Rows 4–6) | # Drivers—Widget Line (Table 19.7, Rows 4–6) | Activity Cost—Innovative ($millions) (#3×#1) | Activity Cost—Functional ($millions) (#4×#1) | Activity Costs—Widget Line ($millions) (#5×#1) | Activity Cost per Unit—Innovative ($) | Activity Cost per Unit—Functional ($) | Activity Cost per Unit—Widget Line ($) |
| A3 | Receive and store incoming merchandise | # Pallets handled | $320 | 20,000 | 80,000 | 25,000 | $6 | $26 | $8 | $2 | $4 | $2 |
| A4 | Fill store orders and transport merchandise | # Pallets handled | $227 | 40,000 | 160,000 | 75,000 | $9 | $36 | $17 | $3 | $5 | $3 |
| A5 | Stock and sell merchandise in stores | # Items sold | $10 | 3,000,000 | 7,000,000 | 5,000,000 | $29 | $67 | $48 | $24 | $4 | $9 |

**Table 19.10  Product Line Profitability**

| | 1 | 2 | 3 | 4 | 5 | 6 | 7 | | 8 | 9 | 10 | 11 |
|---|---|---|---|---|---|---|---|---|---|---|---|---|
| Product | Average Unit Selling Price | Purchase Cost | Merchandising Cost | Order Cost | Inbound Logistics Cost | Outbound Logistics Cost | Selling Cost | Total Activity Cost per Unit Sold | Profit per Unit ($) | Units Sold | Total Profit ($millions) | Cost Markup (percent) |
| | | | A1 | A2 | A3 | A4 | A5 | | | | | |
| Innovative | $250 | $100 | $5 | $6 | $2 | $3 | $24 | $39 | $111 | 3,000,000 | $332 | 139 |
| Functional | $102 | $71 | $18 | $22 | $4 | $5 | $4 | $53 | ($23) | 7,000,000 | ($158) | 174 |
| Widget line | $122 | $30 | $7 | $9 | $2 | $3 | $9 | $29 | $62 | 5,000,000 | $310 | 196 |

# References

1. Nelson, Brett, "Stuck in the Middle," *Forbes*, August 15, 2005, pp. 88, 89.
2. Kaplan, Robert S. and Anderson, Steven R., "Time-Driven Activity-Based Costing," *Harvard Business Review*, November 2004, pp. 131–138.
3. Hicks, Douglas T., *Activity-Based Costing: Making it Work for Small and Mid-Sized Companies*, 2nd ed., New York: John Wiley, 1999.

# Chapter 20

# Barriers to Addressing the Root Causes for Cost

This book's Section IV, Supply Chain Process Improvement, describes ways to enlist one's own organization, trading partners, and process designers in the effort to become more competitive. This includes providing better service to customers, lowering costs, and increasing profits. Chapter 19 attacked the issue of often-hidden costs through activity-based costing (ABC). Once costs are documented with ABC, the tools in this chapter will guide teams to the next steps. Topics of the chapter include root causes for costs and the barriers that exist to addressing them.*

## 20.1 Root Causes for Supply Chain Cost

The list of root causes for cost addressed in this book includes the following:

1. *Lack of clarity.* As described in Chapter 19, this root cause includes the ways cost accounts are organized and presented; these often obscure cost drivers. ABC is a solution for this root cause.
2. *Variability.* The variability root cause includes anything in the supply chain that creates uncertainty in operations such as missed deliveries, demand fluctuations, unforeseen demand, and poor-quality materials arriving at the doorstep. Such uncertainty generates costs that show up in contingency inventory; overtime pay; expedited freight; lost sales; returned products; and, at the retail level, lost customers.

---

* Many of the ideas for this chapter were previously published in ref. 1.

3. *Product design.* A product's cost is "baked in" during design through decisions related to material choices, component obsolescence, suppliers, and ease of fabrication and assembly. Leaving such considerations out of the design will increase product direct costs, customer image, and after-sales service.

4. *Lack of information sharing* between involved parties. Information exchanges range from sharing operating costs as part of cost reduction collaboration to sharing operating data needed to make day-to-day decisions.

5. *Weak links.* Managing links encompasses make-or-buy decisions, the choice of partners, and the connections between one partner and another.

6. *Unintended consequences.* The best intentions can produce bad results. An effort to reduce costs in one area of the supply chain might raise costs elsewhere. For example, choosing the lowest-price supplier might not result in the lowest total cost because that partner might practice some of the cost-raising practices described above.

Most incidents of supply chain waste can be tracked to one or more of these six causes. Chapter 21 addresses #5 and #6 in greater depth, focusing on when and how to enlist trading partners in the effort to reduce cost.

Identifying and addressing root causes of costs should be an essential part of any supply chain improvement project. The model for implementing supply chain change, introduced in Figure 15.1 (Chapter 15), points to the need to uncover the gap between where the company is and where it wants to be. *Gaps* include those related to costs, as well as other gaps in service, delivery, and flexibility. The model also identifies the barriers that exist in making such a transition. This book defines *barriers* as factors that can be overcome if properly managed, while a *constraint* is a given and beyond the organization's power to change.

Table 20.1 lists chapters and sections that prescribe methods to address costs attributable to these root causes. This chapter seeks to explain why root causes for cost do not get addressed in many supply chains. Table 20.2 serves as a guide. It lists five barriers and the principal root causes that apply to each barrier. The remainder of this chapter will prescribe approaches to overcome these barriers.

## 20.2 No Focus

Supply chain projects are, by definition, ambitious. The need for formal project management arises when attempting great things, particularly beyond the boundaries of one's own company. This was seen in the West Marine case introduced in Chapter 15. At West Marine, as with many other companies, focus was achieved in a crisis brought on by too-fast growth. Sometimes, a crisis does not exist to jump-start the change process and sustain it, so a focused effort that includes disciplined project management should be established. Disciplined project management for

**Table 20.1  Root Causes for Cost**

| | Root Cause for Cost | What It Is | Chapter or Section Addressed |
|---|---|---|---|
| 1 | Lack of clarity | An inability to attach costs to processes. Cost accounting obscurity and inaccuracies. Lack of sharing of costs. | 11.1 The Product Life Cycle<br>11.2 Innovative and Functional Products<br>11.3 Market Mediation Costs<br>12.2 Market Segments<br>17.2 The Path from Forecast-Driven to Demand-Driven<br>19 Understanding Supply Chain Costs |
| 2 | Variability | Any variable factor that affects supply chain flow. | 17.3.1.1 Lean Supply Chain Approaches<br>17.3.1.2 Constraint Management |
| 3 | Product design | Designs that are hard to manufacture, maintain, or service. | 17.3.1.3 Quality Improvements<br>17.3.1.4 Design for Commonality |
| 4 | Insufficient information sharing | Failures to provide or to manage for information accuracy. | 17.3.2.1 Synchronization and Fixed-Interval Planning<br>18 Product Tracking along Retail Supply Chains |
| 5 | Weak links | Poorly performing trading partners or trading partner interfaces. | 14 Retail Supply Chain Management—Skills Required<br>16 Collaboration with Supply Chain Partners<br>21 Multicompany Collaboration to Reduce Costs—Who, What, and How |
| 6 | Unintended consequences | Well-intentioned actions that hurt more than help. | 12.3 Spheres—Modules for Supply Chain Design<br>13 Activity Systems and Process Definition<br>15 Organizing to Improve Retail Supply Chain Performance<br>17.3.2.2 Simplification<br>21 Multicompany Collaboration to Reduce Costs—Who, What, and How |

**Table 20.2  Root Causes and Related Barriers**

| | | | Barriers to Cost Reduction | | | | |
|---|---|---|---|---|---|---|---|
| | | | No Focus | Confusion | Motivators | Boundaries | Rigidity |
| Root causes for cost | 1 | Clarity | • | | • | | • |
| | 2 | Variability | | • | • | | |
| | 3 | Product or service design | • | • | | | • |
| | 4 | Information sharing | | • | | • | |
| | 5 | Weak links | | • | | • | |
| | 6 | Unintended consequences | | • | • | • | • |

large projects requires a top-down commitment because a bottom-up continuous improvement mentality will not be sufficient if strategy-level changes are needed.

Unfortunately, many retail supply chain companies give half-hearted support, if any, to project management. Often, there are no commonly understood project management practices adopted by the company. Improvement efforts are boot-strapped, that is, assigned to employees already working in other roles to complete in whatever time is left over after their regular duties are dealt with. This often means no time at all.

When teams from various departments meet on occasion to work on the project, the result may be muddled. Total Quality Management (TQM) and more recent Six Sigma efforts are like this. Managers tout success in terms of number of people trained or number of projects launched. Also, in manufacturing companies, the engineering department is a frequent omission. They are needed to address #3 on our list of root causes for cost in Table 20.2. In summary, we have not deployed the right "army" to uproot the root causes.

An unintended result is a superficial effort with local savings far below the potential of a focused project with broad participation. A common response is, "We don't have the budget for a dedicated team." Fair enough, but do not expect meaningful results. With a focused approach to a limited number of projects, more improvement will be achieved. The following sections describe two solutions for this barrier: project management basics and team building.

## 20.2.1 Project Management Basics

Projects displace ongoing, repetitive operations as a share of all work. Consequently, most leaders need to better understand how to manage projects. *Projects* are "temporary efforts that produce a product, service, or result." In fact, there is a "body of knowledge" for managing projects maintained by the Project Management Institute.[2] In a bow to the impact of globalization, the guide is available in French, German, Chinese, Italian, Spanish, Portuguese, and Japanese in addition to English.

A start for a retail supply chain project is establishing a project infrastructure within the company using this body of knowledge.* Making this commitment recognizes that the challenge requires a dedicated effort and raises the visibility of the effort. Definition of the reason for a project is important to achieving focus. How we define the deliverable makes a difference in how we do the project. For example, a *product* definition for a supply chain project might be to "establish a truck route between point A and point B." A *service* definition might be to "establish transportation links between point A and point B." A *result* definition might be to "lower logistics costs between point A and point B." The first, the product definition, is very specific and easily verified. However, it is limited in the choice of method

---

* For a description of how to do this, see ref. 3.

employed. The second, the service definition, opens options to the project manager. For example, roads, railways, or air options are candidates. The third, the result definition, expands the options to not only transportation links but also logistics services such as warehouses, common carriers, and so forth.

In framing the definition of the expected project, the company has a huge opportunity to declare its intent if it wants to reduce costs. This occurs by emphasizing the result sought, not the means to achieve it. A technology company did the same thing for a bill of material (BOM) cost reduction effort. The result was a series of measures ranging from value engineering to renegotiated prices that slashed material cost by 20% annually on a base of $250 million. As described in Chapters 15 and 16, retailer West Marine followed a two-stage approach, starting in its own operation and then involving its trading partners in pursuing what they called "breakthroughs."

### 20.2.2 Team Building

Startup is the time to select key project team members. As recommended in Chapter 16, Section 16.4, insiders should include a project manager and staff (if necessary), a steering committee, and a design team. Supply chain partner-participants should include the keepers, those you want for long-term relationships. This is an excellent time to rationalize a supplier base or review distribution channels for poor-performing partners and unprofitable products. Keep in mind that an important criterion for being a keeper is the willingness of the partner to collaborate on cost reduction.

The project manager, if a significant impact is sought, should be dedicated, full time If possible. Company executives should populate the steering committees, with the CEO or COO included for the most important efforts. The design team is a midlevel management team who will do the early work on the project. Participating functions, depending on the echelon organization and project needs, could include merchandise planning, engineering, finance, procurement, distribution, and manufacturing.

It is not too early to start a stage 3 multicompany steering committee, as described in Chapter 6, Section 6.7.2. Supply chain cost reduction is a multicompany effort; costs include any incurred all along the chain, not just in one's own company. Some suppliers may greet this with suspicion. That is why creating a dialog early on is important. It should be emphasized with suppliers that this is not a quarterly business review where price reductions are sought, but a focused effort seeking sustainable solutions.

## 20.3 Confusion

A second barrier is confusion within management and the project team, and among partners, about what the mission is or should be. The opportunities for confusion are many. In particular, there may be different ideas about just what is included and what is not—what is called *scope* in the project management discipline. In fact, some of these misunderstandings are related to varying definitions of the supply chain, certainly a source of confusion. If there are ongoing efforts already underway, there can also be confusion about whether a proposed new project is already underway in another form. No progress is made if different projects are running at cross purposes.

Another source of confusion is technology—often for the purpose of sharing information. There is no shortage of "solutions providers" ready to address information gaps. Many managers do not have the time and training to match these solutions to the needs of their supply chains. In particular, proposed claims for software are often confusing and may be inappropriate for the business at hand. Retailers are particularly prone to problems in this area because most of industry's business information technology (IT) was developed for manufacturing companies. When there is pressure to accomplish something, however, the current management fashion or slickly marketed software package may be the easy choice, absent an understanding of the real needs.

Often, product design is overlooked as a possible root cause for costs. Managers are confused because "the horse is already out of the barn" in cases of products already in the marketplace. Closing the door does not solve the problem. Cost reduction is a reactive strategy to high cost. The most effective cost reduction effort would have been cost avoidance captured during product design. Here we describe two actions to avoid confusion: promoting supply chain management (SCM) and the graduated approach.

## 20.3.1 Promoting SCM

Often, people in supply chain functions are second-class citizens, considered less important in a strategic sense. This may be particularly true in retail organizations where merchandising, not operations, is the priority. In a recent visit to a technology company further up the supply chain, it was apparent that the supply chain department managers had a huge inferiority complex. The company's fortune was based on high-tech products, and engineering and finance ruled the roost. Many supply chain functions were afterthoughts and taken for granted. Because of this attitude toward SCM functions, there was little interest and skill inside the group in going outside their comfort zone—purchasing, warehousing, and distribution. Many retailers see the supply chain as requiring less expertise than the selection of merchandise to carry even though its execution can determine the level of profitability of items selected for sale.

## 20.3.2 Graduated Approach

A source of confusion mentioned earlier is matching the right solution with the real problem. This is complicated if the supply chain is extended with three to eight partners and the accompanying interfaces. Each partner has two internal interfaces, represented by departments or important processes. We are now up to 6 interfaces for a simpler chain and 16 for a lengthier one. At each interface, decisions to replenish and stock are made.

The as-is review of the supply chain will uncover sources of delay that extend the lead time for a product. As described in Chapter 17, it should also uncover the degree to which planning decisions are based on forecasts or on actual demand. Long lead times, naturally, make forecast-based planning a necessity. Shorter lead times enable demand-driven decisions. Figure 17.3 and the accompanying discussion described a programmatic way of shifting to demand-driven decision making. The approach also yields requirements for technology, including information systems, where it is needed along the chain. The multicompany steering committee can review and approve proposals for these solutions.

## 20.4 Motivators

Implicit or explicit performance measures drive reward and punishment in an organization. Although many organizations are turning to broader approaches like the balanced scorecard, most organizations still stress company financial success as their essential measure. This is natural because the company that does not make money has failed in one of its most important missions—to earn a return for its investors.

The 2016 crisis at Wells Fargo Bank's retail operation illustrates this point. A corporate goal was to increase the number of Wells Fargo services that each customer used. For example, a credit card holder might be recruited to take out a home or auto loan with the bank as well as maintaining checking and savings accounts. Pressure to make this happen resulted in bank employees opening accounts for various services for customers without their knowledge in order to make the individual retail units' performance figures look better. A federal investigation was the result of this fraudulent practice.

Complicating the landscape, currently used tools for financial measurement are outmoded. Accountants concoct their budgets following accounting practices developed decades ago, with performance in internal supply chain functions tied to budget adherence. A typical result is an oft-encountered measure like "supply chain costs as a percentage of sales." Broader measures, such as those including multiple companies, are hard to come by. Chapter 19 describes how to use ABC to address this issue.

Excellence in SCM requires something different. Defining better measures and what is needed in terms of flexibility, described in the following sections, will motivate desirable results from the project team.

### 20.4.1 Measures

Just as occurred at Wells Fargo Bank, selected performance metrics for a retail supply chain organization can drive dysfunctional behavior, resulting in unintended consequences. If the measure is supply chain costs as a percentage of sales, mentioned above, the person being measured will surely ratchet down on supply chain costs without regard to the fallout or increased costs in other parts of the business, often on the critical sales floor. The broader supply chain mission of matching supply and demand is lost. For example, if the company is selling hot products with short life cycles, the cost-conscious supply chain manager, trying to reduce transportation cost possibly by using slower transportation means, will leave money on the table and destroy customer goodwill. Ample inventories, expedited airfreight, and extra manufacturing capacity can be a good thing if it means supply is chasing fast-growing demand.

The commodity or staple product manager or buyer whose measure is lowest price paid for merchandise also may make bad source-selection decisions. In addition to quarterly price decreases, one company shifted raw material inventory to its suppliers to relieve its own balance sheet. Total supply chain costs remained the same, but investment in inventory was lower thus increasing the return on investment (ROI).

Another original equipment manufacturer (OEM), in the last 2 weeks of each quarter, turned production control over to corporate finance—not because they were great schedulers but to book as much business as possible by the end of the accounting period. The result was a crash program that pulled finished products out of inventory and reconfigured them to get them out the door. Therefore, a lot of work was duplicated, and also, as a result, the company was exposed to shortages in the next quarter.

Another public company nearing the end of its fiscal year put its high-ticket products on sale at a large discount to boost year-end earnings. The manufacturing vice president was alarmed but went along as a "team player." This cost him his job. The plant choked on the fire-sale orders, and the new year brought the pink slip. The stock also collapsed as the factory dropped further and further behind its sales commitments.

### 20.4.2 Flexibility Defined

Perhaps it is unrealistic to purge all of these habits; however, it is possible to manage them better. To address situations like the ones described, marketing strategies for each product line should define the need for supply chain flexibility. Section 6.5 in Chapter 6 recommends how to do this.

If final demand is uncertain or fluctuates up and down—and it's hard to conjure up a product that does not fit this situation—then flexibility is the most important supply chain design objective. Achieving other objectives in the categories of cost and customer service depend on supply chain flexibility.

If one asked 150 people what supply chain flexibility means, that person might get 150 different answers. The American Production and Inventory Control Society (APICS), for supply chains, defines *flexibility* as the ability to neutralize the risks of variability in demand, supply, cycle time, and other factors during up or down volume changes. So, consequences, such as added cost or reduced responsiveness, from any of these sources of variability will be minimal in a flexible supply chain.

The Supply Chain Operations Reference (SCOR) model uses time and volume change to gauge flexibility. An example is "so much volume change" in "such and such time." As with the APICS definition, changes must also occur without cost or inventory penalties. So, upside production flexibility is defined as "the number of days to achieve an unplanned sustainable 20% increase in production." Interestingly, downside production flexibility is defined as the "percentage order reduction sustainable at 30 days prior to shipping with no inventory or cost penalties." It's strange that upside flexibility is expressed as number of days, whereas downside flexibility is defined as percentage of production.

Although the process may be complex, a multicompany steering committee, in a process such as that described in Chapter 16, Section 16.4, will make a strong contribution by defining supply chain flexibility requirements. This *strategic* definition should be in terms that partners affected by changes in demand can understand and embrace, providing clear direction for investments and performance measures.

## 20.5  Boundaries

At the risk of being too obvious, physical and organizational boundaries complicate supply chain improvement efforts. They qualify as barriers in both the literal and figurative sense. The individual, whether a frontline worker or the CEO, has the most control over his or her environment. As additional players are introduced into a business process, an individual's control and visibility diminish. By extension, the same is true for the company level where several work groups take part, and certainly for the supply chain level where multiple companies are involved. West Marine, in taking back control of its inbound material flow, eliminated a troublesome boundary—coordinating supplier deliveries—that had disrupted its stores' operations.

Effective SCM means we must manage improvement not only across our own department boundaries but also across company boundaries. To be successful, we must somehow enlist those in other departments in our own company and those in our partners' organizations to assist in developing and implementing supply chain strategies. This requires skills that many lack, such as an inclination to be proactive in leading change, powers of persuasion, and creativity in devising win–win solutions in collaboration with partners.

One example of the impact of boundaries is the *bullwhip effect*. Small changes in final, end-user demand are amplified into wide swings in demand as one goes backward up the chain due to each level's desire to carry additional inventory to avoid stockouts in the fact of change. West Marine was motivated to work with its suppliers to eliminate supply chain bullwhips. Prior to the effort, supply chain synchronization was not incorporated in the design of participant linkages, an example of weak links. That said, the latest and greatest technology is even less likely to fit the differing levels of capability among companies along the chain. So, unless our company is a channel master that dictates to partners, such as West Marine or Wal-Mart, we are stuck with supply chain performance levels determined by the weakest link. The next sections describe the divide-and-conquer approach and mechanisms for multicompany participation.

## 20.5.1 Divide and Conquer

This approach encourages organizations to bite off one piece of their supply chain at a time. It builds a firewall around what might be a risky endeavor if too much is undertaken at once. It also allows the company to focus limited resources on priority supply chain activities. Retailer West Marine almost failed from its too-rapid effort to integrate a merger partner.

As an example of the divide-and-conquer approach, companies may focus on one customer segment. Segments have different requirements for customer service, products, and other supply chain features. Also, companies differ in terms of the importance of various supply chain functions. A retailer specializing in high fashion or a high-tech, engineering-intensive company depends heavily on its suppliers, but a manufacturer relying on commodity products or a discount retailer depends less on individual supplier relationships because there are multiple suppliers for their products.

A company can divide and conquer by carving its supply chain into *spheres*, as described in Chapter 12. The term refers to three-dimensional customer–product–operations combinations. These define multiple supply chains in a single company set aside for focused improvement. The divide-and-conquer strategy creates workable projects and reduces the risk of designing a one-size-fits-all supply chain. It is also a tool for setting priorities if resources are limited. The highest-priority first project can address the needs of the most important "businesses within the business."

## 20.5.2 Multicompany Participation

Once a piece of the supply chain has been chosen for a makeover, the willingness of a partner to cooperate will be put to the test. If a multicompany steering committee does not exist, then it should be formed. Partners whose operations are important must contribute to gain full benefit from the effort. Contributions will take various forms; examples include the following:

- Providing information on and guarding the integrity of the retail format
- Supplying data for process flowcharts for cost and time across the chain
- Providing points of contact across boundaries in a variety of functions, the "diamond" model of Figure 16.1 (Chapter 16)
- Costs and cost driver information
- Technology improvements that would enhance the supply chain
- Ideas for cost reduction that address root causes
- Contracting that encourages innovations for cost reduction

Balky partners are an occupational hazard. A company's steering committee should anticipate lack of cooperation and have a contingency plan in place. Such a plan should include the work-around option, partner replacement, or suspension of the effort until cooperation is forthcoming. The major mistake is not confronting the situation and allowing the effort to muddle along when success is doubtful.

## 20.6 Rigidity

The press reminds us frequently that the pace of change, or "clockspeed,"* has quickened. Fashion-oriented and technology industries have always had to move at fast clockspeeds, whereas the older, so-called staple or smokestack industries have poked along. In the latter, slowness afflicts decision-making speed. Changes in the environment, if they are even detected, are not translated into timely action plans. Of course, initiation of new supply chain projects or modifying ongoing ones is also slow.

Clockspeeds have increased, whereas processes for decision making have not. A barrier exists if company processes continue to move more slowly than the pace of change needed to stay competitive. Slowness may be a symptom of a conservative, isolated management. It can also be the symptom of fast-paced environments where no one has time to reflect on what is needed for the longer term. Such organizations may not unlock their doors for collaboration.

One wholesale distributor of electronic products was contracted for an ambitious enterprise resource planning (ERP) system. A constraint was that all the built-in forms and reports had to be identical to the legacy system format. This and other project pitfalls led to the unintended consequences of overruns and the necessity of employing a unique high-maintenance system. The financial bleeding triggered a rapid pullback in the company's fortunes, putting the company out of business.

Rigidity is both subtle and unsubtle. Subtle rigidity besets the mindsets of people in the organization and is hard to identify. The solution is to change these

---

* A term originated by Charles Fine of MIT.

mindsets, often not an easy task. Unsubtle rigidity produces slowness in coping with needed change during the execution of supply chain change projects.

### 20.6.1 Mindset Changes

Supply chain change projects surface in many instances where a steering committee or management team faces a subtle change decision. How and what they decide reflects their collective mindset and values. The electronic product distributor discussed earlier had one such decision. Essentially, that decision was to change the software or the way people worked. The choice to change the software, not retrain the people, mucked up the software implementation and irreparably damaged the company.

The solution to this barrier lies in bringing in new mindsets through replacement or addition of people. Often, facilitating consultants fill a devil's-advocate role to help a client team make the shift. There are no objective yardsticks for measuring mindsets. In fact, a positive mindset for implementing effective supply chain change might be measured by the absence of the barriers described in this chapter.

### 20.6.2 Changing the Project

Another rigidity source comes from sticking too long with a previously developed project plan. To many project managers, persistence through thick or thin is a virtue. These managers take pride in staying the course despite the fact that forces for change are hard at work.

Postmortem research into ERP implementation projects supports this proposition.[4] Professors Robert Austin of the Harvard Business School and Richard Nolan of the University of Washington Business School maintain that executives drop the ball when they treat large-scale ERP implementations as "rigid" IT projects.

A better model, they suggest, is the new business venture. Such a venture needs to change frequently in response to new circumstance. The Project Management Body of Knowledge (PMBOK), cited earlier, refers to this as "progressive elaboration" requiring processes to realign the project if needed in response to each new reality.

To be successful, supply chain projects must have well-oiled change management processes. In addition to changing project tasks and schedules, management must also be willing to change people or add people with absent skills. The steering committee should also avoid giving a project team too long a leash. Coming back for regular approvals is a good way of making sure the effort has not run amok.

## 20.7 Barriers to Cost Reduction—Summary

Awareness of barriers to improvement is the first step toward neutralizing them. This chapter has described five barriers to supply chain cost reduction and described ways to counter or circumvent them. The barriers act to keep us from dealing with the six root causes of cost listed in Table 20.2. The threat here is wasted time and effort on ineffectual supply chain improvement efforts. Also lost is competitive advantage that can never be recovered, possibly a life-threatening consequence.

# References

1. Ayers, James B., "Costs: Getting to the Root Causes," *Supply Chain Management Review*, November–December, 2003, pp. 24–30.
2. *A Guide to the Project Management Body of Knowledge (PMBOK Guide)*, 5th Edition, January 2013, Project Management Institute.
3. For a description of how to do this, see *Supply Chain Project Management* by James B. Ayers, published by St. Lucie Press, Boca Raton, in 2003.
4. Cliffe, Sarah, "ERP Implementation: How to Avoid $100 Million Write-Offs," *Harvard Business Review*, January–February 1999, pp. 16 and 17.

*Chapter 21*

---

# Multicompany Collaboration to Reduce Costs—Who, What, and How

---

This chapter guides the reader toward decisions about *who*, *what*, and *how* to achieve retail supply chain collaboration to reduce costs.* The *who* discussion proposes a screening process for confirming which partners are worth the teaming effort. The *what* discussion focuses on the type of collaboration using models for information exchange and decision making described in Section 16.1.2. The *how* lists types of collaboration appropriate for initiation by different supply chain partners—retailers, service providers, distributors, or manufacturers.

Chapter 20 listed root causes for costs and reasons why they are not systematically addressed. In particular, three of the root causes—confusion, weak links, and unintended consequences—likely involve trading partners. Being multicompany in nature, these root causes can be the most challenging to fix. Despite the difficulty, multicompany partnerships to reduce cost are bound to increase as the globalization of retail markets increases. And, as if there are not enough options now, more will come into being as trading partners become creative in implementing solutions.

---

* The authors thank David Malmberg for his review of this chapter and his contributions to the analytical framework described in Chapter 21.

## 21.1 Case Study—Frozen and Refrigerated Foods "Cold Chain" Distribution

Models of demanding supply chains already exist. One of the most demanding is that for frozen and refrigerated foods, the so-called cold chain.* According to the Grocery Manufacturers Association (GMA), the U.S. consumer packaged goods industry annually generates over $2 trillion in revenue. Frozen food sales by manufacturers are about $30 billion. The refrigerated segment is thought to be larger in revenues than the frozen segment, and both have higher growth rates of dollar sales volume than other food categories. Important retail supply chain issues that are related to frozen and refrigerated food are as follows:

- Temperature variance control (a quality issue)
- Higher costs of warehousing and transportation versus dry products sold at ambient temperatures (financial)
- Dating and stock rotation (quality)
- The necessity for high inventory turnover and effective application of just-in-time concepts (financial and quality)
- Frequent requirements for store-door delivery from manufacturers/processors (financial and quality)
- Opportunities for self-distribution versus use of wholesalers (financial)
- Feasibility of using Automatic Identification and Data Capture (AIDC) technologies [bar coding/radio-frequency identification (RFID)] with moisture and frost on the packaging (quality and cost effectiveness)
- The potential for tracking temperatures with sensors as merchandise moves through the chain—an application with near-term feasibility, as described in Sections 18.3 and 18.4.

The following are examples of projects aimed at dealing with these issues. They illustrate the breadth of projects required of a demanding supply chain.

1. *Retail grocery store-door delivery ice cream manufacturer*: Larger or outside warehouses versus tighter production scheduling and safety stocks; separate storage from odorous products such as fresh fish, to avoid odor transfer from the fish to the ice cream
2. *Retail chain of ice cream parlors*: Use of contract copackers or self-manufacturing; product dating due to freezer burn; implementation of time-of-day delivery precision
3. *Refrigerated fruit juice processor*: Multistop scheduling of less-than-truckload (LTL) deliveries and automatic product identification

---

* The authors wish to thank Peter A. Crosby for contributing the cold chain example.

4. *Dairy food product processors*: Scheduling and routing of delivery vehicles for milk, ice cream, yogurt, and sour cream
5. *Frozen microwave dinner entrees*: National location of plants and warehouses to minimize supply chain costs
6. *Refrigerated third-party logistics (3PL) public warehouses*: Outsourced inventory customer service to chain distribution centers
7. *Frozen and refrigerated food warehouses*: Order processing and warehouse productivity

The retail part of the cold chain requires higher inventory turnover and higher levels of service than the manufacturing/processing echelon of the supply chain. Comparing the supply chain performance metrics for retail supermarkets, mass merchandisers, convenience stores, and food service (restaurant) chains illustrates the differences.

|   | Metrics | Processing/Manufacturing | Retail Stores/Outlets |
|---|---------|--------------------------|-----------------------|
| 1 | Annual inventory turns | 5–10 | 20–50 |
| 2 | Fill rates | 85–95% | 98–99% |
| 3 | On-time delivery | 90% | 95–99% |

In summary, frozen and refrigerated cold chain products require more resources to plan, schedule, store, deliver, and manage than other food products, as well as other categories of merchandise. The amount of care and quality provided need to be at higher levels due to the perishable nature of the product and the demand that there be little variance in temperature all throughout the temperature-controlled chain.

# 21.2 Recognize Root Causes

The need for collaboration is obvious in the frozen and refrigerated food cold chain, but it is not always so in others. However, once the desire for collaboration has been established, the sponsoring company needs to pursue correction of root causes for cost. An article in the *Harvard Business Review* by V. G. Narayanan and Ananth Raman reports cases and research as examples of several of these causes.[1]

■ *Confusion*. Technology company Cisco relied on subcontract manufacturers. These manufacturers had incentives to build inventories of parts, not what Cisco was selling. A sales slump left too much material in the supply chain and ambiguous accountability for the unneeded inventory. In fact, it was not clear what was actually ordered and what was actually made. Cisco was forced to take the write-offs.

■ *Confusion.* There are "hidden actions" that are not shared by trading partners. The authors point to manufacturer Whirlpool not knowing whether retailer Sears is pushing its own Kenmore brand instead of Whirlpool, making it hard to plan for efficient production.

■ *Confusion and weak links.* One party often possesses information or knowledge that its trading partner does not possess. This particularly applies to cost information. In the case of suppliers, they may fear that retailers will use that information to negotiate lower prices.

■ *Unintended consequences.* The authors conducted research of over 50 supply chains. They found that incentives were not aligned, so companies acted in their own interest, not the joint interests of themselves and their trading partners.

■ *Unintended consequences.* Badly designed incentives play a role in adding costs. The authors describe a Canadian bakery that paid deliverymen for sales based on their allotted space in stores. The deliverymen's incentives promoted overstocking, necessitating disposal of large quantities of stale pastries.

Narayanan and Raman recommend correcting the relationships by targeting these hidden actions, information gaps, and incentives. Their solutions include rewriting contracts, documenting costs with activity-based costing to develop appropriate charges, and collaborating on information sharing and tracking. This chapter offers specific suggestions for pursuing these ends.

Just how one's trading partners should be involved with a company will depend on their relative power in the relationship, the business arrangements among partners, and how broadly and deeply they interact. This chapter refers to a number of concepts (whats) and methodologies (hows) already described elsewhere. For ready reference, Table 21.1 lists candidate collaboration topics described elsewhere in this book.

# 21.3 Types of Collaboration

Figure 16.3 in Chapter 16 depicted different types of collaboration. These types vary in terms of the need for mutual adjustment during the collaboration and the associated risks. As needs for adjustment increase, more intense collaboration is required. The four levels of collaboration described in Section 16.1.2, ranked from lower to higher levels, were the following:

■ *Data exchange collaboration*, where partners exchange information as required to complete day-to-day transactions. Data exchange can have two forms: one-way (type A) or two-way (type B). These types of collaboration are often automated and seek to improve supply chain speed and efficiency.

**Table 21.1 Candidate Topics for Collaboration**

| | *Partnership Topics* | *Topics Defined* | *Chapter or Section Addressed* |
|---|---|---|---|
| 1 | Product-related collaboration | Considerations related to the base (physical) product and extended (related services) product | 11.1 The Product Life Cycle<br>11.2 Innovative and Functional Products |
| 2 | Market-related collaboration | Understanding the needs of different customers and end users | 12.2 Market Segments<br>13.1 Activity System Example |
| 3 | Demand-driven supply chain | Process designs that utilize actual demand rather than forecasts, in decision making, leading to the lean supply chain | 13.2 Defining Processes<br>17 The Demand-Driven Supply Chain |
| 4 | Partnership types and structures | Nature of the multicompany relationship and governance | 12.3 Spheres—Modules for Supply Chain Design<br>14 Retail Supply Chain Management—Skills Required<br>15.2 Continuous Improvement Cycles<br>15.3 S&OP Process and Functional Roles<br>16 Collaboration with Supply Chain Partners |
| 5 | Financial incentives | Recognizing opportunities and rewarding | 11.3 Market Mediation Costs<br>19 Accounting for Supply Chain Costs<br>20 Addressing Root Causes for Cost |
| 6 | New technology | Innovations in merchandise tracking, transportation, and handling | 18 Product Tracking Along Retail Supply Chains |

- *Cooperative collaboration* (type C), where partners share systems and tools so each partner has simultaneous access to information needed for decision making. One or both will make an independent decision after the sharing. Examples include sharing sales and forecasting data provided by a system, as well as personal interactions for capacity planning and product development. A non-supply-chain example is consulting a stockbroker about the purchase of a security. The broker must understand the investor's goals and recommend the "right" investment, but the investor must ultimately decide what to purchase.

- *Cognitive collaboration* (type D) involves joint, concurrent, intellectual, and cognitive activity between partners to reach joint decisions. This level includes knowledge exchanges, included in this book's definition of supply chain flows in Chapter 1. Such collaboration could change the "space" in the supply chain, lead to new products, or produce investments in facilities and information systems. In this case, the broker and investor invest together.

Using inputs from this book, sourcing-team brainstorming, and other sources, Table 21.2 lists examples of trading partner collaboration candidates of each type. The mission of the list is to trigger ideas for innovation in trading partner relationships. The next section describes a methodology for confirming the trading partners with whom the company wants to collaborate. Following that discussion, this chapter will explain the options presented in Table 21.2 in greater depth.

# 21.4 Who—Rationalizing the Customer/Supplier Base

Pursuing multicompany partnerships should start with a review of existing and candidate trading partners. This look should confirm that you desire a relationship in any form—collaborative or not—with any particular trading partner. A helpful tool from the inventory management discipline is called inventory ABC analysis or distribution. Note that this version of ABC shouldn't be confused with the other ABC described in Chapter 19 that stands for *activity-based costing*.

Many companies use ABC inventory analysis to sort products or stock-keeping units (SKUs) into category *A*, *B*, or *C*, based on parameters such as total sales performance for a retailer or distributor, or percentage of the cost of goods sold for a manufacturer. This type of analysis is particularly useful for nonfashion or staple merchandise.

Note that manufacturers might use the term SKU to refer to their raw materials, and the term products as the finished goods they ship to distributors and retailers. A distributor might use either term, but SKU is common for both incoming and outgoing merchandise when an SKU is not converted but passes through en route from manufacturers to retailers. However, distributors moving into new space in the supply chain may convert an incoming SKU into multiple SKUs for individual

**Table 21.2  Candidates for Collaboration by Type—Whats and Hows**

| Type | Name | Candidate Multicompany Collaborative Tools | Second-Tier Supplier | OEM | Distributor | Retailer | Service Providers |
|---|---|---|---|---|---|---|---|
| A | One-way data exchange | Prearranged exception notices: | | | | | |
| | | 1. Inventory shortages/excesses | | | | | |
| | | 2. Missing product/SKUs | | | | | |
| | | 3. Excessive backlogs | • | • | • | • | • |
| | | 4. Capacity problems | • | • | • | • | • |
| | | 5. POS exception data | | • | | | |
| | | 6. Transportation bottlenecks | | | • | • | • |
| | | 7. Other exceptions | • | • | • | • | • |
| B | Two-way data exchange | Information sharing: | | | | | |
| | | 1. Production schedule sharing | • | • | | • | |
| | | 2. Forecasts as committed orders | | • | | | |
| | | Product- and service-related quality: | | | | | |
| | | 1. Specification flexibility | • | • | | | |
| | | 2. Tolerance relaxation | • | • | | | |
| | | 3. Reporting against standards | • | • | • | | |
| | | 4. Backup inventory availability | • | • | • | | |

*(Continued)*

**Table 21.2 (Continued)  Candidates for Collaboration by Type—Whats and Hows**

| Type | Name | Candidate Multicompany Collaborative Tools | Second-Tier Supplier | OEM | Distributor | Retailer | Service Providers |
|---|---|---|---|---|---|---|---|
| B | Two-way data exchange | Transportation and warehousing: | | | | | |
| | | 1. Freight consolidations | | • | | • | • |
| | | 2. Transportation coordination | | • | | • | • |
| | | 3. Warehousing services | | | • | | |
| | | 4. Production staging | • | | • | | • |
| | | 5. Customs/freight forwarding | | | • | | • |
| | | Life cycle product data: | | | | | |
| | | 1. Configuration status | | • | | • | |
| | | 2. Repair history | | • | | • | |
| | | 3. Asset management | | • | | • | |
| C | Cooperative collaboration | Process improvements: | | | | | |
| | | 1. Yield improvement | • | • | | | |
| | | 2. Synchronized replenishment | | • | | • | |
| | | 3. Technologies like RFID | | | | • | |
| | | 4. Direct-to-store shipments | | | | • | |
| | | 5. Supplier process qualification | | • | | | • |

*(Continued)*

**Table 21.2 (Continued)  Candidates for Collaboration by Type—Whats and Hows**

| Type | Name | Candidate Multicompany Collaborative Tools | Second-Tier Supplier | OEM | Distributor | Retailer | Service Providers |
|---|---|---|---|---|---|---|---|
| C | Cooperative collaboration | Financial incentives: | | | | | |
| | | 1. Incentives to reduce costs | • | | | | • |
| | | 2. Consignment inventory | | • | | • | |
| | | 3. Contract terms | | • | | • | |
| | | Collaborative analysis: | | | | | |
| | | 1. Inputs for QFD analysis | | • | | • | |
| | | 2. Activity-based costing support | | • | | • | |
| | | 3. Multicompany teams | | • | | • | • |
| | | 4. Flexibility definition | | • | | | • |
| | | Compliance services: | | | | | |
| | | 1. Quality audits | | • | | • | • |
| | | 2. Social compliance audits | | • | | | • |
| | | 3. Consulting services | | | | | • |
| D | Cognitive collaboration | Collaboration strategy: | | | | | |
| | | 1. Activity system construction | | • | | • | |
| | | 2. Providing a core competency | | • | | • | |
| | | 3. Service agreements/guarantees | | • | | • | |
| | | 4. Long-term contracts | | • | | | |

*(Continued)*

**Table 21.2 (Continued)  Candidates for Collaboration by Type—Whats and Hows**

| Type | Name | Candidate Multicompany Collaborative Tools | Second-Tier Supplier | OEM | Distributor | Retailer | Service Providers |
|---|---|---|---|---|---|---|---|
| D | Cognitive collaboration | New product development: | | | | | |
| | | 1. Avoidance of capital costs | | • | | | |
| | | 2. Financing new product | | • | | | |
| | | 3. Product design support | | • | | | |
| | | 4. Sourcing/component selection | | • | | | • |
| | | 5. Packaging configurations | | • | | | • |
| | | 6. Component commonality | | • | | • | |
| | | Demand-driven supply chain: | | | | | |
| | | 1. Data sharing/synchronization | | • | | • | • |
| | | 2. Addition/deletion of echelons | | • | | • | • |
| | | 3. Supplier consolidation | | • | | • | |
| | | 4. Postponement—configuration | | • | | • | |
| | | 5. Postponement—location | | | | | |
| | | 6. Inspection reductions | | • | | • | |
| | | 7. Tooling design | | • | | | |

(Continued)

**Table 21.2 (Continued)  Candidates for Collaboration by Type—Whats and Hows**

| Type | Name | Candidate Multicompany Collaborative Tools | Second-Tier Supplier | OEM | Distributor | Retailer | Service Providers |
|------|------|---------------------------------------------|----------------------|-----|-------------|----------|-------------------|
| D | Cognitive collaboration | Life cycle product support:<br>1. Vendor-managed inventory<br>2. Configuration management<br>3. Repair/return support<br>4. Repair parts stocking<br>5. Component refurbishment<br>6. Technical support | | • • • • • • | | • • •   • | |

*Note:* • indicates likely originators of collaborations.

retailers. A retailer might use "SKUs," "products," or even product "categories" in applying an ABC inventory analysis.

Another available tool for spend analysis is the United Nations Standard Products and Services Code (UNSPSC). The UNSPSC allows its users to generate eight-digit codes for over 20,000 products and services. Having common codes puts buyers and sellers on common ground when identifying just exactly what is bought and sold. Coding purchases this way eliminates a source of confusion—that of identifying what is purchased. The eight-digit codes can be extended with other company-specific information.

Regardless of the application, a typical product/SKU split will have about 65% of total value (in cost, contribution margin, "importance," or revenue) in the *A* category. *B* items may account for another 25%, and *C* items for 10%. The percentage of items in each category is reversed, with about 10% of the product/SKUs being the high-value *A* items, *B* items about 25% of all the items, and low-value *C* items the remaining 65% of products/SKUs.

Dividing products and SKUs into categories enables tailored strategies for sourcing, replenishment, handling, and storage (Figure 21.1). *A* products/SKUs receive focused attention for source selection and replenishment. Depending on classification criteria, they likely generate most of the merchandise cost and inventory investment. From a customer loyalty point of view, *A*-item stockouts may also carry the highest penalty. This isn't always the case; Wal-Mart set up a Remix supply chain to avoid stockouts for critical everyday items. Chapter 12, Section 12.3, describes the Wal-Mart effort. Shortages of critical or hard-to-find *C* items sometimes cause manufacturing operations to halt because no one has paid attention to their availability. Because *C*'s are low cost, their transaction costs represent a higher proportion of the total cost of managing them. So, management of *C* items focuses on developing efficient processes. In retail supply chains, the retailer is more likely to purchase *A* items directly from the manufacturer and *C* items from a distributor. *B* items may follow either path, depending on the volumes involved and supply chain economics.

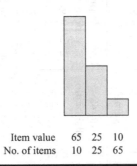

| Item value | 65 | 25 | 10 |
| No. of items | 10 | 25 | 65 |

**Figure 21.1   ABC inventory strategies.**

Figure 21.2 illustrates the landscape for product–supplier strategies using the ABC approach. The table can be interpreted to match the perspective of any player in a retail supply chain: retailers, distributors, original equipment manufacturers (OEMs), service providers, and second-tier component suppliers. Figure 21.2 employs the ABC approach to sort *both* SKUs and suppliers, a technique conceived by David Malmberg of CGR Management Consultants. In the figure, capital letters in italics stand for products/SKUs, and small letters in regular type stand for suppliers. As mentioned earlier, *A* products/SKUs are usually high-price or high-profit products. But they can also be *A*'s by virtue of their importance in the company's strategy for the future—like a new product just launched into the market. *A*'s are likely in the growth or maturity stages of the product life cycle shown in Figure 11.1 in Chapter 11. *B*'s have moderate volumes or importance; *C*'s are usually low-value and high-volume commodities. Sometimes, more than one supplier provides a particular SKU. So, there may be two providers of an *A* product/SKU; one might be an "a" supplier, the other a "b." Likewise, an "a" supplier, like a large distributor, may provide nothing other than *C* products/SKUs.

An "a" supplier will often supply *A* SKUs. *A* items residing with many small "c" suppliers may be a signal to reduce suppliers. This would be even more the case if the SKUs are *C* items, and the suppliers are "c" suppliers. Freeing the company of many small suppliers will reduce hidden transaction costs. The other ABC, activity-based costing, is a good way to document these costs. Note that parameters for supplier classification need not be the same as those for products/SKUs. For example, a "b" supplier might supply a high-margin critical *A* product to a retailer or an important proprietary technology for a manufacturer. This relationship may be a critical one for innovative products promising high growth, thereby promoting the "b" supplier to the "a" list.

| | | **Suppliers** | | |
|---|---|---|---|---|
| | | a | b | c |
| **Products/SKUs** | *A* | Major OEM manufacturers supplying high price products/SKUs to distributors or stores. Collaboration at all levels. **Aa** | Manufacturers or distributors supplying innovative niche product. Alternate sources unlikely. Product life cycle collaboration. **Ab** | A company has produced a new product with high market potential. Sole source. Future growth attractive. Supplier helps with design/production. **Ac** |
| | *B* | Manufacturer or distributor of mid-priced merchandise. Apply activity-based costing. A and B collaboration. **Ba** | For high-performing suppliers, add business to convert from "b" to "a". Level A and B collaboration. **Bb** | Search out alternative sources. Justify continuing relationship with activity-based costing. **Bc** |
| | *C* | Manufacturer or distributor of consumer packaged goods or small items. Level A and B collaboration. **Ca** | Explore moving business to an "a" supplier or, for good performers, expand role. Apply activity-based costing. **Cb** | A supplier–product combination that's a candidate for elimination. Use activity-based costing to make case. **Cc** |

**Figure 21.2  Product–supplier landscape.**

Figure 21.2 lists examples and suggests forms of collaboration that might fit each combination of product/SKU and supplier. Higher forms of collaboration (types C and D) are particularly suitable for all *A* products/SKUs. Indeed, one might define *A* products/SKUs as ones requiring such collaboration. *C* products, on the other hand, are amenable to data sharing to streamline replenishment (type A and B collaboration) or shifting from direct purchase to purchase from a distributor.

The lower right-hand corner of Figure 21.2 (cell *Cc*) represents commodity products from low-volume suppliers. An ABC analysis might prove them uneconomical. Moving their business to another larger supplier (an "a" or "b") could make sense. For the retailer or distributor, low-profit "c" products might also be dropped.

Figure 21.3 suggests what directions collaboration might take. Space does not permit an all-inclusive list. There are two types of strategy in Figure 21.3—one that applies to products/SKUs and the other that applies to suppliers. Strategies for products/SKUs are in italics; those for suppliers are in regular type. For example, the *Aa* cell suggests pursuing a demand-driven supply chain, as described in Chapter 17, for high-volume product/SKUs. For a supplier strategy, financial incentives are suggested for cost reductions that apply to all the products from that supplier. A vendor-managed inventory (VMI) arrangement might also be negotiated with a supplier of multiple products/SKUs. The same strategies could apply to the *Ba* cell. For a high-performing "b" supplier of *A* products, more business with that supplier might be justified if the supplier offers products/SKUs that aren't currently purchased.

The *Ca* cell could include a distributor providing a lot of small-value parts. The total volume of multiple *C* items makes the distributor an "a" supplier. Perhaps there are too many distributors or manufacturers if a large amount of *C* products/SKUs is purchased from "b" and "c" suppliers.

| | | Suppliers | | |
| --- | --- | --- | --- | --- |
| | | **a** | **b** | **c** |
| Products/SKUs | *A* | *Demand-driven decisions* <br> Financial incentives <br> VMI **Aa** | *Demand-driven decisions* <br> Add business <br> VMI **Ab** | Focus on "A" SKUs or transfer business to other suppliers **Ac** |
| | *B* | *Demand-driven decisions* <br> Financial incentives <br> VMI **Ba** | Add business <br> Move to distributor if buying from a manufacturer **Bb** | *Drop product/SKU* <br> *Substitute product/SKU* <br> Find A or B suppliers **Bc** |
| | *C* | Consolidate demand <br> Apply activity-based costing <br> VMI **Ca** | *Drop product/SKU* <br> *Substitute product/SKU* <br> Consolidate demand <br> Move to distributor **Cb** | *Drop product/SKU* <br> *Substitute product/SKU* <br> Consolidate demand <br> Move to distributor **Cc** |

**Figure 21.3 Product–supplier strategies.**

## 21.5 What and How—Pursuing Partnership Opportunities

This section describes in further detail the collaboration scenarios listed in Table 21.2. Five participating supply chain links are shown in Table 21.2: second-tier suppliers, OEM manufacturers, distributors, retailers, and logistics service providers. Examples of the latter category include transportation companies, customs brokers, quality inspection services, freight forwarders, and sourcing companies. An example of the last category is Li and Fung Limited in Hong Kong. This company describes itself as a trading company that manages the supply chain for high-volume, time-sensitive consumer goods. Its services, much of it for apparel merchandise, include product design, sourcing, production planning, quality assurance, and export documentation from any of 40 countries where it operates. On its website, CEO Spencer Fung states that, "We aspire to create Supply Chains of the Future." According to the company, this will be enabled by an ambitious Information Technology Initiatives.

Dots in Table 21.2 show where in the supply chain collaboration initiatives might originate. For example, if all four participants are marked, that collaborative action could be initiated at any link in the chain. If just the retailer is marked, then the collaboration could include any of the other echelons. For example, for a *C*-item shortage, just the distributor might be involved. But for an *A* item, the OEM and the second-tier supplier of the item might be involved.

### 21.5.1 Type A: One-Way Data Exchange Collaboration

Although there is little exotic about one-way exchanges, they can be quite valuable in alerting trading partners to exception situations. Rapid notification of exceptions can head off bigger problems if the condition causing the exception is not corrected. The list in Table 21.2 is an example of exception conditions. Such reports are often prearranged by partners along the chain and generated according to agreed-to business rules. Terms for these arrangements include *proactive* systems and workflow. The rules are a by-product of process designs that have built-in collaboration mechanisms. The communications should be directed at decision makers responsible for reacting to the reported condition, such as an out-of-stock condition.

Inventory mismatches in the form of shortages or excesses are reported by distributors or retailers—those closest to end-user demand. These notices signal upstream manufacturing partners to slow down or speed up. "Missing products/ SKUs" refers to mismatches between what was ordered and what arrived. These can be generated at the OEM, distributor, or retailer level. Backlogs or capacity problems normally occur in manufacturing, but they can also occur when a supply chain manager such as Li and Fung detects a problem.

Point-of-sales (POS) data must originate at the retailer. They do not necessarily have to be streaming data but can be automatically screened to detect conditions when customer demand is running ahead or behind forecasts. Distributors, supply chain managers, and transportation companies might trigger transportation bottleneck reports. Because the world of exceptions is quite broad, any participant might consider generation of exception reports as a feature in its extended product service offerings.

## 21.5.2 Type B: Two-Way Data Exchange Collaboration

This category covers communications that, although routine, require responses to the originating supply chain partner. A common area of collaboration in manufacturing is production scheduling and forecasting, often under the Collaborative Planning, Forecasting, and Replenishment (CPFR) banner. As described in Chapters 15 and 16, West Marine issued its forecasts in the form of committed orders. This is shown as a reasonable method for both the OEM manufacturer to its supplier, and the retailer (like West Marine) to the OEM or the distributor. By accepting the forecast, the receiving partner is agreeing to meet its commitment.

Product and service quality is an area of potential two-way collaboration. Specification flexibility is important in product design to assure that suppliers have the processing capability to meet these requirements. It also applies to assuring that components specified in a product are not at the end of their production lives, especially important in fast-changing electronics. Relaxation of tolerances might occur in production when specifications not critical to product function can be relaxed.

Reporting exceptions to service standards for completeness of orders is a useful technique to spur corrective actions. This can occur at the second-tier, OEM, and distributor levels. Many manufacturers and distributors are now contracted to carry inventory to service retailers; reporting the status for critical items is an option for two-way communication.

The transportation and warehousing category deals with merchandise moving through the supply chain. Transportation and warehousing exchanges can occur at several points, but which points will depend on the supply chain partner with the biggest stake in having the visibility. This can be an OEM, distributor, retailer, or service provider providing visibility as an extended product service. Second-tier manufacturers, distributors, or logistics service providers can support production staging. This staging serves manufacturers' production lines or retailers' stores. Often, the staging involves added services such as store labels, material kitting for production, or light assembly. Customs and freight-forwarding reports from logistics service providers are another forum for two-way communications.

Long-lived retail merchandise such as personal computers, televisions, cameras, autos, and other expensive items require support over their product life cycles in the form of warranties, recall notices, rebates, repairs, and software upgrades. End-user registrations, returns, service contracts, and OEM warranties trigger the requirement for collaboration. The retailer and OEM need to establish responsibilities for these, and they may vary by product category. In actual operations, the end user will trigger these events that require retailers or OEM manufacturers to respond. Chapter 22 discusses the category of aftermarket processes in more detail.

### 21.5.3 Cooperative Collaboration

This category is more intense two-way collaboration. This collaboration is more likely to go on personally, by phone or face to face, rather than through message exchanges. An example is an effort in manufacturing to increase process yields. Small increases in first-pass yield bring outsized benefits in capacity and profit. Often, this requires collaboration between a supplier and its OEM customer. The collaboration should address root causes for yield losses, including too-tight specifications from the OEM. These can be caused by variations in processes such as those that are targets of Six Sigma initiatives described in Chapter 17.

Synchronized replenishment seeks to eliminate bullwhips or to employ pull-type replenishment rules such as those in 3C (capacity, commonality, and consumption) as discussed in Chapter 17. The retailer, OEM, or supply chain manager could orchestrate the synchronization for all or part of the supply chain. Technology deployments are more likely to be less democratic. Technology such as RFID will likely proliferate if demanded by strong retailers like Wal-Mart, who have the best chance of capturing savings from the technology. The same applies to direct-to-store delivery service provided by OEM manufacturers and distributors, thereby avoiding distribution center processing. Supplier process qualifications are likely driven by OEMs to assure reliable components from their suppliers.

The research by Narayanan and Raman highlights the importance of aligning financial incentives.[1] A second-tier supplier or a third-party supply chain manager might propose such incentives to the OEM manufacturer. Consignment inventory rules might avoid a situation like that faced by Cisco where order tracking disappeared and excess inventory caused write-offs. The OEM and the retailer may want to set the rules for inventory for their upstream suppliers. The same applies to other contract terms designed to avoid mismatched incentives.

Collaborative analysis encompasses supply chain efforts directed at improvement. A manufacturer may ask retailers or its customers for inputs into product design. These efforts could employ Quality Function Deployment (QFD) as a way of displaying the "voice of the customer" inputs. Chapter 7, Section 7.5, describes the approach. Activity-based costing inputs could help assure alignment of incentives and provide a clear picture of where supply chain costs reside. These, in turn, could lead to contract terms that reduce conflicts of interest.

The retailer, OEM, or supply chain manager could initiate an effort to define flexibility. The collaboration would set operating ranges for products, SKUs, or categories for capacity setting and response to changes in sales levels. Beyond basic capabilities, flexibility is the most important property of a supply chain. This is because end-user demand fluctuates for all but the simplest products, and other measures such as cost, quality, and delivery depend on being flexible enough to respond accordingly.

A final category for cooperative collaboration is compliance with quality assurance, standards for worker protection, and supply chain troubleshooting. OEM manufacturers will need to collaborate with their suppliers or their supply chain managers to assure compliance. Retailers also are aware of the downfalls of not considering worker conditions in the factories that supply them. This is particularly true in those overseas labor surplus regions, even if these suppliers are two or three organizations removed from the retailer. Nike, after being highly criticized for poor labor practices overseas, totally overhauled its product specifications and its supply chain to meet customer expectations in this area. The supply chain manager and other specialized providers can fill a consulting role to assist OEMs and retailers in designing products and establishing the logistics required to put merchandise on shelves in appropriate quantities.

## 21.5.4 Cognitive Collaboration

This category encompasses high-level decisions made at key points in a relationship. Such points include initiation of the partnership, planning a new product, making decisions on what to make and what to buy, and setting up the supply chain. In fact, the lower levels of collaboration (A, B, and C) will have been considered, and presumably designed, during cognitive collaborations.

Collaboration strategy addresses the basic, up-front need for supply chain partners to work together. These are likely to be initiated by OEM manufacturers or retailers for their supply chain zones—second-tier suppliers and service providers to the OEM, and distributors and OEMs for the retailer. An example is Wal-Mart's reliance on drug distributor McKesson for vendor managed inventory (VMI) services. In some cases, OEMs and retailers may collaborate in the design of an activity system for a new product, service, or territory. These arrangements may lead to service agreements in exchange for business guarantees. An OEM may seek second-tier suppliers for their core competencies, leading to long-term contracts.

New products bring a host of options for collaboration for the OEM manufacturer. This includes choices of suppliers, outsourcing supply chain activities to service providers, and working with the retailer on packaging and tracking technologies such as bar codes and RFID. The collaboration includes the base product, associated extended products, and design and financing of the means of production.

The demand-driven supply chain, by definition, requires collaboration among trading partners. The effort ideally will be driven from the retailer or retailers closest to customers. The OEM may also initiate such efforts, especially if there is a high degree of component commonality or an extensive supply network.

The OEM would likely lead postponement decisions related to configuration—seeking to commit to final configuration as close to final assembly as possible. However, postponement related to location is the logical domain of the retailer.

This type of postponement delays shipments from the distributor (or retailer distribution center) until customer demand signals the retailer to send merchandise to individual stores. This is also consistent with VMI arrangements between retailer and distributor. Inspection and tooling are opportunities to lower cost through automation and elimination of non-value-adding steps in the process.

Product life cycle support also requires collaborative decisions. OEMs will initiate requirements for repair part stocking and component refurbishment. This need is common for large-ticket items where rebuilt parts can be recycled after their initial replacement. For many big-ticket items, this is a lucrative business. Options abound for handling initial warranty repairs and long-term repairs. For example, for laptop computers, Best Buy might do long-term warranty repairs in-house or farm the work out to contractors, or in some cases, return the computers to the manufacturers for service.

## 21.6 Multicompany Collaboration to Reduce Cost—Summary

The process for initiating or bolstering efforts to collaborate with trading partners is a three-step process. First, there is a need to screen both upstream and downstream trading partners. This may lead to pruning unprofitable products, categories, or SKUs, or trading partners that drive up costs. Second, the types of collaboration needed (A, B, C, D) should be derived from company strategies for operations. This might include analysis of costs with activity-based costing, customer requirements with QFD, or an activity system design. Finally, the collaborative tools must be chosen. Table 21.2, along with sections and chapters listed in Table 21.1, provide a candidate list of area for collaboration.

## Reference

1. Narayanan, V.G. and Raman, Ananth, "Aligning Incentives in Supply Chains," *Harvard Business Review*, November 2004, pp. 94–102.

# Chapter 22

# Retail Return Loops

This chapter explores issues that are, for many supply chains, becoming more important; these deal with the "return loop." When the *forward* supply chain has delivered a product to an end user, merchandise, for varying reasons, journeys back through the *reverse* or *return* supply chain. Returns or reverse flows also address issues of sustainability wherein some products must be disposed of in environmentally friendly ways. This is particularly true of products that degrade chemically. Currently, tires and technology products are examples of the types that use the return loop at the end of their usable life.

The return loop is also a service element that is important to many customers and end users. Convenient returns reduce purchase risk when buying from a retailer. Customers may also place considerable value on aftermarket service for equipment repair and maintenance. For durable products, manufacturers and retailers find that aftermarket services are more profitable than initial sales. Retailers or original equipment manufacturers (OEMs) price many products lower in the beginning because the real source of profit will come from the aftermarket. For example, cell phones, cameras, and computer printers require ongoing investment in consumables after purchase in the form of minutes, film or photo paper, and ink cartridges, respectively.

## 22.1  FedEx Supply Chain Case Study— The Rise of the Return Loop

FedEx Supply Chain is a U.S. supply chain services provider specializing in reverse logistics. The company, based in Pittsburgh, is privately held and maintains 26 million sq. ft. of warehouse space in 90 facilities and employs 5500 "team members."

The company, whose revenues are about $400 million, offers several services related to reverse supply chain logistics. These include an online auction of returned merchandise, software to manage return flows, disposition of damaged merchandise, warehouse and transportation services, and consulting in reverse logistics.

FedEx Supply Chain pursued offering the returns service after providing forward flow logistics services beginning in 1898. In an interview, FedEx Supply Chain's CEO, Herb Shear, recounted how his company was drawn into reverse logistics.[1] As with many new business opportunities, FedEx Supply Chain's move into reverse logistics started with a customer request. In 1988, the customer, a discount drug retailer, sought a place to store merchandise returning to its warehouses. Service to that customer evolved into developing software to scan incoming items, identify the merchandise and the store where they originated, and charge back the items to the manufacturer where possible. The first large retailer to buy the software was Target; other large retailers followed, transforming FedEx Supply Chain from a regional into a national company.

## 22.2 Types of Returns

The FedEx Supply Chain case demonstrates that reverse-logistics consciousness is a relatively recent phenomenon, and examination of the types of returns demonstrates the potential for complexity. The Supply Chain Council's Supply Chain Operations Reference (SCOR) model lists three types of returns. The types are listed in the following text along with other observations produced by a publication of the Council of Supply Chain Management Professionals (CSCMP) authored by Dale Rogers of Arizona State and Ronald Tibben-Lembke of the University of Nevada–Reno.[2] These authors add a fourth type of return, the recapture of assets required for shipment, such as special containers, pallets, and totes. This is a routine feature in forward supply chain design, so it's not included here.

1. *Return of defective products.* Interpreted broadly beyond outright defects, this return category also includes cases of customer or end-user "remorse" and mind changes. Included are items that are hard to install or did not fit properly, product recalls, and environmentally hazardous material.
2. *Return of an MRO (maintenance, repair, or overhaul) product.* In retail, this type includes high-value items needing repair or periodic maintenance. Rogers and Tibben-Lembke include product refurbishment and remanufacturing in this category. For appliances, this service can be done on site; for automobiles, it is performed at a dealer location or at a contract repair center. Often, such returns must be authorized through a *return merchandise authorization* (RMA).
3. *Return of excess products.* Examples include unsold merchandise, goods sold on consignment, and obsolete products.

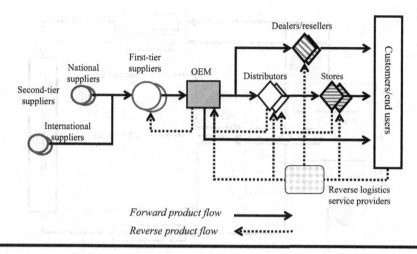

**Figure 22.1 Physical flows in return loops.**

Figure 22.1 is an adaptation of Figure 1.1 in Chapter 1 that depicts the forward supply chain. Figure 22.1 traces both forward and reverse flows for base, or physical, products. Depending on the product, returns can occur between the end user and the retailer, or from the end user back to the OEM manufacturer. Product component flows occur further upstream from the OEM back to first-tier suppliers. A third-party reverse-logistics provider, such as FedEx Supply Chain, may play a role anywhere in this flow. Indeed, transactions associated with reverse flows for many products outnumber those for forward flows. In retail, book sales returns to publishers occur with regularity; the books are restocked at the publisher and sold to other companies as needed

Figure 22.2 models return processes using a three-step process. Large numbers mark each step.

1. *End-user originates return action appropriate to the product.* This is one of the three types described earlier, with the product landing at the retailer, the OEM, a return center operated by the OEM, a first-tier supplier, a distributor, a retailer, or a returns service provider.

2. *Receiver processes the return.* It could process the item back into the forward supply chain without modification ("no fault found"), repair or refurbish the product, or remove the item from the chain for disposal.

3. *Product moves to a forward return path or to disposal.* Paths shown include regular forward paths, a discount or auction option, or direct shipment to end users. This requires a decision based on the action taken, available channels for return, and the nature of the product.

In Figure 22.2, a regular channel, shown at the upper right, can be through the retailer or by the Internet or catalog. A discount channel can include all of the previously discussed types, including "factory stores" or sales to brokers. The

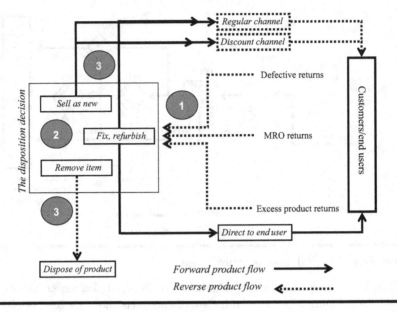

**Figure 22.2    Flow of returned merchandise.**

direct-to-end-user channel is shipment back to the party originating the return—especially appropriate for returning or replacing expensive merchandise.

Table 22.1 provides examples of reverse flows for different types of retail merchandise. These examples illustrate the multitude of paths in return-loop supply chains. For each example, there's a reason for the origin of the return and identification of common configurations of related processes.

## 22.3  Opportunities in Returns

The return loop, for many products, is an afterthought, but the cost and service implications of returns make the design of their processes important. This section describes some of the opportunities available from better design of the return processes. Table 22.2 outlines these opportunities.

### 22.3.1  Reduced Returns

An organization that has returns should adopt a *Lean* philosophy by treating returns as a form of *waste*, but this can only be done if root causes for returns are addressed. For example, Section 21.2 described a bakery with unaligned compensation for its delivery staff. The incentive arrangement based on total sales without considering scrap led to overstocking and returns of unsold product. An apparel manufacturer using multiple Chinese manufacturers sold products with varying sizing standards.

**Table 22.1    Examples of Return Loops**

| # | Example/Reason | 1 Originator | 2 Processor | 3 Return Path/ Disposal |
|---|---|---|---|---|
| 1 | Clothing return (doesn't fit, changed mind, etc.) | Customer, end user | Retail outlet where sold | Same-store resale |
| 2 | Laptop repair (manufacturer's warranty) | End user | OEM | Direct shipment |
| 3 | Laptop repair (extended retailer warranty) | End user | Retailer or service provider | Direct shipment |
| 4 | Books on consignment (unsold, surplus) | Retailer | OEM (publisher) | Regular-channel resale or disposal |
| 5 | Bakery goods (unsold, no longer fresh) | Retailer | OEM (bakery) | Disposal or discount channel |
| 6 | Defective part from first-tier supplier | OEM manufacturer | First-tier supplier | Repair, replace, or dispose of (scrap) |
| 7 | Car battery end of life | End user | Retailer (dealer garage) | Dispose through approved processor or recycling center |

The inconsistencies raised returns because buyers found that garments did not fit properly. Future orders were also deterred by the inability of customers to forecast their own sizes accurately. The lack of reliability encourages the ordering of several units at once with the intent of returning the unacceptable items. Attacking returns with a programmatic Six Sigma approach, such as that described in Chapter 17, should reduce processing costs and overproduction.

Another avoidance technique is targeting no-fault-found situations. These take the form of both returned products at the retail level and between first- and second-tier suppliers. The latter can sometimes be addressed by assuring that quality measurements are consistent between suppliers and OEMs. The former might be reduced by better instructions and troubleshooting direction. Information systems, designed around the return process, can also reduce returns. First, they assure that end-user returns are eligible under warranty and sales terms. Second, such systems

**Table 22.2  Opportunities in Returns**

| # | Opportunity | Suggested Strategies |
|---|---|---|
| 1 | Reduced returns | Understand and mitigate root causes for returns |
| 2 | Improved customer service | Emphasize extended product features that reduce end-user risk |
| 3 | Collaboration with partners | Cooperate in returns to achieve forward process improvement |
| 4 | Customer feedback | Gather early indications with base product or its use |
| 5 | Material source | Use recycled components as parts |
| 6 | Environmental mitigation | Control environmental impact of your product; reduce liability |
| 7 | Additional business | Expand service beyond your own product line |
| 8 | Cash-to-cash cycle reduction | Tighten investment in product circulating in return loops |
| 9 | Process standardization | Assure consistency; provide economies of scale |

alert partners to problems and track what is coming in and where it is. They can also help to diagnose problems in the system or the product so that they can be resolved.

## 22.3.2 Improved Customer Service

The return level is an inverse measure of customer satisfaction—more returns equates to less satisfaction. Smooth return processing is also an index of the ease of doing business with one's company, whether retailer, distributor, or manufacturer. For example, some customers find comfort in a "clicks-and-bricks" model used by retailers such as Eddie Bauer. They know they can return their Internet purchases to the retailer's stores, which makes them more willing to take the risk of shopping online and buying products sight unseen. They may also be able to make exchanges easily in the local physical store. This customer service result should be a powerful incentive to improve return processing.

## 22.3.3 Collaboration with Partners

A supply chain approach to returns requires multicompany collaboration. Such collaboration in the returns domain can build on or lead to collaboration on forward supply chain processes. One aspect of the collaboration can include the determination of which services the OEM and the retailer will provide. Data generated using activity-based costing (ABC), described in Chapter 19, will aid the discussion. This may be particularly necessary because financial reporting of cost in many return processes is weak or nonexistent.

Financial flows are another aspect of collaboration; this topic includes pricing and credits for returned items. For many products such as tires and batteries, there is a fee paid by the customer at the time of purchase to cover the later cost of recycling or disposal. The conditions for issuing an RMA may also be negotiated between the retailer and the OEM to control what is returned and where it is returned.

### 22.3.4 Customer Feedback

An understanding of customer feedback provides rich "voice-of-the-customer" information to improve product design, adjust merchandise assortments, and respond to customer priorities. For example, Rogers and Tibben-Lembke cite IKEA, where customer feedback led to development of easy-to-understand instructions for assembling its knockdown furniture that the customer has to assemble.* Better instructions reduced returns by frustrated assemblers of the product.

### 22.3.5 Material Source

For durable goods and parts, the return loop is a source of refurbished and remanufactured product. For example, Amazon offers both new and recycled books for sale at various prices. For a prior book by one of the authors, the site offers new books for about $77 and used ones for $40. However, many retailers and OEMs take a casual approach to this source of revenue. This does not mean there are no players taking advantage of this role. Smaller remanufacturers or generic part makers often refurbish previously owned goods for resale, a practice reinforced by growing interest in sustainability, as discussed in Chapter 5. The success of Goodwill Industries and Savers/Value Village after 2010 demonstrates the high interest consumers have in purchasing good-quality, previously owned products. Auto manufacturers in the United States compete actively in the aftermarket by touting the reliability of their "authentic," and usually pricier, products. Pulling in more of this business may be an option to consider.

### 22.3.6 Environmental Mitigation

If a product presents an environmental hazard, then close control of the return process can limit liability. It may also, through process reengineering, produce product

---

* See ref. 2, p. 7.

designs and material substitutions that lower the cost of product ownership and produce recycled material for new production. As described in Chapter 5, retailers are making environmental sustainability an important mission. Wal-Mart recently announced its intention of becoming a totally green company. Recent information regarding sustainability and supply chain issues can be found in the 2015 Retail Sustainability Management Report issued by the Retail Industry Leaders Association.[*]

### 22.3.7 Additional Business

Some vertically integrated retailers may choose to handle their own reverse supply chain activities. However, as there are service providers in the form of contract manufacturers serving the forward supply chain, there are service providers doing the same for reverse supply chains. FedEx Supply Chain, described at the beginning of this chapter, is an example. A company that decides to operate its own reverse supply chain might also do so for others as a service provider, creating another line of business.

### 22.3.8 Cash-to-Cash Cycle Reduction

Improvements in this metric, introduced previously, result from reductions in cycle time in return processes. Too often, returned merchandise is put aside for processing "when time is available." If it is not available, then both customer service and cash flow may suffer. A related problem, according to Rogers and Tibben-Lembke, is accounting for returns.[†] For example, the retail store is measured on sales, but returns cut into sales. So, returns are bad news to stores, and, if salespeople are paid on commission, for their paychecks. This may cause underreporting of returns, although most store operations capture this information. More common is inaccurate recording of reasons for returns.

### 22.3.9 Process Standardization

Returns processes will vary as merchandise is sold in different chains, in different countries, and in a variety of store types. Added control at the retailer, distributor, or OEM level assures consistent processes. Rogers and Tibben-Lembke point to the potential for centralized return centers, or CRCs, as ways to shorten cycle times and enforce consistent process guidelines. Benefits cited by the authors include the following:

---

[*] 2015 Retail Sustainability Management Report, Retail Industry Leaders Association, http://www.rila.org.

[†] See ref. 2, p. 13.

- Retail-store space savings by moving returns out of the store quickly or bypassing it altogether.
- Screening out items that have to be discarded, saving the expense of their transport back up the supply chain.
- An extended product service by the manufacturer or distributor trying to win business from a retailer.
- Shorter cycle times because the dedicated facility has returns as its primary mission.
- An ability to spot trends in returns and better understanding of root causes for returns. For the manufacturer or distributor, this could lead to quicker correction of root-cause process problems that cause returns.

## 22.4 Return Loops—Summary

Return-loop opportunities abound for the many retailers and the trading partners that serve them. If these opportunities are being overlooked, addressing returns can pay off in customer satisfaction, market share, end-user feedback, lower cost of sales, and lower working capital. With the movement to a sustainable business model, return loops can also be the source of new profits, reduced liability risk, and improved image with customers and end users.

## References

1. MacDonald, Mitch, "A Fortune in Reversal," *DC Velocity*, October 2006, pp. 25–30.
2. Rogers, Dale S. and Tibben-Lembke, Ronald S., "Returns Management and Reverse Logistics for Competitive Advantage," *CSCMP Explores ...*, Winter, 2006.

## Chapter 23

# Case Application: SeaBear/ Made in Washington

SeaBear/Made in Washington (MIW) is a privately held company that offers three product lines. Each product line has a separate business name and focuses on products made or processed in the state of Washington. This chapter highlights recommendations and techniques addressed in the prior five sections and provides an application of tools and methodologies covered in other chapters. This is intended to serve those seeking to improve a retail supply chain.

Information for this chapter was gleaned from interviews with company president and CEO Michael Mondello, visits to stores and processing facilities, and a review of the organization's three principal websites. The company is complex; however, many other businesses, as they evolve, take on similar levels of complexity.

## 23.1 Introducing the Company: Three Businesses within a Business

The three major subsidiary businesses SeaBear/MIW operates are as follows:

1. *SeaBear Seafoods, purveyor of processed fish products*, targets consumers and corporations through an online site and five company-owned physical stores operated under the name of *Made in Washington*. Wholesale customers include numerous other brick-and-mortar stores and online sales.
2. *Gerard & Dominique (G&D)*, producer of fresh fish specialty products, targets wholesalers and high-end restaurants through its online business and marketing group, as well as other food purveyors.

3. *MIW, a retailer of gifts and food products,* targets consumers and corporations online and through five brick-and-mortar stores.

### 23.1.1 Division 1: SeaBear Seafoods

On its website, the company describes itself as follows:

> In 1957, Anacortes fisherman Tom Savidge and his wife Marie built a backyard smokehouse and began selling smoked wild salmon to local taverns. With that, Specialty Seafoods (later renamed SeaBear after a Native American legend) was born.

The tavern owners loved Tom's smoked salmon but asked him to preserve it longer. Being an inventive guy, Tom answered their request with a whole new idea in packaging: his solution was the *Gold Seal* pouch, which preserves the salmon naturally so no refrigeration is required. This innovation (for which he received a patent) made it easy for tourists traveling through the Northwest to take Tom's salmon back home or to ship it to family and friends. From this, word spread about "the legendary flavor of the Pacific Northwest."

Today, the company ships its full line of seafood to customers in all 50 states and remains dedicated to the its original principles: "Make great food people love, and always listen to our customers. We stand behind everything we do with our unconditional Fisherman's Oath guarantee."*

Major product lines include the following:

- Smoked salmon purchased unsmoked and flash-frozen from suppliers
- Lox-style (cured in brine and cold-smoked) salmon
- Salmon fillets to cook at home
- Ready-to-eat take-anywhere salmon
- Appetizers and foods for entertaining.
- Wild Alaskan halibut and cod for cooking at home
- Chowders
- Gift baskets
- SeaBear apparel gear

### 23.1.2 Division 2: Gerard & Dominique

This 2008 acquisition by SeaBear is a luxury brand. It produces smoked salmon but differs from SeaBear in that it sources only the finest fresh, never frozen, salmon fillets.

> In 1990, acclaimed European-trained chefs Gerard Parrat (proprietor of *Gerard's Relais de Lyon*) and Dominique Place (proprietor of

---

* http://www.seabear.com

*Dominique's Place)* could not find a smoked salmon which met their standards, so they created one.

Over the years, Gerard & Dominique's signature European Style Smoked Salmon has been served at premier hotels and restaurants across the U.S. and around the world. Wine Spectator has called Gerard & Dominique's creation "Simply the best smoked salmon made in the Northwest, and the only one ... I tasted that rivals the best smoked salmons made in Europe."

Made with only the freshest natural ingredients from the Northwest, Gerard & Dominique products are carefully hand-filleted and smoked by Chef Dominique Place per old-world traditions. The process begins with rich, flavorful salmon harvested from the cold, clean waters of the Pacific Northwest. Fillets are specially seasoned, then individually smoked over a select blend of Northwest hardwoods, which imparts a subtle, complex flavor. No preservatives or coloring agents are ever used.*

In 2008, G&D joined the SeaBear/MIW family. Although primarily a wholesaler/restaurant-targeted business, the company also sells products direct to consumers from its online site. Its international reputation for quality has earned its parent the respect of smoked salmon producers, hotels, and other knowledgeable food experts worldwide.

## 23.1.3 Division 3: Made in Washington

MIW is targeted at the corporate and consumer markets and carries foods and beverages, which they divide into specialty foods, as well as production packaged goods; gifts from independent artists and company artists; and other specialty and gift items made in the state.

The company targets consumers directly and corporate gift and recognition purchasers. It offers local, national, and corporate buyers options of ordering from the online site or visiting one of the five MIW stores located in the Seattle–Tacoma area, primary destinations for out-of-state tourists. However, locals make up the clear majority of customers who purchase both for local use and for friends outside the state near and far (Figure 23.1).

In 1984, Gillian and Jack Matthews opened their first MIW store at Seattle's Pike Place Market. That store brought a new concept to our region—a wide variety of gifts made locally, by Washington artists, food makers, entrepreneurs and small businesses.†

---

* http://www.gdseafoods.com
† http://www.madeinwashington.com

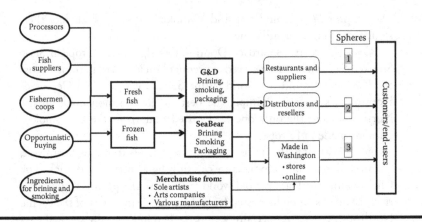

**Figure 23.1 Supply chain spheres for SeaBear, Gerard and Dominique (G&D), & Made in Washington.**

Major product lines include the following:

1. Blown-glass art from Seattle and environs, the national center of this craft
2. Wines from some of the 850 prolific and award-winning Washington wineries
3. Specialty coffees and coffee-related products
4. Smoked salmon, other fish, and fish-related products
5. Many other specialty food items including candies, cookies, jams and jellies, and many others
6. A wide offering of household items including soaps, candles, apparel items, and crafts
7. All types of works from the many artists working and residing in the state

As MIW describes itself on its website,

> The Northwest is a hotbed of culinary innovation. And, smoked salmon of the Pacific Northwest is one of the world's truly great food traditions. All of this—and the never-ending innovation across many, many products provides an endless stream of wonderful gifts which celebrate all that is special about our home.*

## 23.2 Review of Important SCM Management Skills

Using the case described above, this chapter recalls the five SCM tasks identified in Chapter 1 and how these are reflected in the SeaBear/MIW organization. These tasks are as follows:

1. Designing supply chains for strategic advantage
2. Implementing collaborative relationships inside the organization

---

* http://www.madeinwashington.com

3. Forging supply chain partnerships with trading partners up and down the supply chain
4. Managing supply chain information
5. Making money from the supply chain

Selected topics addressed in earlier chapters are reviewed in this chapter using methodologies and tools that apply and demonstrate how the concepts are deployed by one company.

## 23.3 Designing Supply Chains for Strategic Advantage

To be successful financially, retail companies must identify their target markets, build an effective retail format, and create a sustainable competitive advantage. Table 23.1 identifies the approaches used for each of the three subsidiary companies in the case.

Table 1.1 in Chapter 1 displays a generic supply chain model, which applies to all three companies but with distinct differences due to the varying way the products are created and delivered. For example, the fish companies have more echelons

**Table 23.1 Summary of Retail Strategies for Subsidiary Companies**

| Subsidiary Company | Target Market(s) | Retail Format | Sustainable Competitive Advantage |
|---|---|---|---|
| SeaBear | 1. End consumers<br>2. Corporate gift givers<br>3. *Made in Washington* stores and online | 1. Online sales<br>2. Wholesalers selling to *Made in Washington* and other retailers | High-quality smoked salmon and other frozen fish |
| Gerard & Dominique | 1. Restaurants<br>2. Food wholesalers | 1. Online ordering<br>2. Wholesale direct sales | Highest-level lox-style smoked salmon from only fresh fish sources |
| Made in Washington | 1. Local consumers<br>2. Tourists<br>3. Corporate gift givers | 1. Five retail stores<br>2. Online store | Provides food and nonfood goods made in state of Washington from artists and local companies |

than does MIW due to the processing levels required, while MIW primarily purchases its merchandise from outside vendors.

All three companies have similar objectives for the supply chain as delineated in Chapter 2:

- The need for timely deliveries and excellent customer service
- High margins and frequent inventory turns
- Regularly updated products to meet market needs.

Although important for many retailers, drop shipping is not yet important in these subsidiaries' businesses.

In the fish companies, SeaBear and G&D, inventories are built according to monthly forecasts that are updated frequently. SeaBear inventories the cleaned but unprocessed frozen fish in cold storage until they are needed to meet planned sales. This enables the company to take advantage of favorable purchase terms when available. G&D processes only fresh fish, thereby requiring different purchasing procedures that don't allow for long-term storage of the salmon and other fish. This premium level of handling is required to service the very high-end restaurants who are G&D's primary customers.

## 23.3.1 Brief Description of the Fish Supply Chains for SeaBear and Gerard & Dominique

There is considerable similarity between the supply chains of SeaBear and G&D. Figure 23.1 depicts the supply chains of each of the two fish processing subsidiaries.

Sustainability has impacted the fish business with issues related to sourcing, freshness, preservation of a perishable product, labor issues, and contamination from environmental sources such as mercury and pollution. Chapters 4 and 5 discuss the strategic impact of globalization and sustainability on supply chains and suggested issues to be considered by supply chain managers. The major effect on the SeaBear/MIW organization is the ability of products to be shipped all over the world to customers and gift recipients.

Activity systems are discussed in Chapter 13, and IKEA is used as an example. Strategic priorities at SeaBear/MIW are the following:

1. High-quality to very-high-quality products
2. A strategy to drive business to the websites for efficient distribution
3. Maximizing channel position
   a. SeaBear is a small company in the fishing industry and so does not possess a great deal of channel power, *but* the G&D brand gives SeaBear some cachet, and suppliers find importance in the company's business by association.

b. G&D is a respected player in the fresh fish business.

MIW is the major player in much of its business. Artists are anxious to get their products into the stores and on the website.

c. These products can be divided into two categories:

   i. Products from "regular, proven" vendors who are on the approved list

   ii. Products considered more risky from artists new to MIW or very large art pieces

     A. New products are often given a trial period to see if they will be profitable items. If so, they are transferred to the "regular vendors" list.

     B. Some products are purchased by the company, and some are carried on consignment, depending upon the risk.

d. Efficient use of facilities and resources resulting in shared overhead, which is often difficult to allocate to specific product lines. A few years ago, the headquarters location in Seattle was consolidated with processing operations in Anacortes, Washington, to work toward this goal.

If the company seeks to create an activity system, it would use these components to identify themes and activities.

## 23.3.2 Using Metrics to Evaluate Strategy

Strategic review and revision requires good metrics according to the adage that "what gets measured gets managed." Table 23.2 outlines useful metrics for the three major subsidiaries as suggested in Chapter 9. The evaluative measures used by the company are proprietary, but readers may find the following useful as a set of possibilities:

# 23.4 Product Issues

Many of the fish-related products produced by the company are staple in nature. SeaBear's signature smoked salmon is the everyday workhorse product for this division. Similarly, G&D produces a signature salmon product in the lox style, which plays a major role in its product lineup. MIW carries both staple and "fashion" items, the latter being products that have relatively short life cycles. They must be replaced as customers tire of them and seek newer and unique items. In all divisions, there is diligent attention to new product development and discovery with all the attendant product life cycle considerations.

Table 23.2 Important Metrics for SeaBear/Made in Washington

| Service Type | Unit Relevance | Operational Type | Unit Relevance | Financial Type | Unit Relevance |
|---|---|---|---|---|---|
| Market share (%) | S, G&D, MIW | Product quality | S, G&D | Total cost of ownership | SeaBear/MIW Corporate |
| Perfect order (%) | S, G&D, MIW | First-pass quality | S, G&D | Revenue growth (%) | S, G&D, MIW |
| Order fill rate (%) | S, G&D, MIW | Process capability | S, G&D | Profit growth (%) | S, G&D, MIW |
| On-time delivery (%) | S, G&D, MIW | Labor Productivity | S, G&D, MIW | Total operating costs (% change) | S, G&D, MIW |
| Delivery lead time (# days) | S, G&D,MIW | Production productivity by square foot | S, G&D, MIW | Cash-to-cash cycle | SeaBear/MIW Corporate |
| Return rate (%) | S, G&D, MIW | Retail productivity per square foot | MIW | Inventory turns | S, G&D, MIW |
| Back orders (#) | S, G&D, MIW | | | Return on investment (ROI) | SeaBear/MIW Corporate |
| Back order frequency | S, G&D, MIW | | | Gross margin ROI (GMROI) | S, G&D, MIW |
| Product line depth | S, G&D | | | Residual income | SeaBear/MIW Corporate |

## 23.5 Internal Collaboration

Internal collaboration is important at SeaBear/MIW. The three subsidiaries share some supply chain components: incoming transportation for raw materials and outgoing delivery of products in company-owned trucks and by outside transportation providers. Sometimes, shipments are jointly planned for all product sets; shared forecasting and forecast revision by the same staff members; and some shared suppliers, particularly for packaging and other auxiliary products and raw materials. There is also shared warehousing of many products. At the product level, all three companies may be represented in MIW outlets, while MIW merchandise, with a few possible exceptions, does not appear on the websites of the fish-related businesses.

The company plans and forecasts separately for the retail stores and the online businesses and combines these prognostications for final production and purchasing estimates for the season. In addition, acquisition of new items is extremely important since 65% of customers are local and want to see exciting new items in the stores and online.

An important and not-yet-discussed activity is packaging and branding. Special pouches, boxes, labels, printed materials, and inserts are needed for the many different items produced; all of this is internally coordinated. Obviously, product forecasting has an impact on the company's ability to purchase in economical volumes.

CEO Mike Mondello has stressed the difficulty in assigning overhead costs to subsidiaries due to the sharing of resources, creating internal cost accounting challenges.

## 23.6 Partnerships Up and Down the Supply Chain

SeaBear/MIW has relatively few, if any, formal partnerships with companies up and/or down the supply chain from its subsidiaries. However, the links between the three companies inside the organization are strong and varied. All the individual companies have informal partnerships with suppliers. In some instances, fish purchases will be made against a guaranteed forecast, allowing suppliers to plan for their sales of salmon and other fish to SeaBear organizations.

SeaBear does have one contract to make private-label smoked fish for an outside company. Production is estimated by their downstream customer, and the ordering company guarantees to purchase all this production. However, actual purchase time is determined by consumer demand for the private-label product. SeaBear eventually sells all the production to this customer, but the schedule of sales varies with their partner's customer demand.

MIW carries some art-based company product lines where it does high volumes. Informal partnerships with these suppliers benefit both retailer and vendors.

## 23.7 Supply Chain Information Management

SeaBear/MIW relies heavily on a purchasing information system that performs many functions. Based on sales and forecasts, the system produces material requirements for the various businesses, determines a buying schedule, manages inventory, and performs other information delivery functions.

Retail stores use a point-of-sales system, which tracks sales, inventories, and other important statistics. Central merchandise inventory updating occurs corporately. Similar data are produced by the online retail site's support staff.

Currently, warehouse operations are centralized for all nonfrozen inventories, especially for MIW and SeaBear. The G&D product lines are refrigerated but never frozen and must be handled separately. Currently, a pick, pack, and ship system is used for manual picking of all divisions' products, with preidentified bins for optimal order picking.

## 23.8 Financial Challenges

Earlier chapters point out that traditional accounting is designed for reporting, but it is often not useful for business analysis, particularly when there are shared resources. For SeaBear/MIW, monitoring multichannel costs is difficult, particularly when company personnel may be working on one product line one day and another on the next day. Labor is often moved from one subsidiary to another, so these costs are often accounted for as a percent of corporate sales.

There is a carryover effect of this when pricing products. Often, there are many non-product-tied costs that should be included in determining the original selling price of an individual item, including holding costs, cost of interest expense, and other shared expenses. Freight charges are often a challenge for retailers since these are often negotiated and vary frequently. MIW is the most affected by freight agreements.

As mentioned previously, channel power affects the cost of goods for each of the SeaBear/MIW divisions. Overall, the company fish businesses are very small in that industry and wield little channel power. Exceptions are cases where suppliers want the prestige of supplying the G&D fish to enjoy any associated bragging rights. In this industry, information is generally not shared by supply chain partners up and down the chain, and of concern is the frequent inability to determine to whom final sales of the products are made by distributors. Distributors' customers range from restaurants to other retailers.

The changing nature of the art product lines offers additional challenges and financial risks for this system. Artists are often challenged in searching for outlets for their works. In these channels, MIW serves as supply chain captain and possesses considerably more information and clout than other parties in its supply chain. The result is that the company has many financial options in obtaining this merchandise, including the ability to sell unknown or risky products on consignment.

Often artists are happy to have an outlet for their wares and will make pricing and delivery accommodations. There are many successful products in the inventories, but as always, failing products must be marked down and the investment in them recaptured when possible. The opportunity to test products without investing in inventory reduces the riskiness of introducing new items to consumers.

## 23.9 Summary

The SeaBear/MIW case has been presented to give readers insights into how the principles discussed in this book can be applied to any size of company. The discussion here barely scratches the surface but provides a glimpse into the power of strategically evaluating and designing supply chains with the flexibility needed to take advantage of rapidly changing business opportunities.

# Glossary

**3C alternative to MRP:** A method that uses capacity, commonality, and consumption as a basis for control of material in the supply chain. The technique decreases the dependence of the supply chain on forecast accuracy by shifting inventory decision to considerations of actual demand and capacity.

**3D bar code:** A microscopic bar code used to protect high-value items.

**4PL/LLP:** 4PL is a trademarked term from the consulting firm, Accenture. It describes an integrator of supply chain service providers to deliver a comprehensive solution. The Lead Logistics Provider (LLP) is a company's primary supply chain services provider. Clifford Lynch quoted in *DC Velocity*, July 2005, page 57.

**5S:** A foundation for visual controls in a production operation. Characteristic of Lean manufacturing. The approach includes the following:
1. Sort (organization): what is needed and not needed
2. Stabilize (orderliness): a place for everything and everything in its place
3. Shine (cleanliness): keeping the workplace clean
4. Standardize (adherence): maintains and monitors the above
5. Sustain (self-discipline): sticking to the rules, scrupulously

(From Best Manufacturing Practices Center of Excellence.)

**ABC inventory classification:** Division of inventory into groups based on decreasing order of annual dollar volume (annual units × projected volume). "A" items are 10–20% of items but 50–70% of dollar volume. "B" items are about 20% of items and 20% of dollar volume. "C" items are 60–70% of items but only 10–30% of value.

The classification points to places where attention can be focused for improvement. The same principle can be applied to products, product categories, suppliers, customers, and sales. In classification efforts, one must decide at what level the classification should be completed. This will depend on the product's configuration. (Adapted from *APICS Dictionary*, 10th ed.)

**ABCD analysis:** Technique for analyzing technical and administrative functions. "A" activities add value to the customer and require decision-making discretion. "B" activities require decision-making but don't add value. "C" activities don't require decision-making but do add value. "D" items don't require decision-making and don't add value. The classification is useful for process analysis and deciding how to remove or automate activities.

**Accordion theory:** Fluctuations in breadth (wide or narrow) and depth (broad or narrow) of retail product mix according to the strategy of the retailer. (Adapted from *Retailing Management*, 5th ed.)

**Action plan:** A plan that defines a project or projects. They are part of programs or initiatives.

**Activity (project management context):** An element of work performed during a project. It has an expected duration, cost, and resource requirement. An activity can be subdivided into tasks. Activity definitions describe what has to be done to produce deliverables. Formerly called a "work item." (Adapted from the *PMBOK Guide*, 2000 ed.)

**Activity-based costing, management (ABC, ABM):** A method to plan, measure, and control expenses associated with managing and monitoring the supply chain; specific techniques for assigning cost in business processes to activities. ABC is seen to overcome many of the shortcomings of conventional accounting methodologies. *Time-Driven Activity-Based Costing*, from Robert S. Kaplan and Steven R. Anderson, simplifies the administration of ABC.

**Activity system:** A term originated by Michael Porter in defining networks of activities that provide a sustainable competitive advantage. These networks can constitute a supply chain. An activity in this context is a feature of the company's strategy that makes it distinctive. Activities, in turn, are supported by supply chain and other company processes. In this book, groups of supporting processes make up activities.

**Agent:** A party that negotiates supply chain transactions that does not take title to the goods.

**Agile enterprise:** Companies that employ rapid customer/supplier partnering to achieve a short-product development life cycle.

Agility merges competencies in cost, quality, dependability, and flexibility. (*APICS Dictionary*, 10th ed.)

**AIDC (Automatic Identification and Data Capture):** A set of technologies to track material movement in the supply chain. Technologies include bar codes, RFID, GPS, and others. Also ADC, automatic data capture. Includes bar codes, RFID, biometrics, magnetic strips, and voice recognition. (Adapted from *Wikipedia*.)

**Allocation:** The process of deciding which customers should receive products or services that are in short supply.

**APICS:** International not-for-profit offering programs and materials for individual and organizational education, standards of excellence, and integrated resource management topics. Formerly called American Production and Inventory Control Society, now The Educational Society for Resource Management.

**Apparel matrix:** Inventory category.

**Application area:** With respect to project management, an application area is a discipline where project management theory and practice applies. This book adapts SCM to project management. Other example application areas include construction, defense acquisition, and software development.

**Approved material list (AML):** A list of approved suppliers and materials. Some companies seek to expand the AML to increase options for product design and to avoid single-source or end-of-life components.

**APS:** Advanced Planning System. Systems that plan actual logistics and production over short-, immediate-, and long-term periods. Can be separate from or built into MRP/ERP systems. The APS can generate different scenarios for decision support. Components include demand planning, production planning, production scheduling, distribution planning, and transportation planning. (Adapted from *APICS Dictionary*, 10th ed.)

**AS2:** Messages notifying of inbound items and contents. Transmitted by Internet. Used by smaller companies due to lower cost.

**As-is:** The current state, such as how processes in the supply chain process are currently performed.

**ASN (Advance ship notification):** Messages notifying of inbound items and contents. Transmitted by EDI. Used by larger companies.

**ASQC:** The American Society for Quantity Control.

**Assemble-to-order:** An environment where products or services are assembled after receipt of an order. This is useful where there are a large number of options consisting of common components. A basket of groceries is an example. Made-to-order computers are another. In a VAT analysis, this approach might be tried for "T" type product structures. (Adapted from *APICS Dictionary*, 10th ed.)

**Assortment:** The items carried within a category. Can include sizes, styles, and colors of items. Collaboration is often required when setting up and making changes to the assortment.

**ATP:** Available to promise. The uncommitted portion of inventory and planned production maintained in the master schedule. (Adapted from *APICS Dictionary*, 10th ed.)

**Auctions online:** Online negotiations among qualified suppliers. Usually facilitated by software applications.

**Balanced scorecard:** An approach to measurement that cascades measures from the top down through the organization. The method uses four perspectives to achieve balance. These are financial, customer, internal business, and innovation and learning.

**Bar coding:** An automatic identification technology that uses parallel dark bars and spaces to represent characters. Bar coding is an important element in automating the tracking of material in the supply chain. Also called the Universal Product Code.

**Barrier:** An obstacle that hinders the organization's ability to reach its objectives. Many barriers are hidden. Barriers, unlike constraints, can be managed through project planning and execution.

**Batch-and-queue system:** Refers to a production management system that relies on large batches of material. This leads to large queues while waiting to complete a production step. Such systems are characterized by high work in process inventory and low velocity production.

**Benchmarking:** A search for those best practices that will lead to superior performance. Benchmarking is usually executed with those who perform a targeted activity the best, regardless of the industry they are in. Internal benchmarking makes comparisons within an organization, such as developing best practices from several stores who perform similar functions.

**Best of breed:** This term refers to a specialized supply chain application such as demand management or a warehouse management application. These are stand-alone and compete with similar functions that are part of integrated enterprise-level applications such as those from JD Edwards, SAP, or Oracle.

**Bill of Material items:** Inventory category. Assemblies and subassemblies.

**"Blue Ocean Strategy":** In strategic planning, a strategy that makes competitors irrelevant by creating a "monopoly" in the marketplace. The title of a book describing the strategy by W. Chan Kim and Renée Mauborgne.

**Bluetooth:** A technology that uses radio-frequency standards for wireless communication between computers and their peripherals. A line-of-site connection is not necessary.

**BOM:** Bill of material in manufacturing industry.
Beginning of month in retail.

**BPM:** Business Process Management. Broadly, BPM focuses on improving business processes rather than functions or costs. Narrowly, BPMI (Business Process Management Initiative) is a nonprofit group promoting open standards for information technology used in business processes.

**BPO:** Business Process Outsourcing. Contracting out for support services beyond information technology. Examples include human resources, finance and accounting, and logistics services.

**Bracket pricing:** The use of brackets for order volumes. Each bracket has a different price per unit, with larger orders having lower prices per unit. Such prices usually recognize economies in logistics and other supply chain processes.

**Brand, branding:** Vision, position, "space" in the market. Establishing a brand name is a primary way to compete in many industries. SCM can support the strategy for establishing a brand image. Also includes brand equity, or value of the brand.

**Breadman:** A term applied to "automatic" replacement of inventory by third-party logistics providers, normally distributors. The analogy is the breadman who replenishes stock in the grocery store on a regularly scheduled basis.

A related term is "milk run." The term can also apply to types of vendor-managed inventory.

**Break-even analysis:** A calculation that produces the volume required to make a profit on a product. This is called the break-even point. It is also used to calculate the volume required to pay for a cost reduction. (Adapted from *Retailing Management*, 5th ed.)

**Buffer stock:** See *Safety stock.*

**Bullwhip effect:** A term coined by Dr. Hau Lee of Stanford. It describes the phenomenon in which small changes in final demand for a product produce wide swings in production upstream in the supply chain.

**Business model:** A model answers questions such as the following: "Who is the customer?" "What does the customer value?" "How do we make money in this business?" "What is the underlying economic logic that explains how we deliver value to customers?" A *strategy* defines how the organization competes. Competing effectively requires being different from your competitors. (Why Business Models Matter, *Harvard Business Review*, May 2002.)

**Business process reengineering (BPR):** Taking a holistic customer-focused systems view to changing processes in the organization. BPR encompasses vision for the organization's future, workflow along the supply chain, information technology, organization theory, the Internet, computer-supported collaboration, and other approaches.

**Buyback:** The purchase of a competitor's stock at a retailer in order to substitute the buying company's product.

The purchase of a retailer's slow-moving stock by the manufacturer. (Adapted from *Retailing Management*, 5th ed.)

**Capacity strategy:** A strategic choice for adjusting strategy to business levels. A "leading" strategy adds capacity in anticipation of demand. A "lag" strategy waits until the demand has materialized. A "tracking" strategy means attempts to match capacity and demand. (Adapted from *APICS Dictionary*, 10th ed.)

Such a strategy should consider product life-cycle position and profitability.

**Capital recovery costs:** The equivalent expense to recover the cost of an investment, such as that for fixed assets and working capital. The calculation normally uses asset life, salvage value, and the cost of capital to make the conversion. Also called "equivalent uniform annual cash flow."

**Cash-to-cash cycle time:** The time between payments for product components to suppliers and the time customers make payments. This parameter has become an important measure of supply chain performance, reflecting both financial and inventory management process performance. Most have negative measures ranging from 30 to 80 days. Some, notably Dell, have a positive cycle time, meaning they collect payments from customers before they have to pay suppliers.

**Category:** Items that are substitutes for each other. There are many ways to determine categories. (Adapted from *Retailing Management*, 5th ed.)

**Category captain:** Supplier who works with a retailer to improve customer satisfaction and profits across a category. (Adapted from *Retailing Management*, 5th ed.)

**Category management:** A structure that focuses on management of products or product families. With respect to SCM, this could also include incoming material, production planning, and distribution shifting away from a structure based on commodities or manufacturing plants.

**Cause-and-effect diagram (fishbone diagram):** A tool that uses a graphical description of contributing elements to identify root causes of process variation.

**Cellular manufacturing:** A manufacturing process that produces families of parts within a single line or cell of machines with operators who work only within the line or cell. The cellular concept is applicable to administrative and technical process. In this context, it means clustering unlike operations to increase processing velocity.

**Center of Excellence (COE):** A formal or informal committee that focuses on benchmarking and continuous improvement. Has expertise in identifying project management tools. (Adapted from Strategic Planning for Project Management.)

**Centralized Return Center (CRC):** Process facility to handle returned merchandise. The CRC collects the items and makes decisions on its processing based on retailer and manufacturer guidelines. (Adapted from Rogers, Dale S. and Tibben-Lembke, Ronald S., Returns management and reverse logistics for competitive advantage, *CSCMP Explores ...*, Winter, 2006.)

**Certified partner:** A trading partner that has met its customer's supplier requirements.

**Certified supplier:** A supplier that has been approved for providing defined components for manufacturing or distribution. Certification levels may have varying conditions related to quality management, such as needs for quality control. Suppliers are often qualified before financial terms are negotiated.

**Channel:** A group of businesses that take ownership title to products or facilitate exchange during the marketing process from the original manufacturer to the final buyer. Effective SCM requires an understanding of the needs of each customer and segment and the correct channel to reach them.

**Channel master:** The single, most powerful company in a supply chain. The channel master dictates terms of trade for the channel. The presence of a master depends on the nature of the industry and competition. Channel mastery is often the goal of SCM programs.

**Charter:** A document that authorizes a project. It enables the project manager to apply resources to project activities. (Adapted from *PMBOK Guide*, 2000 ed.)

**CLM:** Council of Logistics Management. A worldwide professional organization of logistics personnel. CLM has contributed heavily to the discussion of supply chain issues. Beginning January 1, 2005, the organization was renamed the Council of Supply Chain Management Professionals (CSCMP).

**Closed-loop supply chain:** A supply chain with finite boundaries. Such a situation provides a domain for implementation of advanced RFID and other technologies. Examples are single companies in which parts containers are tracked or high volume flows between two trading partners, where benefits can be readily identified.

**Closeout:** An offer of discontinued or slow-moving merchandise at a discount. Often made in bulk quantities.

**Collaboration:** CGR defines it as joint planning and execution of supply chain activities. These activities can range from new product development to day-to-day operations. Collaboration includes all aspects of the relationship related to physical movement, information sharing, financial flows, and exchange of intellectual property. Collaboration is also defined as internal between people and functions, and external between supply chain companies. The Supply Chain Council defines collaboration as

*A relationship built on trust that is benchmarked by the commitment to the team objective and where consensus may not always be achievable but where nothing takes place without the commitment of all involved.*

**Collaborative execution systems:** Category of application software that enables the effective coordination and flow of information across the entire value chain. Automating tasks required to manage each transaction and providing real-time visibility to information, collaborative execution systems are designed to improve productivity and reliability.

**Collaboratory:** A term coined by participants in the Supply Chain Council's SCOR update technical committee. It refers to the entity that includes the business, cultural, and system environment needed to build and operate a linkage between partners.

**Comparative advantage:** This concept, sometimes called a "theory" or a "law," holds that trading partners gain when countries specialize in what they can do most efficiently (use the fewest labor and capital resources) and trade for the products they don't produce as efficiently. This is not to be confused with absolute advantage, where a trading partner can make all products more efficiently than others. Absolute advantage would hold that the best producer should not specialize, making everything and not trading for any goods.

**Concurrent engineering:** The process of coordinating product and process, including supply chain, development. Also called simultaneous engineering.

**Configuration:** The arrangement of components specified to produce an assembly. (*APICS Dictionary*, 10th ed.)

Configuration has a major impact on supply chain design. For example, different configurations affect postponement strategies. In application of the 3C approach, configuration figures in commonality among end items.

**Configurator:** A system used by design-to-order, make-to-order, or assemble-to-order companies. They enable direct customer or sales engineer configuration of the product. Configurators can generate solid models, drawings, costs, and bills of material. (Adapted from *APICS Dictionary*, 10th ed.)

**Consignment:** 1. A shipment by a common carrier. 2. Terms of a contract in which a supplier is not paid until the goods are used or sold. (*APICS Dictionary*, 10th ed.)

**Consignment inventory:** Inventory provided for sale but not paid for until it is sold to an end-user/customer.

**Constant-cycle (fixed-cycle) reorder model:** An inventory reorder pattern with fixed time intervals and variable quantities. Advantages include

- Better for close operations with minimal transportation requirements.
- Can take advantage of EOQ economies for operations involving high setup costs.
- Fast, doesn't require counting or tracking of inventory.
- Simplicity. Compatible with visible signaling. Examples are the two-bin system and Kan-Ban approaches.
- Easier to predict time requirements once orders are placed.

Disadvantages include that the model can cause excess inventory in the system. It is better for low-cost, "C" items. Some companies expense items in this category. (*Handbook of Supply Chain Management*.)

**Constant-quantity (fixed-quantity) reorder model:** An inventory reorder pattern with fixed-quantity delivered variable time intervals. Advantages include

- Establishes a regular rhythm in the supply chain
- Decreases variability from uncertainty about schedules
- Can take advantage of setup economies when setup times depend on sequence, for example paint lines where different color sequences require different setup efforts

Disadvantages arise when variation in quantities can cause production to run behind. One must also track production through the chain, with a requirement to know usage at various points to signal correct quantity. The approach fits higher-value "A" items.

**Constraint:** Any element that prevents a system from achieving a higher level of performance. Constraints can be of many kinds, including physical steps in production and the limits on customer desire for the product. Constraints are "givens" or limitations that can't be changed in the course of designing or redesigning a supply chain. A barrier is an obstacle that may be mitigated by management action.

**Continuous Replenishment Planning (CRP):** The practice of partnering between distribution channel members that changes the traditional replenishment process from traditional purchase orders based on economic order quantities, to the replenishment of products based on actual and forecasted product demand.

**Control points:** In the theory of constraints, these are strategic locations that are tightly planned and scheduled. Other work centers are not, simplifying scheduling and control. (Adapted from *APICS Dictionary*, 10th ed.)

**Cooperative advertising (co-op):** Joint advertising agreements between supply chain partners (OEMs and retailers).

**Core assortment:** A large proportion of stock carried by every store in a chain. Seen to be essential to the image of the store. (Adapted from *Retailing Management*, 5th ed.)

**Core competence:** An organizational capability that can be applied to a variety of core and end products. The capability is usually technology based, but can also be competence in facets of supply chain management.

**Core processes (project management context):** Processes with clear dependencies that are likely to be performed in the same order on most projects. These processes may be iterated several times. Examples are scope planning, performance reporting, and project phase initiation. (Adapted from *PMBOK Guide*, 2000 ed.)

**Cost (retail):** Amount paid to vendor for merchandise item or items plus the cost of shipping the goods to the retailer.

**Cost baseline:** A time-phased estimate of cost. It is used to monitor performance on cost throughout the project. (Adapted from *PMBOK Guide*, 2000 ed.)

**Cost driver:** In activity-based costing, volume variable used to calculate the total cost of an activity or process. The activity cost may be expressed in a unit cost – (cost)/(unit of volume). The unit of volume used is the cost driver.

**Cost of quality (COQ):** COQ may be viewed as a subset of activity-based costing and can provide the information necessary to drive service improvements and reduce costs. Components of COQ usually include prevention, detection, and correction. Some will divide correction into internal (before-the-sale) and external (after-the-sale) components.

**Country portfolio analysis (CPA):** An analysis of country market attractiveness using statistics such as income, population, and product consumption. It is recommended that this analysis be adjusted for cultural, administrative, geographic, and economic distance. (Distance Still Matters, *Harvard Business Review*, Sept. 2001, pp. 129–147.)

$C_p$, $C_{pk}$: Process capability and the index of capability, respectively. Typically, a process is considered "capable" when capability and/or the capability index are 1.33 or greater.

$C_p$ = (upper – lower specification limit)/$6s$, where $s$ = standard deviation of process output

$C_{pk}$ = (mean – nearer specification)/$3s$

**CPFR®:** Collaborative Planning Forecasting and Replenishment. A set of business processes used for supply chain collaboration. The term is a trademark of the sponsoring organization, the Voluntary Interindustry Commerce Standards (VICS) Association.

**CPIO:** Chief process improvement officer. A senior management role to lead the reengineering of processes. Facilitates process improvement across internal and external boundaries. (AMR Research.)

**Critical path:** The series of activities that determines the duration of a project. It is the longest path through the project. The critical path method (CPM) is a technique to predict the project's duration by analyzing the path of activities with the least amount of scheduling flexibility. (Adapted from *PMBOK Guide*, 2000 ed.)

**Critical to quality (CTQ):** A feature in a product that's important to customers. Such a feature can be translated to processes for delivering the feature. The term is used in connection with Six-Sigma efforts to improve processes.

**CRM:** Customer Relationship Management. "CRM aligns business processes with customer strategies to build customer loyalty and increase profits over time." (Quoted from Rigby, Darrell K., Reichheld, Frederick F., and Schefter, Phil, Avoid the Four Perils of CRM, *Harvard Business Review*, Feb. 2002, pp. 101–109.)

Computer applications that deal with the "front office" interface between the company and its customers.

**Cross docking:** At a warehouse or distribution center, providing quick turnaround of incoming stock by backing supplies truck up to loading dock where merchandise is immediately transferred to retailer's distribution truck. This avoids storing inventory for any time in the warehouse.

**CSCMP:** Council of Supply Chain Management Professionals. Formerly the Council of Logistics Management.

**CTP:** Capable to promise. The ability to commit to orders with available capacity and inventory. (Adapted from *APICS Dictionary*, 10th ed.)

**Customer:** A person or organization that decides to purchase a product or service or that receives a product or service if no purchase is involved, such as an internal customer for information. An end user is the person or organization that uses or consumes the product or service. The end user is not necessarily the customer or buyer.

**Customer service ratio:** In a make-to-stock company, the percentage of items or dollars shipped on schedule. In a make-to-order company, the percentage of items or dollars shipped on time. Synonymous terms include fill rate and customer service level.

**Customer-centric organization:** An organizational structure built around customer segments. Desirable when segments have different requirements, style-driven products with short product lives requiring fast responses, and higher-margin products. (*Handbook of Supply Chain Management.*)

**Customer-centric supply chain:** Supply chains or organizations whose construct centers on the requirements of targeted customer segments. Alternatives are functional and product-centric supply chains.

**Customs-Trade Partnership against Terrorism (C-TPAT):** A voluntary government-business initiative to build cooperative relationships that strengthen international and U.S. border security. The effort involves owners of the international supply chain such as importers, carriers, consolidators, licensed customs brokers, and manufacturers. (Adapted from http://www.cbp.gov /xp/cgov/import/commercial_enforcement/ctpat/)

**Cycle time:** A property of processes along the supply chain. The minimum theoretical cycle time for a product's supply chain is the sum of individual process cycle times.

Cycle-time reduction is achieved through process reengineering, including new technology along the chain. Examples include automated sharing of information about final demand, introducing postponement through product design, and automation in production processes.

Lead time is a market-oriented property that is driven by competitive forces. A competitor that works to reduce cycle time can also end up with the shortest lead time. Throughput time is a synonym.

**Data warehouse:** A repository for data organized in a format that is suitable for ad hoc query processing. Data warehouses are built from operational databases used for day-to-day business processes. The operational data are "cleaned" and transformed in such a way that is they are amenable to fast retrieval and efficient analysis. A single-purpose data warehouse is sometimes referred to as a data mart.

**Dealer:** A representative of a manufacturer or distributor who directly services end users/customers.

**Decomposition (forecasting):** A method of forecasting where data are divided into trend, seasonal, and cyclical components. Another component may be random—where no pattern exists. Forecasts are made using each component. (Adapted from *APICS Dictionary*, 10th ed.)

**Decomposition (WBS, IDEF):** Breaking a category down into lower levels for sharper definition of requirements. The term can apply to project scope, activities, tasks, and projects. IDEF decomposes functions in a supply chain in a similar way. (Adapted from *PMBOK Guide*, 2000 ed.)

**Deficiency, discrepancy:** Failure of a quality system to comply with requirements.

**DELIVER processes:** SCOR processes to provide finished goods and services to customers.

**Deliverable:** Any measurable, tangible, verifiable outcome, result, or item produced to complete a project or part of a project. Often refers to a work product delivered to and approved by a sponsor or customer. (Adapted from *PMBOK Guide*, 2000 ed.)

**Demand:** End-user requirements for a product or service. This is what would be consumed if sufficient product were available at prices that yield a profit. End users aren't necessarily purchasers who pay for a product. A "customer" may buy a product or service on behalf of the end user.

**Demand chain:** A term sometimes applied to the "outgoing" side of the business. Supply chain, in this context, only applies to the "incoming" side. To the end user, all activities to produce the product or service are part of the supply chain.

**Demand flow®:** A technique to speed product final assembly. Demand flow uses the concept of a "pile of parts" that can be assembled in response to actual customer orders. The term is trademarked by the John Costanza Institute of Technology.

**Demand-driven supply chain:** A term developed by CGR that applies to supply chains using tools that enable decisions to be made on the basis of actual customer demand rather than forecasts. The extent to which a supply chain is "demand-driven" is measurable. Most supply chains will require some level of forecasting for advanced planning. However, it is desirable to reduce dependence on these forecasts.

**Demand (independent, dependent, and derived):** Independent demand is driven by end-user or customer needs. It comes from outside the sphere or enterprise. Dependent demand is derived from independent demand by a direct link between the end product through the bill of materials and triggers replenishment within the sphere or enterprise. Derived demand also depends on final demand but is not directly linked through the bill of materials, such as steel being derived from the sale of automobiles. *(APICS Dictionary,* Mentzer & Moon, SCMR May/June 2004.)

**Dependent demand:** See *Demand (independent, dependent, and derived).*

**Derived demand:** See *Demand (independent, dependent, and derived).*

**Design team:** A team, usually of operations managers involved in included supply chain processes, which designs new supply chains. Design teams may be called upon to develop spheres, activity systems, requirements for IT systems, and process improvements.

**Discount:** A price reduction to promote or clear inventory of an item.

**Discounted cash flow:** A method of financial analysis that recognizes the time value of money as measured by the cost of capital. DCF is used to convert capital costs into "equivalent uniform cash flows." This makes it possible to combine expense and capital items when weighing capital investments.

**Disintermediation:** The elimination of echelons or stages in the supply chain. This can reduce cycle time and operating expense. The term is often used with respect to distribution and the number of warehouses a product passes through between the manufacturer and the end user/customer.

**Distribution requirements planning (DRP):** Replenishment procedures at distribution control points. Can use MRP logic or other rules.

**DMAIC:** Define, measure, analyze, improve, and control. A process for implementing supply chain changes associated with the Six-Sigma improvement process. (A Foundation for Operational Excellence, *Supply Chain Management Review,* March/April 2003.)

**Downstream:** The end of the supply chain nearest to end users. Upstream refers to the beginnings of the supply chain, probably suppliers of components or raw materials. Some reverse this convention.

**Driving force:** A strategic planning concept developed by Michel Robert. The concept holds that there is one and only one driving force around which a company competes. Company management may acknowledge this; however, often it is not.

**Drumbeat:** The pace at which an organization produces product. Used to pace all the operations in a factory or in a supply chain. Similar to takt time.

**Drum–buffer–rope:** In the theory of constraints, a generalized process to manage resources to maximize throughput. The "drum" sets the pace of production to match the system's constraint. "Buffers" protect the system from disruption and uncertainty. They are often placed to assure that the constraint always has work. The "rope" communicates between the constraint and the gating operation that controls release of work into the system.

The model can be applied at the factory and supply chain levels. (Adapted from *APICS Dictionary*, 10th ed.)

**DSD (Direct Shipment to Stores):** A form of disintermediation in which a manufacturer or distributor ships directly to a customer's stores often bypassing that customer's distribution centers.

**EAN*UCC:** European Article Numbering/Uniform Code Council. Standard codes for supply chain commerce administered by EAN International, now GS1, and the Uniform Code Council, Inc., now GS1 U.S. The latter is U.S.-based and, since 2002, is a member of GS1. Joining facilitated the generation of global standards.

**Early manufacturing and supplier involvement (EMI/ESI):** Inclusion of the manufacturing department and suppliers in product design. The result is a more producible and durable design.

**EAS tags:** Electronic article surveillance tags. A tag that is part of a price tag that protects merchandise against shoplifting. The tag is deactivated when the purchase is made. The manufacturer often installs it. (Adapted from *Retailing Management*, 5th ed.)

**Echelon:** A term that refers to layers of distribution or to stages in the process. Each echelon can include the storage, transportation, and handling of the product between the source (presumably a factory) and its point of use. A trend is toward reducing echelons to speed the supply chain and reduce its cost. Also, competitors at any echelon may seek to add services, reducing the roles of other echelons.

**E-Commerce:** Electronic commerce has come to mean many different things to many different people. Originally, the term meant selling things online. The term has evolved to mean conducting business online, which can include customer service functions, sales, marketing, public relations, advertising, and more.

**Economic order quantity (EOQ):** A fixed order quantity model that determines the amount of an item to be purchased or manufactured at one time. The model minimizes the combined costs of acquiring and carrying inventory. When production rates are closer to consumption rates as in a synchronized supply chain, the production quantity approaches infinity or continuous operation.

**Economic value added (EVA®):** The dollar amount of value added by an enterprise over a specified period of time. EVA takes into account the capital employed in the business. EVA is a trademarked term by Stern Stewart.

**ECR:** Efficient consumer response. Refers to technologies to match supply and demand in the retail sector.

**EDLP:** Every-day low prices. A pricing strategy that calls for continuing lower prices with few sales. A high–low pricing strategy uses premium prices and sales.

**Electronic data interchange (EDI):** The computer-to-computer transmission of business information between trading partners. The information should be organized in standard file formats or transaction sets following guidelines administered by the Uniform Code Council (UCC). Standards have been developed for all regular business-to-business communication, including purchase orders, invoices, shipping notices, and funds transfer. By eliminating the clerical, mailing, and other costs associated with paper-based information, EDI reduces costs, time delays, and errors. (*ECR Best Practices Report.*)

**Electronic draft capture (EDC):** Integration with leading credit card services to reduce fraud and error. (Microsoft.)

**Enable process:** A SCOR process that prepares, maintains, or manages information, relationships, or other factors to support planning and execution processes. EP processes enable PLAN processes, ES enable SOURCE processes, and so on. EP.1 establishes and manages PLAN rules, ES.1 plans SOURCE rules, and so on.

**Enable sphere:** Spheres that involve activities used by product-producing spheres. These are often supporting activities. Customer requirements are set by the needs of the product-producing spheres. Examples can include support systems, organization, logistics services, and sourcing.

**End user:** The person or organization that uses or consumes a product or service. The end user is at the end of the supply chain. The user is not necessarily the customer or buyer of the product or service.

**Engineer-to-order:** Products that need unique engineering design, customization, or new materials. Each order results in a unique bill of material, some unique part numbers, and custom routings. (Adapted from *APICS Dictionary*, 10th ed.)

**Enterprise resource planning (ERP):** ERP systems are composed of software programs that tie together all of an enterprise's various functions—such as finance, manufacturing, sales, distribution, procurement, and human resources. This software also provides for the analysis of the data from these areas to plan production, forecast sales, and analyze quality.

**EPC:** Electronic Product Code. Industrywide standards for RFID communication of product information through standards organization, EPCglobal, Inc. (EPCglobal is a joint venture between GS1 and GS1 U.S.). It is a unique number that identifies a specific item in the supply chain. The EPC is stored on RFID tag, which combines a silicon chip and an antenna. EPC data can include changing data such as origin and production date, much like a GTIN (Global Trade Identification Number). The EPC identifies the manufacturer, product, version, and serial number. A large amount of related data can be stored in a linked database. The items referred to can be individual items, cases, or pallets. (Adapted from the GCI Glossary.)

**EPCglobal Network:** Organization that grew out of the Auto-ID Center, an academic research project headquartered at the Massachusetts Institute of Technology (MIT). The focus is on RFID using Electronic Product Codes (EPC). UCC and EAN (Standard setters GS1 U.S. & GS1) are participants. (Adapted from epcglobalinc.org.)

**Event:** An occurrence in the supply chain that triggers the need for action. Supply chain event management (SCEM) refers to software solutions that monitor operating data to determine if such an event has occurred.

**Execution process:** A SCOR process that changes the state of material goods. It includes scheduling/sequencing, transforming products through manufacturing processes, and moving products.

**Executive information system:** Software providing operating information for direct access by executive users.

**Extended product:** Those features of a product that aren't part of the base, or physical, product. Many supply chain attributes are extended product features such as availability of product, method of delivery, customer service, ability to return the product, and so forth. (Adapted from *Handbook of Supply Chain Management.*)

**Facilitating processes (project management context):** Processes that may or may not be needed, depending on the needs of the project. These are likely to be performed intermittently or as needed. Examples include staff acquisition, risk response planning, team development, and solicitation of suppliers.

**Fashion product:** A product has high margins and uncertain demand. The supply chain for such products should be designed for responsiveness to demand, rather than efficiency. The term, innovative product, includes fashions, new technology, and other fast-growing products.

**Five focusing steps:** A theory of constraints process to continuously evaluate the production system and market mix to make the most of the system constraints. There are five steps:

1. Identify constraints in the system.
2. Decide how to exploit the constraint.
3. Subordinate nonconstraints to the constraints.
4. Elevate the constraints in the system.
5. Return to step 1 if the constraint is broken.

(Adapted from *APICS Dictionary*, 10th ed.)

**Flexibility:** The ability to change or react with little penalty in time, effort, cost, or performance. Categories of flexibility include product mix variation, volume variations, labor flexibility, design-change flexibility, and routing flexibility. (David Upton, *California Management Review*.)

**Focused factory:** A concept originated by Wickham Skinner arguing that factories or parts of factories perform best if they are designed to fulfill customer requirements as efficiently as possible. The focused factory uses manufacturing capability to support strategies for competing.

**Forecast error:** The difference between actual and forecast demand, stated as an absolute value or a percentage. Forecast errors are used to adjust production and inventory plans in supply chains with high dependence on forecasts for decision-making. (*APICS Dictionary*, 10th ed.)

**Forecastable demand:** Applies to certain patterns of demand that contain enough history to provide a forecast of future demand. The opposite is lumpy demand, for which forecasting isn't possible.

**Form factor:** A term used to describe product features that have different meanings depending on the product. Commonly includes linear dimensions and configuration of a product. (Adapted from *Wikipedia*.)

**Format:** The design of a store or other retail outlet. Includes layout, décor, location, advertising and promotion, product selection, and services provided.

**Fourth-party logistics service provider:** A fully integrated supply chain partner who plays a substantial role in its customers' supply chain operations. Some, such as UPS Logistics, evolve from their parent company. Some are joint ventures such as Vector, a joint venture between General Motors and CNF. Others focus on specific industries, such as Li & Fung for apparel. (*Collaborative Global Logistics* by William W. Goldsborough.)

**Freight forwarder:** This is a manager or handler for the shipment of goods. The responsibilities of a freight forwarder include arranging shipment details and completing documentation. Because of their brokering role, freight forwarders have a good understanding of market trends and insurance and transport alternatives.

**Frontline team:** A group of people working in a process who test new designs and provide recommendations for process design and changes.

**Functional organization:** An organizational structure built around functional tasks such as marketing, accounting, manufacturing, and customer service. Works best where product lines are narrow or mature businesses. Not a good alternative where speed is required or products and customers have diverse requirements. (*Handbook of Supply Chain Management.*)

**Functional product:** A category of product with lower margins and low uncertainty regarding demand. The supply chains for these products should be designed for the lowest possible cost. This type of product is also called a staple or a frequently purchased consumer good (FPCG). See *Innovative product.*

**Fuzzy front end:** Refers to the beginning of the development cycle when new product and service concepts are not clear. Many organizations are defining processes and systems to manage the "fuzziness" of the front end of new product development cycle.

**GCI:** Global Commerce Initiative. An effort by retailers and manufacturers to implement best practices and standards in supply chains. Effort includes a global data dictionary. (Adapted from GCI Web site.)

**Gemba:** Japanese term meaning "the place where truth can be found." Refers to going to the manufacturing flow or the customer's place of business to observe what takes place and what needs improving. (Adapted from *Wikipedia.*)

**Glass pipeline:** A term describing a supply chain in which the visibility over the status of the product is high. One is able to track physical movement through the pipeline easily.

**Global Positioning System (GPS):** A satellite technology for tracking position. Supply chain tracking systems use GPS for locating materials along the supply chain.

**Globalization:** Doing business across country boundaries. In the supply chain context, this can include upstream sourcing and downstream channels to customers or both.

**GMROI:** Gross Margin Return on Investment. A financial performance measure that incorporates sales, profit margin, and assets employed. It is calculated by multiplying the traditional gross margin by the ratio of Net Sales to Average Inventory. (Gross Margin/Net Sales) × (Net Sales/Average Inventory). The latter is also called the sales-to-stock ratio. (Adapted from *Retailing Management*, 5th ed.)

**Greenfield vision:** An ideal state based on specifications for future operations. The greenfield should ignore constraints inherent in the current situation. It should serve as a "stretch" target for implementing improvements in the supply chain. The use of the greenfield approach is based on the premise that, without ambitious targets, only incremental change will occur.

**Group technology:** A technique used to develop manufacturing cells that are similar but not identical. The practice gains economies that are spread over a large volume of similar parts, each of which has relative low volume. The routing in the work cells need not be the same for each part. The technique can be broadly applied in designing supply chain logistics processes. (Lean Direction, Society of Manufacturing Engineers, February 9, 2004.)

**GSMP:** The Global Standards Management Process. Development and maintenance of the EAN•UCC System. (Adapted from GCI Glossary.)

**GTAG:** Global TAG. An RFID standard developed by EAN*UCC. The standard addresses data content specifications and performance guidelines.

**GTIN:** Global Trade Identification Number. UCC/GS1 global data structures that employ 14 digits. Currently, GTIN is used exclusively within bar codes, but could be used in other data carriers such RFID. For North America, the UPC is the existing form of GTIN. Current standards covered include EAN/UCC-8, UCC-12, EAN/UCC-13, and EAN/UCC-14. Products at every level of product configuration (consumer selling unit, case level, inner pack level, pallet, shipper, etc.) require a unique GTIN. (Adapted from http://www.gtin.info/)

**Hedge stock:** A form of safety stock implemented for a specific period. Reasons can include interruptions due to strikes, price increases, or a currency reevaluation. (Adapted from *APICS Dictionary*, 10th ed.)

**Heijunka:** Heijunka, or production smoothing, is a technique used to adapt production to fluctuating customer demand. The Japanese word Heijunka (pronounced hey June kah), means literally "make flat and level." Customer demand must be met with the customers preferred delivery times, but customer demand is "bumpy," whereas factories prefer "level" or stable production. So, a manufacturer needs to try and smooth out these bumps in production.

The main tool for smoothing is frequent changing of the model mix on a given line. TPS advocates small batches of many models over short periods of time, requiring fast changeovers. (Adapted from Frederick Stimson Harriman at FredHarriman.com)

**High–low:** A pricing strategy that relies on both premium prices and sales over a product's life cycle. The opposite is EDLP, or every day low prices. (Adapted from *Retailing Management*, 5th ed.)

**Hosted software vendors (HSV):** A model of offering software packages over the Internet. The term has supplanted "ASP." Applications can be in categories such as accounting and CRM or vertical solutions for specific industries. (Adapted from *Infoworld*, Jan. 20, 2003, p. 35.)

**HPC:** High productivity computing.

**IDEF:** Integrated computer-aided manufacturing (ICAM) definition methods are used to perform modeling activities in support of enterprise integration. The original IDEF methods were developed for the purpose of enhancing communication among people who needed to decide how their existing systems were to be integrated. The technique of decomposing a process into activities is useful for supply chain process analysis. The product is a "node tree" of supply chain process functions. $IDEF_0$ modeling is supported by Visio software.

**Implosion:** The process of determining where a component is used. Implosions can be single level; showing only the parents of the next higher level; or multilevel, showing the ultimate top-level parents. (Adapted from *APICS Dictionary*, 10th ed.)

**Independent demand:** See *Demand* (*independent, dependent, and derived*).

**Inert stock:** A term used by CGR to define slow-moving categories of inventory. Components can include defective items, obsolete items, "stranded" odd-quantity components with no demand, and lumpy demand items. The inert category can be a large portion of total inventory. Reducing it may require a concerted effort on several fronts.

**Initiative:** A broad program to improve supply chain operations. Initiatives can last several years and evolve with changing requirements. An initiative can have multiple projects. A synonym is program.

**Innovative product:** An innovative product has high margins and uncertain demand. The supply chain for such products should be designed for responsiveness to demand, rather than efficiency. Also called a fashion product in retail. See *Functional product*.

**Integrated supply:** An alliance or long-term commitment between two or more organizations for the purpose of achieving specific business objectives by maximizing the effectiveness of each participant's resources. The relationship is based upon trust, dedication to common goals, and an understanding of each other's individual expectations and values.

**Integration:** The extent to which components of the production process are inextricably linked. A software design concept that allows users to move easily between applications.

Supply Chain Integration. Coordinated data sharing between companies to improve customer service and reduce cost. (Adapted from *Supply Chain Management in the Retail Industry*.)

**Interleaving:** Task interleaving is a warehouse productivity improvement technique in which software directs workers to perform unrelated tasks such as put-away and picking where feasible. This reduces travel time in the warehouse. (*Supply Chain Digest*, Logistics Ed.)

**International Standards Organization (ISO):** An international organization charged with setting broad-ranging standards that can lead to certification including those of process discipline, RFID, and communications.

**Internationalization:** The process of designing a software or Internet application to handle different linguistic and cultural conventions without additional engineering. Central to internationalization is the separation of language and cultural data from the source code. (globalization.com)

**Inventory turnover:** Ratio of sales (at cost) to average stock. Can be calculated by multiplying sales-to-stock ratio by (1-gross margin). Usually intended for performance measurement over an annual period.

Adjustments are required for shorter selling periods. If the average inventory required to support a 6-month sales effort that produces $200,000 in monthly sales ($1,200,000 total sales) is $100,000 at cost, the sales-to-stock ratio is 2. The inventory turns calculated conventionally are $1,200,000/($100,000/2) = 24 turns. (Adapted from *Retailing Management*, 5th ed.)

**Inventory turns:** The number of times each year that the inventory turns over. It can be in units, but is more often in dollars. It is computed by dividing the average inventory level into the annual cost of goods sold.

**Issue, issues list:** Issues are questions that define the scope of the supply chain strategy. A running list keeps track of these issues and the response implicit in the strategy. Issues are often tracked in categories such as financial, organization and measures, product development, processes, and so forth.

**Item level tagging (ILT):** RFID passive tag attachment to individual items. Used to combat counterfeiting, track expiration dates, support inventory control, provide rapid checkout, and track product quality, among others.

**Jikoda:** A principle of the Toyota Production System that allows workers to stop the production line in the event of defects.

**Joint replenishment:** Coordination of lot sizing and order release for related items. The purpose is to take advantage for setup, shipping, and quantity discounts. It applies to material ordering, group technology production, and distribution. The commonality component of the 3C approach is a form of joint replenishment. (Adapted from *APICS Dictionary*, 10th ed.)

**Just in time (JIT):** A philosophy of manufacturing based on planning elimination of all waste and continuous improvement of productivity. It encompasses the successful execution of all manufacturing activities required to produce a final product, from design engineering to delivery and including all stages of conversion from raw material onward. The primary elements of just in time are to have only the required inventory when needed; to improve quality to zero defects; to reduce lead times by reducing setup times, queue lengths, and lot sizes; to incrementally revise the operations themselves; and to accomplish these things at minimum cost. In the broad sense, it applies to all forms of manufacturing, job shop, and process, as well as repetitive. (Adapted from *APICS Dictionary*, 10th ed.)

**Kaikaku:** Innovation. As applied in Lean approaches to operations, the implementation of novel, original, and likely more radical change. Contrasts with kaizen or continuous improvement.

**Kaizen:** A Japanese word that means loosely translated, constant improvement.

**Kaizen blitz:** Conceived of as five days and one night applying Toyota Production System principles that include process observation, cycle time calculation, calculation of takt time, calculation of value-added fraction, elimination of work, and preparation of standard worksheets. (*Lean Directions*, Society of Manufacturing Engineers.)

**Kanban:** A method of just-in-time production that uses standard containers or lots sizes with a single card attached to each. It is a pull system in which work centers signal with a card that they wish to withdraw parts from feeding operations or suppliers. The Japanese word Kanban, loosely translated, means card, billboard, or sign. The term is often used synonymously for the specific scheduling system developed and used by the Toyota Corporation in Japan. (Adapted from *APICS Dictionary*, 10th ed.)

**Kano model:** The model describes three different types of quality. The first is basic quality, items that one assumes are part of a product. The second is performance quality. The customer will be able to articulate this type of quality and can be captured by surveys. The third is excitement quality that is unexpected and cannot be articulated by the customer. The supply chain has the potential for assuring all three types of quality. (*The QFD Handbook.*)

**Key characteristic:** A feature whose variation has the greatest impact on the fit, performance, or service life of the finished product from the perspective of the customer. Key characteristics are a tool to help decide where to focus limited resources. They are used for process improvement purposes. Key characteristics may or may not be "critical characteristics" that affect product safety.

**Key process parameter:** A process input that is controllable and that has a high statistical correlation with the variation in a part key characteristic. Key process parameters are most effectively determined by the use of designed experiments.

**Knowledge management:** Refers to efforts to capture the "knowledge" resident in an organization. Such efforts are often centered on information technology. Some have dismissed knowledge management as a fad, but the concept has value in supply chain management across multiple enterprises.

**KPI:** Key performance indicator. Measures of supply chain performance.

**Lead time:** Lead time is associated with a product or service delivered by the supply chain. It is "imposed" on the supply chain by the competitive environment. It is driven by customer expectations, supply chain innovations, and competitive pressure.

All these factors are in constant motion, moving toward "faster, cheaper, better." Competitors that can't deliver products and services within the established lead time will likely perish. Competitors that have the shortest lead time have an advantage.

**Lean enterprise:** A term coined by James Womack and Daniel Jones to extend the idea of "Lean manufacturing" along the supply chain, including production partners. The Lean enterprise is operationally synchronized with end-user demand. Womack and Jones were the originators of the "Lean" terminology. (Adapted from *APICS Dictionary*, 10th ed.)

**Lean manufacturing:** Production approach based on using multiskilled workers, highly flexible machines, and very adaptable organizations and procedures to manufacture an increasing variety of products while continually decreasing costs. "Lean" means more productive use of labor, material, and inventory along the supply chain.

**Legacy systems:** A network or hierarchical database system, usually running on a mainframe. Replacement of legacy systems is often a motivator for installing new supply chain information systems. Implementing supply chain improvements may be limited by the capabilities of legacy systems.

**Level (of a product):** Components of product structure. Each level is coded with the end item as the 0 level. Level 1 has level 0 components; level 2 has level 1 components, and so forth. Also, see *Decomposition*. (Adapted from *APICS Dictionary*, 10th ed.)

**Level 1 processes:** SCOR has five core management processes: PLAN, SOURCE, MAKE, DELIVER, and RETURN. There are separate definitions in this table for each. When used in SCOR, these core processes are spelled with capital letters.

**Level of effort (LOE):** A support-type activity that is hard to measure. It is usually characterized as a uniform rate of activity. (Adapted from *PMBOK Guide*, 2000 ed.)

**Level plant loading:** Efforts to reduce variability in production at the business unit and supply chain levels. Level plant loading is considered a best practice for achieving effective supply chains. Drumbeat and takt time are related terms.

**Levels (SCOR):** SCOR processes decompose to three levels. Level 1 is composed of the five core management processes. Level 2 is the configuration level and depends on supply chain design. Level 2 process examples are a letter and a number, such as PP for plan supply chain and M1 for make-to-stock. Configuration types include ake-to-stock, ake-to-order, and engineer-to-order. Level 3 activities are process elements supporting level 2. Level 4 processes are company-specific and fall outside SCOR.

**Localization:** The process of adapting a product to the requirements of a target locale. This involves the translation of the user interface (UI)—including text messages, icons, buttons, etc., of the online help, and of any documentation and packaging, and the addition of cultural data and language-dependent components, such as spell checkers, input methods, and so forth. (globalization.com)

**Logistics management:** That part of supply chain management that plans, implements, and controls the efficient, effective forward and reverses flow and storage of goods, services, and related information between the point of origin and the point of consumption to meet customers' requirements. (Council of Logistics Management.)

**Lot Matrix:** Inventory category.

**Lot operation cycle time:** Length of time from the start of setup to the end of cleanup for a production lot at a given operation. (*APICS Dictionary*, 10th ed.)

**Lumpy demand:** An infrequently occurring demand that can't be forecast. The usual result is a need to carry an insurance level of stock. Also called "discontinuous demand."

**Maintained markup:** The markup a retailer actually makes over the life of the product. It is expected to cover direct costs of selling the product, shrinkage, and discounts offered as the product ages and to provide a profit. This may differ from the initial markup, which is set when the product is originally put on the floor.

**Maintenance, repair, and overhaul (MRO):** A class of activity occurring after the sale of the product. MRO often demands special supply chain design and can be an important factor in the success of a product that has a long life cycle.

**MAKE processes:** SCOR processes that transform material into finished products.

**Make-to-order:** A production environment where the product is made after receipt of the order. The product is often a combination of standard and custom items. Make-to-order is similar to assemble-to-order. (Adapted from *APICS Dictionary*, 10th ed.)

**Make-to-stock:** An environment where products are finished before receipt of a customer order. The customer orders are filled from stock. Production orders replenish the stock. (Adapted from *APICS Dictionary*, 10th ed.)

**Manufacturing Execution System (MES):** An MES is a manufacturing software application, not a "MIS" system. MES focuses on execution and management of production processes. It provides synchronization of the following as they are used to make the product: labor, machinery and equipment, tooling, and other resources, e.g., power, raw material, and work-in-process inventory. MES usually operates in time increments from subshift to real time.

MES applications may serve as interfaces between MRP scheduling applications and machine controllers. They also collect quality and production data.

**Manufacturing strategy:** The concept that manufacturing can support other strategies for competing, such as product, marketing, and financial strategies. A related term is a "supply chain strategy" where supply chain design contributes to competitiveness.

**Market mediation cost:** The often hidden cost to a business due to mismatches in supply and demand. Too much supply causes disC.

**Markup or Margin (for retailers):** Retail selling price for an item minus retail cost. Margin is used to pay all expenses. Any remainder is profit.

Retail Selling Price – Cost = Markup or Margin

Retail Selling Price – Margin = Retailer's Cost of Goods

**Mass customization:** Creation of individual variations of a high-volume product with many options for configuration.

**Matrix bill of material (BOM):** A method for identifying common components. Components are arranged on one dimension; end products on the other. This is a useful tool for establishing commonality in applying the 3C methodology.

**Maturity model:** A framework for measuring progress toward some goal. The model consists of descriptive "levels" to help users assess their progress toward higher levels of maturity. Harold Kerzner's project management maturity model (PMMM) has five levels: common language, common processes, singular methodology, benchmarking, and continuous improvement.

**Mean absolute deviation (MAD):** The average of absolute values of the deviations between observed and expected values. MAD can be calculated to evaluate forecasting processes as the difference between actual sales and forecasts.

**Merchandise management:** The process of providing the right product in the right quantity in the right place at the right time. (This definition is similar to Supply Chain Management.) (Adapted from *Retailing Management*, 5th ed.)

**Merge-in-transit:** A technique for combining order components from various sources while those components are in transit from sources to customers.

**Milestone:** A significant event in the project usually associated with completion of a deliverable. (Adapted from *PMBOK Guide*, 2000 ed.)

**Milk run:** A transportation link in the supply chain characterized by regularly scheduled shipments to one or more points. By combining shipments, more frequent shipments are economically feasible. The milk run lowers the incremental cost of filling an order, enabling continuous flow in the supply chain.

**Minimum shelf quantity:** Also MSQ. The quantity of stock to maintain at a shelf location.

**Min–max:** A type of order point replenishment where the reorder point is the "min," and the "max" sets the order quantity.

**Mixed-model production:** A production scheme where the production line product mix matches what is sold each day.

**Monopsony:** A market dominated by a few large customers who have power over pricing. The effect is to put pressure on suppliers to these customers for price reductions. Examples cited in this context include tobacco companies, blueberry processors, and Wal-Mart. Antitrust focus is on monopoly situations where control of end-user markets is deemed excessive. Monopsony suits are less frequent. (*The Wall Street Journal*, January 27, 2004, p. A1.)

**MRP, MRP II:** Materials Requirement Planning—a concept developed in the 1970s to make use of high-speed computers to model the requirements of material for a manufacturing operation. It is viewed as a method for planning all resources of a manufacturing company. It addresses operational planning in units and financial planning in dollars, and has simulation capability. Output from MRP is integrated with financial reports, purchase commitments, shipping budgets, and inventory projections. "Closed-loop" MRP implies feedback to keep plans valid with regard to constraints such as capacity. (Adapted from *APICS Dictionary*, 10th ed.)

**Network diagram:** A logical display of project activities. It shows sequence and dependencies among activities. (Adapted from *PMBOK Guide*, 2000 ed.)

**Noninventory items:** Inventory category. Services and warranties.

**NTEP:** National Type Evaluation Program. Standards for weights and measures to protect commerce. Administered in the United States by the National Council on Weights and Measures (NCWM). Program provides a one-stop evaluation process that satisfies the initial requirements for introduction of weighing and measuring devices.

**Offshoring:** The movement of operations from one country to another within the same company. Outsourcing transfers responsibility for a process to another entity that may be in the same country or not. Often, outsourcing involves a transfer of employees as well.

**Omni-channel retailing:** Multichannel approach to retailing that provides the customer with the opportunity to choose any of the channels as sources of product information, sales assistance, purchasing opportunities, pick-up and returns locations, and customer service in a seamless manner.

**Operation:** A step in a process. Can include a changing of physical configuration, a quality control action, temporary or long-term storage, an administrative task, or transportation.

**Operational excellence (OE):** A term used by Michael Porter in discussions of strategy. His contention is the OE is a necessary but not sufficient condition for sustained competitiveness. It reflects the belief that "you can't save your way to prosperity." Porter advocates the development of activity systems to distinguish the company from its competitors.

**Optimization:** The application of operations research tools to a supply chain function. Examples include distribution planning (warehouse location and transportation planning) and planning a scheduling production. Optimization technology applies in complex supply chains and when the potential for improvement justifies its use.

**Order penetration point:** The point in a product's flow where an item is earmarked for a particular customer. Downstream processes are driven by customer orders; upstream processes are driven by forecasts and plans. However, the plans themselves can reflect actual customer orders in a demand-driven supply chain. (Adapted from *APICS Dictionary*, 10th ed.)

**Outsourcing:** The transfer of responsibility for a process to another entity that may be in the same country or not. Often, outsourcing involves a transfer of employees as well. Offshoring moves a process to another country, but retains the process within the company.

**P:D ratio:** According to the *APICS Dictionary*, 10th ed., "P" is the manufacturing lead-time. "D" is the customer required delivery time. If the ratio exceeds 1.0, the customer order will be delayed or production will start as a result of a forecast (make-to-stock). The demand-driven supply chain approach argues that different segments of the supply chain can be driven by either forecasts or actual demand. In general, actual demand is more desirable than forecasts. In this book, we use cycle time to refer to processes for manufacture and distribution, and lead time as a market-driven requirement for delivery.

**Panelization:** A construction practice of fabricating building components in a factory and assembling them at a building site. A case is the 2000 panels (140 truckloads) for the Salt Lake City library fabricated in Mexico. (*The Wall Street Journal*, March 3, 2004, p. B1.)

**Partner:** An entity with which one does business, either upstream or downstream in the supply chain, whose performance is important to your success. The relationship between you and the partner may or may not include partnering.

**Partnering:** A management approach used by two or more organizations, often, but not always, a buyer and a seller, to achieve mutual business objectives by maximizing the effectiveness of each partner's resources. Partnerships can take a number of forms from arms-length sharing of information to acquisition. Examples include collaboration in design, measures to reduce cost, and simplified replenishment procedures.

**Partnership classification:** A classification of partnerships has three dimensions: purpose, direction, and choice. The purpose defines whether the partnership creates new space or not. Direction refers to the supply chain. Horizontal means partners are at the same echelon. Vertical is a partnership along the supply chain—probably between a customer and a supplier. Choice refers to the relative strength of each partner. A "many to one" means your company has many competitors and you are seeking a partnership with a dominant partner. (*Handbook of Supply Chain Management.*)

**PDCA:** Plan–Do–Check–Act. Also called the Shewhart cycle for implementing process improvement.

**Perfect order:** A flexibly defined metric that measures error rates in filling customer orders. Components include the completeness and correctness of the items picked, the delivery of the order on time, delivery without damage, and proper invoicing and collection. (Adapted from http://www.supplychain metric.com)

**Performance-based pricing:** Basing prices on value to the customer, not necessarily what the product costs. The supply chain can influence value to the customer. Applies specifically to "innovative" products as opposed to "functional" ones where prices are cost driven in competitive markets.

**Periodic replenishment:** Aggregating requirements to place deliveries of varying quantities at evenly spaced time intervals, rather than variably spaced deliveries of equal quantities. The term fixed cycle also refers to this method. The milk run is also a tool for implementing this approach. (Adapted from *APICS Dictionary*, 10th ed.)

**Phase:** A project phase is a collection of logically related project activities, usually culminating in a deliverable. (Adapted from *PMBOK Guide*, 2000 ed.)

**PLAN processes:** SCOR processes that balance supply and demand. PP processes cover long-range planning at the supply chain level. PS, PM, PD, and PR cover shorter-term planning for source, make, deliver, and return.

**Planning process:** A SCOR process that aligns expected resources with expected demand.

**Planogram:** Diagram that shows the location of specific SKUs in a retail store. Uses drawings, computer-generated graphics, or photographs. (Adapted from *Retailing Management*, 5th ed.)

**PMMM:** Project Management Maturity Model. A five-level model developed by Dr. Harold Kernzner. The levels are common language, common processes, singular methodology, benchmarking, and continuous improvement.

**Point of sale (POS):** 1. Place where the purchase is made at the checkout stand or scanning terminals in a retail store. The acronym POS frequently is used to describe the sales data generated at the checkout scanners. (From ECR Best Practices Report.) 2. The relief of inventory and computation of sales data at a time and place of sale, generally through the use of bar-coding or magnetic media equipment. (*APICS Dictionary*, 10th ed.)

**Point-to-point integration:** Building a customized computer connection. The software for such integration is usually expensive to build and maintain. When systems change on either side of the connection, expensive changes are needed.

**Portfolio, PPM:** A set of initiatives or projects being pursued to improve supply chains. Portfolio management is deciding the priority of the projects and making resources available for their completion. PPM stands for Project Portfolio Management.

**Postponement:** A product or supply chain design strategy that shifts product differentiation closer to the end user. The approach encompasses identity changes such as assembly or packaging. (Adapted from *APICS Dictionary*, 10th ed.)

**Price-taker:** A buying organization that typically takes the low price every time. Generally requires a functional supply chain in the face of competitive alternatives. Prices often become the basis for selection in online auctions.

**Private-label brand:** An exclusive brand made for and sold by a retail enterprise.

**Privatization:** Transfer of product or service delivery from the public to the private sector.

Privatization is the transfer of assets or service delivery from the government to the private sector. Privatization runs a broad range, sometimes leaving little government involvement, and other times creating partnerships between government and private service providers where government is still the dominant player. (Privatization.org)

**Proactive systems:** An approach to designing information systems to focus on the needs of decision makers. The approach may rely on computer-based tools to disseminate the needed information. Noncomputer-based approaches may also be used.

**Process owner:** The central figure in organizations organized around processes. Owners are charged with end-to-end responsibility and authority for a cross-functional process.

**Process, process group (project management context):** A series of actions bringing about a result. A process either manages the project itself (a project-management process) or creates the output of the project (a product-oriented process). In the former group are initiating, planning, controlling, and closing process groups. Project-management processes call for project-management knowledge and practice expertise. In the latter are executing processes. Executing processes call for application-area knowledge and practice expertise. (From *The American Heritage Dictionary of the English Language*, 3rd ed., Boston: Houghton Mifflin Company, 1992, and *PMBOK Guide*, 2000 ed.)

**Process type:** At level 2, SCOR uses three processes types: planning, execution, and enable. Planning processes are preceded by a P, Enable by an E, and Execution by S (Source), M (Make), and D (Deliver).

**Product description:** In a project, the product description documents the characteristics of the physical product, service, or result sought in pursuing the project. It is established prior to project initiation and should be embellished as the project progresses. The product description should have sufficient detail to support project planning throughout the project. (Adapted from *PMBOK Guide*, 2000 ed.)

**Product group, product line, product family:** A grouping of products or SKUs for planning and forecasting requirements.

**Product life cycle:** A well-known marketing concept that holds that products pass through phases in their market lives. The phases are inception, growth, maturity, and decline. The presence of the product life cycle has implications for supply chain design.

**Product pipeline, product funnel:** Visual models of the way new products are developed. The concept infers a repetitive pattern for producing products. SCM should be a part of the product-development process.

**Product-centric organization:** An organization structure built around different product lines. Preferred in cases of multiple products with different technologies, homogeneous customer bases, and capital-intensive and cost-driven businesses. (*Handbook of Supply Chain Management.*)

**Product-centric supply chain:** Supply chains or organizations whose construct centers on the production of products. Alternatives are functional and customer-centric supply chains.

**Product-producing sphere:** A sphere that produces products for external customers. The other type is an enable sphere that provides a support service. The product-producing sphere is a "business inside the business." It merits its own supply chain design.

**Product tree:** A graphical representation of the product and its SKUs. The tree can also show manufacturing locations and multiple geographic markets for the same or similar SKU.

**Program:** A group of related projects managed in a coordinated way. A synonym is initiative. A program can include project and ongoing operations work. For example, a new product program includes product design (a temporary project) and ongoing manufacturing and sales (an operation). (Adapted from *PMBOK Guide*, 2000 Ed., and the *Handbook of Supply Chain Management.*)

**Progressive elaboration:** A property of projects that arises from the "temporary" and "unique" nature of projects. At the beginning of a project, the resulting product, service, or result is defined broadly. As the project proceeds, the final result is "progressively elaborated." For example, a building project progressively proceeds from concept to design on paper to construction. (Adapted from *PMBOK Guide*, 2000 ed.)

**Project:** An organized change effort usually associated with an initiative or program, with a manager, budget, objectives, and schedule. A project is temporary and produces a unique product, service, or result. Several projects may support an initiative or program. Action plans define the goals for the project. (Adapted from *PMBOK Guide*, 2000 ed., and the *Handbook of Supply Chain Management.*)

**Project life cycle:** A collection of generally sequential project phases needed for control of the project. Life-cycle phases generally include the initial phase, intermediate phase, and final phase. Different industries define these differently. For example, the construction industry might call the initial phase "feasibility," and the final phase "turnover and startup." A software project might start with "business requirements" and finish with "test and deploy." (Adapted from *PMBOK Guide*, 2000 ed.)

**Project manager:** A person responsible for managing a project. The project-management function may rest with an individual for smaller projects, and with a larger project office for larger ones. The project manager function coordinates the logistics involved in the project, including the activities of steering committees, design teams, and employee teams testing new ways of working.

**Project manufacturing:** Manufacturing processes designed for large, often unique, products requiring custom design. These processes require flexible processes and multiple engineering changes. (Adapted from *APICS Dictionary*, 10th ed.)

**Project office:** A permanent line function for project manager with expertise in project-management processes and tools, a repository of lessons learned, and a champion for project-management methodology. A project office can administer a larger supply chain project. (Adapted from *Strategic Planning for Project Management*.)

**Promotion:** A term used by CGR to describe risk pooling to lower inventories. In promotion, products, product families, or SKUs are moved higher in the tree (promoted) to concentrate demand.

**Promotion:** Activities to inform customers about a product or service. Also used in connection with short-term efforts to increase sales of a product or service.

**Provider service models (PSMs):** A tool for defining the staffing requirements to meet defined service objectives. Often used in managing the staff required to support operations focused on delivering services.

**Public warehouse:** A warehouse that is rented or leased. Services are provided under contract or on a fee-for-service basis. (Adapted from *APICS Dictionary*, 10th ed.)

**Pull system:** In production, replenishment only when items are taken for use as a result of a pull signal. For material control, an issue of material is made only in response to a pull signal from using entity. Similarly, in distribution, a pull signal comes from the downstream warehouses close to the end user. (Adapted from *APICS Dictionary*, 10th ed.)

**Push-and-pull systems:** Production control systems are often describes as "push" where decisions are based on forecasts, or "pull" where decisions are based on actual demand. A demand-driven supply chain is an example of a pull system. Most organizations try to move from "push" to "pull" decision-making.

**Push system:** In production, replenishment from a schedule driven by forecast requirements. In material control, it is the issue of material based on forecast requirements. In distribution, replenishment is based on forecasts likely to be generated centrally. (Adapted from *APICS Dictionary*, 10th ed.)

**QR Code:** A two-dimensional data exchange medium such as a bar code with more information. ("Enterprise Integration in Japan," *CASA/SME Blue Book*, 2004.)

**Qualitative risk analysis:** Use of tools to identify the probability and potential outcomes to identify high-, moderate-, and low-risk conditions to set priorities for response planning. (Adapted from *PMBOK Guide*, 2000 ed.)

**Quality function deployment (QFD):** A system engineering process that transforms the desires of the customer/user into the language, required, at all project levels, to implement a product. It also provides the glue necessary, at all project levels, to tie it all together and to manage it. Finally, it is an excellent method for assuring that the customer obtains high value from your product, actually the intended purpose of QFD.

**Quality standard:** A set of rules for those seeking to qualify under the standard. Standards are either general or industry-specific. Standards bring consistent practice to large numbers of participants in the supply chain.

**Quality threshold:** The expected features of a product and its supply chain. Any participant must at least operate at the threshold to maintain market share. Those falling below the threshold lose market share and may have to exit the business.

**Quantitative risk analysis:** Measurement of probability distributions and potential results to calculate a distribution of possible outcomes. (Adapted from *PMBOK Guide*, 2000 ed.)

**Quick response program (QRP):** A program to shorten cycle times in supply chains. Elements include strong relationships among trading partners, elimination of waste, and the use of technology for information exchange. (*APICS Illustrated Dictionary.*)

**Radio-frequency (RF)/automatic data collection:** Technology frequently deployed in distribution centers for rapid processing of operating information.

**RAG:** A system for better shop-floor control through use of Red, Amber, and Green lights. Red calls for "urgent action." Amber for "going out of control," which is on the borderline, and Green is for "no problem." RAG is used with kanban systems, inventory management, customer service, and statistical process control. (*Lean Directions*, Society of Manufacturing Engineers.)

**Rapid replenishment:** Denotes frequent or fast response to signals for inventory restocking. Rapid replenishment enables demand-driven supply chain approaches.

**Real-time location systems (RTLS):** Technologies capable of locating and tracking assets along the supply chain. Such systems must have fixed reference points for ranging or must use triangulation. Applications that track people carrying small electronic tags.

**Reduced Space Symbology (RSS):** Bar-code technology allows greater use of bar codes on smaller products with limited space for bar-code labels.

**Reengineering:** Analysis, redesign, and implementation of process changes. Can involve new technology, new methods of performing process steps, and organizational change to support the process. The idea of reengineering should not be confused with downsizing or staffing cutbacks, although they may occur in conjunction with process change. Also, see *Business process reengineering.*

**Replenishment cycle time:** The total time from the moment a need is identified until the product is available for use. The *APICS Dictionary*, 10th ed., uses "lead time" to define this. Here we refer to cycle time as a physical property and lead time as a market-determined property, or expectation by customers for performance. (Adapted from *APICS Dictionary*, 10th ed.)

**Representative product:** A typical product flowing through a process that is used as the basis for process design. The term is applied in developing manufacturing cells or maps of supply chains with many product variations. (From Bourton Group.)

**Reseller:** A party that sells to end users/customers. Many add value to manufactured products and software.

**Return Merchandise (Material) Authorization (RMA):** Documentation required before a customer can return purchased items to the retailer or OEM manufacturer. This is to allow for on-the-phone troubleshooting and assuring that the cause wasn't customer-induced damage. (Adapted from *Wikipedia*.)

**RETURN processes:** SCOR processes addressing return and receipt of products for repair, overhaul or refurbishment, or for resale. Includes postdelivery customer support.

**Reverse logistics:** The processing of returned merchandise from end users. This process includes matching returned-goods authorizations, and sorting salvageable, repairable, and nonsalvageable inventories. The flows involved reverse typical flows of physical goods, information, and funds in the supply chain. The purpose is to either recapture value or dispose of the merchandise.

**RFID:** Radio-frequency Identification. Emerging technology that uses passive (short-range) or active (battery-powered long-range) tags to identify inventory items. RFID allows for distance reading of product information.

**Risk:** An uncertain event or condition that could have a positive or negative effect on a project's objectives. Risk identification determines what risks might affect the project; a risk management plan will help manage project risks. (Adapted from *PMBOK Guide*, 2000 ed.)

**Risk pooling:** The process of reducing risk among customers by pooling stock, reducing the total inventory required to provide a customer service level. CGR uses the term promotion to describe movement up the product tree resulting in pooling of lower levels of inventory. (Adapted from *APICS Dictionary*, 10th ed.)

**Routing guide:** An instruction from a retailer regarding shipping to its locations. Increasingly, the guides have become complex as retailers seek to reduce their costs and improve their services. VICS is seeking to standardize terminology and content. (Adapted from VICS standard.)

**S&OP or S&IOP:** Sales, (inventory), and operations planning. Processes for matching supply and demand. Usually an intermediate (1–3) planning horizon. Also refers to a category of software to perform these tasks.

**Safety factor, safety stock:** Factor used to calculate the amount of inventory required providing for uncertainty in forecasts. This is a numerical value based on a service standard, such as 95% certainty that orders will be filled. The factor usually ranges between 1 and 3 and is applied to the mean absolute deviation (MAD) or standard deviation ($\sigma$) to compute the safety stock required.

The need for safety stock is reduced from risk pooling, more frequent replenishment, or taking advantage of commonality among SKUs using the 3C methodology.

**Safety stock:** A quantity of stock planned to be in inventory to protect against demand fluctuations. The level of safety stock is a function of the uncertainty of the demand forecast during the replenishment period and uncertainties in the length of time required for replenishment. High uncertainty (such as for an innovative product) and longer lead times increase the need for safety stock. Also referred to as "buffer stock."

**Sales-to-stock ratio:** Ratio used in merchandise budgeting to calculate GMROI, which is the product of Gross Margin times the Sales-to-Stock ratio. Sales in the ratio are at retail, whereas stock is at cost. The sales-to-stock ratio may be calculated from required GMROI, and anticipated contribution margins from merchandise sales. (Adapted from *Retailing Management*, 5th ed.)

**Scan-based trading:** Supplier retention of ownership until the merchandise is sold (scanned). The effect is to shift inventory cost and control to the manufacturer or distributor. Some see benefits and risks for manufacturers. Manufacturers may enjoy more business and will have increased visibility into final demand. Other might see a threat to the manufacturer. (Adapted from *Wikipedia*.)

**Scan-based trading:** The practice of shifting risk from retailers to manufacturers. The manufacturer is paid when merchandise is sold (scanned). Similar to consignment sales.

**Schedule baseline:** The approved schedule developed in project planning. It is the standard by which subsequent progress is measured. Throughout the project, the baseline is updated based on actual progress. (Adapted from *PMBOK Guide*, 2000 ed.)

**Schema:** From the Greek for "form" or "figure." The organization or structure of a database. It is the product of data modeling. In retail supply chains, the term refers to the information objects used in commerce, such as a freight invoice, a receiving advice, or a replenishment request. Plural is schemata.

**SCO:** Supply chain orientation. A term coined by the University of Tennessee Supply Chain Research Group. It is a management philosophy that recognizes the implications of proactively managing both the upstream and downstream flows of products, services, finances, and information. See Chapter 2.

**Scope:** The sum of the products and services to be provided by a project. Product scope includes the features and functions in the products and services produced by the project. Project scope is what has to be done in the project to produce those features and functions. (Adapted from *PMBOK Guide*, 2000 ed.)

**SCOR:** Supply Chain Operations Reference model. An activity model developed by the Supply Chain Council to standardize descriptions of supply chain processes.

**SCPM:** Supply Chain Event Management. Used to describe software that tracks supply chain operations. Includes Supply Chain Event Management (SCEM) and Supply Chain Performance Management (SCPM). (ARC Advisory Group.)

**Segmentation, segment:** Breaking the market down into definable subcategories. For instance, Coca-Cola may segment its audience based on frequency (one can a month or five cans a day), location (Bangkok or Bangladesh), and many other criteria. Supply chains should be designed with the differing needs of multiple segments in mind.

**Sell–Source–Ship (3S):** A supply chain characterization in which the seller doesn't hold inventory. Once an order is placed, the seller channels orders to single or multiple sources. This is the opposite of the Buy–Hold–Sell model in which the seller does hold inventory.

**Seven wastes:** Shigeo Shingo developed these waste categories as part of the just-in-time philosophy: overproduction, waiting, transportation, stocks, motion, defects, and processing.

**Single Minute Exchange of Dies (SMED):** A theory and the techniques for performing setup operations in fewer than 10 minutes, the number of minutes expressed in a single digit. The SMED philosophy is important in moving from "batch-" to "flow-" oriented supply chains.

**Single sourcing:** Selection of one supplier when there are alternatives. (Adapted from *Supply Chain Management in the Retail Industry*.)

**Six Sigma:** Sigma is a letter in the Greek alphabet. The term sigma is used to designate the distribution or spread about the mean (average) of any process or procedure.

For a business or manufacturing process, the sigma value is a metric that indicates how well that process is performing. The higher the sigma value, the better. Sigma measures the capability of the process to perform defect-free work. A defect is anything that results in customer dissatisfaction. The sigma scale of measure is perfectly correlated to such characteristics as defects-per-unit, parts-per million defective, and the probability of a failure/error.

A Six-Sigma capability means no more than 3.4 parts per-million defects. Recently, Six-Sigma programs have become more general in their approach, reflecting overall efforts to make improvement as well as error-free production.

**SKU (Stockkeeping unit):** An inventory item whose status is maintained in inventory-tracking systems. In the distribution system, different SKUs may represent the same item at different locations. Pronounced "skew." For clothing, SKU definition includes size, color, and style (configuration). (Adapted from *APICS Dictionary*, 10th ed.)

**Slotting allowance (fee):** Fee paid by a manufacturer to a retailer for shelf space.

**SOA:** Service-Oriented Architecture. An approach to developing software that capitalizes on the ability to reuse software modules. In the supply chain context, this practice is an example of commonality and postponement.

**SOAP:** Simple Object Access Protocol. An XML-based communications protocol between Web services. The protocol allows programs to communicate via standard Internet HTTP. (WWW Consortium.)

**Sole sourcing:** Purchasing from one supplier when there are no alternatives. (Adapted from *Supply Chain Management in the Retail Industry*.)

**SOURCE processes:** SCOR processes related to incoming material and services.

**Specification:** A description of performance required from the supply chain for a process based on an evaluation of the as-is. The specification only states what is required, not how that goal will be reached.

**Sphere:** A description of entities derived by dividing complex supply chain operations for the purposes of improvement. A sphere consists of market–product–operations combinations, or "businesses within the business." There are two types of spheres: product-producing and enable. The former has external customers. The latter provides support to multiple product-producing spheres and has internal customers.

A related, but not synonymous, term from the Supply Chain Council is "threads." (*Handbook of Supply Chain Management*.)

**Sponsor:** An executive champion for a supply chain improvement effort. The level of the individual will depend on the level of the project—functional (department level), business unit level, or supply chain level.

**Stage 3 supply chain organization:** Stage 3 refers to the multicompany organization needed to implement supply chain-level changes. A common goal, multicompany staffing, a third-party "honest broker," creative win-win contracting, and a senior management steering committee mark stage 3.

**Stage gate approach to product development:** Formal processes used for the development of new products and services in companies of all sizes. It includes (1) clearly defined stages in which specific tasks are undertaken, (2) the development of compelling, comprehensive business cases, rigorous, and demanding, (3) go/no-go decision points at the end of each stage using clearly defined measurable criteria, and (4) the objective review of actual versus planned performance for every new product, after its introduction to the marketplace. (Adapted from *Winning at New Products*.)

**Staple product:** A category of product with lower margins and low uncertainty regarding demand. The supply chains for these products should be designed for the lowest possible cost. This type of product is also called a functional product or a frequently purchased consumer good (FPCG). (See *Innovative product*.)

**Statement of work (SOW):** A narrative description of products or services to be supplied, often part of contract terms. (Adapted from *PMBOK Guide*, 2000 ed.)

**Statistical process control (SPC):** A set of techniques and tools that help characterize patterns of variation. By understanding these patterns, a business can determine sources of variation and minimize them, resulting in a more consistent product or service. Many customers are demanding consistency as a measure of high quality. The proper use of SPC provides a powerful way to assure that the customer gets the desired consistency time after time.

**Steering committee:** An executive level group responsible for SCM projects. The steering committee makes decisions and sets policies. Membership depends on the levels represented: level 1 is functional, or departmental; level 2 is the business unit level; level 3 is the multicompany or supply chain level. The steering committee is responsible for project results. It will also make important organization-related decisions. A project may have two steering committees. The first is inside the company that initiates the project. Later a multicompany steering committee may oversee intercompany relationships including processes and terms of agreements.

**Stock-to-sales ratio:** Ratio of expected sales for a period to the inventory (at retail price) needed to support the sales. Corresponds to the weeks of supply or months of supply. Used in merchandise budget planning to set beginning-of-period inventory that drives replenishment requirement for the prior period. See also *Sales-to-stock ratio*. (Adapted from *Retailing Management*, 5th ed.)

**Strategic sourcing:** The use of the overall acquisition function as a tool for strategic improvement rather than one focused on transactions only. Involves both cost reduction from better purchasing and effective partnerships across the supply chain.

**Strategy:** The ways in which the company will be different from competitors. Strategy is different from a business model that defines the customers, their needs, and the underlying economic logic for the organization. (Why Business Models Matter, *Harvard Business Review*, May 2002.)

**Subproject:** A smaller portion of a larger project. A subproject is likely to be managed just like a stand-alone project. (Adapted from the *PMBOK Guide*, 2000 ed.)

**Supplier clustering:** Deliberate sole sourcing of remote suppliers within a small geographic area to gain economies in shipping. (Adapted from *APICS Dictionary*, 10th ed.)

**Supply chain:** 1. Life-cycle processes comprising physical, information, financial, and knowledge flows whose purpose is to satisfy end-user requirements with products and services from multiple, linked suppliers. 2. The global network used to deliver products and services from raw materials to end customers through an engineered flow of information, physical distribution, and cash. (*APICS Dictionary*, 10th ed.)

**Supply Chain Council (SCC):** A nonprofit association of companies interested in supply chain management (SCM). The Council was incorporated in June 1997 as a not-for-profit trade association. The Council offers members an opportunity to improve the effectiveness of supply chain relationships from the customer's customer to the supplier's supplier. Its primary mission is to develop and maintain its Supply Chain Operations Reference Model, or SCOR.

**Supply chain design:** According to the *APICS Dictionary*, 10th ed., facets of design include selection of partners, location and capacity of warehouse and production facilities, the products, the modes of transportation, and supporting information systems.

**Supply chain event management (SCEM):** Software feature that monitors supply chain transaction data for predefined "exceptions" or events that require intervention. An example could be a late order. In such a case, the SCEM software would alert designated parties to inform them and suggest interventions.

**Supply chain management (SCM):**
1. Design, maintenance, and operation of supply chain processes, including those that make up extended product features, for satisfaction of end-user needs.
2. The design, planning, execution, control, and monitoring of supply chain activities with the objective of creating net value, building a competitive infrastructure, leveraging worldwide logistics, synchronizing supply with demand, and measuring performance globally. (*APICS Dictionary*, 10th ed.)
3. Encompasses the planning and management of all activities involved in sourcing and procurement, conversion, and all logistics management activities. Importantly, it also includes coordination and collaboration with channel partners, which can be suppliers, intermediaries, third-party service providers, and customers. In essence, supply chain management integrates supply and demand management within and across companies. (CSCMP.)

**Supply chain orientation:** The idea of viewing the coordination of a supply chain from an overall system perspective with each of the tactical activities of distribution flows viewed within a broader strategic context. Actual implementation of supply chain orientation is supply chain management. (Council of Logistics Management.)

**Supply chain strategy:** The idea that supply chain design should support overall strategies for competing—that supply chain operations themselves can be used to differentiate a company's products and services and can protect it from competitors.

**Surface acoustical wave (SAW) RFID:** An emerging RFID technology that offers advantages over microchip-based technology.

**SWOT analysis:** Strengths, Weaknesses, Opportunities, Threats. A technique to use in planning to identify issues related to competition.

**Synchronized supply chain:** A general vision of having all links in the supply chain producing at the same rate as customer demand. Obstacles include coordination, batch size limitations in production, and inability to share information. However, synchronization is a useful goal because it is likely to provide high levels of customer service at low cost relative to unsynchronized supply chains. The term is somewhat synonymous with a Lean supply chain.

**Tag:** Notifications or commands written into Web documents. (WWW Consortium.) A small object attached to or incorporated into a product, animal, or person. The tags contain silicon chips and antennas to receive and respond to radio-frequency queries. Passive tags require no internal power source; active tags require a power source. (Adapted from *Wikipedia*.)

**Tag-along items:** Inventory category.

**Takt time:** The interval that sets the pace of production to match the rate of customer demand. It is the "heartbeat" of the Lean production system. The term is derived from the German expression for a metronome beat. (Adapted from *APICS Dictionary*, 10th ed.)

**Target costing:** A strategic profit-planning and cost management system that incorporates a strict focus on customer wants, needs, and values, and translates them into delivered products and services. A variation is using cost as a design criterion in product development.

**Task:** The lowest level of effort on a project. Not included in a work breakdown structure but could be part of the decomposition of work by individuals responsible for the work. (Adapted from *PMBOK Guide*, 2000 ed.)

**TCP/IP:** Transmission control protocol/Internet protocol. The communications protocol used by the Internet.

**Template:** An activity list containing skills, resources, deliverables, dependencies, and risks that is appropriate for reuse from one project to another. (Adapted from *PMBOK Guide*, 2000 ed.)

**TEU:** Twenty-foot equivalent unit. The standard for measuring ocean-shipping containers. The dimensions are 20' × 8' × 8'6" (6.1 m × 2.44 m × 2.59 m). Two TEUs are one FEU (40-foot equivalent unit).

**Theory of constraints (TOC):** A portfolio of management philosophies, management disciplines, and industry-specific "best practices" developed over the past 20 years by physicist Dr. Eliyahu M. Goldratt and his associates.

**Third-party logistics (3PL) provider:** A company specializing in performing logistics-related services for its customers. Examples include warehouse, transportation, and product assembly.

**Thread:** A multientity supply chain that uses different Level 2 SCOR execution processes. For example, a make-to-stock company supplies a make-to-order company. Sphere is a related work with a broader meaning in Section I.

**Throughput:** In the theory of constraints, the rate at which the system generates money through sales. This does not necessarily mean output in terms of physical production, so it excludes inventory building. (Adapted from *APICS Dictionary*, 10th ed.)

**To-be:** The future state, or how a supply chain process will be performed in the future. Determined after examining trade-offs between an ideal goal (greenfield) and constraints standing in the way of implementing that ideal.

**Total cost of ownership (TCO):** All the costs associated with buying, supporting, and operating a product or a component.

**Total productive maintenance (TPM):** A systematic approach to minimizing machine "downtime" resulting from unexpected breakdowns. TPM emphasizes the role of the machine operator, who becomes more involved with routine checks and fine-tuning. TPM enables machinery to operate more efficiently and reliably, decreasing the risk of a "broken link" in the supply chain.

**Total quality management (TQM):** An approach that involves all employees in continually improving products and work processes to achieve customer satisfaction and world-class performance. TQM is generally associated with "bottom-up" incremental improvement.

**Toyota Production System:** A manufacturing process model developed by Toyota that contributed to reputation for quality in the auto industry. The Toyota Production System was built on three key factors that differentiated it from practices being employed by their competitors in the auto industry: (1) reduced lot sizes, leading to production flexibility, (2) controlling parts required in production to enable them to be provided when and where they are needed for specific tasks, and (3) arranging production equipment in the order that people work, and value is added instead of grouping by equipment function. All these elements involved suppliers and customers to some extent.

**Traceability:** An attribute that allows for ongoing location of items in the supply chain.

**Tracking signal:** A signal that forecasting techniques should be reevaluated. (*Handbook of MRP II and JIT.*)

**Transfer pricing:** The pricing of goods and services between entities in the supply chain. These entities can be internal or with outside organizations. Supply chain partnerships require agreements on pricing.

**Triad:** This concept from a research paper by Alan Rugman and Alain Verbeke shows that few so-called multinationals in the North America–European Union–Japan "triad" focus on home or regional markets. The conclusion is that these multinationals are not really global and leave much autonomy to national or regional decision makers.

**Trigger, trigger events:** An indication that a risk has occurred or is about to occur. A trigger may activate a risk response or a replanning of supply chain operations.

**TRIZ:** Russian acronym for theory of incentive problem solving. TRIZ is a methodology for eliminating conflicts that arise in product design. (From *QFD Handbook*.)

**Truckload/less-than-truckload (LTL) carriers:** Carriers that cater to the needs of different classes of shippers. "Truckload-only" carriers generally serve larger shippers. LTL carriers generally serve smaller shippers.

**Two-bin system:** An inventory rule that calls for a new order when one bin (either real or conceptual) runs out. The second bin then becomes the source of new requirements. The reorder quantity is equal to the bin size and depends on lead times and usage quantities. The method is one of the simplest to implement and lends itself to visual approaches.

**Unit time:** In activity-based costing, the labor required expressed in time or money to process one unit of a driver through an activity or process.

**UNSPSC:** United Nations Standard Products and Services Code. An open, standard, voluntary method for codifying products and services. Uses two-digit codes to define segments, families, classes, and commodities. For example, a "photocopier" is in Segment 44, Office Equipment and Accessories and Supplies, Family 10, Office Machines, Class 15 Duplicating Machines, and Commodity 01, Photocopiers. So, the UNSPSC would be 44101501. Codes are utilized to analyze spend categories. (Adapted from "Introduction and Overview UNSPSC" a presentation available from the UNSPSC.)

**UPC:** Universal Product Code found on products in the form of a bar code. Used for identification throughout the supply chain.

**Upstream:** A reference to the "front-end" component and raw material suppliers in the supply chain. Downstream is the end of the supply chain nearest to end users. Some reverse this convention.

**Utility computing:** Acquiring systems capability on a pay-as-you-go basis. This reduces the investment required by the user. "Grid computing" relies increases computing resource utilization by linking together computing resources into a grid capable of executing large computing tasks. (*SupplyDemandChain Executive*, January 18, 2004.)

**Value chain:** The source of strategic advantage within the firm. It stems from the many discrete activities a firm performs, including those associated with the supply chain. Value is created through cost efficiencies or differentiation from competitors. Value will be reflected in the profitability of value chain (or supply chain) members. Those making the highest profits are, by definition, adding the most value. (Adapted from *Competitive Advantage: Creating and Sustaining Superior Performance* by Michael Porter.)

**Value-added network (VAN):** A network for automated information sharing between trading partners. Can be administered by a third party. Uses standards for common transactions.

**Variable costing:** An accounting approach to support management decision making. Variable costs normally consist of direct labor and material plus variable overhead. Fixed overhead, which is allocated, is not included, although it is included in the cost of goods sold, the basis for inventory costing.

Variable costing is more valid in making decisions related to make or buy, economic order quantities, and other decisions. Supply chain design may transform variable into fixed costs. For example, a milk run will be made regardless of a decision to replenish for any single SKU. Therefore, the reorder cost (including transportation) assumption related to the decision should be reduced accordingly.

The approach is consistent with the theory of constraints, which maintains that operating expense is relatively fixed over a range of production.

**VAT analysis:** Analysis of product structure from the theory of constraints. A "V" structure has a few raw materials and many products. An "A" structure has many raw materials and a few end products. A "T" structure has numerous similar finished products assembled from common components.

Describing the product structure is a foundation for supply chain design. (Adapted from *APICS Dictionary*, 10th ed.)

**Velocity:** A term that describes how much time a unit of production spends in actual process steps as a percent of total time in the process. It is also the ratio between cycle time and lead time. Low velocities mean much of the time required for processing is spent in waiting on value-adding steps in the process. A goal of supply chain design is often to increase velocity. The term is increasingly applied to administrative as well as physical processing.

**Vendor-managed inventory (VMI):** The practice of partnering between distribution channel members that changes the traditional replenishment process from distributor-generated purchase orders, based on economic order quantities, to the replenishment of products based on actual and forecasted product demand. (From CRP Best.) (*See also Vendor-managed replenishment* [*VMR*]).

**Vendor-managed replineshment (VMR):** A process by which a supplier automatically replenishes customer stock based on actual sales or shipments. Also called continuous replenishment. (*APICS Dictionary, 10th ed.*) Some practitioners view VMR as an enhancement of VMI, requiring more collaboration. (*See also Vendor-managed inventory* [*VMI*]).

**VICS:** Voluntary Interindustry Commerce Standards Association. Maintains CPFR and other processes for commerce. Promotes a "vision for the future" in which products move through the global supply chain. Promotes voluntary rather than compulsory standards. (Adapted from http://www.vics .org/home)

**Virtual enterprise:** A team of individual companies organized to meet a market opportunity as if they were all part of the same company with a common goal.

**Virtual private network (VPN):** A private network that uses Internet technology. It is only accessible by authorized users. It is seen as a cost-effective alternative to dedicated lines.

**Virtual value chain:** The virtual, information-based equivalent of the value-chain model where value is created by gathering, selecting, synthesizing, and distributing information. (From J.F. Rayport and J.J. Sviokla, *Harvard Business Review*, "Exploiting the Virtual Value Chain," November–December, 1995.)

**Voice of the customer:** A component of quality function deployment (QFD) that provides customers' requirements as the basis for design of a product or process.

**Voice-directed picking:** In warehouses, delivering orders to stock pickers via a wireless network. Such orders are usually produced by warehouse management systems. Usually, data are transmitted from the WMS; the picker's terminal translates the data into voice messages.

**Voucher item:** Inventory category. Gift card/gift certificate.

**W3C:** World Wide Web Consortium. An organization of public and private sector organizations that maintains standards for the World Wide Web (WWW). (WWW Consortium.)

**Wall-to-wall inventory:** A technique in which material enters a plant and is processed into finished goods without entering a formal stock area. Also four-wall inventory. (*APICS Dictionary*, 10th ed.)

**Warehouse management system (WMS):** A system that tracks and controls the movement of inventory through the warehouse, from receiving to shipping. Many WMSs also plan transportation requirements into and out of the warehouse. The WMS allows visibility to the quantity and location of inventory, as well as the age of the inventory, to give a current and accurate picture of the available to promise (ATP).

**Web services:** Supply chain application-to-application communications delivered over the Internet. These reduce the cost and complexity of forming links between supply chain partners and customers for products in the chain. They use shared standards to speed the job of developing links. (Adapted from "The Strategic Value of Web Services" in *The McKinsey Quarterly*, and *"Business Processes and Web Services"* by Alan Kotok.)

**Weight Item:** Inventory category.

**WERC:** The Warehousing Educational and Research Council. An international professional association dedicated to the advancement and education of people involved in the management of warehouses and distribution facilities.

**Wireless fidelity (Wi-Fi):** A technology that follows the IEEE 802.11x standard for wireless communication over the Internet. The technology uses "hot spots" where personal computers, particularly laptops, and other devices can access the Internet.

**Work breakdown structure (WBS):** A deliverable-oriented grouping of project elements that organizes and defines the total work scope of the project. Descending levels add detailed definition to the project work. (Adapted from *PMBOK Guide*, 2000 ed.)

**Work flow:** A class of software application that includes automation of the flow of information according to process rules. Similar to, but not as encompassing as, a proactive systems approach in which the requirements of decision makers are part of the redesign of the supply chain.

**Work in progress (WIP):** Units of production that have started, but not finished, the production process. Material entering the factory usually starts as raw material, then becomes WIP, and then proceeds to finished goods. High WIP levels are characteristic of long cycle times or low velocity in production.

**Work package:** A deliverable at the lowest level of the work breakdown structure, when that deliverable may be assigned to another project manager. A work package can be divided into activities. (Adapted from the *PMBOK Guide*, 2000 ed.)

**World class:** Being the best in your industry on enough competitive factors to achieve profit goals and be considered one of the best in satisfying customers.

**World Trade Organization (WTO):** A global international organization (over 140 countries) dealing with the rules of trade between nations. WTO agreements, negotiated and signed by the bulk of the trading nations, are ratified in their legislative bodies. The goal is to help producers of goods and services, exporters, and importers conduct their business.

**XML:** Extensible markup language. This is a flexible cousin of the HTML, the format for Web pages. HTML just describes how the document will look. XML describes what's in the document and is not concerned about the display but the organization of the information. XML enables transfer of data among databases and Web sites without losing descriptive information. It also speeds searches because the search engines can look at tags rather than lengthy text. A standard syntax is required in order for companies to share information. ("Explaining XML", *Harvard Business Review*, July–August 2000.)

**Yield management:** Using price and other promotions to maximize the return on investment. Usually infers a fixed capacity, such as airline seats, that is filled with customers from segments paying different prices.

# Bibliography

*A Guide to the Project Management Body of Knowledge (PMBOK Guide®)*, Newtown Square: Project Management Institute, 2000.

Abernathy, Fred, "Marketing, Merchandising, and Retailing: The Role of Intermediaries in Global Value Chains," presentation at the University of Washington, June 6, 2004.

Agrawal, Mani, Kumaresh, T.V., and Mercer, Glenn A., "The False Promise of Mass Customization," *The McKinsey Quarterly*, 2001, Number 3.

Andraski, Joe, Joe Andraski discusses collaborative planning, forecasting and replenishment with Larry Smith of West Marine, Interview Transcript at http://www.vics.org/committess/cpfr.

Ansberry, Clare and Aeppel, Timothy, "Surviving the Onslaught," *The Wall Street Journal*, October 6, 2003, p. B1.

Arntzen, Bruce C. and Shumway, Herbert M., Driven by Demand: A Case Study, available at http://www.manufacturing.net, January 1, 2002.

Arruñada, Benito and Vázquez, Xosé H. "When Your Contract Manufacturer Becomes Your Competitor," *Harvard Business Review*, September 2006, pp. 135–145.

"As U.S. Quotas Fall, Latin Pants Makers Seek Leg Up on Asia," *The Wall Street Journal*, June 16, 2004, p. A1.

Ayers, James B. and Malmberg, David R., "Supply Chain Systems: Are You Ready?" *Information Strategy: The Executive's Journal*, Fall 2002, pp. 18–27.

Ayers, James B., Backbone of the Lean enterprise, SME Technical Paper TP04PUB138, Detroit: Society of Manufacturing Engineers, 2004.

Ayers, James B., "Costs: Getting to the Root Causes," *Supply Chain Management Review*, November–December, 2003, pp. 24–30.

Ayers, James B., Gustin, Craig and Stephens, "Scott, Reengineering the Supply Chain," *Information Strategy: The Executive's Journal*, Fall, 1997 (14/1), pp. 13–18.

Ayers, James B., *Handbook of Supply Chain Management*, 2nd ed., Boca Raton, FL: Auerbach Publications, 2006.

Ayers, James B., *Making Supply Chain Management Work: Design, Implementation, Partnerships, Technology, and Profits*, Boca Raton, FL: Auerbach Publications, 2002.

Ayers, James B., *Supply Chain Management (SCM), the Wheel and the Manufacturing Engineer*, Detroit: Society of Manufacturing Engineers, 2002.

Ayers, James B., *Supply Chain Project Management: A Structured Collaborative and Measurable Approach*, Boca Raton, FL: St. Lucie Press, 2004.

Ayers, James B., "Supply Chain Strategies," *Information Strategy: The Executive's Journal*, (15/2) Winter, 1999, pp. 2–10.

423

Ayers, James, Rooting out supply chain costs, *Optimize*, October 2003, available at http://www.optimizemagazine.com.

Banker, Steve and Snitkin, Sid, "A Foundation for Operational Excellence," *Supply Chain Management Review*, March–April 2003, pp. 42–48.

Beavers, Alex N., *Roadmap to the e-Factory*, Boca Raton, FL: Auerbach Publications, 2000.

Beer, Michael and Eisenstat, Russell A., "How to Have an Honest Conversation about Business Strategy," *Harvard Business Review*, February 2004, pp. 82–89.

Bensaou, M. and Earl, Michael, "The Right Mind-Set for Managing Information Technology," *Harvard Business Review*, September–October 1998, pp. 119–128.

Bermudez, John, "Supply Chain Management: More Than Just Technology," *Supply Chain Management Review*, March–April 2002, pp. 15–16.

Bhagwati, Jagdish, *In Defense of Globalization*, Oxford: Oxford University Press, 2004.

Bhote, Keki R., *Strategic Supply Management: A Blueprint for Revitalizing the Manufacturer–Supplier Partnership*, New York, AMACOM, 1989.

Blackman, Andrew, "Is Consensus Wisdom on Oracle—"Buy"—Wrong?" *The Wall Street Journal*, May 12, 2004, p. C3.

Blackwell, Roger D., *From Mind to Market: Reinventing the Supply Chain*, New York: Harper Collins Publishers, 1997.

Blumberg, Donald F., *Managing High-Tech Services Using a CRM Strategy*, Boca Raton, FL: St. Lucie Press, 2003.

Bowersox, D.J. and Closs, David J., *Logistical Management: The Integrated Supply Chain Process*, McGraw Hill, 1996.

"Breakthrough Ideas for 2004," *Harvard Business Review*, February 2004, pp. 13–37.

Brussee, Warren, *Statistics for Six Sigma Made Easy!* New York: McGraw-Hill, 2004.

Burt, David N., "Managing Suppliers Up To Speed," *Harvard Business Review*, July–August 1989.

Buss, Dale, "Little Giants," *Chief Executive*, May 2004, available at http://www.chiefexecutive.com.

Cahill, Joseph B., "Whirlpool Experiences Shipping Delays over Computer Glitches in SAP software," *Wall Street Journal*, November 3, 1999, p. A3.

Camp, Robert C. *Benchmarking*, Milwaukee: ASQC Quality Press, 1989.

Campoy, Ann and Rhoads, Christopher, "As EU Expands, It Re-Examines Old Ways: Sleepy Economy of Europe May Get Jolt by Low Prices and Vigor of New Members," *The Wall Street Journal*, April 29, 2004, p. A14.

Cantwell, Dick, "Procter & Gamble's EPC Advantage Strategy," Presentation to RFID Journal Live 2006 Conference, May 1–3, 2006.

Cavinato, Joseph L., "What's Your Supply Chain Type?" *Supply Chain Management Review*, May–June 2002, pp. 60–66.

Chakravorti, Bhaskar, "The New Rules for Bringing Innovations to Market," *Harvard Business Review*, March 2004, pp. 59–67.

Chapman, Timothy L., Dempsey, Jack J., Ramsdell, Glenn, and Bell, Trudy E., "Purchasing's Big Moment—After a Merger," *The McKinsey Quarterly*, 1998, Number 1, pp. 56–65.

Christensen, Clayton M., "The Law of Conservation of Attractive Profits," *Harvard Business Review*, February 2004, pp. 17–18.

Cliffe, Sarah, "ERP Implementation: How to Avoid $100 million Write-Offs," *Harvard Business Review*, January–February 1999, pp. 16–17.

Conner, Martin P., "The Supply Chain's Role in Leveraging PLM," *Supply Chain Management Review*, March 2004, pp. 36–43.

Cooper, Robert G., *Winning at New Products*, 3rd ed., New York: Perseus Publishing Company, 2001.

Cooper, Robin and Chew, W. Bruce, "Control Tomorrow's Costs through Today's Designs," *Harvard Business Review*, January–February 1996.

Corcoran, Elizabeth, "Making over Motorola," *Forbes*, December 13, 2004, pp. 102–108.

Council of Supply Chain Management Professionals, *Supply Chain Management Process Standards*, Council of Supply Chain Management Professionals, 2004. The standards are in six volumes: *Plan Processes, Source Processes, Make Processes, Deliver Processes, Return Processes, Enable Processes*.

Cox III, James F. and Blackstone, Jr., John H., *APICS Dictionary*, 10th ed., Alexandria: APICS—The Educational Society for Resource Management, 2002.

DC Velocity Staff, "The Rainmakers," *DC Velocity*, July 2006, pp. 33–49.

Denend, Lyn, West Marine: Driving growth through shipshape supply chain management, Stanford Graduate School of Business Case Study GS-34, 2005.

Duffy, Mike, "How Gillette Cleaned Up Its Supply Chain," *Supply Chain Management Review*, April 2004, pp. 20–27.

Dyer, Jeffrey H., "How Chrysler Created an American Keiretsu," *Harvard Business Review*, July–August 1996, pp. 42–56.

Dyer, Jeffrey H., Kale, Prashant and Singh, Harbir, "When to Ally & When to Acquire," *Harvard Business Review*, July–August 2004, pp. 109–115.

Eisenhardt, Kathleen M. and Brown, Shona L., "Patching: Restitching Business Portfolios in Dynamic Markets," *Harvard Business Review*, May–June 1999, pp. 72–82.

Fahey, Jonathon, "Just in Time Meets Just Right," *Forbes*, July 5, 2004, pp. 66–68.

Farrell, Diana, "The Real New Economy," *Harvard Business Review*, October 2003, pp. 104–112.

Fawcett, Stanely E., Magnan, Gregory M., and Williams, Alvin J., "Supply Chain Trust Is Within Your Grasp," *Supply Chain Management Review*, March 2004, pp. 20–26.

Feitzinger, Edward and Lee, Hau, "Mass Customization at Hewlett-Packard: The Power of Postponement," *Harvard Business Review*, January–February 1997, pp. 116–121.

Feld, Charlie S. and Stoddard, Donna B., "Getting IT Right," *Harvard Business Review*, February 2004, pp. 72–79.

Ferdows, Kasra, Lewis, Michael A., and Machuca, Jose A.D., "Rapid-Fire Fulfillment," *Harvard Business Review*, November 2004.

Fernández-Rañada, Miguel, Gurrola-Gal, F. Xavier, and López-Tello, Enrique, *3C: A Proven Alternative to MRPII for Optimizing Supply Chain Performance*, Boca Raton, FL: St. Lucie Press, 2000.

Fish, Lynn A. and Forrest, Wayne C., "The Seven Success Factors of RFID," *Supply Chain Management Review*, September 2006, pp. 26–32.

Fisher, Marshall L., Hammond, Janice H., Obermeyer, Walter R., and Raman, Ananth, "Making Supply Meet Demand in an Uncertain World," *Harvard Business Review*, May–June 1994.

Fisher, Marshall L., "What is the Right Supply Chain for Your Product?" *Harvard Business Review*, (75/2), March–April 1997, pp. 105–116.

Fites, Donald V., "Make Your Dealers Your Partners," *Harvard Business Review*, March–April 1996.

Ford, Henry, Henry Ford on continuous improvement, *Lean Directions*, available at http://www.sme.org, July 9, 2003.

Foster, Thomas A., "The Trends Changing the Face of Logistics Outsourcing Worldwide," *Global Logistics & Supply Chain Strategies*, June 2004, pp. 32–43.

Friedman, Thomas L., *The World Is Flat: A Brief History of the Twenty-first Century*, New York: Farrar, Straus and Giroux, 2005.

Geary, Steve, Childerhouse, Paul and Towill, Denis, "Uncertainty and the Seamless Supply Chain," *Supply Chain Management Review*, July–August 2002, pp. 52–61.

Ghemawat, Pankaj and Ghadar, Fariborz, "The Dubious Logic of Global Megamergers," *Harvard Business Review*, July–August 2000, pp. 64–72.

Ghemawat, Pankaj, "Distance Still Matters: The Hard Reality of Global Expansion," *Harvard Business Review*, September 2001, pp. 137–147.

Gibson, Brian J., Rutner, Stephen, M. and Manrodt, Karl B., "How Trigger Events Can Get the CEO's Attention," *Supply Chain Management Review*, November 2005, pp. 40–45.

Gilliland, Michael, "Is Forecasting a Waste of Time?" *Supply Chain Management Review*, July–August 2002, pp. 16–23.

Global Reporting Initiative, *Sustainability Reporting Guidelines*, Version 3.0, 2006.

Goldratt, Eliyahu M. and Cox, Jeff, *The Goal*, Croton-on-Hudson: North River Press, 1984.

Goldratt, Eliyahu M. and Fox, Robert E., *The Race*, Croton-on-Hudson: North River Press, 1986.

Goldsborough, William W., *Collaborative Global Logistics*, Report R860, SRI Consulting Business Intelligence, 2002.

Gouillart, Francis J. and Sturdivant, Frederick D., "Spend a Day in the Life of Your Customers," *Harvard Business Review*, January–February 1994.

Gould, Stephen A., "How to Source Logistics Services Strategically," *Supply Chain Management Review*, September–October 2003, pp. 48–54.

Gupta, Rajat and Wendler, Jim, "Leading Change: An Interview with the CEO of P&G," *The McKinsey Quarterly*, Web exclusive July 2005.

Hagel III, John and Brown, John Seely, "Your Next IT Strategy," *Harvard Business Review (79/9)*, October 2001, pp. 105–113.

Hamel, Gary and Prahalad, C.K., "Strategic Intent," *Harvard Business Review*, (67/3) May–June, 1989, pp. 63–76.

Hamel, Gary and Prahalad, C.K., "The Core Competency of the Corporation," *Harvard Business Review*, (68/3) May–June 1990, pp. 79–90.

Hammer, Michael, "Deep Change: How Operational Innovation Can Transform Your Company," *Harvard Business Review*, April 2004, pp. 84–93.

Harbison, John R. and Pekar, Peter, *Smart Alliances: A Practical Guide to Repeatable Success*, San Francisco: Jossey-Bass, 1998.

Hauser, John R. and Clausing, Don, "The House of Quality," *Harvard Business Review*, (66/3), May–June 1988, pp. 63–73.

Hayes, Robert H. and Pisano, Gary P., "Beyond World-Class: The New Manufacturing Strategy," *Harvard Business Review*, January–February 1994.

Hayes, Robert H. and Wheelwright, Steven C. *Restoring Our Competitive Edge: Competing through Manufacturing*, New York: John Wiley & Sons, 1984.

Hayes, Robert H., Wheelwright Steven C., and Clark, Kim B. *Dynamic Manufacturing: Creating the Learning Organization*, New York: Free Press, 1988.

Hicks, Douglas T., *Activity-Based Costing: Making it Work for Small and Mid-Sized Companies*, 2nd ed., New York: John Wiley & Sons, 1999.

Hofman, Debra, "Getting to World-Class Supply Chain Measurement," *Supply Chain Management Review*, October 2006, pp. 18–24.

Hope, Jeremy and Fraser, Robin, "Who Needs Budgets?" *Harvard Business Review*, February 2003, pp. 108–115.

House, Charles H. and Price, Raymond L., "The Return Map: Tracking Product Teams," *Harvard Business Review*, January–February 1991, pp. 92–100.

Hugos, Michael and Thomas, Chris, *Supply Chain Management in the Retail Industry*, Hoboken: John Wiley & Sons, 2006.

Hyland, Tricia, "Logistics Is Not Supply Chain Management," *CLO/Chief Logistics Officer*, October 2002, pp. 32–34.

Iansiti, Marco and Levien, Roy, "Strategy as Ecology," *Harvard Business School*, March 2004, pp. 69–78.

Iansiti, Marco and West, Jonathan, "Technology Integration: Turning Great Research into Great Products," *Harvard Business Review*, (75/3), May–June 1997, 69–79.

Imai, Masaaki, *Kaizen*, New York: Random House, 1986.

"In Bow to Retailers' New Clout, Levi Strauss Makes Alterations," *The Wall Street Journal*, June 17, 2004, p. A1.

Ittner, Christopher D. and Larcker, David F., "Coming up Short on Nonfinancial Performance Measurement," *Harvard Business Review*, November 2003, pp. 88–95.

Iverson, Steven, "When Clear Communication Matters," *World Trade*, July 2004, pp. 58–59.

Jackson, Bill and Winkler, Conrad, "Building the advantaged supply network, *strategy + business*," September 15, 2004, available at http://www.strategy-business.com /resilience/rr00011.

Jennings, Dana and Kling, Greg, "Integration of Disparate Enterprise IT Systems," Presented to Supply Chain World Conference sponsored by the Supply Chain Council, April 1999.

Johansson, Juliet E., Krishnamurthy, Chandru, and Schlissberg, Henry E., "Solving the Solutions Problem," *The McKinsey Quarterly*, 2003, Number 3.

Johnston, Peter, "Onsite Manufacturing Is a Lean Strategic Advantage," *Lean Directions*, September 9, 2003, available at http://www.sme.org.

Juran, J.M., *Juran on Quality by Design*, New York: The Free Press, 1992.

Jutras, Cindy M. *ERP Optimization: Using Your Existing System to Support Profitable E-Business Initiatives*, Boca Raton, FL: St. Lucie Press, 2003.

Kahn, Gabriel, "Invisible Supplier Has Penny's Shirts All Buttoned Up," *The Wall Street Journal*, September 11, 2003, p. A1.

Kahn, Gabriel, "Tiger's New Threads," *The Wall Street Journal*, March 26, 2004, p. B1.

Kaplan, Robert S. and Norton, David P., "Measuring the Strategic Readiness of Intangible Assets," *Harvard Business Review*, February 2004, pp. 52–63.

Kaplan, Robert S. and Norton, David P., "The Balanced Scorecard—Measures That Drive Performance," *Harvard Business Review*, January–February 1992, pp. 71–79.

Kaplan, Robert S. and Anderson, Steven R., "Time-Driven Activity-Based Costing," *Harvard Business Review*, November 2004, pp. 131–138.

Kerzner, Harold, *Project Management: A Systems Approach to Planning, Scheduling, and Controlling*, 7th ed., New York: John Wiley & Sons, 2001.

Kerzner, Harold, *Strategic Planning for Project Management: Using a Project Management Maturity Model*, New York: John Wiley & Sons, 2001.

Kim, W. Chan and Mauborgne, Renee, "Creating New Market Space," *Harvard Business Review*, (77/1), January–February 1999, pp. 83–93.

Kim, W. Chan and Mauborgne, Renee, "Value Innovation: The Strategic Logic of High Growth," *Harvard Business Review*, July–August 2004, pp. 172–180 (first published in 1997).

Knemeyer, A. Michael, Corsi, Thomas M., and Murphey, Paul R., "Logistics Outsourcing Relationships: Customer Perspectives," *Journal of Business Logistics*, (24/1), 2003, pp. 77–109.

Knemeyer, A. Michael, Corsi, Thomas M., and Murphy, Paul R., "Logistics Outsourcing Relationships: Customer Perspectives," *Journal of Business Logistics*, 2003, pp. 77–109.

Kotsuka, Yoshibumi, "Case Study: Securing Cargo with E-Seals," Presentation to RFID Journal Live 2006 Conference, May 1–3, 2006.

Kumar, Nirmalya, "The Power of Trust in Manufacturer-Retailer Relationships," *Harvard Business Review*, November–December 1996.

Lahiri, Sandip, *RFID Sourcebook*, Upper Saddle River, NJ: IBM Press, 2006.

Lambert, Douglas A. and Knemeyer, A. Michael, "We're in This Together," *Harvard Business Review*, December 2004, pp. 114–122.

Laseter, Tim and Oliver, Keith, "When Will Supply Chain Management Grow Up?" *strategy + business*, Issue 32, Fall 2003, http://www.strategy-business.com/reprints/03304

Lee, Hau I., "The Triple-A Supply Chain," *Harvard Business Review*, October 2004, pp. 102–114.

Lee, Hau L. "What Constitutes Supply Chain Integration?," *IEEM Network News*, Stanford University School of Engineering, Summer 1998.

Leimanis, Eriks, *APICS Illustrated Dictionary*, 11th ed., APICS—The Educational Society for Resource Management, 2004.

Levitt, Theodore, "Marketing Myopia," *Harvard Business Review*, July–August 2004, pp. 138–149. (First published in 1960.)

Levy, Michael and Weitz, Barton A., *Retailing Management*, 5th ed., New Delhi: Tata McGraw-Hill, 2004.

Lewin, Marsha, Kennedy, Keith, and Ayers, Jim; "Transformation through Proactive Systems: A Case Study, *Information Strategy: The Executive's Journal*, (12/3), Spring 1996, pp. 29–35.

Lewis, William W., *The Power of Productivity*, Chicago: University of Chicago Press, 2004.

Liker, Jeffrey V. and Choi, Thomas Y., "Building Deep Supplier Relationships," *Harvard Business Review*, December 2004, pp. 104–113.

Luhnow, David, "As Jobs Move East, Plants in Mexico Retool to Compete," *Wall Street Journal*, March 5, 2004, p. A1.

Lutz, Robert A., *Guts*, New York: John Wiley & Sons, 1998.

Magretta, Joan, "Why Business Models Matter," *Harvard Business Review*, May 2002, pp. 87–92.

Marglin, Stephen A., "Outsourcing Common Sense," *Los Angeles Times*, April 25, 2004, p. M3.

McAfee, R. Bruce, Glassman, Myron, and Honeycutt, Jr., Earl D., "The Effects of Culture and Human Resource Management Policies on Supply Chain Management Strategy," *Journal of Business Logistics*, 2002, pp. 1–18.

McCormack, Kevin P., Johnson, William C., Walker, William T., *Supply Chain Networks and Business Process Orientation: Advanced Strategies and Best Practices*, Boca Raton, FL: APICS/St. Lucie Press, 2003.

McGee, Ken, "Give Me That Real-Time Information," *Harvard Business Review*, April 2004, p. 26.

McGrath, Rita Gunther and MacMillan, Ian C., "Discovery-Driven Planning," *Harvard Business Review*, July–August 1995, pp. 44–54.

McWilliams, Gary, "Lean Machine: How Dell Fine-Tunes its PC Pricing to Gain Edge in a Slow Market," *The Wall Street Journal*, June 8, 2001, p. A1.

Mentzer, John J. and Moon, Mark A., "Understanding Demand," *Supply Chain Management Review*, May–June 2004, pp. 38–43.

Mercer, Glenn A., "Don't Just Optimize—Unbundled," *The McKinsey Quarterly*, (3), 1994, pp. 103–116.

Moffett, Sebastion, "Canon Manufacturing Strategy Pays Off with Strong Earnings," *The Wall Street Journal*, January 30, 2004, p. B3.

Monden, Yasuhiro, *Toyota Production System*, Norcross, Georgia: Institute of Industrial Engineers, 1983.

Montcrief, Bob and Stonich, Mark, "Supply Chain Practice Maturity Model and Performance Assessment," Presentation by the Performance Management Group (PMG) and Pittiglio Rabin Todd & McGrath (PRTM), November 6, 2001.

Moody, Kavin W., "New Meaning to IT Alignment," *Information Systems Management*, Fall 2003, pp. 30–35.

Moore, Geoffrey A., "Innovating within Established Enterprises," *Harvard Business Review*, July–August 2004, pp. 86–92.

Morais, Richard C., "I Want It Yesterday," *Forbes*, November 24, 2003, pp. 134–136.

Morris, Steven A. and McManus, Denise Johnson, "Information Infrastructure Centrality in the Agile Organization," *Information Systems Management*, Fall 2002, pp. 8–12.

Muller, JoAnn, "Global Motors," *Forbes*, January 12, 2004, pp. 62–68.

Myerson, Judith M., *Enterprise Systems Integration*, 2nd ed., Boca Raton, FL: Auerbach Publishers, 2002.

Naik, Sapna, *Fight for Consumer Mind Space: Dynamics in Food Retailer-Supplier Relationships*, Rabobank International Food & Agribusiness Research and Advisory, May 2004.

Narayanan, V.G. and Raman, Ananth, "Aligning Incentives in Supply Chains," *Harvard Business Review*, November 2004, pp. 94–102.

Narus, James A. and Anderson, James C., "Rethinking Distribution: Adaptive Channels," *Harvard Business Review*, July–August 1996.

"New Study Reveals Changes in Supply Chain Management Best Practices," *Supplier Selection & Management Report*, Institute of Management & Administration (IOMA), November 2004, p. 1.

Norek, Christopher D., "Throwing It into Reverse," *DC Velocity*, January 2003, pp. 54–58.

Nunes, Paul F. and Cespedes, Frank V., "The Customer Has Escaped," *Harvard Business Review*, November 2003, pp. 96–105.

O'Brien, Kevin P., Value Chain Report—Cats & Dogs: Objective Approaches to SKU Rationalization, available at http://www.iwvaluechain.com, October, 7, 2002.

O'Brien, Kevin, "Vendor-Managed Inventory in Low-Volume Environments," *Industry Week's the Value Chain*, available at http://www.valuechain.com, July 7, 2003.

"Outsourcing 101 (Editorial)," *The Wall Street Journal*, May 27, 2004, p. A20.

Parker, Bob, "Building a 'House of Productivity,'" *Supply Chain Management Review*, March 2004, pp. 12–13.

Parker, Ginny, "Going Global Can Hit Snags, Vodafone Finds," *The Wall Street Journal*, June 16, 2004, p. B1.

Petroff, John N., *Handbook of MRPII and JIT: Strategies for Total Manufacturing Control*, Englewood Cliffs, NJ: Prentice-Hall, 1993.

Poirier, Charles C., "The Path to Supply Chain Leadership," *Supply Chain Management Review*, (2/3), Fall 1998, pp. 16–26.

Poirier, Charles, "Achieving Supply Chain Connectivity," *Supply Chain Management Review*, November–December 2002, pp. 16–22.

Porter, Michael E., *Competitive Advantage: Creating and Sustaining Superior Performance*, New York: The Free Press, 1985.

Porter, Michael E., *Competitive Strategy: Techniques for Analyzing Industries and Competitors*, New York: The Free Press, 1980.

Porter, Michael E., "Strategy and the Internet," *Harvard Business Review*, (79/3) March 2001, pp. 62–78.

Porter, Michael E., "What Is Strategy?" *Harvard Business Review*, (74/6) November–December 1996, pp. 61–78.

Porter, Michael E. and Kramer, Mark R., "Strategy and Society," *Harvard Business Review*, December 2005, pp. 78–92.

Prohalad, C.K., and Ramaswamy, Venkatram, The collaboration continuum: Understand the full goals and complexity of collaboration before moving forward, November 2001, available at http://www.optimizemagazine.com.

Project Management Institute, *A Guide to the Project Management Body of Knowledge (PMBOK Guide—2000 Edition)*, Newtown Square, PA: Project Management Institute, 2000.

Ptak, Carol A., Schragenheim, Eli, *ERP: Tools, Techniques, and Applications for Integrating the Supply Chain*, Boca Raton, FL: St. Lucie Press, 2000.

Quinn, Francis, "Alliance Builder: An Interview with Lorraine Segal," *Supply Chain Management Review*, April 2004, pp. 43–47.

Quinn, Francis J., "Ready for the Digital Future? An interview with M. Eric Johnson," *Supply Chain Management Review*, July–August 2006, pp. 26–32.

Rangan, V. Kasturi, "The Promise and Rewards of Channel Stewardship," *Supply Chain Management Review*, July–August 2006, pp. 42–49.

Rayport, Jeffrey F. and Sviokla, John J., "Exploiting the Virtual Value Chain," *Harvard Business Review*, November–December 1995.

Reichheld, Frederick F., "The One Number You Need to Grow," *Harvard Business Review*, December 2003, pp. 46–64.

ReVelle, Jack B., *Manufacturing Handbook of Best Practices: An Innovation, Productivity, and Quality Focus*, Boca Raton, FL: APICS/St. Lucie Press, 2002.

ReVelle, Jack B., Moran, John W., and Cox, Charles A., *The QFD Handbook*, New York: John Wiley & Sons, 1998.

Rice, Jr., James B. and Hoppe, Richard M., "Supply Chain vs. Supply Chain—The Hype and the Reality," *Supply Chain Management Review*, September–October 2001, pp. 46–54.

Rigby, Darrell K., Reichheld, Frederick F., and Schefter, Phil, "Avoid the Four Perils of CRM," *Harvard Business Review*, February 2002, pp. 101–109.

Riggs, David A. and Robbins, Sharon L., *The Executive's Guide to Supply Chain Management: Building Supply Chain Thinking into All Business Processes*, New York: AMACOM, 1998.

Robb, Drew, "The Virtual Enterprise: How Companies Use Technology to Stay in Control of a Virtual Supply Chain," *Information Strategy: The Executive's Journal*, Summer 2003, pp. 6–11.

Robert, Michel, *Strategy Pure & Simple II*, New York: McGraw-Hill, 1998.

Roche, Eileen, "Explaining XML," *Harvard Business Review*, (78/4), July–August 2000, p. 18.

Rogers, Dale S. and Tibben-Lembke, Ronald S., "Returns Management and Reverse Logistics for Competitive Advantage," *CSCMP Explores ...*, Winter, 2006.

Ross, David F., *Competing through Supply Chain Management: Creating Market-Winning Strategies through Supply Chain Partnerships*, Chapman & Hall Material Management Series, 1997.

Ross, Jeanne W. and Weill, Peter, "Six IT Decisions Your IT People Shouldn't Make," *Harvard Business Review*, November 2002, pp. 85–91.

Roztocki, N. and Needy, K.L., An integrated activity-based costing and economic value added system as an engineering management tool for manufacturers, 1998 ASEM National Conference Proceedings, Virginia Beach, October 1–3, 1998, pp. 77–84.

Rugman, Alan M. and Verbeke, Alain, *Regional Multinationals and Triad Strategy*, August 5, 2202.

Rutner, Stephen, Waller, Matthew A., and Mentzer, John T., "A Practical Look at RFID," *Supply Chain Management Review*, January–February 2004.

Schragenhiem, Eli and Dettmer, H. William, *Manufacturing at Warp Speed: Optimizing Supply Chain Financial Performance*, Boca Raton, FL: APICS/St. Lucie Press, 2001.

Schroeder, Michael, "Outsourcing May Create U.S. jobs," *The Wall Street Journal*, March 30, 2004, p. A2.

Shapiro, Benson P., Rangan, V. Kasturi, and Sviokla, John J., "Staple Yourself to an Order," *Harvard Business Review*, July–August 2004, pp. 162–171 (first published in 1992).

Shirouzu, Norihiko, "Chain Reaction: Big Three's Outsourcing Plan: Make Parts Suppliers Do It," *The Wall Street Journal*, June 10, 2004, p. A1.

Skinner, Wickham, "The Focused Factory," *Harvard Business Review*, May–June, 1974.

Slater, Derek, "The Ties That Bolt," *CIO Magazine*, April 15, 1999.

Slone, Reuben E., "Leading a Supply Chain Turnaround," *Harvard Business Review*, October 2004, pp. 114–121.

Smeltzer, Larry R. and Manship, Jennifer A., "How Good Are Your Cost Reduction Measures?" *Supply Chain Management Review*, May–June 2003, pp. 28–33.

Smith, Rob, *Global Supply Chain Performance And Risk Optimization: The Value Of Real Options Flexibility Demonstrated In The Global Automotive Industry*, Weisbaden: Deutscher Universitäts-Verlag GmbH, 2002.

Smith, Larry, "A CPFR Success Story," *Supply Chain Management Review*, March 2006, pp. 29–36.

Smith, Hedrick and Young, Rick, "Is Wal-Mart good for America?" Frontline program, available at http://www.pbs.org/wgbh/pages/frontline/shows/walmart/, Hedrick Smith Productions, 2004.

Snyder, Bill, "When Should You Sell the Factory?" *Stanford Business*, November 2003, p. 31.

Soloman, Ira and Peecher, Mark E., "Does Your Auditor Understand Your Business?" *The Wall Street Journal*, May 25, 2004, p. B2.

Spear, Seven and Bowen, H. Kent, "Decoding the DNA of the Toyota Production System," *Harvard Business Review*, September–October, 1999, pp. 97–106.

Spear, Steven J., "Learning to Lead at Toyota," *Harvard Business Review*, May 2004, pp. 78–86.

Stalk, Jr., George and Lachenauer, Rob, "Hardball: Five Killer Strategies for Trouncing the Competition," *Harvard Business Review*, April 2004.

Starinsky, Robert W., *Maximizing Business Performance through Software Packages: Best Practices for Justification, Selection, and Implementation*, Boca Raton, FL: Auerbach Publishers, 2003.

Swank, Cynthia Karen, "The Lean Service Machine," *Harvard Business Review*, October 2003, pp. 123–129.

Thurm, Scott, "Lesson in India: Not Every Job Translates Overseas," *The Wall Street Journal*, March 3, 2004, p. A1.

Timme, Stephen G., "The Real Cost of Holding Inventory," *Supply Chain Management Review*, July–August 2003, pp. 30–37.

Tinnirello, Paul C., *Project Management*, Boca Raton, FL: Auerbach Publications, 2000.

Trebilcock, Bob, "The Seven Deadly Sins of Reverse Logistics," *Logistics Management*, June 1, 2002, available at http://www.manufacturing.net.

Turbide, Dave, "What is APS?," *Midrange ERP*, January–February 1998.

Turrettini, John, "Remade in America," *Forbes*, January 12, 2004, p. 190.

Upton, David M. and McAfee, Andrew, "The Real Virtual Factory," *Harvard Business Review*, July–August 1996.

Upton, David M., "The Management of Flexibility," *California Management Review*, (36/2), Winter 1994, pp. 72–89.

Upton, David M., "What Really Makes Factories Flexible," *Harvard Business Review*, July–August 1995.

Vitasek, Kate L., Manrodt, Karl B., and Kelly, Mark, "Solving the Supply Demand Mismatch," *Supply Chain Management Review*, September–October 2003, pp. 58–64.

Vitasek, Kate, Manrodt, Karl B., and Abbott, Jeff, "What Makes a Lean Supply Chain?" *Supply Chain Management Review*, October 2005, pp. 39–45.

W. Chan Kim and Renée Mauborgne, *Blue Ocean Strategy*, Boston: Harvard Business School Press, 2005.

Walker, Marcus, "Reunification Policies Flopped, Germany Admits, as East Faces Competition," *The Wall Street Journal*, April 29, 2004, p. A14.

Walker, William T., *Supply Chain Architecture: A Blueprint for Networking the Flow of Material, Information, and Cash*, Boca Raton, FL: CRC Press, 2005.

Walton, Mary, *The Deming Management Method*, New York: The Putnam Publishing Group, 1986.

Wheelwright, Steven C. and Clark, Kim B., *Revolutionizing Product Development*, New York: Free Press, 1992.

Whelan, David, "The Slipper Solution," *Forbes*, May 24, 2004, p. 64

White, Erin, "For Retailer Mango, Frenzied 'Fast Fashion' Proves Sweet," *The Wall Street Journal*, May 28, 2004, p. B1.

Witte, Carl L., Grünhagen, Marko, and Clarke, Richard L., "The Integration of EDI and the Internet," *Information Systems Management*, Fall 2003, pp. 58–65.

Wohleber, Curt, "The Shopping Cart," *Invention & Technology*, Summer 2004, pp. 10–11.

Wolf, Martin, *Why Globalization Works*, New Haven, CT: Yale University Press, 2004.

Womack, James P. and Jones, Daniel T., "Beyond Toyota: How to Root Out Waste and Pursue Perfection," *Harvard Business Review*, September–October 1996, pp. 140–158.

Womack, James P. and Jones, Daniel T., "From Lean Production to the Lean Enterprise," *Harvard Business Review*, March–April 1994, pp. 93–103.

Womack, Jim, Taking a value stream walk at Firm "A", *Lean Directions*, available at http://www.sme.org, May 8, 2003.

Woods, John A. and Marien, Edward J., *The Supply Chain Yearbook*, New York: McGraw-Hill, 2001.

Zook, Chris and Allen, James, "Growth Outside the Core," *Harvard Business Review*, December 2003, pp. 66–73.

# Index

Printed in the United States
by Baker & Taylor Publisher Services

Printed in the United States
by Baker & Taylor Publisher Services